The Rise of

Mystery Babylon

Vol. 3: Seeds of the Serpent (Part 1)

Brett Lee Thomas

Parallel World Books

The Rise of Mystery Babylon:
Vol. 3: Seeds of the Serpent (Part 1)

Copyright © 2024 by Brett Thomas

All rights reserved. This book or any portion thereof may not be reproduced or used in any manner whatsoever without the express written permission of the publisher except for the use of brief quotations in a book review.

ISBN-13: 978-0-9995257-5-3
Parallel World Books

Email:
  mysterybabylon@1791.com

www.mysterybabylon.com

It all makes sense once you realize they want to kill us.

- Mike Whitney

Table of Contents

Chapter 1
The Four Apocalyptic… <Groups>
1

Chapter 2
The Black Horse - Pagan Connection
14

Chapter 3
*The White Horse -
An Extension of the "Black"?*
31

Chapter 4
"Hebrews" Against the World
55

Chapter 5
The Real Story of "At-lantis"?
87

Chapter 6
The Great Cover Up(s)
108

Chapter 7
*Archetypal Pagans Fleeing…
To Godly Areas?*
136

Chapter 8
*More Corruption… in Rome
and in Judaism*
191

Chapter 9
A Second Group of Edomites
221

Chapter 10
From the "Old" World to the "New"
247

Chapter 11
Where They May Have Went
271

Chapter 12
Ushering in those (Catholic) "Dark Ages"
307

Chapter 13
Sciences, Explorations, and Reformations
337

Chapter 14
Beginnings of "Western Civilization"
366

Chapter 15
Bringing Down the Protestants
399

Chapter 16
Making their Moves… Whilst Covering Their Backsides
429

Preface

Timeline of the Apostasy, And Deeper Answers

*Professing themselves to be **wise**, they became fools, And changed the glory of the uncorruptible God into an image made like **to corruptible man**... Wherefore God also gave them up to uncleanness through the lusts of their own hearts... Who changed the truth of God **into a lie**...*   - *Rom.* 1:22-25 (KJV)

In this third volume, we will not be spending as much effort on the understanding those "parallels in time," as we did before - those parallels representing the early times of Genesis as compared to today. At least, we won't be talking about it very much. We've already discovered what paganism *really* is, and where it had originally come from. We've found out that, most probably, it originated with Cain and his father the Serpent. Also, we're not going to continue on with the early history of *Mystery Babylon*, and the *systems* it manifested itself into over the years. We've already done a lot of this as well. What we are going to do in this volume is to look at a number of topics that we may not have been able to get into yet, or things that may have seemed a little irrelevant... until *now*. There is a lot more to all of this, as we soon shall see. And, this time, we are going "for the throat" in a manner of speaking, pulling no punches. We need to go right to the (relevant) points, and start expanding on them!

Identifying a number of these *other* elements, in this whole *serpentine*-led process, will help us to understand the very magnitude of all that's really going on around us. This volume will help us discover just how many more things are out there... with a *Babylonian* connection. It's shocking, once we go down the rabbit hole a while.

Another thing that will make this volume a bit different will be the way information will flow. We will go in chronological order - from the very "beginning" (once again), all the way to this present day. This time, however, there will be no "parallels." We will show an unbroken line of serpentine progress and deceit.

We will also go on to divide the entire volume into *four* sections. Why? Because, as we soon shall see, the Bible gives us *four* elements to help us make sense of the up-and-coming "end times." And, although some information will be brought back to us from previous volumes, they're only there to assist in our understanding of the rest of it. Hopefully, the third volume will help to "fill in the gaps," in regards to any missing information that we might need. It should help to "bring everything together," if you will.

So, with all of this in hand, let's begin our *third* - and most important - journey, a journey into the little-known (and often obscured) elements of the past, present and future.

Mystery Babylon - a "Reintroduction"

> *And upon her forehead* was *a name written,* **MYSTERY, BABYLON** *THE GREAT, THE MOTHER OF HARLOTS AND ABOMINATIONS OF THE EARTH.* - *Rev.* 17:5 (KJV)

It's time to reiterate some information from the previous volumes, and expand on it all a little bit. Even though it may not completely necessary to read these previous works, they do help to understand this current rendering, quite a lot. Also, while we cover a vast number of different (yet relevant) topics here, we highly suggest that the reader take his or her own time to do some *independent* research. We advise people to use their own discernment abilities, and take their own investigations to the next level. Why? Because space is fairly limited here; and, there is so much going on in our world today that it's almost easier to glance over all of these relevant topics, give some examples of each, and let the reader decide what to do with what they now have. As long as it's all out there, it helps us to be understand the veracity of all that we may be facing, and how to deal with it! We won't know how to combat anything if we don't really know what we're up against.

Exposure is the first step to allow us any comprehension. And, through the words of this volume, we should be able to understand just how *vast* the sacrilege is against us, and how deep it all really goes! There's just *so much* out there that it's next to impossible to fit everything related to Cain, the Serpent and *Mystery Babylon* into a nice little bubble. At least, if we gather a little bit of everything, in little tidbits (as we're about to do), we could begin to see the relationships between them all, and how to utilize the knowledge we have in our fight against the enemy. Information *truly* is the key.

Now, for the sake of review, let's take another look at the term "*Mystery Babylon*," and go from there. This term, of course, comes from the Bible (in Rev. 17:5). The word *mystery* is fairly easy to understand: something that's going on, right out from under our noses, and unbeknownst to most people. If we examine the word *Babel* (the root of *Babylon*), we might recall (from previous volumes) that it actually could be a conglomeration of two words: **Ba** (i.e. "the gate") and **Bel** ("of Bel"). And, from previous volumes, we also understand how *Bel* was just another name for the *Serpent* (in the Garden of Eden). Put the two together, and we understand how the term *Babel*, or *Babylon*, stands for a "gateway" to the *Serpent*, and all that he stands for! Of course, we know that this Serpent stands for everything ungodly, and opposing to the Bible. It's that simple. The term *Mystery Babylon*, then, stands for all things that work to bring us *away* from God, and, subtly, towards elements of the "Other Side." It happened back then; it continues today.

As we've also discovered, *Mystery Babylon* splintered off (over the years) into a vast number of influencing "systems," subtly doing a number on the masses. The ultimate goal of these *systems* - whether they be religious, political, cultural, or whatever - is to take the entire human race *down*, as far away from God as possible! We also recall that the "Other Side" signifies anything from the fallen, supernatural plane - the plane of fallen angels, demons, and what have you. It's basically anything and everything from satan's realm. It also represents everything that's separate from God, or totally the *opposite* of Him.

And, in order to lure people into becoming a part of these "systems," things have to seem inviting to them - "enlightening," "humanistic," or even "compassionate" (as we soon shall see). What these systems do is to put something out there, which looks "good" to the individual, or to humanity as a whole, and then, after people are lured in, things slowly start to change. It doesn't seem the same as before, as time goes on. It ends up becoming something entirely different later on. But, that's how the enemy works! There's usually something a lot *deeper* to things we see around us; and there's almost always a deeper agenda to things that sound wonderful to be a part of… at least regarding elements of this world. That's what "worldly temptations" are all about!

Once we begin to discover what these systems truly are, and discover their true roots, things won't look as rosy any more. True intentions will always seem to come "out," through time. Sadly, the deceptions of this "Other Side," are, quite often, *very* subtle, and also very harmful. That's why so many get "sucked into" these ways of Cain and the Serpent in the first place. There's just so much deception in this world.

As we begin to get to the "meat" of discovering these temptations, we might begin to wonder: just how could those ancient mysteries of *Babylon still* be around today, influencing world events? How could these elements of our society - which were thought to have come straight out of the Garden of Eden - *still* have relevance in our daily lives? It's all just so ancient…or *is* it? We'll soon see how those *Mystery* systems of *Babylon* are a lot like people - they *breed*, they create descendants, and they fight for survival. Don't be fooled. They haven't left. It's all still here. And, hopefully, this volume will us discover a good deal of evidence to support all of what we're initially saying, here.

We can refer to a couple of these remnant, Babylonian "systems" as the present-day "deep state," or "shadow governments" if you will - the deeper and darker the ruling classes are, the more apt they are to be under the spell of this ancient, sacrilegious force. Often, these shadowy cabals are made up of social "elites" - those at the very top of a number of ruling classes, complete with evil, self-absorbed intentions. They may even pride themselves as being in the upper echelons of our organized religions as well. And, so often, these people feel a need to manipulate, or control, people… just so they could get as many other individuals on their own side.

Yes, they may begin act as (ideological) *vampires* might. As a typical bloodsucker, they slowly try to drain the *souls* out of people, in order to make *themselves* more alive and stronger. And, of course, their major enemy would be anyone who considers themselves a follower of God, or believes in Judeo-Christian ethics. To those elites, the Godly represent a major "stumbling block," as far as the achievement of their ultimate end game: to make everyone think and act the same as *they* would. To them, it's all about gathering more and more strength to their side, *weakening* the other side at the same time.

Their utopia, of course, is to make the entire world go along with them, which, ultimately, would bring the entire world under the influences of Cain, and, ultimately, of the Serpent himself. No matter how long it takes, no matter how many tiny increments it takes for them to advance a little bit… they will try to do it. It's their end-game; it's their goal. They are also very patient. *He* (the Serpent) began this whole process, even before the city of Babylon. It just takes quite a while, sometimes, to turn people (with a conscience) into believing the *opposite* of what they once knew, and accepted, is now correct. Nothing has changed, as far as their methods, since the Fall!

How do we stop this, or, at least, slow it down? As usual, their mortal enemy - God and the Bible - keeps throwing monkey-wrenches into this march towards the "Other Side." As Jesus himself once said:

Ye are the salt of the earth…
- *Mat.* 5:13 (KJV)

The "ye" in this verse is *us*. We represent the "salt." We are among the individuals who actually want to do what's right, and not what's popular, or what everyone around us *tells* us may be right. We are the ones who try to "preserve" (as salt) what is good and decent in the world, according to the Bible. But, if we begin to fail, Jesus also stated:

*…but if the salt have lost his savour, wherewith shall it be salted? it is thenceforth **good for nothing**, but to be cast out, and to be **trodden under foot** of men.*
- *Mat.* 5:13 (KJV)

In other words, if we lose our fortitude, and or motivation to "keep up the good fight," our zest for remaining a Godly human being may also start to fragment. Our struggle could, eventually, be "good for nothing," and we will begin to be "trampled underfoot" by those around us, with corrupted philosophies and ideologies. It's truly a struggle - the *ultimate* struggle for our existence as a moral, human race (whether many may consciously understand this or not)! Don't be fooled by a lot of those naysayers out there, because they are either oblivious to what's really going on, or are hard at work, trying to advance things of the *other* side.

Their push towards world domination has always been *progressing* - sometimes slow, sometimes fairly rapidly. In this current day and age, however, it all seems to be gaining a lot of momentum! We can tell this by noticing all of the harsh "blowback" against anyone trying to promote Judeo-Christian values. And, also, let's not be fooled by all of the flowery and "compassionate" rhetoric out there, trying to replace Godly values with something that sounds "good." These ways are not necessarily God's ways... they are the ways of man. But, in reality: it's only *one* way or the *other* - it's either the ways of God or ways which, ultimately, will begin to point one towards the "Other Side." There really is no "middle ground." We'll see a number of examples soon enough.

With that said and done, how would we be able to push back a lot of this corruption today? There's just so much around. And, what forces might *we* have at our disposal, to carry on with the good fight? Well, we have the Creator of the universe for one thing. Wouldn't that be enough to at least get us started? God is more powerful than any living thing on this earth, as well as anything pagan. He was even the One who created the Serpent himself - not the other way around. With One more powerful that anything of the "Other Side," how could we really lose? We also have the wisdom and knowledge of the Bible at our disposal, as well as these three volumes, to help inform us, and aid in our discernment. There *are* truths out there; and, if we have the patience and desire to seek it all out, it is possible to get somewhere. They say that knowledge is power, and these volumes, hopefully, will be a good place to start our process.

So, let's begin by discovering some things that we may not have already known before. Let's use it all to assemble a database of esoteric knowledge and experience, and then put it to good use: to help us become good warriors for all that is *truly* Godly.

...To Have an Open Mind

We, undoubtedly, will hear our neighbors out there, hearing information about fallen, terrestrial angels or the seeds of the Serpent, and concluding that these volumes are just a bunch of nonsense. With the way things are taught to us today it's totally understandable to understand how they'd think that. But, we can't just go by the negativity we might receive, and can't reach everybody to our side. Some may attribute a lot of this as "fairy tales," no longer relevant in today's society… and that's okay. They may not even believe that evil exists in our present-day world, the only evil that happens is in the inside of one's mind, and that's also okay. We need to pursue what *we* believe may be out there, regardless; because that's what the evil one wants - disbelief. So, what about the belief in fallen, terrestrial angels - those with the ability to live (and even copulate) like human beings? What about that existence of God? What about the supernatural world? Are we the ones who are actually going crazy, trying to make sense of it all, or could there have been a number of preconceived notions *propelled* upon us, throughout the years, to make *us* think that we are barking up some wrong tree? One thing's for sure: many, upon *many*, individuals sure believed that these things existed a long time ago… were they all ignorant? They believed in these things so much that they decided to write a lot of their experiences down, or even make them part of their religious dogma. Back then, these were forces to be reckoned with. Did they *really* disappear, in today's world?

And, of course, just because a vast number of "experts" believe that science only has the answers, does that really make it so? Everyone has the right to their own opinion, but not their own facts. There are so many things they can't explain. Now what do they do? Yes, it's truly up to the critical, well-informed (and open-minded) individual, to be able to take the chance, and make up their own minds regarding this all… not some "expert" who believes only what they've been *taught* to believe, and is afraid to go out of their ideological bubble. Ideological sabotage *is* alive and well with us today, and always has been.

In one example of this, we'll soon be looking at how the *Smithsonian Institution* - a well-known governmental agency - was reportedly behind the suppression of ancient, archaeological evidence, evidence that was contrary to what they believed in, and were promoting at the time. They, then , reportedly worked to suppress it all. Why would they be so afraid of examining ancient evidence of *giant* human beings living in North America? The bones that they collected (and confiscated) would have supported a lot of the information in this book, as well as the Bible; but, they reportedly took it, put it all on a barge, and dumped it in the middle of the ocean. Why? Was it because it wasn't considered "scientifically viable" in their eyes, not part of their bigger, political agenda? There's probably a lot of bones and other ancient artifacts out there, that could give us a lot of information about our past, but some people have made sure that it never sees the light of day. Again, *why*? Was it because this information could actually head us in a *different* direction than what they have been pushing? Most probably. Yes, some are very sneaky. Could this institution be just an arm of one modern *system* of *Mystery Babylon*?

Many in the past have accepted the existence of giant human beings, however. Many ancient **pagan** cultures also believed the same. They believed in supernatural spirits, angels, as well as demons. Why would anyone try to cover things up… unless they had something to hide? Assuredly, there's a lot more to our world than what a few, modern intellectuals might want us to think, or know about. With so many bits of information coming at us from so many different directions it becomes hard for an individual, nowadays, to accept any points of view that may be contradictory to "popular demand." From pop culture, from the media, from various other religions, as well as politicians and the government, we are being bombarded by a host of things… things that, quite easily, could be considered opposing to God and His ways (and that's all by design). With the influences of the "Other Side" so strong out there in society (whether we know it or not) it's not very hard to want to want to dismiss a lot of the information in this book. It's fascinating (and scary) to see just how much disbelief, and how much sacrilege, we see around us today, continually downplaying things that, once, represented common knowledge. Majority seems to rule nowadays, and so does peer pressure. And, of course, anything that they don't like - such as Christianity - "needs" to become a thing of the past, being no longer viable.

With all of this said and done, a number of individuals might read this volume and truly "get it" - it will be fairly easy to understand, and make sense of. Others will become enlightened by the information, but wonder why it hasn't been presented to the masses like it should have. Still others will begin to question it all, because it's so new to them. Still others won't really "get" any of it, and, most likely, never will. All of the above scenarios are okay. Some people may even be a little "turned off," or "offended," and that's okay too. It's not for everybody, and we're not out for hateful purposes… just to expose and inform.

One thing we need to say about these writings: *both* political sides (i.e. the left and the right) can have good elements to them. Both can make sense, if you look at what people are saying. Yet, both sides also have serious issues, as well… and that is what we are looking at here. **Exposure** needs to be injected into both, to inform the populous about *all* of the corruption ahead of them. We're not out to promote one sex over another, one race over another, one sexual orientation over another, whatever… just one *ideology* over another. That's the difference.

The best advice for understanding it all is: have an open mind, and try to give it all a good reading. Most of it should come together as time goes on… if we really want to see these other elements of the world. We will see things that aren't in the history books, that's for sure. We'll provide a good deal of information, coming from a number of ancient texts, alternate views of history, etc., and then let the reader decide on what they might want to believe. Damn any "politically correct" insertions here, because (as we'll know) a majority of the drives these needs for political correctness are, often, brought about as political tools - and ways to silence people. This the real world, and there are things in what we see all around us that might not be the most savory, or have the best past behind them.

So, in conclusion, we need to understand that the theme of this volume is trying to expose *corruption*, pure and simple - corruption on *both* sides of the political/theological coin. We are here to show *truths* - as close to the truth as ancient accounts have given us. An open mind, with a desire not to jump to conclusions, will reign here, and allow us to be able to "connect all the dots."

Follow the Bread Crumbs

So, let's begin by taking our third - and *deepest* - venture into what's really going on in our world, and who's really "pulling the strings" at the top. And, a third time, we'll need to start "in the beginning." This time, however, we'll begin to discover a lot *more* about the "history of things to come" by following their trail of sacrilege… directly from the Garden of Eden, to all of what's going on now.

Chapter 1

The Four Apocalyptic… <Groups>

*…How much more when I send my **four** sore judgments upon Jerusalem… to cut off from it man and beast?*   *- Ezek.* 14:21 (KJV)

Let's take a good, hard look at those four sections that were previously mentioned. Why four, and what could each one represent? Essentially, there were four massive *routes* that the ancient Serpent, Cain, and other members of their entourage would end up manipulating (ever since the beginning), to be able to influence mankind, and we really did not have the capacity to understand just what, exactly, these four route were… until the modern era! The people who found themselves a part of these four routes were, throughout the ages, taken advantage of, corrupted, and subsequently "rewoven" to allow the "Other Side" to gain more and more power. The four were used as part of their end game. And, yes, this manipulation has been going on since the early days of Genesis… all the way up to now! Let's begin to discover just what these four routes were, and are today, and how each of them have been (stealthily) hijacked.

In this volume, we are going to identify these four routes a four groups of *human* beings… and all groups with have a bit of relevancy during the "end times" of our world. Assembling people into four groups, of course, may be a far cry from what a lot of Biblical scholars, today, might consider as part of the apocalypse. But, as we'll soon see, it will all make sense, once we really stop to think about it.

First, it must be understood that *all people* within each group are not intentionally pushing agendas of the "Other Side"… not by a long shot. In fact, a **vast majority** of people in these groups don't even know how Cain and the Serpent (and their future sympathizers) have used their group over time, to expand their negative tentacles over almost everything! Yes, it's a sad fact of life. And yes, there are only a small fraction of individuals - usually at **the top** - who really know what's going on, or are really out there to do nefarious things with their power! So, of course, it's not really fair to assume that *any* individuals (who *doesn't* really know what's going) is guilty of working for the devil… not at all. These people are just trying to live out their own lives, and do according to what they were always told was right. And, those "top dogs" are the problem, for the most part, because they are the ones that do the majority of the pushing, as well as deceiving. And, *they* are also the ones who are the focus of our discussions.

Expanding on all this, we'll need to look at these four groups, and understand what may actually he going on within their upper echelons. The four, in actuality, end up sounding a lot like another well-known element of Bible prophecy. Yes, in the final book of the Bible we'll see many scholars assuming the beginning of our "end-time" perils manifest through *four* swift world occurrences… actually symbolized by four "**horses**." Yes, these are the infamous "**Four Horsemen of the Apocalypse**" (in Rev. 6:2-8). And, yes, the four groups of our discussion, in actuality, parallel these same four temporal horseman of Revelation… they're just groups of *people*, rather than major events. It should all make more sense as we go on.

So, for the sake of these four groups and their identification, we've also divided this entire volume into *four* different sections… each section supplying a detailed history of one particular horse, and their affects on the world. There are definitive *reasons* why we need to go this particular route, and explain each "horse" individually, in these ways. It will all make sense soon enough.

"Four (Groups) of the Apocalypse"

Next, one of the first things we might need to understand is how the following information will, almost certainly, be a lot *different* than what most other religious authorities teach out there, in Sunday School. And, it's also very interesting to see just how many Christian intellectuals will hold fast to this *one* particular interpretation, and dare not stray. We'll also, eventually, discover why things seem to be so "tightly-knit" in the Christian community nowadays.

And, to further the understanding of each horse, the Bible does seem to *color code* each individual one, pointing out differences between all of them. So, with all of this at hand, let's begin to look at these Four Horsemen, as mentioned by the apostle John (in a vision):

Rev. 6:
*2 And I saw, and behold a **white horse**: and he that sat on him had a bow; and a crown was given unto him: and he went forth conquering, and to conquer...*
*4 And there went out another **horse** that was **red**: and power was given to him that sat thereon to take peace from the earth...*
*5 ...And I beheld, and lo a **black horse**; and he that sat on him had a pair of balances in his hand.*
*8 ...And I looked, and behold a **pale** (or **green**) **horse**: and his name that sat on him was Death, and Hell followed with him. And power was given unto them over the fourth part of the earth...*[1]

Along with the identification of these "horses," we receive a little bit more information regarding the *color* of each. But, before we get deeper into it all here, let's take a look at the "cookie-cutter" approach that so many Christians seem to have out there, in regards to identification. Many accept that these horses as *chronological* events. And, the events all starts with the "White Horse," eventually trickling down to the "Pale Horse" (just like they're listed in the above). And, by the time the "White Horse" comes onto the world's scene, it, supposedly, marks the beginning of our "end times." But, in our reinterpretation, we need to understand that these verses **don't** actually state that these horses are events, nor do they even *have* to be in any chronological order. The Bible just states that there are four of them, and details them somewhat!

Regardless, most theologians hold that the first event of our end times will associate with this White Horse, and whatever he brings, followed by another major chronological event, symbolized by the Red Horse, and then another (symbolized by the Black Horse), and then another (symbolized by the Green Horse).[2] And, to the Christian "elites" who only want to follow this line of logic, the arrival of the White Horse is the horse we really need to watch out for!

With that said and done, a number of people hold that this White Horse will be associated with an (up-and-coming) era of **world peace**. There is a bow that seems to be associated with this White Horse - a bow with no arrows. And, to many, this clearly represents an upcoming (yet short) time of peace and prosperity for the human race. The color *white* is also a symbol of this peace.

Next, this peace would be broken up, quickly followed by the era of the Red Horse - a time of *bloody* war. Many have interpreted the color *red* as the color of blood. Many have also interpreted this time as the beginning of **World War III**. One third of the population reportedly dies. To follow this horrible even, the Black Horse of **death** states his claim over a number of individuals left on the earth. Lastly, the Green Horse of *famine* hits the world's stage, and hits it very hard - claiming even more lives (because of the death and instability that World War III had brought to mankind).[3]

Now, as we continue to examine these claims, it makes a lot of sense… to a point. But, as we'll now see, there's the potential for a few problems. First, as we begin to dig a little *deeper* into all of it, we have the era of the White Horse giving rise to the man known as the *Antichrist* (the evil one who, in actuality, is instrumental in establishing this era of world peace). Sounds good, at least so far. Next, war breaks out - thermonuclear war. All manner of "red" blood is spilled. Still makes sense. But, next, we have the blackness of *death* dropping in, killing a large number of people. But, what about the **final** *Green* Horse of famine? Shouldn't that really be going on before all of this death? It seems a little out of order. But, if we "stretch it" a little bit, it just might seem to work. But, still, the first question that might come to a skeptics mind may be: why wouldn't mass famine and disease come before the blackness of *death*? Yes, both may result from war; but, it makes a lot more sense to have the mass sickness, disease and poverty come right after the war… then, a lot of dead. Not trying to split hairs here, but it already seems as if there's some cracks in their chronological argument.

And, to top it all off, we need to ask ourselves: just because things were listed in this Biblical way does it mean that is all *has* to be in this particular order? Not really. The Bible never says it has to. What if the Bible just lists them that way in order to have them listed? What about the possibility of these four groups being groups of people as well, and not necessarily major chronological events? By the time we finish with this volume, we will discover that these horses could, indeed, mean something entirely different - and, potentially, a lot more *frightening* - than what traditional Christians could have ever dreamed. We're not saying, here, that there definitely was not *any* "Four Horsemen of the Apocalypse," there may also be! Who knows? We are just saying that these horse might mean something else, in addition. There may actually be *another* meaning to them and their characters.

The frightening thing about this *new* way of thinking is: it does not only show us what may be coming in the near future - it also shows us that the "end times" may already be here... the "four horsemen" are *already* present, in the "here and now!" They are already in place. That's the scary thing, if we think about it. And, yes, these horses could very well be established, and something we already experience in our daily lives.

So, if these "four horseman" are *already* four groups of human individuals in this world, then they might, indeed, represent *four* segments of our world's population - those with specific commonalities, a number of things in common possibly, whatever. It may not necessarily be a racial thing; it may be some kind of common nationality. It's definitely not a gender thing. It may not even some kind of "class struggle" parameter. It, probably, is associated with something that a person chooses to do, or live by - a specific *moral* pathway or belief system adopted into one's life. Each "horse," then, could be thought of as a **conglomerate** of like-minded individuals, all drawn together with "common threads." What might all of it mean, in regards to *Mystery Babylon*? Plenty. We'll also see how some *systems* of Cain and the Serpent have slithered their way into each and every one of them, commandeering them and twisting them around just enough to guide every participant towards the *opposite* moral direction of what the Bible might considers of God, or Godly.

So, now, let's begin by understanding how each horse came about, and how each has grown to such a massive size. And, if this particular postulation on those four horses is correct, then each group theoretically should represents around a *quarter* of the earth's population (if we think about it)! Yes, if it's really here, then it's really something massive. Could there be such a set up in our world today? The kicker seems to lie in the latter part of those verses, above:

*...And power was given unto **them** over **the fourth part of the earth**...*
- Rev. 6:8 (KJV)

It's funny how a number of modern Biblical scholars seem to ignore *this* half of the verse. Why? It's because the verse doesn't exactly say that there will be four chronological events; it seems to say that each horseman will hold influence, or power, over a **fourth of the earth**. Fairly straightforward, right? Could this "quarter" actually be a quarter of the world's population, or even a quarter of all the land where people live? Could many of these educated elites have gotten it a little wrong? Could we, indeed, be able to divide the people of the earth into a four, general "groups?"

Also, if we are really talking about four massive human groups here, we may need to reiterate that the vast majority of people in these groups (probably) do not have a deeper, nefarious agenda - they probably do not have a deeper understanding of all that's *really* going on within their leadership. They probably don't know who might really be "pulling the strings" here, in regards to the top levels. Of course, it was all configured to be that way, over time… by you-know-who (in the Garden of Eden). It may have been a slow process, but the progression would continue, on and on. So many common people, here, might even believe that they are doing everything right, or according to God's will… unaware that their top brass have "sold their souls" right out from under them. It's so sad.

As we continue to dig deeper into it all, we'll begin to see how each group could have grown, to become as large as they are now. We'll also discover how a group or two may have even "emerged" out of another one (at least as far as ideologies are concerned). Regardless of their histories, regardless of just "who" may have sprung out of "whom," these four horses, today, are able to stand on their own, each thriving independently from one another. And, if this all is real (and each one represents about a *quarter* of the world's population during the **time of the apocalypse**) then maybe this is telling us something deeper, and a little disturbing: maybe we are close to those "end times!" Maybe we're a lot **closer** to a number of up-and-coming apocalyptic events than we may have ever realized.

On top of what we already discussed here, there seems to be *more* to these four horses (at least according to the Bible). This additional information could us to pinpoint - even more succinctly - just who the four horses might represent. The Bible, essentially, refers to this additional information as something negative, or even "atrocities" - each atrocity corresponding to a particular *domineering* technique, or modem that usually used by a particular horse, in to maintain control over their populations.

We see one example of these verses in the Book of Revelation:

> *...And power was given unto them over the fourth part of the earth, to kill with* **sword**, *and with* **hunger**, *and with* **death**, *and with the* **beasts of the earth**.
> - *Rev.* 6:8 (KJV)

Along these same lines, there's another set of verses in the Book of Ezekiel which seems to state a lot of the same:

> *For thus saith the Lord GOD; How much more when I send my four sore judgments upon Jerusalem, the* **sword**, *and the* **famine**, *and the* **noisome beast**, *and the* **pestilence**, *to cut off from it man and beast?*
> - *Ezek.* 14:21 (KJV)

Both of these verses are important. Let's take a premature stab at understanding it all, by assigning a few atrocities to one of these four horses. For reasons that we will discuss later, we'll assign:

- *the Black Horse, and how it works through* **"death"** *or* **"pestilence"** - this signifies that the leaders of the Black Horse could, quite often, control people by perpetuating or selling *death* as a major means of achieving one's own personal potential, or self-actualization. They also may spread infectious, ideological *pestilence*, or dangerous ideals, among their own people - convincing them to glorify the *opposite* of all that's needed to achieve a healthy and fulfilling life.[4] They even may front *death* as some kind of spiritual "stepping stool," in order to help one achieve their own spiritual "utopia."

- *the White Horse, and how it works through* **"hunger"** *or* **"famine"** - This signifies how the leaders of the White Horse could, quite often, control people by (continually) heading them into a meek or humbled direction, towards a state of yearning, of need, poverty, etc. They keep people just a little shy of having enough physical, material or (especially) *spiritual* fulfillment - they keep them *hungry*!

- *the Green Horse, and how it works through* **"the sword"** - This signifies how the leaders of the Green Horse could, quite often, be able to control people through intimidation, with the use of weapons, guns, etc. - even with the *sword* itself!

- *the Red Horse, and how it works through* **"the noisome beasts of the earth"** - this signifies that the leaders of the Red Horse could, quite often, control people by harsh ideological tactics. They do not use religious "trickery;" instead, they may act "beast-like," regarding their methods of keeping people in line, or making someone more subversive. Adherence to "beast-like" ideologies are important to this individuals; they don't mind using fear, violence, threats of torture, and etc., to maintain their power and control.

Each horse, and their respective "atrocities," will be analyzed more as we go on; and (hopefully) we'll understand what it all might mean.

But, first, let's take a look at the **Black** Horse. We'll also take a look at the group of individuals who may have gotten caught up in those "death-loving" ways of this particular "blackened" quarter.

The "Black Horse" - An Introduction

*...And I beheld, and lo a **black** horse...*
  - Rev. 6:5 (KJV)

If our "alternate" look at those Four Horsemen contains any shreds of viability, we need to begin it all by examining this third horse (as mentioned in the Bible). Why the third? And, why the Black Horse and not the others? Well, for one thing, we already know that the Bible doesn't necessarily say that there *has* to be a particular order to them all. It, again, just says that there are four. Logic tells us that, because of this, one horse doesn't necessarily have to come right before or after another. And, as we begin to proceed, we'll begin to discover a few reasons *why* this particular horse needs to be put out there at the beginning.

To "let the cat out of the bag" a little early here, a major reason why we need to begin with this horse is because (in certain ways) it could be considered the "foundational" horse, if you will… with other horses possibly stemming from it, or utilizing elements of it. We'll understand more about this as time goes on. It also could be thought of as one of the "earliest" horses out there - originating all the way back to the *Garden of Eden*! So, yes, because of all this, it only seems fitting to begin our study right here, at this point.

Those Quarter Totals

Now, let's provide a little bit more evidence of this horse being a representation of a quarter of the world's population. If there are, roughly, six or seven billion people on the earth today then each horse should, roughly, hold sway over about a *quarter* of the world's population - approximately 1.5 to 1.7 billion people![5] Do we *really* have the ability to "split" the world's stage into four "population centers" here? Can we divide the world into four general commonalities of human thought, political belief or religious dogma - at least, approximate it? The answer may indeed be *yes*.

For starters, we may hypothesize that this Black Horse could represent a group of individuals who, in one way or another, lie under some means of **pagan** influence, share some collective pagan attributes, or possess the desire to go in some worldly, or *pagan*, direction. After a while, and by continuing to hold onto this assumption, it'll be hard to believe that the Black Horse could be anything but *black*.

Let's now bring in a few major religions into the picture, and discover how a number of them do seem to identify as having the same pagan elements, and, how a number of them could, quite possibly, form the population of this Black Horse.

To refresh our understanding on just what may be the power structure behind the Black Horse, we, first, need to recall a definition of who "pagans" are:

*...those who practiced a religion **other** than Christianity, Judaism, or Islam.*
("Paganism", 2024, p. 1)[6]

Sounds pretty straightforward (at least, in a good number of ways). Paganism, essentially, involves *any* religion or form of worship that doesn't particularly point towards the God of the Bible. The other three faiths (above) do, for the most part. The majority of people under this pagan "umbrella" do not give the God of Scripture a lot of consideration, if any. It'll all makes total sense here, because, as we'll soon see, paganism and the Black Horse **both** seem to stand for any religious belief, or religious dogma, which is *diametrically opposed* to most all of what the God of the Bible may stand for. They, quite often, seem to head the believer into completely *opposite* ideological directions (as we'll soon see). Let's look at a few of the larger pagan religions out there, as well as some (approximate) human numbers that belong to each.

They are:

-**Hinduism**, with approx. 1,100,000,000 followers
-**Buddhism**, with approx. 500, 000,000 followers
-**Shintoism**, with approx. 104,000,000 followers
-**Sikhism**, with approx. 25,000,000 followers
-**Daoism**, with approx. 12,000,000 followers
-**Muism/Shinism/Shingyo**, with approx. 10,000,000 followers
-**Confucianism**, with approx. 6,000,000 followers
-**Cao Dai**, with approx. 4,400,000 followers
-**Janism**, with approx. 4,500,000 followers
        ("The 10 Largest Religions in the World", 2022, p. 22)[7]

Add them all together, and we have approximately **1.766** billion people! Wow. That's very close to our 1.5 to 1.7 billion person "requirement." It's practically a quarter of the world's population! And, yes, as we notice, all of them do share a commonality: their dogmas really don't point them towards the God of the Bible (in the slightest), but, rather, point them towards something pagan.

Here's another source on the subject:

*We'll count Hinduism, Buddhism, Taoism, and Shintoism (etc.)... Buddhists and Hindus combined make up about **21%** of the world's religious leaning... **007%** of the world is Pagan... **3-5%** of the world's population follows Shinto. So now that brings us up **to about 24%-26%** of the world's population following a collective **Pagan definition**.*
        ("What percentage of the world is Pagan?", 2012, p. 1)[8]

It's interesting, once again, to see the pagan element, here, ending up with a quarter of the world's population - with 24%-26% of those participants identifying as having some kind of *pagan* affiliation. Could there really be something to paganism and that Black Horse?

Major Characteristics of this "Black Horse"

As we've previously mentioned, a vast majority of people in the world - pagans included - probably want to do the right thing by others, and by themselves, finding their own pathway to spiritual "enlightenment." Pagans, for the most part, just do not want to go via the route of that God and the Bible have laid out for them. Pure and simple. And, again, the typical, everyday pagan is not the real problem here. It's not really the faithful who might be lower on the totem pole, but the *top* brass, once again, as the ones who are "in the know."

So, without getting too involved in each of these religions, let's begin by looking more at the common core to them all, and what these fundamentals might mean to the Black Horse itself. First, we need to recall those negative "atrocities" of the Black Horse, as mentioned in the Bible. We, once again, have them as:

- **pestilence**
- **death**

We may recall that the word *pestilence* comes from Ezekiel 14:21. Now, does this mean that the majority of people associated with the Black Horse will have some kind of *disease* or something? Of course not. A quarter of the world's population, surely, do not have any kind of physical illness. In Biblical terms, however, the illness could be considered of as more of a "falling away" from God, or an *unhealthy* relationship with all things ungodly… that turns their soul "ill," if you will.

Actually, the original Hebrew word for *pestilence* here, as translated into the modern English, can mean to "speak," to "declare," "promise," even to "**lead away**" (or "put to flight") something.[9] Could these definitions help to better explain the real *significance* of this "pestilence" atrocity, at least according to the Bible? Could it stand for subtle, religious rhetoric, or certain philosophies or theologies, that may truly *hurt* an individual, at least as far as their relationship with God? Could it really be what those "top" elites are trying to spew out to people, working to sway the masses towards the *opposite* of most everything that the Bible calls Godly? It could easily be an *infection* of ideas, if you will, or (according to the Bible) a number of *toxic* words, poisoning the souls of the people in these groups.

What about the other "atrocity" of *death* (as in Rev. 6:8)? What could this be all about? Well, it's fairly simple, if we really think about it. The leaders of this Black Horse would also be out there, trying to perpetuate (or "sell") *death* as a means of personal redemption, or even salvation. As we'll soon see, with their particular approach towards a personal "utopia," a person may begin to feel that their own death has something special to offer them… a lot more than just the end of their one and only life. These elites may have even been able to convince many that this is a time of departure, a gateway into another stage of existence, far greater! Of course, it may begin to sound a lot like Christianity, and their belief that one might go to heaven after their death. But, there's actually a vast difference between the two ideologies (as we soon shall see). Instead of death being thought of as something a person may want to avoid, or even *loath*, it now is considered another rung up that pagan "ladder towards perfection." This life, according to pagan ideology, represents only a personal "springboard" if you will, where the individual might be able to find ways to better themselves… the next time they are born again. It's all about them, with no God in any of the process. There's no real savior… except *themselves* (and their own actions).

Yes, so many of those religions under this pagan umbrella seem to subscribe to this same particular ideology. And, as we'll soon see, the Black Horse also seems to hold onto similar ideologies… those that try to take people far away from God and those that try to get people to look forward to their death. And now, for the sake of identifying a few of these parallels, we'll now postulate that paganism, as well as this Black Horse, both:

- **head people in a "darkened" direction (or, away from God).**
- **glorify death/reincarnation.**
- **believe in natural (i.e. earth-based) spiritual forces, nature spirits, etc.**
- **front multiple deities/gods (and not just one).**
- **promote ancestor worship.**

In the next chapter, we'll look into each one of these links a bit more, and see how we can begin to link paganism and the Black Horse - as one in the same. We already know (from the last two volumes) what *paganism* is all about, and where it really had come from. This may help us connect the two together even more, and in ways we may have never really thought of! Let's go.

Chapter 2

The Black Horse - Pagan Connection

*And the light shineth in **darkness**; and the darkness comprehended it not.*
                              - John 1:5 (KJV)

*And this is the condemnation, that light is come into the world, and men **loved darkness** rather than light...*   *- John 3:19 (KJV)*

What is paganism really all about? Could it just be an *innocent* religious platform, emphasizing a love for nature, or a love for all things of this lower world... as a representation of the *real* gods and goddesses we have? Is it all just benign, or could there be something a lot *deeper*, and a lot less innocent, to it all?

As we're beginning to discover, elements of pagan thought *do* seem to point a person in the direction of all things *opposing* God, or whatever's diametrically opposed to all that God might want for His people... and they're fine with it! What, traditionally, was wrong is now **right**... according to paganism. What was once down is now *up*. All of the *chaos* that may end up resulting from this falling away from God is now considered the *new* order for the ages. The list goes on and on.

As we begin to focus on a few examples of pagan thought, we'll also begin to see how that Black Horse seems to be the embodiment of this pagan community as well, and a lot of what they stand for. We've already postulated that there are parallels between paganism and the Black Horse. Paganism, we know, works to:

- head people in a "darkened" direction (or, away from God).

Interestingly enough, we've already understood that (from previous volumes) there was an actual (spiritual) "location," known as the *Darkness*, located deep beneath our physical existence here on earth. And this *Darkness* could easily have been considered a "holding cell" of sorts, for a number of human souls in transition. Some call it Hades;

some refer to it as Sheol. Still others refer to it as Hell. But, ultimately, it's essentially believed to be some kind of spiritual place, where one's soul has to exist… **without the heavenly God**.

We this, we could assume that: if one really wants to lead a decent, Godly life then they should not be looking to head in any direction that might direct them to any *lower* plane, or anything away from God's light. We should always be looking *upward*, towards something in the heavenly realms, because that's where God is. Yet, in pagan belief, we'll see that a number of ideologies seem to coax an individual into going the *opposite* direction of this. Again, as we continue to see, it's either one way or another - either *up* or *down*.

Let's look at a few examples.

The "Darkening" of One's Mind

Most things around us, including our physical bodies, are made up of physical, earthly material. We also could figure that God considers this entire world a corrupted and fallen cosmos, thanks to the Fall. Naturally, this would include our *physical* bodies as well. So, if everything *down* below, here - in the fallen world around us - is a part of this same corrupted situation, then it makes perfect sense to assume that we are all separated from God, at least to certain degrees. And, it also makes perfect sense to assume that: the farther *down* one begins to head, the *darker* everything may become for him or her. They understand that what's behind a lot of this *darkness* could really hurt them and their spirit overall; yet, paganism would rather push for the opposite of all this.

In one example, it's fairly easy to understand that *darkened* thoughts are a reality in most every person, something that we all may have to encounter. Everyone probably feels a little *low* at certain times. Yet, many of us also know that, in order to keep ourselves healthy and stable, our minds cannot stay in that state for very long. For a vast majority of the time, our minds need to be in a healthy, stable position… with clear (and not clouded) thoughts. To be fully functional, a person really need to be calm, rational and level headed… without resorting to a number of extreme *emotional* responses (in order to help guide them). We can't often be out there, losing our composure, or allowing our minds go to a *dark* place. However, with the pagan "love affair" with all things *opposing* God, this all seems to extend over to how one *thinks* as well.

Pagans may, quite often, try to push an individual in the opposite direction of where a typical Christians might - towards some manner of **conscious *darkening*** as well. They may say that, in order for a person to score their spiritual "points," they might need go **out** of their conscious mind in some way. Some, for example, may be required to involve themselves in intense sessions of **meditation**. Others might feel the need to take drugs or hallucinogenic herbs, to help them reach different (i.e. "higher") intellectual planes. Still others might begin to feel the need to participate in the higher degrees of yoga, Tantric sex, or what have you. Again, in all of these scenarios, it's about inhibiting one's own ability to use *conscious* thought, all the while using an impaired state to help them import *other* insights or inspirations. And, of course, it doesn't take a genius to figure out *where* these other thoughts may come from. If these individuals almost always seem to claim that you have to go into another, "altered state" of consciousness, in order to achieve something "higher," then we may really need to contemplate where all of these changes may really be taking us, and what they *really* may be opening up to us!

To Soul or Not to Soul...

Also, as we've already discussed (in previous volumes), one's **soul** could also be considered:

...where the spirit of God interacts with the body... (and the) area of "mind," "will," (and) "intellect"...
    ("Little Creatures: The Gates of Hell are Opening", 2015, p. 1)[1]

Could a person's *soul* parallel a person's own intellectual capacity - their **consciousness**? Could it represent that part of a human being where everyday thoughts occur - a place where one use rationality, reason, etc? These abilities indeed could have been part of what God *uniquely* wanted to give to human beings, and to them alone. Animals do not have such capabilities, and there's a reason for this. Our consciousness could easily be thought of as our soul, because our consciousness seems to allow us a way to set a good moral standard for ourselves, and for others. Yet, once again, paganism would rather have us diminish this capacity.

We also recall (from previous volumes) that God came down to earth (before the Fall) and gave Adam, the man He just formed, a "living soul" (in Gen. 2:7). We've also discovered that, from that point on, Adam was known as the "Thinker" - a man who, most probably, used a considerable amount of rationality, reason and logic. He now had a reflective *soul*... being self-conscious and aware of his surroundings. And, ultimately, he used it to temper all of his other thoughts... with self-control and humility. It's a very important part of the mind.

Ultimately, with his consciousness, Adam also seemed as though he wanted to be *closer* to God! That also seems to be another reason why God gave not only Adam a living soul, but all of mankind! He wants people to be closer to Him. Yes, the conscious *soul* does seems to be something really special... something of immense spiritual value! And, if one's *soul* is considered to be something special (given to us by God), then why would we want to be in a number of positions that may require us to start wasting it away? It just doesn't seem right.

And, as long as Adam remained conscious and self-aware, he (most probably) didn't really feel a need to act out in very many negative ways, nor would he allow any negative things from the outside in. His conscious *soul* stopped him from becoming too overly-emotional, from acting out on a number of those inner feelings of *pride*, envy, etc. It represents that great **barrier** to so much negativity. Yet, paganism wants us to open our mind up, and get rid of any barriers to what they might want us to allow in. It's pretty much the *opposite* of what God wants: to diminish our souls, and rely a lot more on *emotions* to help us made decisions, and open up our minds to whatever things this lower (and often *darkened*) world might have to offer.

Extreme Emotions, Passions and Feelings

Well, what about some of those *other* things that might begin to enter the mind (after the conscious mind is diminished)? What about **emotions**, for example? Are they all bad?

Do they always head us in the wrong direction? No, not necessarily. But, leaving them unchecked, allowing people to "fly off the handle" at times (with continued emotional responses) could, quite easily, get a lot of us into trouble. People **need** to be in their conscious mind - a vast majority of the time - to help them "block out" potential interferences… especially emotional interferences. They need to use rationality and reason to evaluate what might be going on around them, to help them make proper decisions overall. Relying on sheer emotion really doesn't really seem to "cut it."

Interestingly enough, some versions of the Bible even state something much to this effect:

> *Whatsoever thy hand is able to do, do it earnestly: for neither work, **nor reason**, nor wisdom, nor knowledge **shall be in hell**…*
> *- Eccl.* 9:10 (Douay-Rheims 1899 American Edition)

Well, if the use of *reason* doesn't help to point us in the direction of hell, than what might?

Some of us may have even seen a "witch doctor," or tribal doctor, on television, who might come from remote areas of Africa or South America (for example), and many will explain to the cameraman that, in order for them to achieve their magical outcomes, they either need to take some kind of hallucinogenic drug, or need to go into some kind of extreme **emotional** state (or **emotional** "frenzy"). Either way, they needed to go *out* of their conscious mind in some way… all for their pagan results. Yes, they're surely not petitioning to God here, with their actions!

Yes, it seems that: those from the pagan realm would either want a person to go out of their conscious mind, or become extremely emotional in some way, before their protocols will be effective. Doesn't *that* tell us something, here?

The "Fiery Seraph"

Let's also recall (from previous volumes) a bit of information about the two most powerful beings of the "Other Side" - those ultimately rooted in the entire pagan process. The *Serpent* was once considered a "**Fiery Seraph**"... before his downfall, of course. To understand what this title may have originally meant, let's break it down a little. As we may also recall, the Serpent was once considered a *Seraph* - a high-ranking angel with a great deal of medicinal knowledge. But, what about the word "fiery?" Did he actually breathe *fire*, or could it have stood for something else?

Throughout history, we've had various descriptions of the Devil (i.e. the Serpent): he was (and *is*) a type of *dragon*, with horns, tail, and a stream of "fire" coming out of his mouth. But, are these accurate descriptions, or are they, for the most part, just esoteric symbols? The whole sense of having "flames" firing out of one's mouth could easily symbolize how much *passion* - or, *fevered* passion - that comes out. In other words, a person (or angel) who continually speaks with a strong emotional cadence, or seems extremely fire branded to a particular cause, could easily be symbolized as one who's breathes out "fire." It, most probably, was all symbolic. And, from what we may already know (from previous volumes), both Samuel and the Serpent were thought to be *very* vocal, and over-zealous… which was a part of their fall from grace. Now, if intense, emotional expressions could have had a part in bringing even *these angels* down, then wouldn't the same be able to affect a vast numbers of mortal people in our world the same way?

Reincarnating… into Something Better?

Speaking of these processes of diminishing (or even "destroying") something that's considered a natural part of us - such as our mind - let's take a look at how agents of paganism, as well as the Black Horse, might also want us to get rid of something *else*, beyond our souls… our own physical bodies! Yes, could they really be out for *everything* that we possess on this earth: our minds, our souls, *and* our entire bodies? Apparently, so.

We recall how pagan ideology seems to:

- glorify death/reincarnation.

Well, talk about destroying *every* part of a human being! First we diminish the mind; now we have them trying to entice people to *look forward* to their own deaths! They make it sound as if death a good thing, a means towards achieving a higher plane of existence, or another "rung up" that "divine" ladder. Pagans truly believe that they could reach a state of godhood… without any intervention from the God of the Bible. They don't need anything that God has to offer. One can do it *on their own*. And, of course, all they need to do is to realize that their pathway to divinity is found in the world *around them*, or is *already* inside of them... all they have to do is to just reach out, and take the "fruits" of the world around them.

This, essentially, is what **reincarnation** is all about. If certain criteria are met, an individual could keep heading towards a "higher" plane of existence, every time they die, until they ultimately obtain "enlightenment," or their own spiritual "perfection." Wow. Who wouldn't want to look forward to their own death then, with these promises in hand! It essentially states: one could reach a state of godhood, all they need to do is "play their cards right" in their current life, and **die** a virtuous pagan... and then, "utopia!"

The reincarnation process, according to them, was modeled after the victories of early pagan "gods":

> *While the initiates of the mystery cult enacted the life cycles of gods who **triumphed** over death and who where reborn, they also assured **their own path** of wisdom that would enable them to conquer death, accomplish resurrection in the afterlife, and undergo rebirth in a new body, in a new existence.*
> (Steiger, 2006, p. 308)[2]

God, of course, is nowhere to be found... these "gods" did it all. Wow. But, what these pagan elites won't tell you is that you might only have one life. What if their way is not entirely correct? They won't tell you that, after this life, it's all about God's judgment, with no second chances at doing it by yourself. It's obviously stated in the Bible that God wants people to make the *most* out of their lives, and make the most out their time in this world... not look towards their death as being some kind of "stepping stone." He wants us to have the best life that we can possibly have. Yet, with both paganism and the Black Horse, it seems to be about the ***opposite***. The darkening of one's mind, as well as looking towards one's own *death*, takes a person in the direction of something better... but, if we think about it, it really takes one in the direction of all things *black*. People don't conquer *darkness* (without God)... they get *absorbed* by it!

As any student of history may also be able to tell us: the ancient Egyptians (as well as other ancient empires) were run by leaders who almost seemed *obsessed* with death. It's like they concentrated so much on this (supposed) time of transformation that they went out and continually prepared for it, in many extensive and expensive ways. The Egyptian pharaohs, for examples, had his people building massive burial structures, all the while inserting a large number of priceless objects inside… all waiting for that "special" time, and all of it to "help him out" in that next life. He would even command everybody to celebrate his death with extreme pomp and circumstance! Again, the *blackness* is what a number of these people began to fall in love with, not the light.

This obsession with death did not stop with ancient peoples, however. Even today, in Central America (for example), a vast number of people *still* celebrate the "Day of the Dead" - a yearly festival honoring all things *death*! What a concept to behold.

Many Bible scholars may already recall how the "Angel of **Death**" (in the Bible) is none other than Sammael (or Satan) himself! Go figure. Who would know more about *death*, and how to manipulate this topic, than he would!

> *… that through death He (Jesus) might destroy him who had the power of* **death***, that is, the devil.*   - Heb. 2:14 (KJV)

It only makes sense to assume that this particular angel would absolutely love to show human beings how to look forward to their own deaths, or even celebrate it! To the "Other Side," it's all about death and blackness. On the other extreme, God wants us to strong, blessed and successful - He wants it to be about His light, above.

> *Renowned psychologist Erich Fromm comments that these (death-loving) "necrophiles" have "precisely the* **reverse of the values** *we connect with normal life: not life, but* **death** *excites and satisfies them" - death in all of the sensational downward spirals of a* **selfish, purposeless existence***.*
>   (Clare Prophet, 2000, p. 38)[3]

How true, here, it all seems. It's truly either one way or another.

Again, what if all of these glorious references to death could be an outright scam? Once again, although reincarnation may sound quite alluring to a vast number of people, we need to ask ourselves: what if it really does not work? Not only would a person be focusing on the wrong things in life, but they also may be giving away their one and only chance at personal redemption! If God gave us the means to make it to heaven already, and we've decide to ignore it, then what? We're stuck.

And then, our mind, body *and* soul would be lost... forever.

"Nature" Spirits, "Earthly Elementals"

To gather a few more parallels between paganism and this Back Horse, let's take a look at more meanings of *black* in the Bible. Obviously, this color - the color behind the Black Horse - could also stand for the *abyss, emptiness* and *gloominess*, and it seems that this *blackness* could manifest itself, quite a lot, in our *lower world* around us. And, if we really think about it, it does make sense. All that is in heaven, and from heaven, would, naturally, be bright - illuminated by the light of God. All that is of this fallen world, however (which is farther and farther away from God), would begin to manifest as the opposite of what's God: darkness, blackness, etc. It only makes sense.

And, if this truly is the case, it only makes sense to assume that our fallen world would be subjected to those who have authority over all this darkness, such as those of the "Other Side." And, wouldn't these same forces that pagans everywhere tell us that we need to communicate with, or even submit to, to get us our "divine assistance?" What if there is a lot more to it?

Yes, according to a number of these individuals, there are spirits down below, *in the trees, in the water*, and even *inside animals*, influencing their environment. These spirits could even be in the rocks, in the wind, and in fire... almost anything. The world is alive with spirits in the elements. This, in actuality, is one cornerstone of pagan thought.

As well, a number of pagans may begin to claim that spiritual entities - behind all of these things we see around us - represent what's *really* working "behind the scenes," so they need to be appeased to, or worshiped. *They* are the elements behind most of the changes in our world, so they must be revered as "gods."

As we've already postulated, paganism seems to:

- believe in natural (i.e. earth-based) spiritual forces, nature spirits, etc.

There really is a lot of knowledge to be had out there, especially supernatural knowledge. There's power to be gathered. A lot of individuals, in the past, desperately wanted to know about what the future might hold for them (and still do), and wanted to know how to manipulate the world around them (to achieve results that favor them). Now, with these uses of natural (or elemental) spirits, people believed they had a means to gather a lot of this. But, of course, they're, most probably, petitioning forces of the "Other Side," and usually will not get what they want… without a price.

And, what might a number of these fallen angelic spirits or demons want in return for their services? They want power and control… ultimately, power and control over *you*. They don't like to give human beings something for nothing. They also have agendas. Ultimately, they want to bring as many members of the human race *down* to the same levels that they are. It's that simple, but that's the dirty little secret we're not told about elemental spirits.

Also, they want to have as many people to go out, and begin worshiping *them*, and not God. Of course, because of their fallen situations, they are filled with a great deal of hate, rage and anger… all towards God (the One who put them there), so why wouldn't they want to bring human beings down with them? It'll make them feel a little better, in a pitiful sort of way. To them, the more people that they can bring *down* with them, the better! Where does that lead the typical pagan parishioner, just trying to gather a little power for themselves?

The Bible, especially, mentions the attempt to communicate with earth spirits as a big "no no." It does not want us to worship *any* beings that may be around us - *angelic* or otherwise:

Let no man beguile you of your reward in a voluntary… **worshipping of angels**, *intruding into those things which he hath not seen…*
                - *Col.* 2:18 (KJV)

Ultimately, people should not be petitioning to, or praying to, *any* spiritual being around them, for any of their help (even if these spirits may have referred to themselves as a member of God's host). If an angel of God ever wanted to appear to mankind, it's probably because they were sent there by God. They won't just come there "on their own," or via the result of petitioning. True angels of God are *not* to respond to any person's petition. It just doesn't work that way, and, don't be fooled into believing anything otherwise. The "Other Side" wants you to be confused on just "who's who" here, or believe that there could be "good" or "neutral" spirits out there... beyond anything that's just *dark*. Again, these spirits are either from one side or another.

Institutionalized Deities?

What started out as a number of human petitions to various spiritual elements of this lower world would, eventually, turn into something much bigger. Eventually, a number of these early pagan "gods" would begin to take central stage, and become the major gods we may have heard of today. According to a number of pagan intellectuals, a good deal of these minor nature (or elemental) spirits have, over time, made their way into the "big time," transforming themselves in **major** gods and goddesses! And, as we recall from the above, there's another characteristic that may link paganism to the Black Horse. Paganism seems to:

- front multiple deities/gods (and not just one).

Way back in the Old Testament, idolatry - or the worshipping of multiple spiritual entities as gods - was already considered to be a "big thing." This was the reason that God decided to place two very important commandments at the top of the original 10 Commandments! With this particular step, it seems obvious that these commandments were important to Him, and He did not want competition. He still doesn't.

Yet, the worshipping of *many* deities seems to be another hallmark, or foundation, of this pagan faith. It, as well, shows us how paganism is related to what comes out of our lower, *darkened world*. And, once again, this seems to give us evidence for a relationship between the pagan cause and that particular Biblical *horse* of darkness, known as the Black Horse.

One's Own "Ascension"… Into Ancestor Worship?

On top of accepting these "natural," or elemental, spirits as gods (who are, in actuality, fallen angels or demons), there's a bit more to this whole pagan take on godliness they also believe that ordinary humans could turn into gods, as well (if all the right steps are taken, of course). Our human *ancestors* could also become pagan "gods," straight away. And, this does make sense, understanding *their* take on reincarnation. So, according to them, when a noble pagan reaches their "end game," through reincarnation, they *also* can become divine, and a deity to be worshipped. Wow, who wouldn't mind ending up becoming a "god," being worshipped by your own descendants (if one follows the proper pagan protocol of course)? See how seductive it all could end up being?

As we've already postulated, paganism seems to:

- promote ancestor worship.

We already might recall what happened at the time of the Garden of Eden, where the Serpent tried to convince Eve that she could become a "goddess," knowing good and evil (if she only followed *his* particular ways, of course). Sound familiar? Yes, it's all the same - even today. Today, it still seems to be a cornerstone of this whole reincarnation concept!

We also recall (from previous volumes) how ancestor worship had roots in none other than Cain and (his father) the Serpent… the grand *ancestors* of all this paganism. The worshiping of particular ancestors began here, with none other than these two founders. It's all makes a lot more sense, once we begin to attribute those missing pieces.

And yes, again, paganism seems to be a lot about "smoke and mirrors" though, with a number of demons and fallen angels mimicking the likeness of certain dead ancestors…

in order to fool the living into calling on them, and worshiping them. Yes, it's all the same; and yes, they're also very sneaky! The spirits of these "ancestors," once again, aren't who they say they are. They're out for blood… literally. They're out here, pulling the strings of deception, and causing people to go from bad to worse.

From all of this, it's easy to understand how the many avenues of pagan "enlightenment" eventually head people towards something that is, in reality, *dark*, or even *blackened* to the core. It definitely turns people in the opposite direction of all things Godly, which assists us in understanding how that *Black* Horse could also be related to all things *dark*, or things of this *lower* world. It also helps us explain how almost a quarter of the world's population got caught up in a what the **Black Horse** is, and is all about.

More Worldly "Contributions"

Now that we've looked into a number of pagan foundations, and discovered how they might also be related to that which comprises the Black Horse, let's take a quick look at early propagators of this pagan faith, and what they were able to accomplish so early on. One could only imagine how much of an entrenchment it all might have had to our ancient world, if "properly" handled (at least, according to them).

From previous volumes, we may already recall how the pagan religion actually originated with Cain and the Serpent. After the garden, things would seem to take on a life of its own (thanks to those two above individuals, as well as a whole number of fallen, terrestrial angels around them). It's incredible how much this ancient religion was able to expand out because of this, influencing the ancient world to such a degree.

We might also recall (from previous volumes) how, after the Fall of Man, Cain and the Serpent were able to promote their *own* ways of channeling water to the masses, to make it more useful in this post-Fall world. People were already using irrigation techniques before the Fall, in the Garden of Eden; but, this time, they would no longer be subjected to Adam, or having to work under Adam's authority. They began to be the ones who were taking *all* of the credit for any more irrigation advancements here. And, since this time, the two provided a system of aqueducts for the people, which delivered **water** accurately, to where it needed to go, and on a massive scale.

We also recall how Cain, eventually, was known as the god of *techne* - a discipline by which we get the word *technology*. Cain eventually became known as the "god of the forge," from which we get the industrial uses of *fire*. Cain (thanks to his father, once again) understood how to utilize this element, and pushed it to a whole number of people. It's surely became a lot easier for people to construct tools and metallic pieces of equipment with this knowledge; and, as time went on, they were able to work their fields a bit easier, as well as do bigger and bigger things, such as formulate new and effective **weapons**.

All of these talents allowed Cain to start taking people (mentally and physically) *away* from their former lives - a lifestyle of cloth tents and accomplishing things "by hand." After this, Cain also began to show people how to construct large stone structures, even into individual homes. Of course, Cain would, over the years, want to go beyond the construction of a few simple homes and buildings. He wanted more. And, as ancient sources tell us (even the Bible), Cain was originally supposed to wander the earth, thinking about his murder of Abel. God dictated he was not really supposed to stay in one place, for very long. Yet, as a typical pagan might respond to anything Godly, Cain strived to do the *opposite* of what God instructed him to do. Why stop now, with the construction of ordinary homes? Why not go bigger?

Yes, later on, Cain would commission the construction of larger and larger stone structures. He was also more than willing to help out this new pagan cult by making sure that there were religious edifices going up, as well. And, of course, a lot of that terrestrial, angelic knowledge was being put into "proper" practice here. As well, a number of giant, hybrid offspring seemed more than happy to help Cain out, with the enormous feats of labor required to complete such ancient feats of construction. Things would eventually take off. And yes, thanks to his father, Cain knew that he had the Nephilim, as well as those antediluvian giants, in his back pocket. All of it helped Cain to achieve as much of his vision as possible, which was a lot.

Ancient sources even tell us that Cain was responsible for the building of at least seven antediluvian **cities**:

- Eridu (or Edin... the city closest to, and probably named after, the Garden of Eden)
- Erech (i.e. Uruk?)
- Sumer
- Kish or Kush (i.e. Akkad?)
- Calneh
- Ur of the Chaldees
- **Babylon**, the great (of course)

Of course, practically all of the sins that emerged out of this pagan powerhouse of *Babylon* would end up "escalating" the city into a city like no other (at least, according to the Bible)... and it wasn't to be for something honorable:

> *...Babylon the great is fallen, is fallen, and is become the habitation of **devils**... For all nations have drunk of the wrath of the wine of her fornication. and the kings of the earth have committed fornication with her, and the merchants of the earth are **waxed rich** through the abundance of her delicacies.*
> - Rev. 18:2-3 (KJV)

> *...how is **Babylon** become a desolation among the nations!*
> - Jer. 50:23 (KJV)

So many things went on in our ancient past. Great structures, indeed, were built. Intricate pagan temples and edifices were raised, and utilized. Paganism all took off, and was promoted.

And, once again, modern history tells us that, even though a number of these advancements **should not** have been able to take place, they it did at this time, with remnants of these ancient advancements still being seen today! *How* did they do it, if we're supposed to be thousands of years "ahead" of these ancient societies? How could archaeologists - with a straight face - explain these ancient boosts of knowledge and understanding? They can't... but, we can.

There are even a number of items out there which have (over the years) been discovered by archaeologists and lay people alike, known as "OOP" (or "Out Of Place") artifacts. They are so-called because the "experts" of today cannot really give their public a good reason as to *how* the people of ancient times were able to construct such a thing, nor where they may have received their information to do so... but, *we* know.

Of course, if you add the fallen, terrestrial angels (i.e. the Nephilim) into the mix (and all the knowledge that they're able to provide to the ancient world), supplement it with the contributions of their giant, hybrid offspring were able to provide, over the years since, and there's no telling what the ancient populous could have accomplished with these additional elements added to their world.

The dignitaries of these ancient times, most probably, became a **huge** part of what helped to spur paganism and the Black Horse to new horizons, and into many, many different households. They definitely helped to launch these ways into becoming more and more appealing to the vast majority of people out there.

And, as we continue on with this volume, we'll need to continue with more of the history of these gigantic offspring, and how they progressed throughout the ages. A vast majority of these individuals, assuredly, became very troublesome to the post-Fall world, largely due to a reflection of their original ancestry. They were *especially* troublesome to all of those seeking the ways of God. These beings would also end up bartering that "forbidden" knowledge of their forbearers, allowing them become some of the biggest propagators of all things *lower*, or of this *darkened* world, as well as all things **pagan**. Yes,. it all seems to be interrelated. And, because of their infusions, the entirety of the ancient world was about to become a lot more complex, as well as corrupt.

Chapter 3

The White Horse -
An Extension of the "Black"?

Now that we've looked into a number of pagan foundations, and discovered how they might, often, parallel the Black Horse, we'll begin to go a bit *further* down this "rabbit hole" of Biblical corruption, and, hopefully, gain a much *deeper* understanding of how certain forces from the "Other Side" work to manipulate the populous at large, or even work to influence *more* of these other colored "horses."

Well, where should we go from here? Could this *second* horse - the White Horse - have at least some kind of relationship with that (former) Black Horse? And, if so, just what could this second horse be all about? And, what might be its modus operandi, especially if it, on the outer surface, seems to portray an image the opposite of all that's *black*, or *darkened*. It's got to be called the White Horse for a reason. If this was the case, then it, assuredly, would not want to advertise itself as anything pagan, or anything of this lower world (at least, not publicly). To be true to its color, it should be standing for things a lot different than the Black Horse, even more of the *opposite*! Now, what could this be?

It only makes sense, then, to believe that this White Horse could have represented those *Judeo-Christian* and *Catholic* populations of our world - the chaste *as well as* **the corrupt**. With that White Horse, we'll need to take into account the orthodox as well as the liberal; the fundamental as well as the superfluous; the serious individuals as well as those "Christmas and Easter only" attendees!

With that being said and done, we end up with this Judeo-Christian/Catholic total as a little over 25% of the world's population (once again). Those claiming to follow Judaism were about 15 million people, or only about .2% of the world's population. But, to round things out, we have many, many more Protestants and Catholics:

In 1900, around 16 percent of the world population was Catholic. This number peaked at around 18 percent in 1970, before falling back some to the same level of 16 percent in 2020.
    ("Global Catholicism: Diverse, Troubled, Holding Steady", 2021, p. 4)[1]

The current Catholic total, as we see, floats from around 16%-18% of the world's population, with Protestantism ending up around the 11.6% mark.[2] Adding in Eastern Orthodoxy (about 4% of the total population), and we, supposedly, have a little over 30% of the world's population taking this stand.

Of course, these are just estimates; but, if we really think about it, we also need to take into account the many, *many* people who may go around, stating that they are a member of one of these faiths, but, in reality, are (more or less) just "going through the motions." They might feel a need to attend church, or mass, on major holidays, and that's all. We've all, assuredly, met a number of these individuals over the years. But, if we really think about it: to be *truly* of a particular faith one needs to really involve themselves in a change of heart, maintaining an aura of seriousness. Of course, there's nothing wrong with one associating themselves with a faith. And, there's also nothing wrong with one just "going through the motions," if that's all they want out of it. But, of course, to become a serious contender in all things Godly, one needs to adopt a certain Godly lifestyle - desiring to live out most every moment in the service of God, and, according to His life directions.

So, now, if we're able to subtract out those who are just "not really into" their faith (and, assuredly, there are a good number of them out there), then our percentage of the world's population would easily be reduced, probably around to 25%. And, if we also believe that Catholicism and Protestantism are, most probably, on the *decline*, then it also supports a reduced percentage. Given the contemporary political climate of our world today, we have educational systems removing these faiths from almost all schools and universities. We also have the current, ungodly media, knocking out Judeo-Christian values left and right. And, we also have a massive rise of humanism and politically correct thought… all against the God of the Bible. With all of this, we cannot help but believe that this 30% estimate may be a little high, or is quickly going *down*.

Either way, if these White Horse faiths had what it took to be able to draw a least a quarter of the world's population into them (over time), then at least *something* must have been working in their favor (even if a good amount of it has turned corrupt)! So, now, in order for us to discover just *why* the faiths of Protestantism, Catholicism as well as Judaism could have been a inserted into one of these "horses," let's begin our journey - to make sense of all that may have happened in our past, as well as how *corruption* could have been allowed to eventually settle in.

Earlier on (in this volume), we've understood the "atrocities" of the former horse: what Black Horse elites may often use to control and manipulate the masses. We know that they used (and still use) *death* and (spiritual) *pestilence* to subtly draw people into their own fold. Yet, we might recall that the "atrocities" of this White Horse are not exactly the opposite of this all, not even close - they represent **hunger** and ***famine***. Well, just what might they mean, and what could they stand for? Do these attributes - those of which the White Horse elites use to manipulate *their* masses - stand for some kind of *impoverished* state? Not exactly what me might think. We'll soon discover that these types of *hunger* and *famine* might actually represent some kind of *spiritual* hunger, or *spiritual* famine, driven by a lack of spiritual "nutrition." It would be because the White Horse elites would contribute to the "starvation" of their people... for something more. Deep down in their soul, their lack of "nutrition" cannot seem to be fulfilled.

Sure, there might already be a number of people in this White Horse group who are physically hungry, or poor, just as in any other group out there... it's just that the White Horse would stand alone, here, for what their leaders might often do: they would work to lead individuals into a *Biblical* or God-fearing direction, but not totally, and not solely. They're different because they will not quite deliver what they may need to, ideologically... which leaves their patrons essentially "starving!"

This is also why the White Horse is considered "white": they will claim that they are not pagan. They appear to be a "pure as the driven snow," and are individuals who are on "God's side." The elements of the pure Judeo-Christian faith are altered just enough. Cain it be? Apparently, yes. That's why each horse in Revelation might have a few sinister elements to it as well, subtly seducing a whole number of people.

And, to add insult to injury, a number of White Horse elites may have, over the years, even brought in some elements of the *Black Horse* into their mantras, to further dilute and further confuse the pureness of what was once true Judaism and Christianity.

Both are "Spiritual"

Yes, it's a little different than the Black Horse, but the elites still could do the same amount of damage to the people involved… even more so. The people might actually want something different, and they're not getting exactly what they're seeking. In the end, it all might begin to leave White Horse patrons a bit confused. There are certain elements missing, or enough elements of the faith have been switched around, just enough, to leave the individual continually yearning for more. Trust and assurance becomes wobbly at best. People cannot help but question a number of things in life. Over time, they can't help beginning to feel a bit weak, or helpless, because their foundation seems to be built on ideological sand. Ultimately, a number of people begin to feel like they're a "shell" of what a powerful believer in God (and follower of the Bible) could have been, and they're just "going through the motions" of their belief.

"False Lights"

So, if we look at how diluted and maladjusted the true faiths of Judaism and Christianity had become over the years, it's not too hard to conclude that *this* is the real modus operandi of this next horse… a "new" or "good-looking" take on Judeo-Christian beliefs and values, but not exactly (and not the same). Those heading in the direction of this White Horse want to head towards the "light," but, this time, their "lights" aren't exactly what they may have bargained for.

If we think about it, at least the elite members of the Black Horse are upfront about their paganism, and embracing it as being apart from God. They don't need to go to these deceptive extremes. And, as we may already recall (from previous volumes), Cush, Nimrod and Semiramis (of ancient Babylon) were extremely open about their paganism, and how opposing and sacrilegious they intended to be against God. They didn't really have to trick people. They wore their adherence to paganism on their shoulders, and could be able to feel this, quite easily.

Antichrist... Once Again

Most of us, as well, have heard of the Antichrist, with the topic being discussed in previous volumes. And popular interpretations will define this *Antichrist* as a man of pure evil - the *opposite* of Christ (in practically every sense). But, what this popular interpretation, often, does not tell us the whole story? What if the definition of "anti" could mean a bit more? Could it also stand for is that which is "not quite" Christ, or something "near (or close) to Christ"... but not quite?

A few modern dictionaries even seem to define the word *anti* as:

> ...*of **the same kind*** but situated opposite, exerting energy in the opposite direction, or pursuing an opposite policy
> - Merriam-Webster Dictionary[3]

> ...***identical to** in form or function*, but lacking, opposite, or **contrary in essential** respects
> - The Free Dictionary[4]

Now, if we apply these definitions to the White Horse, we'll see a whole new world emerging - one that also supports those two "atrocities" (of spiritual *hunger* and *famine*). If the word could also stand for something that is "close to" something of Christ, but a *little* different or not exactly the same, then isn't this the M.O. of that corrupted White Horse? Wouldn't that be exactly what they are involved in? Wouldn't that be what a **rival** of Christ may want to do - to vie for a position that's *like* Christ, but is utilized to be *instead of Christ, in place* of Christ, or even (subtly) *against* Christ?[5] Understanding this alternate definition of *anti*, is oh, so important.

Now that these other definitions might help us redefine a few traditional ways of thinking, we now see how the *Antichrist*, and a number of his *antichrist* systems, may be able to "win over" a number of people, over time. Acting as though you are "on their side" is a perfect way for the Serpent to **slither** his way through the hopes and dreams of so many new Judeo-Christian converts… presently and in the future!

The White Horse - An Introduction

Well, just what might the Bible say about this White Horse, and the modems of propaganda that a vast number of "antichrists" have used to wiggle their way into the hearts of subjugated populations? Let's see how that "White Horse" is portrayed in the Book of Revelation:

> *And I saw, and behold a white horse: and he that sat on him had a **bow**; and a **crown** was given unto him: and he went forth **conquering, and to conquer**.*
> *- Rev. 6:2 (KJV)*

We have a few interesting reveals here, in regards to what this horse is all about. It also helps us to understand just how those in the upper echelons of this White Horse actually work. First, the "rider" of this horse (i.e. the leadership within it) has a **bow**. Funny, it only has a bow here, with no arrows. Why? What could this be all about? Well, it's obvious that the forces (or systems) that make up the hierarchy of this particular horse probably have the ability (and the overall might) to fight an enemy. They have a lot of fortitude, and an ability to conquer others, if necessary… but, choose not to. They, rather, seem to be out for peace.

They almost appear to be too altruistic and compassionate to start a war. They, also, seem to wear a victor's crown upon its head, as if it had been given a lot of people and land over or time. In other words, the White Horse represents something very powerful, which has inherited (or conquered) a lot in the past. It already seems to possess a great deal of influence or domination over the world… but, now, promotes peace and compassion.

Apparently, it *still* has a lot of say-so over what goes on in our present (and future) world. Because the horse is colored *white*, it also seems obvious that it will go around the world claiming that it's all about humanitarian relief and understanding… and will manifest itself as a great and wonderful force for mankind. We'll see about how this will all come together soon enough.

It's obvious that it acts as compassionate and altruistic as Jesus would. And, interestingly enough, we do see a Biblical verse that mentions Jesus, and his return - on a white horse nonetheless. In Rev. 19:11-12, we see a "white horse," with crowns as well. This time, it's not the phony horse of the antichrist, it's the *real* Christ, on a horse, at the time of his second return:

> *And I saw heaven opened, and behold **a white horse**; and he that sat upon him was called **Faithful and True**, and in **righteousness** he doth judge and make war. His eyes were as a flame of fire, and on his head were many **crowns**…*
> *- Rev. 19:11-12 (KJV)*

Wow. Doesn't that sound somewhat like that other White Horse? The apocalyptic White Horse, of course, is not exactly faithful and true, but close. It's not purely righteous, but "almost there." Yes, this horse probably has a number of deeper agendas, beyond all of this altruism. Do we seem to have "type" and "anti-type," here?

In the above, we have Christ riding in on a white horse, ready to save the world - being called Faithful and **True**, one who acts in truth and righteousness. The returning Christ will also be proficient in waging war, and already has many crowns. Wow. It truly sounds a lot like some "purified" form of this White Horse of the Apocalypse, now doesn't it? Yes, a vast **majority** of people will indeed fall for the claims of this apocalyptic White Horse, over time, by assuming that their glorious "outer shell" has their best interests in mind.

One thing that true Christians have going for them, however, is that, although this apocalyptic White Horse may be able to deceive a whole number of people, over a long period of time, they cannot hide their true intentions forever, or they cannot fool *all* of the well-wishing seekers out there. The Bible truly is their worst enemy; it exposes a lot of their agenda. And, there are also a number of other ancient works out there that could help to blow their agendas wide open… if we look deep enough. With proper research, cracks will begin to develop in their augmented ideologies. Some adulterous elements will bleed out of the mix. God will also aid a number of people in their attempts at discernment, to see through a lot of this deceptive muck. Yes, the White Horse will, over time, end up showing a lot of its true "colors"... to a number of those really seeking to find out more.

And, as those at the top might begin to sense a number of these defections, they become more and more desperate for control, and, as a result, smarter in what they do to keep people under their thumb. They already have a lot of might, as well as history, in regards to their ability to deceive, so it won't be as hard to turn things around on people as one might think.

But, one thing we may need to ask ourselves is: why would so many White Horse leaders out there (even their lower-level "activists") want to do this to their constituents? Why would these individuals want to "sell out" purehearted seekers of the Jewish and Christian faiths anyhow? It just seems so contrary to what the faiths are supposed to be all about!

As we'll now see, there could be a lot that goes on inside almost every person's head, to bring them into desiring these particular ways of working… it all depends on if they would be willing to "take the bait," or not. The evil one is a master of psychological manipulations, and uses it to seduce a whole number of those in the upper echelons of the White Horse. Let's see how.

The "Reptilian" or "Lizard" Brain

Once again, as with a quarter of the world's population already caught up in the Black Horse, the vast majority of another quarter of the world's population will fall for the spell of this one… thanks greatly to those in charge, seducing them into it. As we've mentioned something to this effect before, the majority of people caught up in clutches of this White Horse are not really the problem - they are just trying to do what they were always taught, or do what they thought was right. Again, the vast majority of this White Horse problem are those "at the top."

If we think about it: assuredly, preaching the ways of God (however diluted it all might become) cannot be **all** bad. A great number of people might be given the opportunity to see some of the *true* light here, of course, by standing under the umbrella of this particular horse. Inadvertently, the White Horse could bring a whole number of people to Christ, or towards God, and that's great. It's just that the problem begins with what often happens *afterwards*, as the person begins to look for deeper elements of the faith. And this, of course, is all due to just where those "powers that be" may begin to take a person, once they decide to come on board.

Speaking of those at the top, what *really* might be going on here, inside the heads of so many White Horse minions? What really could be going on in their heads, to allow them to feel justified about doing some of the things they do to the public? How could so many - knowingly or even *unknowingly* - push the "snake oil" of a conglomerated Godly belief with something that's not really supposed to be there, along with it?

Of course, a number of these leaders may just be out there, doing what they were taught or were told… but, of course, that doesn't make it any better for the poor parishioners (just trying to figure it all out). Yes, there's usually *some* kind of deeper motivation behind the outward persona of these particular elites, and even behind a number of priests or preachers out there. What's driving this whole process, allowing people to turn out like they have?

Of course, many will say that it's personal: for "the love of money," or some other desire for worldly materialism… and that makes perfect sense. This may end up being a part of one's personal driving force **over time**… but, not necessarily at first! There *is* actually one element of the human thought process that's even recognized by today's psychological community, and it also seems to have a very fitting name: the "Lizard" or "Reptilian" Brain! Ah, yes. We recall how the *Serpent* was (and still is) behind so much evil in our world today; and a serpent is also considered a *reptile*. What an interesting title we have been given here.

This psychological term seems to refer to how a thinking human being might begin to "regress," or resort to some kind of *lower* (or, even "animal-like") way of thinking, while subject to certain circumstances, or while reacting to certain environmental stressors:

> ...the **limbic** system of the brain has been implicated as the **seat of emotion**, addition, mood, and lots of other mental and emotional processes. It is the part of the brain that is phylogenetically very primitive. Many people call it "The **Lizard Brain**" because the limbic system is about all a lizard has for brain function. It is in charge of fight, flight, feeding, fear, freezing-up, and fornication. The limbic system is much **more powerful** than we humans credit it to be.
> ("Your Lizard Brain", 2014, p. 1)[6]

> *(It is)... that prehistoric brain stem that **all of us** must contend with...*
> ("The Lizard Brain and the Resistance", n. d., p. 1)[7]

As we recall from a previous chapter, once a person begins to *go out* of (or *lose*) their conscious thought, some *other* modems of thought might, naturally, have to come in and take over. What if, in a number of human beings, the Lizard Brain was continually allowed to take over, and affect their thoughts?

Notice how the above definition also seems to mention **emotional** responses! Once again, we know how those under the spell of the Black Horse are, quite often, encouraged to *leave* their consciousness, to be able to gather for themselves supernatural knowledge and power. Emotions are also a part of this processes. And, we now see how the Reptilian Brain seems to be part of that same *limbic* system as where one would go to involve themselves with emotional responses! And, as we also recall, a **conscious** mode of thought, quite often, points one in the direction of rationality, reason and "good old fashioned" common sense… essentially, a lot of what is moral. Not so with the Reptilian Brain.

Let's look a little bit more into some of the recognized characteristics of this Reptilian or Lizard Brain, and see how it all might begin to influence even the "nicest" of people around. We'll also see how these ways of thought could start to parallel that most infamous *reptilian* out there - the **Serpent** himself.

Reptilian Emotion

> *When **emotions** get out of whack, the reptilian brain will soon **take command** of the body and then 'all hell breaks loose'.*
> ("The Reptilian Brain in Humans", 2024, p. 11)[8]

First, we'll relate that Reptilian Brain to the way people under the spell of the (former) Black Horse may want to utilize their thoughts. It's interesting to note that: in a number of individuals - when their emotional thoughts begin to get "out of whack," or go awry - the Reptilian Brain seems to take over! Could this be another reason why the top leadership of the Black Horse wants their people to go *out* of their conscious mind (in order to get some kind of divine favor)? This, of course, seems to head them *down* (instead of up), right in the direction of how a reptile (or, even the *Serpent*) may think!

Let's begin to dig deeper into this all.

Reptilian Survival Instincts

*Once people **fear not surviving**, the brain's fear center takes over, and we are at the mercy of its reactions to **perceived** threats… It's all about **survival**… **Emotional** responses are based on the fear of not surviving…*
                ("The Reptilian Brain in Humans", 2024, p. 3)[9]

*Lizards… **seek survival**. They don't make a risk to produce something artistic or generous. They… live fearful of others…*
                ("Lizard Brain: Seth Godin's Christian Theology", 2024, p. 1)[10]

People who resort to this Lizard Brain may, quite often, be living out their lives in a sea of fear and anger. They may harbor resentment for certain negative situations in their past; they may question, or be angry with, God; etc. From these things, they may begin to feel a little bit of low self-esteem, or might become a little unhappy with life in general. And, because of these negative thoughts, they, quite often, may begin to look for a number of ways to *act* on these emotions, or act out *against* any of those perceived threats that might be levied against them (real or imaginary).

Because of all these unstable situations, many of them may (quickly) begin to utilize the Lizard Brain, to help them get out of their particular situation, or to get some kind of vengeance. Deep down inside, they might often feel the need to quickly respond to whatever negative elements they come across, or perceive… in order to stop their own self-esteems from being "crushed" in some way.

We'll also see that:

> *Anxiety is a state caused by the reptilian brain even when nothing is happening that should cause us to feel anxious…*
> ("The Reptilian Brain in Humans", 2024, p. 8)[11]

Eventually, the use of this Lizard Brain may even become "second nature" within the mind of certain individuals… always close by, and always affecting them (in one way or another).

There is more, a lot more.

Reptiles Do Not Like Criticism… nor Change

> *The lizard brain… doesn't like being laughed at… It's the part of our brain that worries about **safety** and **dishes out anger**. Being laughed at is the lizard brain's worst nightmare…*
> ("The Lizard Brain and the Resistance", n. d., p. 1)[12]

> *The lizard brain **cares** what everyone else thinks…*
> ("The Reptilian Brain in Humans", 2024, p. 1)[13]

A lot of this becomes so telling - not only does it help us to understand what might be going on in the minds the upper echelon of this White Horse, but also a vast number of those priests or preachers beneath them! Now, we see that a level-headed person, in a whole number of situations, might just be able to go on with their life… without caring (too much) about what someone else might think or say. They really have no need to utilize excessive emotions, nor the Lizard Brain. But, with those who often might resort to using it, it may *really* begin to affect them, and their lives, a good deal over time.

Because so many of these people might become a little self-conscious, or might feel a bit concerned about the lowering of their self-esteems, many may also find it almost impossible to laugh at themselves, or have any real sense of humor:

> *The Reptilian Brain is programmed to **reject** the unfamiliar and **trap us** in our comfort zones - where less energy is spent, and less risky action is taken.*
> ("The Reptilian Brain in Humans", 2024, p. 9)[14]

> *The reptilian brain doesn't like change or new viewpoints. That is why it seems **near impossible to enact any real change as far as politics** goes. The reptilian brain **fears change** and any real change as far as policy goes can be a real "nightmare" to get enacted. **New** views in science, politics, **religion**, education, medicine, the reptilian brain sees this as a threat and will always defend itself... the reptilian brain doesn't like surprises either.*
> ("The Reptilian Brain in Humans", 2024, p. 8)[15]

Wow. What a way to successfully reprogram or brainwash an individual (if done correctly)! A weapon that the top elites of this White Horse might have, now, is: if they could keep people afraid of new ideas, or afraid of change, then they could keep them using their Reptilian Brain... which stops them from wanting to try anything new (or face anything "threatening" to them)! It works. And, yes, if they could get their priests, preachers and even their educators to fall into this same trap, then they have them "stuck" within their current positions. Talk about being able to keep people thinking (and doing) the same thing over time, all the while keeping them under your thumb!

Those Cynical Reptiles

> *It's the voice that **haunts** you. The voice that tells you that you will certain(ly) fail and make a fool of yourself.*
> ("Lizard Brain: Seth Godin's Christian Theology", 2024, p. 1-2)[16]
>
> *We become reactive, **suspicious**, **paranoid**, and delusional.*
> ("The Reptilian Brain in Humans", 2024, p. 9)[17]

Negative thoughts seem to rise within each one of us. And, those who often think with their Reptilian Brain might handle a number of these situations quite differently (than most). So, to allow an individual the ability to "save face" from a number of these negative experiences ahead of them, they, often, have *little trust* for almost anything coming their way, or any new ideas in front of them - *especially* those by which they might not currently agree with. In other words, their minds, so often, stay "closed."

Cynicism is often employed at the same time. And yes, (from previous volumes) we also know *who* was that great cynic of ages past: **Cain**! Yes, what a coincidence. Do we sense a deeper agenda here?

As a result of a stressful, ever-changing world, so many "threats" coming to an individual might begin to push them to the specific extremes. Mistrust and pessimism, quite often, become their social norms. And, if a person begins to harbor enough low self-esteem, they may begin to look for specific ways to help them get out of a particular situation - enter their feelings of *pride*!

Towards Reptilian Pride (And those "Animal Instincts")

The lizard brain is hungry, scared, angry, and horny.
("The Reptilian Brain in Humans", 2024, p. 1)[18]

The lizard brain will fight (to the death) if it has to… It likes a vendetta and has no trouble getting angry.
("The Reptilian Brain in Humans", 2024, p. 1)[19]

Wild animals *are wild because the **only** brain they possess is a lizard brain.*
("The Reptilian Brain in Humans", 2024, p. 1)[20]

As we might recall (from previous volumes): when a person begins to act *wild*, or more "beast-like," their feelings of pride, quite often, become involved. **Emotions**, such as fear, guilt and anxiety, could easily prompt a person to revert to their pride, to help them raise any lowered self-esteem. They may lash out verbally, or even physically. They might say things they would not normally say.

If the need for their pride becomes strong enough, they may even begin to act as an animal would, taking on **beast-like** qualities. The Lizard Brain also seems to *thrive* in this environment, pushing civility and logic into a dusty corner..

There are actually a few more Reptilian Brain characteristics to discover, and a number of them are not necessarily violent, nor destructive… at least on the surface:

*Territoriality, a hierarchical structure of **power**, **control**, ownership, wars, jealousy, anger, fear, hostility, worry, stuck or frozen with fear, aggressiveness, conflict, extreme behavior, competitiveness, cold-blooded, dog-eat-dog beliefs, might is right, and survival of the fittest. OCD, hoarding, looting, superstitions, deception, fight or flight, obesity from fear of lack of food, daily rituals, ceremonial re-enactments.*
("The Reptilian Brain in Humans", 2024, p. 7)[21]

We also see, in the above, that there is a need for personal **power** or **control**. Could people who, quite often, resort to the Lizard Brain resort to these same particular vices as well?

Power and Control

*The desire to **control**, whether it be in relationships, circumstances, or life, in general, is a **primary trait of the reptilian brain in action**. We often call people displaying this behavior "control freaks" and "freak like" is what they appear to be.*
("The Reptilian Brain in Humans", 2024, p. 6)[22]

*When someone is being controlled by the reptilian brain their behavior can affect **other people's brain responses** as well.*
("The Reptilian Brain in Humans", 2024, p. 5)[23]

Now we see how a person may feel compelled to *control* others, or have power over them! It, once again, seems to fall back to the Lizard Brain! These thoughts often might come about, to assist one's own attempt to keep their world the way they've always had it, or to bring it to the way they feel that it should be. No detractions are welcome.

And, to help them keep up their own self-esteems, they may feel the need to influence others, or intimidate others into following their own lead. They can't just let sleeping dogs lie. And, if others begin to think the same ways that they do, it easily begins to "validate" their own thoughts (inside their own heads). So often, it's connected with the Lizard Brain, as well as a few other things:

> *Power, status, reputation, basically the **sense of self**.*
> ("The Reptilian Brain in Humans", 2024, p. 8)[24]

It's also so important to understand how those desires for *power* and *control* can become an integral part of so much of this White Horse. It helps us to discover just how a person might be able to act *Christ-like*, or *Godly*, all the while using these "outer shells" as tools of manipulation. We also might be able to see how the "mover and shakers" of this White Horse could use their Lizard Brain to help them seduce people into their own causes, and keep them there - thinking exactly what they want them to think.

To a number of these top individuals, they want to make the purveyors of the White Horse look compassionate or altruistic; but, so often, things no longer become fronted for the sake of God alone, but also for the sake of a one's own individual desire.

A Reptile Without a Conscious

Yet, with all of this psychology, God *does* seem to give us a number of "safety protocols," ingrained within each individual. God gives us certain ways of thinking, which might actually stop people from allowing the Lizard Brain from going too far, as well as these White Horse deceptions. Most people have a conscience, which appears to tell them what truly may be right or wrong out there. Most also have the use of their conscious mind (when they choose to use it). These represent those "still small voices" inside of almost everyone, giving them common sense ideals, as well as challenging the traditional ways that one may have been already been using, to react to negative stimuli.

Sadly, when a person continually feels the need to utilize their Lizard Brain, it seems that their thoughts (inside) often end up becoming *diametrically opposed* to individuals who insist on using their conscious mind, or their inner conscience - the things that God gave them.

> *The reptilian brain **overpowers** the ability to have calm and **rational** thought. "Losing our heads." These traits all stem from a belief of **not enough** or **a lack mentality**.*
> ("The Reptilian Brain in Humans", 2024, p. 1)[25]

*Repeating patterns such as rituals, automatic responses **without conscious thought**, predictability, fear of losing a job, or spouse, or home, or dying, lack of money & resources, and the unknown are all responses **created** by the reptilian brain.*
("The Reptilian Brain in Humans", 2024, p. 3)[26]

We now see that:

Consciousness *is the **only** way to be free from the effects of the reptilian brain.*
("The Reptilian Brain in Humans", 2024, p. 9)[27]

No surprise here. Again, as we've seen (a number of times), it's usually one way or another. And, it's so amazing to discover these diametrically opposed extremes here, as well (in regards to how we think)! It's also amazing to discover how those hypocrites at the top of this White Horse, as well as a number of preachers, priests or instructors that may find themselves underneath them, could actually be partaking in those thought patterns that *aren't exactly* of God… but more attuned to all of what the *Serpent* of the Garden of Eden might actually want to promote!

Concluding Quotes

*The lizard brain is not merely a concept. It's **real**, and it's living on the top of your spine…*
("The Reptilian Brain in Humans", 2024, p. 1)[28]

*…from a Christian point of view, Lizard Brain can also refer to that which **is Satanic and diabolical.***
("Lizard Brain: Seth Godin's Christian Theology", 2024, p. 2)[29]

Wow. Interesting choice of words here, in that above statement! Again, it seems to hit the nail right on the head here, as far as what direction the Reptilian Brain might take one. And, we're not just making this all up - it's an actual, psychological term!

And, with all of this information, we can now see how it could be possible for a number of "Godly" or "Christ-like" individuals to begin thinking in ways that are **not** really the most Godly! The mind is fragile, and can (over time) be corrupted by certain pressures in this world... and, we all have the potential for going down a few dark pathways, at one time or another.

Ultimately, a number of White Horse "movers and shakers" might *openly* appear to have a compassionate shell, or seem altruistic on the *outside*, but, on the inside, a lot of their flesh could actually be **rotting** away (ideologically)... so often, because they are involved with what their Lizard Brain might have to tell them, and they've made the decision to follow along.

Fronting These "Antichrist" Systems

Now that we delved into a few **base thoughts** behind a number of White Horse "influencers" (and what they really could be thinking), let's take a look at a few *personality* characteristics that, quite possibly, could be associated with these individuals, as well... their "fruits."

As we've previously stated, a whole number of things might have been behind the decision of specific individuals to go down that "Lizard Brain" path: there may have been some kind of early personal abuse; family trauma; anger at God; what have you. Of course, traumatic things can happened to a large number of people, things which could have really hurt or shamed someone. It's truly sad. But, God isn't always the One at fault here. He gave people their free will, to think or do things as they pleased. We're not robots. And, with the ability to utilize this free will, people could easily begin to choose a number of *dark* pathways to go on, or even do things that might hurt others. But, again, these are *choices* - and *people* are deciding to go down these particular pathways, not God.

Could a number of those who decided to go into these religious occupations *still* harbor a bit of shock, or resentment, from times before? Could they *still* hold onto lingering thoughts of anger or resentment - against other people, their environment, or against God? Yes, sadly, a lot of people might begin to harbor up some emotions over time, and, eventually, they'll also decide that a lot of it will have to come back out (sooner or later). With these particular thoughts, a lot of times, people might end up looking to God as the entity behind a majority of their problems... as if everything wrong was *all* of His doing; as if *He* was the one who orchestrated their entire situation.

Yes, sometimes, God does allow people to feel the negative results of this fallen world. But, what about free will, and the *people* who made the decisions that actually might hurt someone else? Also, what about the evil one, who helped to bring about this fallen world in the first place?

So many of us have heard the quote: "If God was *truly* good, then why does He allow bad things to happen to good people?" Interestingly, thoughts like this do seem (indirectly) state that the evil one has successfully diverted a lot of humankind from putting the focuses of their blame on things that's *below*... and back to God. What do we find in this statement that allows us to think anything otherwise?

Mankind as a whole should understand that the **Serpent** was the one who helped to bring about this present, evil world, and, a lot of time, the choices of fallen *man* represent so many of the real problems we face... not God. He allows the ramifications of it all to come to the surface, sometimes. We also know that the fallen world is the result of Serpentine temptations, and man's sacrilegious choices to go against their God. God, once again, was just the reacting force here. De we sense some corruption here, on a number of levels?

Maybe a number of people who go into these positions of religious power want to go into their fields of study to try and "figure things out," regarding the whole spiritual thing. Maybe human *pride* and the Reptilian Brain also began to have their way with the minds of a number of White Horse elites, in order to con them into believing that God (and His Bible) *have* to be the real problems in the world. Maybe that is what leads them to desire a *change* in what traditional Christianity has to offer, to "fix it" in some way. Maybe a number of individuals, deep down inside, still hold onto a lot of anger and resentment towards God, and it makes them feel a bit better to subtly manipulate or corrupt other people's chances at receiving what He may truly have to offer (all out of spite, or "not wanting to be alone," etc.). Things begin to make sense, once we look deeper into the spiritual side of things.

Forerunner to a Modern Psychopath?

We may also recall (from previous volumes) how Cain had acted, way back in the earliest of times. He mercilessly killed his brother Abel, by ambushing him. Because of what led up to this, Cain could have easily been considered the first example of someone who resorted to these same overuses of pride and the Reptilian Brain… and even acted upon them. Those outward behaviors became most evident around the time that he was just about to kill his brother. Cain was full of hatred, anger and bitter envy. He was also very cynical of what **God** wanted from him, and from this world. He also seemed full of anger and resentment.[30] Cain, ultimately, seemed to have fallen in love with everything of this **lower** world.[31] Immoral or "beast-like" responses began to emanate from his mind, as well as through his outward actions.

We also recall that Cain was considered a "blackened" individual - not because of any kind of change in his outer appearance, but because of some *inner*, darkened soul! He may have looked normal on the outside, but, inside, so much was swelling up inside of him… even allowing him to acted as a ravenous wolf might have! Could Cain's reaction (in regards to his murder of Abel) indicate that he was, quite obviously, acting as what many today would call a **psychopath**?

Here's how modern psychologists might define a typical psychopath:

> *…a mentally unstable person… a person having an **egocentric** and antisocial personality marked by a **lack of remorse**…*
> ("Psychopath", n. d., p. 1)[32]
>
> *Psychopaths lack empathy & remorse, are manipulative & lie compulsively.*
> ("How to Defend Yourself Against Psychopaths", n. d., p. 1)[33]

Well, what's the different between a cold and calculating *Cain* and the above? Nothing really. Cain was very self-centered. It was all about him. He utilized his pride a great deal. He also seemed to be the earliest purveyor of all that the Reptile Brain had to offer him. Could some of these psychopathic tendencies be harboring in a number of those corrupted, White Horse dignitaries?

Yes, if we've ever wondered why there seems to be so many hypocrites in this world - outwardly preaching the ways of God, while still having a bit of a shady side - we now may have an answer to why so many may actually feel good about their deception of others: they are beginning to develop those same psychopathic tendencies. If we've ever wondered **how** some people could act so deceptive, or so immoral, all the while acting as though they are "Mother Teresa," we now know. We also seem to see how a number of these particular individuals would rather follow in the footsteps of those first two "grand fathers" of this pagan world, rather than God.

Psychopathic "Predators"

As we begin to dig deeper into the minds of those upper White Horse echelons, there actuality could be a bit more - a couple of *levels* to their leadership, actually. Yes, it's a bit fragmented, with some of them in *the know*, and some of them a little more oblivious. Let's take a quick look at these two authoritarian levels, to help us make more sense of how these people are able to manipulate others. One level of White Horse "authority," here, could be coined the ***predators***.

The **predators** may, in fact, represent those "in the know." They're the ones who may know a number of deep, dark secrets behind this White Horse group, and any of the nefarious elements behind it. They know the deception that's really going on, and *why*. These people, as well, may *willingly* be contrary to the true messages of God, deep down inside, working to deceive people in a true, antichrist manner.

These individuals are usually few and far between, however. There's not a lot of them in the general populous; they're mainly in the upper echelons, or highest levels of power. They, for the most part, could be thought of as the "guardians of the terrible secret."

The **wolf** is a perfect example of a predator. They go after sheep (and other animals), with the intent to hunt and ultimately take them down. And, sometimes, it has been discovered (by naturalists) that a wolf could kill, not only for food, but for a few more reasons! Sometimes, they're not even hungry and they'll end up killing. Why? Sometimes, they may do it for sport, or to show other wolves their particular status, etc. Research has shown that, sometimes, they even seem to *enjoy* the killing aspect of their hunt (believe it or not)![34] They howl in enjoyment in front of other wolves. Well, what might this have to do with our particular argument, here? Maybe some of these *human* predators enjoy the same thrills of doing this to other people as well! Maybe they enjoy the "hunt," and how they can manipulate people into thinking what they're thinking. Maybe there's such rottenness in their bones that they actually enjoy the thrill of taking the motivation out of people truly to seek out the will of God, because they are the same way. And, if we picture Jesus as the "good shepherd," and Christian preachers as the contemporary "shepherds" of the world, then this all seems to fit. What animal is out there, quite often having the desire to pick off a number of sheep, one by one (for whatever self-fulfilling reason they might have)? Yes... we have the wolf.

As we also might notice, many top "movers and shakers" of the White Horse are rich (sometimes beyond belief), and they don't really seem to need to do whatever they could to get money. A lot of times, things are done more for the *sport* of it... to give the individual some kind of *purpose*, or fulfillment. A lot of their enjoyment in life may even involve the thrill of making mincemeat of their prey, or bringing other people *away* from God, as much as possible, and towards *their* own ways of thinking. The thrill of *their* chase, then, involves turning things south for the true sheep of the "Good Shepherd."

Lower-Level "Whores"

Beyond (and beneath) those top-level predators, we also have the *whores*. But, of course, this title doesn't sound like a very good title for any person working inside of the Christian beltway, or does it? Why refer to some people as spiritual *prostitutes*? It's simple: although these individuals might not necessarily be "in the know" (as with the above predator group) about what's going on with the White Horse, they are informed enough, to help them get what they want out of their working positions... and they'll go about getting what they feel they actually deserve, regardless if they might actually believe it's wrong. They may **not** know that the Serpent is the architect behind so many of these twists in their faith. They might not even know how aligned their upper leadership is... with all that's against God. They just know the role that *they* are in, and what they need to continue to do, in order to keep receiving their *material* rewards (for their religious services, that is).

As a prostitute would do what they do for the money (and not necessarily for the moral implications behind it), the spiritual *whore* also wants what the world around them could give. These might be preachers, priests, or even upper (or lower) level educators, all attempting to show the populations beneath them what the "ways of God" presently are… the ones that will still keep *them* on their current payrolls. They are just "going through the motions" of religious practices, saying whatever they might need to say (and regardless of what they *actually* might believe, themselves).

Yes, both levels are what the evil one may begin to use… as his own foot soldiers. This fragmented leadership level of the White Horse, quite often, could be thought of as an *onion*: the more layers one peels off this onion the more mysterious (and corruption) become visible, just under the surface. These *whores* represent the outer layers of this onion of corruption, with the *predators* being somewhere in the middle. Both, however, end up hurting the *true* seekers of the faith, slowly bringing them under their White Horse spell.

This reminds us of what the word "tare" might stand for, in the Bible. In previous volumes, we've discussed what some of those *tares* might actually be, and how they might actually work. We recall that (in a *symbolic* way) the human "tares" - those corrupt people within the White Horse - would actually end up growing up, right alongside the human "wheat" (i.e. the good people who honestly want to follow God). And, for a period of time, the two are almost indistinguishable. In other words, they will both seem to be part of the same bunch. **But**, *eventually*, the true colors of those tares will begin to show through, and a number of people will see through them, and begin to question their theologies (as well as their true motivations). The corruption is out there. We just have to watch out for these "fruits."

As we look into a couple of meanings of the word "tare," we have:

> …(the word **tare**) is derived from zonah, meaning 'degenerate' or 'degraded' though the roots in Hebrew mean literally '**a harlot**', 'unfaithful'.
> ("The Biblical Tare of Saint Matthew's Gospel", n. d., p. 2)[35]

Wow, we also have the word *whore* here. It seems that the *whore*, in ancient times, was a little bit more than just a woman looking for some quick money. She was also considered *unfaithful* to the original cause of marriage. She was accused of "going against the grain" of her society's view on the whole sexual process: she had sex purely for the sake of material gains, and not for any sense of companionship, or wifely "duty." An ideological "whore," here, could easily represent an individual who is willing to "sell" his or her own soul… for the sake of some worldly, material gain. He or she is going "against the grain" of how to properly teach their congregations the true ways of God, for the sake of something self-serving in the end. It's the same here; and they're out there, en masse', doing this to people. Don't be fooled.

Now that we see what may be a few *driving forces* inside the human mind, it helps us to understand just what some of these upper echelon elites are made of. Now that we have a fairly good understating of the kind of people that might claim that they are out for the "best interests" of their constituents, when, in reality, they are not, this also makes it quite easier for us to understand what in a number of people in these leadership roles are actually all about. These individuals could, very well, be the ones out there trying to convince others into believing that *they* represent the true Godly faith, when, in fact, it's more like they are the ones who are, ultimately, using a serpent-like mind, as well as selling Serpent-like ways. It's either one way or another.

Next, we'll begin to discover just how this White Horse powerhouse would have, eventually, come into existence, and how it, over time, was able to begin seducing so many. We'll also begin to discover a number of individuals who became part and parcel to the set up of this horse. Let's, now, see how certain dissenters of God would have, just after the Flood, gotten their foot in the door, and what they exactly did to further their own sacrilegious, antichrist causes.

Chapter 4

"Hebrews" Against the World

*And there came one that had escaped, and told Abram **the Hebrew**…*
  - *Gen.* 14:13 (KJV)

Abram (or Abraham) - the father of so many nations - was also considered a *Hebrew*, at least in the Bible. Now, just what might have been the significance of *this* particular title, and why was he called that? He wasn't to be considered an Israeli, and he wasn't even Jewish (at the time) - for his grandson Jacob (i.e. Israel) was not even born yet! Could this have meant something else, way back then?

Now, for the sake of providing a successful history of the White Horse (and its early beginnings), we'll need to discover just what or who was behind a lot of it all, as well as why these particular individuals may have reviled the people of God enough to do so (and continue doing so, over the generations). There truly was a battle about to brew here, way back in these most ancient of times. And yes, this battle is *still* going on today (to the understandable disbelief of so many we see around us today, assuredly).

So, in order to see how these confrontations began, and what they're really all about, we need to go back a good number of years, into the early times of Genesis once again. We'll also need to initiate a chronological timeline here, beginning soon after the Flood of Noah. That White Horse - and the manifestation it now finds itself under - has an *extremely* extensive history, with *layers* upon *layers* of obscured information to comprise it. And, all of this information really needs to be brought to the surface, and uncovered, to make it all believable. There are a number of *onion* layers, here, that really need to be peeled away, so the process may take a little time.

In previous volumes, we've already uncovered a lot about what may have happened before the Flood, and soon after. In this volume, we'll expand on all of this. To do so, we'll need to return to that occurrence of the Tower of Babel, and begin there. This tower building project was brought about, as we might recall, by prominent pagan leaders: Cush, Nimrod and Semiramis. Looking at this history will show us how there are really *two* major players intertwined within this post-Flood conflict, and how one side would eventually go on to form the skeleton of the entire **White Horse**.

From previous volumes, we already understood how God - through this confusion of tongues - was able to allow for the division of many of those who were rebellious to Him. Because of the fact that most people could not communicate with one another, it facilitated the desire of many to relocate, and go to different locations abroad (with people of their same tongue). Paganism, sad to say, was extremely prominent around the tower, and the religion, as well, began to go along with most of these migrating people.

The Biblical giants, as we may also recall (from previous volumes), were around after the Flood as well; and, for the most part, they may have followed along with a number of these migrating individuals. At first, most of them started out pious. But, of course, after Cush and Nimrod began to bring those old ways of paganism back into the forefront, a lot of people - including the *giants* - began to turn their backs on God once more. They, for the most part, would *not* continue on, with pious behaviors after the Flood. In fact, it would be more like the opposite.

So, this dispersion of tongues not only allowed for a vast number of people to spread out around the world, it also allowed for these giants to expand their presence as well, and spread out their sacrilegious "wings." As the apostate religion began to ignite within each new area that people settled, the giants, quite often, exploded the rate by which it all was taking hold. They began to seize as many opportunities as they possibly could now, in order to advance *themselves*, and their causes, in some way.

It sounded like a parallel to this antediluvian world coming about, once again; but, the one difference between that antediluvian world and what was about to transpire in this new, post-Flood world was that there were a number of Biblical patriarchs out there, on the side of God, who were willing to step up, and **resist** this pagan revival (at least for a time). The people who survived the Flood surely remembered the horrors of what the Flood had brought to the world, and a number of those born since understood why God's judgment had to be upon them - they saw the ramifications of this Flood everywhere, and didn't want anything so destructive to ever happen again. The stakes were high, and these early people were ready to fight.

The initial resistance seems to have been spearheaded by a couple of Biblical patriarchs. Noah - that well-respected "father" of the post-Flood world - was against these pagan advancements (of course); but, he, because of his age, did not really have a lot of "fight" left inside of him. His son **Shem**, however, was still fairly young, and was strong enough to do something about it… and do something he did! Shem's son, as well, may have helped out with his cause.

Being the patriarch to so many descendants under him, Shem was able to recruit a large amount of people to assist him in this fight, and decided to *vigorously* go after those troublesome people of the day, as well as the **giants**. Pagans began to be afraid of him… really afraid. And, being in such a position of authority, Shem eventually decided that it was, ultimately, up to *him* to chase around these top pagan leaders (including Cush, Nimrod and Semiramis), to stop them in their tracks. Who would be better at this job? He was the direct son of Noah. He was one of those who actually made it through the Flood, and knew what everything was all about. Tremendous respect was given to this particular individual, almost as much as given to his father Noah.

Most of us have heard of the mythological title of **Titan**, or *Triton*. It, most probably, was another ancient avatar of *Shem*, as a giant, **powerhouse** of a figure![1] With his resistance underway, the "movers and shakers" of this post-Flood pagan world began to look over their shoulder. It just wasn't as easy to practice their sacrilege anymore, at least out in the open, and get away with it. Shem wasn't just out to use harsh language; he played for keeps. He would have killed any top people if he felt the desire to do so; and a majority of the population around would, probably, not be in any position to do anything about it, because Shem, apparently, was too powerful. The people probably believed that the **God** of Noah was also with Shem, and feared him for that very reason. A number of pagans probably noticed the remnants of this same Flood as well, and did not want Shem's God to instigate anything like that again, so they were hesitant to react!

So, whenever those Godly patriarchs were in town, any pagan heads of state usually felt the need to duck for cover, or even leave the area. They "bobbed and weaved," in regards to their physical locations… to make it look as though Shem was chasing shadows. Yet, we do know (from previous volumes) that Shem did have some success, in regards to his venture to take out certain leaders. He, apparently, was able to take out **Nimrod** - that famous leader of Babylon - and cut his body up into little pieces.

The entire story of Shem's rise to power will be detailed a bit later, and in much more detail. But, for now, we'll need to know that: even though Shem and his immediate followers were initially successful in their endeavors, they couldn't continue on with their mission forever, not without continued help over time. Shem, naturally, was getting older, and needed subsequent, post-Flood generations to continue stepping up, and stay as passionate about displacing paganism, and their pagan leadership (and killing giants) as he was. Sadly, the Godly "fire" of Shem and a few of his subsequent patriarchs were not to continue for very long, at least not for many generations in the future. The later generations did not seem to have this same fervor, probably because they were once-removed from the horrors of the Flood, and how horrible it all really was. People just became a little complacent over time, and this resistance would, eventually, fall apart.

"It takes courage to fight evil. It takes no real courage to fight good."
- The Dennis Prager Radio Program (1/2/24)[2]

And, because the strength of those subsequent patriarchs was slowly beginning to wane, those wanting the pagan experience were beginning to grow, eventually overshadowing a lot of those Godly people over time. Yes, the tables were beginning to turn, one more time, and the world was heading right back in the direction of how it was before the Flood. What could these Godly people do - those of Shem's day - to maximize their attempts to slow any progression of this pagan expansion, at least to a degree?

Eber - Great-Grandson of Shem

Interestingly enough, there may have, indeed, been a reason why Abraham was known as a *Hebrew*! Pagans everywhere may have begun to refer to those who resisted their religious "progression" (such as Noah, Shem, and etc.) as the **Hebrews**, and we'll soon see the reason *why*. Of course, we may be told an entirely different story today, however. Contemporary intellectuals may try to imply that the word equates to Israel itself, or that it is the name of their language. Of course, these are correct statements. But, the word may have an earlier meaning as well. And yes, it could have been related to that same, great patriarch: *Shem*. Let's see.

Shem had a great-grandson named **Eber**. This descendent would end up becoming another great patriarch of the cause, one who would eventually become a powerhouse of Godly teaching and values. Eber would go on to instruct a good number of Godly seekers, not only verbally, but also in the instruction of the written word. And, if we really think about it, that word *Hebrew* could actually be a corruption of this particular patriarch. According to *The New Strong Exhaustive Concordance of the Bible*, the Hebrew word for *Hebrew* is no. H5680, *Ibriy*, which refers to "an Eberite or descendant of **Eber**, which is #H5677, *Eber*, which is the name of two patriarchs." Also, the term, *Hebrew* may also mean: "belonging to Eber; patronymic of Abraham and his offspring." Now, we see that a typical *Hebrew* (of Abraham's time) may also have been called that because he or she voluntarily followed along with the teachings of *Eber*, or wanted to be, somehow, "under his wing."

Thus, the descendants of Abraham (Abram) will be Hebrews… By definition, the word, Hebrew, can be traced back to Eber and no further.
("Who's Who?", n. d., p. 1)[3]

Yes, it probably originated as a *derogatory* term - directed to these people by the vast number of practicing pagans around them.

Shem and Eber would, then, go on to be the early "titans" of this anti-pagan resistance. Shem taught his great-grandson a great deal of Godly information; and, subsequently, Eber began to utilize it all, and greatly expand upon it. And, because of them (and other Godly individuals out there), Eber seemed to be destined to shape the thoughts and moral compasses of so many Godly people out there! It also was reported that Shem and Eber were the ones given the credit for teaching *Abraham* those ways of God, and Abraham was no small character of the entire Biblical scene!

Even though Eber ended up being the instructor of these righteous ways, Shem was still the patriarch who ran the show, and did a majority of the "dirty work" - chasing down prominent pagans and killing a number of troublesome giants. He was the one trying to reform the lands, and keep everything pure. Shem was also thought to have been able to live a *very* long time after the Flood, up to five hundred years after! So, yes, with all of this on his side, he truly became the "alpha-dog" of his day, the "hunter" of all things outwardly pagan.

He may have had other titles, or epithets:

Sem - *meaning "famous".*
Melchizedek - *the man (who) built Salem (i.e. Jeru**salem**) and lived until the time of Abraham.*
("The Travels of Noah into Europe", 2002, p. 2)[4]

In the above, we see that Shem (as Melchizedek) could have also been the one accredited for building the city of *Salem* - i.e. that Holy City of *Jerusalem*! Yes, go figure. God really seemed to have had a soft spot for this particular patriarch, and was probably watching over him (and his causes) for a very long time. In fact, the word "Semite" could actually be a description of those numerous descendants emerging out Shem, and his loins. Wow.

Not only did Shem go to a number of pagan lands, and "cleanse" them, he even "set up shop" there, at some of these areas. Interestingly enough, we *do* see that there are historical texts out there, claiming that "foreigners" decided to come into Egypt, and take it over for a period of time. One group was called the "Shepherd Kings":

Shepherd kings, a series of foreign rulers in Egypt, whose domination must have occurred **about the time of the sojourn of the Hebrews there**.
("Shepherd Kings", 2024, p. 1)[5]

Wow, it even seems to have a few Hebrew connections to it all. These kings also seemed to be connected with the people who built the city of Jerusalem! And, it's also interesting to note that this information was scribed (as well) by none other than that famous Jewish historian **Josephus**!

He (Josephus) professes to cite the exact words of (the ancient historian) Manetho… (and the) extract from Manetho further states that these refugees were the builders of Jerusalem, a statement with which Josephus joins issue, as identifying them with the Hebrews…
("Shepherd Kings", 2024, p. 1)[6]

Talk about credibility! Josephus was, indeed, a very creditable historian of his day. Yes, could this have been one historical account of *Shem* and his posse entering into foreign lands, and trying to purify the people from their pagan infestations?

Those two patriarchs (Shem and Eber), not only laid out the ideological foundations of what a Godly world should have looked like, but were also the genetic ancestors of the people who would go on to form the Israeli nation! And, of course, it makes sense that this *Hebrew* title would be applied to the early patriarchs - they, rightfully so, went off of the (pagan) "plantation."

Regardless of the fact that the followers of God were slowly being outnumbered, the Hebrews were still a force to be reckoned with… of course, because God was on their side! It took a lot for Shem to be able to go out and destroy a top player of post-Flood paganism - in the heart of *Babylon*, nonetheless! It took a lot for Shem and others to come into the land of Egypt as well, to begin the reformation of this area.

To continue on with his battles, Shem, of course, probably spent a lot of his time in the Middle East. But, he might not have stayed in this area forever, though. Noah, as we also know (from previous volumes), ended up retiring in the Italian Peninsula. And, along with this intention of Noah, Shem could have also eventually migrated into central Europe (not too far from Noah), leaving the rest of his descendants to carry on the work in the Middle East. Yes, Shem and his entourage would end up traveling to a number of areas, forcing a number of pagan defectors (as well as giants) to either "change their tunes," relocate, or face something far, far worse.

The Fowl and the Giants… Both "On the Lamb"

Because of people like Shem, a vast number of pagans found themselves in somewhat of a pickle - none as bad, however, as the post-Flood **giants**. And, there appears to be a good reason for all of this. So many giants seemed to have been heading right down the same proverbial "gutter" as they were before the Flood. And, on top of this, the giants couldn't even seem to go away fast enough from their fellow *pagans* as well, because it seems that they became problematic to almost *everyone* they came across! Easily, they ended up becoming overly aggressive, explosive, militaristic, perverted and thieving - very exploitive to the human beings around them. People were getting sick of being of being raided, and even attacked. They were sick of all the debauchery, for the giants ended up participating a number of things that seemed beyond human belief (such as cannibalism). Nobody really felt comfortable with neighbors who might, eventually, become hungry for human flesh! Because of all these things, their human counterparts, no matter what their faith and no matter where they lived, began to group together, and did whatever they could to keep these giants at a safe distance.

True, the giants possessed a lot of occult knowledge and power, and a number of pagans would loved to have bartered for some of that (which they did). But, even this wasn't worth having to deal with a lot of their atrocious behaviors over time. So, people did just enough to use them for what they may have initially needed then for, and then work to push them away! So many people would end up chasing these giants out their immediate vicinities that the giants would, in a way, end up becoming those "first people" in a whole number of new areas. *They* may have ended up becoming the **aboriginals** of a number of different ancient lands (believe it or not) - being met up by expanding human beings later on!

And, as we might also recall (from previous volumes), the *Owph (or Fowl) of the Air* were not too popular as well (with their human neighbors), and ended up being chased away just the same. This group, as we may recall, fled the Middle East the same way the giants did… once again, chased away by Godly people and pagans alike. This, of course, was because the *Owph* also became troublesome to their neighbors in a lot of the same ways.

These *Owph*, as we may also recall, were also thought of as those *fairies, elves, leprechauns*, or even the *sidhe*. Most of them were diminutive in size, and able to maintain an existence between the natural and supernatural worlds. It also seemed that, after the Fall, a majority of these individuals ended up be very mischievous to their neighbors. They ended up engaging in a number of mischievous practices of their own, all the while possessing a lot of this same supernatural knowledge. It was a lot like the situation with the giants, so much so that the two groups were, quite often, treated in much the same way - both being targeted for mass evictions as well.

So, as more and more people began to spread out from the Middle East, the more those giants and fairy *Fowl* were forced to expand out, ahead of their human contemporaries. And, once again, these fairies were considered to be the *first* ones into a good number of lands that were previously uncharted. So, if we think about it, the giants and *Owph* (*both* of them) were among the first to settle into a vast number of virgin lands… becoming the "native people" of these areas!

And this, as well, helps to explains why there was so many advanced, archaeological remnants in a good number of ancient areas - the giants had a hand in most of it. Yes, there were actually a good number of ancient stone monuments and structures in these ancient lands as well, attributed to the *giants* (and, to a degree, the *Owph*) via a number ancient oral traditions and legends! Yes, they're often in there… just trivialized to a vast degree.

The famous ancient rock structure, known as **Stonehenge** (in the United Kingdom), is one great example of this. Stonehenge was originally said to have been built by *giants* (in Ireland), with all of those huge stones being set into place by the use of "magic" (and, eventually being transported into its present location in England). We have a vast number of standing stones and ancient stone structures in the United Kingdom, as well as a good number of traditions that speak of huge giants or diminutive fairies as being a part in it all… so, it all makes perfect sense to assume that there could have been a number of relationships between the two.

Yes, there seems to be so much *more* to this history of migrating giants (as well as the migrating *Owph*), and what they were able to "contribute" to a number of ancient nations than we may have ever assumed. Let's, then, look a bit more into a few examples of these unwanted giants, and the routes they began to take, in order to locate themselves into a few new areas. Yes, there truly is an "untold story" to it all. Let's go.

The Original "Aryan Nation"?

We recall how Shem, his son, and an army of their close descendants (and volunteers) had set out to, not only to take out a number of top pagan influencers, but to also chase away (or even kill) a good number of undesirable giants. Shem could have even been able to (eventually) chase them to the farthest reaches of the Europe continent over time (i.e. to northern Scandinavia, to the islands of England and Ireland, etc.). It just had to take a little time.

Early on (as we may already recall), Shem's primary directives involved the cleansing of major pagan strongholds in the Middle East, such as in Babylon and Egypt (*especially*). And, for a good long time, Shem and his people would begin to cement their hold over a number of these places.

With that, what could have been a number of escape paths for these particular giants, once they began to be "on the run?" Could a number of these giants have been known by *other* names over time? Well, for one, if we think about the *Aryan Nation*, one thought that might come into a person's mind is Adolph Hitler, and the twentieth century Nazis. We may recall the rhetoric of these particular individuals as something like this: the

Aryans were the "master race" of the entire world, and they, themselves, were their descendants. But, what if these original *Aryans* were a little more than human? What if this "master race" was, in actuality, those hybrid *giants* of old - powerful and knowledgeable terrestrial beings who sprung from those antediluvian Nephilim? Let's see if all of this could actually be the case.

A number of historians may begin to ascertain that, during this purge of giants from the Middle East, a number of them could have traveled up, through the Caucasus Mountains (a mountain range at the intersection of Asia and Europe).

After passing through this particular chain, they, then, were thought to be among the first to expand upward, and eventually outward, towards an easterly route (in the direction of India and China) and towards a westwardly route (in the direction of Europe). Could these giants (and Owph) be the same as that one particular group of individuals (believed to have done practically the same thing): the **Aryans**? Could there have been a number of parallels here, between the two? And, if so, could these Aryans have easily been considered amongst the "first peoples" of a number of different areas, as well - the same as the giants? Both groups seemed to have been suffering from this same kind of "displacement anxiety," from being pushed around so much.

And, as we've already sated, those diminutive "fairies," or Owph, were probably chased out of a number of human living areas as well. And, assuredly, these particular individuals were amongst the easiest to be targeted for those human evictions (because of their diminutive sizes).

> *Bronze Age people **tried to exterminate** them… (and) as their lands were finally taken over by other cultures, such **as that of the 'giants,' the tall, fair Aryans,** the fairies **retreated to swamps and islands.***
> (Virginia Stumbough, 1957, p. 85)[7]

It makes sense to believe that these *Owph* would not able to offer as much resistance (as their fellow giants might have). Yet, regardless of who may have been easier to move, a number of giants were not far behind this particular group, assuredly.

Now, if we apply these missing elements of the story into our study of early human migrations, it could easily turn that whole concept of "first peoples" on its head. What if there were a number of people - the descendants of Shem, Ham and Japheth - who began to migrate all over the place (after the fall of the Tower of Babel)? What if a number of these individuals began to dispute each other (over arable land and resources)? Why do we find so many traditions and legends out there, pointing us in the direction of *giants* as being the early inhabitants in so many ancient lands? What if certain individuals had to be chased out, with the Owph and giants amongst the *first* to relocate to a vast number of ancient and arable lands? What if a number of ancient *human* beings - human races, creeds and tribes - became the *secondary* inhabitants of so many of these lands?

Of course, if this could all be a possibility, then it would be a perfect reason for a number of modern "intellectuals" to try and make the existence of these giants (and fairies) to just "go away" Why? It could surely upset the "first nation" status of so many human beings; and this, by extension, could also upset the power grab of a lot of intellectuals and government officials out there (as we soon shall see)! This is just one out of a number of reasons why the existence of giants (and the fairy Owph) need to be thwarted, or even silenced. We will begin to understand the full extent of these silencing attempts a bit later. But, for now, let's assume that no people or nation had just "sprung up" from out of the ground. People migrated from a central location in the Middle East, where Noah's ark came to rest. And, we shall also see (soon enough) how Noah was the one who ended up dictating where a lot of these ancient people would end up going (after the Flood). And, if the giants were, indeed, a big part of those migrating populations, could we have even more evidence of their early migrations, as well as some more connections to other migrating individuals of these same general areas (such as the *Aryans*)?

Blonde Hair and Blue Eyed… Giants

Next, we'll delve more into a few of these possible connections between migrating giants and that so-called "master race" of Aryan peoples. Let's look at another possible name for these ancient Aryans - the **Kurgans**.

> *The Kurgan are believed by some to be **the** prototypical Indo-European or "Aryan" race…*
> ("Giants in the Earth Part II: Giants of the Americas", 2003, p.9)[8]

Reflecting back on some Nazi theology, many of us may also begin to picture the members of this Aryan race as having blonde hair, with blue eyes. A lot of those Kurgans, apparently, had a lot of those same attributes:

> *The Kurgans were quite literally the original Caucasians, having originated from the area around the Caucasus from which the term has derived. They were **tall, blonde-haired, and blue-eyed**…*
> ("Giants in the Earth Part II: Giants of the Americas", 2003, p.9)[9]

We also notice that the individuals in the above quote were believed to be fairly **tall** as well. Go figure. When we look into ancient giant lore, we'll see a vast majority of the Anakim giants as having blond hair, or even red hair, with piercing blue eyes as well. And, if so many of these beings were thought to have had blonde hair and blue eyes then it might be able to help us link them with these ancient Kurgans, and Aryans.

What if this particular color of hair, and color of eyes, were originally sported by those fallen, terrestrial Nephilim? What if a lot of this had indeed passed on, genetically, to their cross-bred human offspring over time? And, if so, then a few things in our world might really be starting to make more sense. That is why the Nazis were so obsessed with people with blonde hair and blue eyes. That is why they elevated the characteristics of these otherworldly and extremely knowledgeable hybrid human beings to such a degree - essentially, holding onto the thought that they were, indeed, some kind of **"master race"** (or "demi-gods")!

In previous volumes, we've also discovered how the *Owph of the Air* group were associated with a number of those who had *red* hair. Now, if we begin to follow this same train of logic, it does become a bit interesting here: we have a number of red-haired individuals coming from the land of Ireland (for example), which also represents a place known for its fairy lore! Could there have been a connection? Could there, possibly, have been some interbreeding going on here, between a few groups, in their distant past? Who knows? People, assuredly, ended up interbreed with those giants over the centuries, believing that they were a special group to be a part of, or even semi-divine. The same might apply here.

Yes, a number of people, back in the times of old, surely believed that these giants (and Owph) had divine attributes… and the same thing would go on here, with twentieth century Nazi Germany.

"Earth Born"… or "Demi-Gods"?

> *The title Arya, Englished into "**Aryan**"… literally means… "the exalted or noble one;" and it is derived… from the Sumerian Ar, Ara "exalt, lofty, **shining**, glory;" which is also disclosed as the remote Sumerian root of our modern word "**Aristocrat**" or "noblest or most excellent governor"…*
> ("On the origin of the Aryans", 2015, p. 5)[10]

This above quote seems to speak volumes. We recall (from previous volumes) that the serpentine Nephilim, as well as the Serpent himself, were believed to have been noble *judges* over people, before and after the Fall. They also were believed to have had a *shining* outer countenance (while on the earth) - much like a celestial angel! Yes, this above definition of *Aryan* does seem to fit in with a lot of what those ancient giants were all about - almost *perfectly*.

Of course, the giant, hybrid offspring of these early Nephilim could have also had a shining appearance (at least somewhat), as well as a number of their subsequent generations afterwards! And, we also recall that those giant hybrids (known as the Anakim) were, quite often, held in high regard by pagans for their knowledge (at least initially). Isn't it also interestingly to see, in the above quote, how the Aryans could have been described as early *Aristocrats*? They were also the 'noble" or "special" ones, the **masters, lords, or worthy teachers** - just like the giants![11]

> *The **Aryan** who is spiritually and technically advanced automatically **benefits** and **civilizes the world he inhabits**. No amount of ordinary men can achieve what he achieves.* ("Michael Tsarion Quotes", n. d., p. 8)[12]

Pagans, at least at first, seemed to have loved what these giants (or *Owph*) could give to them (at least until they got sick of living next to them). Again, "like attracts like." And this also makes sense to why so many of those pagan Nazis would want to look to *these* individuals (of old) as a way to harness a good deal of "sacred" knowledge and power, as well to possibly give them a way take advantage of some kind of "sacred" bloodline... incorporating it all into their own genes.

Yes, during World War 2, the Nazis actually did brag about having Aryan blood, as well worked very hard to access a number of the mystical, or spiritual, realms. They were well-known for using this occult to aid themselves in various life decisions, as well as a number of war strategies. And yes, it all seems as though they wanted to be *on par* with the giants of old, in a whole number of ways! Yes, the Bible does say that: "there is nothing new under the sun." Makes sense here, once again.

We even find that, during World War II, the so-called "Hitler Youth" - the children of high-ranking Nazis and other devotees - were taught to sing a very simple song, with lyrics such as:

We are the joyous Hitler youth,
We do not need any Christian virtue
Our leader is our savior
*The **Pope and Rabbi** shall be gone*
*We want to be **<u>pagans</u>** once again.*
                - Song chanted by Hitler youth

Yes, those Nazis were indeed **pagans**, and modern remnants of them, as well, still are, apparently… clear and simple. They, at least, acted as though they were. A true Christian would have nothing to do with the occult, or any veneration of these ancient giants, that's for sure! Don't be fooled with anything that may sound contrary, here. The swastika is also considered an ancient *pagan* symbol (borrowed from ancient India). Yes, their occult ideologies do seem to have a great respect for anything and everything of this lower world, and nothing *truly* of Judaism or Christianity. Don't be fooled into believing anything different.

Where Aryans May Have (Really) Went

*The **Aryan race** is a racial grouping… describe(d) (as) people of*
***Indo-European heritage**.*
                ("Behistun Inscription", n. d., p. 1)[13]

Based on archaeological, cultural and philological evidence, this theory
*posits that the **Kurgans** and **other Indo-European "Aryan" peoples** had*
*at one time invaded Europe, Asia and the Middle East, bringing their **language,***
***religion and culture with them**.*
                ("The Kurgans", n. d., p. 1)[14]

Now, if those Aryans (or Kurgans) ended up traveling in the same *Indo-European* routes as these early giants may have, then it only makes sense to assume that all three groups (the giants, the Aryans, and the Kurgans) could have possibly been one in the same, going up through the Caucus Mountains and branching out from there.

Although most of our conversation will focus on their *westward* travels (to the European Continent), we (interestingly enough, do seem to have a number of references to semi-divine, or "god-like," individuals arriving in the east, as well. In one example, we have the ***Nagas***, or "serpent people," migrating into the Indian subcontinent:[15]

How fitting the name is, here. Yes, we have another example of wise, semi-divine beings, once known as *serpent* people, this time coming from *the east*. They, at least, have some associations with *a serpent*, or the wisdom of some kind of serpent! We also have a great number of references to a serpentine **dragon** in China, as well as other eastern areas. Go figure! Could most of these things be related to those migrating, hybrid offspring of the **serpentine** Nephilim, or could they have even be related to the Serpent himself, or a few elements of his pagan belief?

One thing that we do know is: a number of these beings (with some kind of *serpentine* affiliation) did seem to have been among the ***first*** to "civilize" a number of ancient eastern areas. They were accredited for bringing the early people of the land a good amount of divine information and supernatural power. Sound familiar?

Beyond the far east, and even beyond the Middle East, those ancient giant *Aryans* may have also ventured to a good number of *other* areas:

> *The Kurgans were a real people who lived in the steppes of Russia (i.e. near the Caucasus Mountains) between 5000-2000 b.c., thereafter apparently migrating from that region to settle practically **every part of the world**... conquering as far **east as Mongolia**, as far west as **Britain**, as far north as **Russia**, and as far south as **southern Canaan**. Evidence suggests that they may have also made it as far as the **South Pacific**, and even to the **Americas**.*
> ("Giants in the Earth Part II: Giants of the Americas", 2003, p.9)[16]

Wow... what a variety of places for them to travel? It appears that these giant offspring could have migrated to a vast number of areas, even expanding much *further* than Europe. And, with them, we'll end up having a lot of their divine knowledge, their arts and sciences, as well as their advanced architectural technique migrating to these same particular places, as well. This, of course, would allow a good deal of those ancient advancements to take root, resulting in so many of those archaeological artifacts we come across, nowadays. Yes, things may begin to make a lot of sense, at least in regards to our ancient world, once we include a lot of this displaced information. The pagan remnants of this Tower of Babel had, indeed, spread out, from their centralized location in Babylon... with the giants (and *Owph*) helping to sprinkle a lot of their occult seeds practically everywhere they went, or had to go.

In the above quote, we see how the giants ended up, early on, locating in the land of Canaan (in the Middle East). Canaan, of course, was located where the nation of Israel now sits. And yes, this land, in these earliest of times, was well-known for having a fairly bad giant infestation. Think of Goliath, for example.

We may also recall that, even our modern-day, there lies a *Circle of the* **Refaim** in northern Israel:

Could these (Refaim) giants be amongst the *earliest* inhabitants of this area? There are none there now, and, of course; but, it's obvious that this circle is extremely old.

Also, as we may recall, the ancient Israelites (in the Bible) saw that those (Anakim) giants were already in the land, and believed that they were of a very *ancient* origin - even remnants of the antediluvian Nephilim!

<u>Josh. 14</u>:
> 12 *Now therefore give me this mountain, whereof the LORD spake in that day; for thou heardest in that day how the **Anakims** were there, and that the cities were great and fenced: if so be the LORD will be with me, then I shall be able **to drive them out**, as the LORD said.*

<u>Deut. 1</u>:
> 28 *Whither shall we go up? our brethren have discouraged our heart, saying, The people is **greater and taller** than we; the cities are great and walled up to heaven; and moreover we have seen the sons of the **Anakims** there.*

<u>Num. 13</u>:
> 32 *...The land, through which we have gone to search it, is a land that eateth up the inhabitants thereof; and all the people that we saw in it are men of a **great stature**.*
> 33 *And there we saw the giants, the sons of Anak, which **come of the** giants (i.e. the **Nephilim**): and we were in our own sight as grasshoppers, and so we were in their sight.*

Once again, it seems as though the ancient Israelites knew about them, and where they were from, and they also felt the need to *evict* them from the land (and any other lands that they may have met them in), because they seemed to *taint* a lot of the lands by which they ended up inhabiting.

And, once again, we see more evidence to help us answer the question: could those **giants** - the hybrid offspring of these antediluvian Nephilim - be a vast percentage of those *real*, "first nation" peoples out there?

As we've seen (in the above quote), they, as well, may have went:

*...even to the **Americas**.*
   ("Giants in the Earth Part II: Giants of the Americas", 2003, p.9)[17]

What a wild concept, here! Yet, as we soon shall see, it all seems to be quite probable (based on the amount of *giant* bones, skeletons and large tools found in so many areas of our New World)! They, apparently, must have been a large part of the "civilization" process, in regards to a number of ancient lands:

*The Kurgan were a **very ancient people**, who… begun to aggressively expand outwards… As a result, "fragments of their religion, language and culture can be found **all over the world**."*
   ("Giants in the Earth Part II: Giants of the Americas", 2003, p.9)[18]

*…various authorities have mounted a case for them being "**THE** proto-Indo-European culture, from which all Indo-European cultures descend.*
   ("Giants in the Earth Part II: Giants of the Americas", 2003, p.9)[19]

So much of the pagan-influenced world we now live in, and so many things that we now see in everyday societies, could have been sourced to these early giant migrations. That is why the ancients had so much knowledge - such as astrology, alchemy, geometry, etc. - before "their time."

"Downplaying" the Obvious?

Things really may begin to make sense, once we open our minds and account for these esoteric elements to it all. But, of course, a number of people, today, may want to *twist* things around a bit, because of the agendas of certain "higher-ups" around us. Many might want to say that their *own* ancestors were the ones who, somehow, thought up these things, or just "stumbled" across it all in some way. Because of some kind of *pride* thing, it seems that might, wholeheartedly, strive to believe that those untimely advancements must have come from some organic, *human* source, without the possibility for any sacrilegious giants (or Owph) to come in and supplant human progression. Of course, it sounds great for a number of human *self-esteems* out there, but is that how we should be presenting history?

There are more reasons for the feverish denial of giants today. For one, there is a lot of paganism in our modern world, and any talk of something that supports the Bible is a big "no no." And, there is power to be gained from being able to say that certain people were the first in the land.. If you have power over certain people, and those people claim to be the "first peoples" of the land, then, by extension, you can have more power over the land as well. It's a lot like a person saying "one's history is their power," and this concept will be expanded on in another upcoming section.

But, for now, the following quote seems to fit perfectly with the kind of denial that a lot of people, today, *automatically* seem to regurgitate, once any talk of those ancient giants come into the picture. Again, maybe a lot of this rhetoric was instigated *by design* - to *automatically* activate person to feel in these ways! Here is a typical reaction we see by many today:

> *"I don't believe there is any solid evidence for a 'race' of such people in North America or anywhere else that descend from the nephilim. Nephilim descendants and races in North America is, of course, part of the modern Moundbuilder **myth**. It is a **<u>fact of history</u>** that the Moundbuilder myth **was created to deny** the indigenous native North American races **the ability and credit** for such creations."*
> ("The Myth of Double Row Teeth and Elongated-Skull Nephilim", 2017, p. 2)[20]

We do seem to see this as a typical, and politically correct, quote today. It seems that there's not really any chance for a person to address any possibilities of giants here, or any other concept other than what is usually assumed here. That is how they work.

Yes, we find that even some prominent members of this American Indian Nation, themselves, say something different:

*"...what's happening now is, with the implementation of NAGPRA (the National American Grave Protection & Repatriation Act)... if you find skeletons, if you find remains, if you find artifacts, or whatever, it's **protected** by the federal government, and the tribe who's assigned to that region takes custody of those items. The problem with that is: that, a lot of these mounds, the native people didn't build. We didn't build them. **Our ancestors didn't build them**. So, we are taking responsibility for something **we didn't make**..."*
- *Chief Joseph Riverwind* (Author, Lecturer)[21]

So much for it being a solid fact of history! Still, this is how they gather consensus, and keep it.

*"Think about: what better way to keep people from going into the mounds, and finding seven, eight, nine foot tall skeletons, then that to have a standing force of Native Americans that are going to come, and they're going to protest, and they're going to **stop** anything like that from happening."*
- *Chief Joseph Riverwind* (Author, Lecturer)[22]

To so many today, they won't even *entertain* an idea such as the Biblical giants - it can't be **just because** "it can't be." Everything gets immediately "shut down."

Yes, this humanistic and pagan world truly **does** have a grip on our modern-day reality, or tries to. There's usually a lot of politics in everyday thoughts and conversations… even though many may not consciously see it! To many, today, it'd be easier to just "let sleeping dogs lie."

Bad Times in Babylon?

We've discovered how a vast number of "first people" may not have exactly been what we've once thought. And, we've also discovered how many of those who eventually settled in a lot of these ancient areas could have been influenced by giants (or *Owph*) in some way. We also recall that a vast number of human beings were forced to leave the tower-building project of **Babylon**, and eventually entered into a number of the same areas that these giants had migrated into (at least for a little while). We also recall (from previous volumes) that Noah was the one who was pivotal in directing certain groups of people to go into certain areas.

Soon, we'll need to return to those early battles in the Middle East, and understand more about what Shem and his posse were doing. But, for now, we'll take a look at some possible aftermaths of these conflicts, and learn about a few more possible migrations.

Even though Shem and his followers may have done a bit of damage to this pagan expansion, over time, it seems that God might not have finished with these particular areas, at least not yet. He punished the people at the tower for their insolence, by dividing a number of people up; quite possibly, He may have still taken issue with a lot of this continuing pagan sacrilege going on.

Battles were assuredly raging in these areas, but, there could have even been more negativity going on here, as well. Maybe there was some kind of drought, famine, or even pestilence going on, or another kind of environmental catastrophe. If we look into the history of this area, we discover that, once upon a time, there was a whole segment of land, known as the "Fertile Crescent":

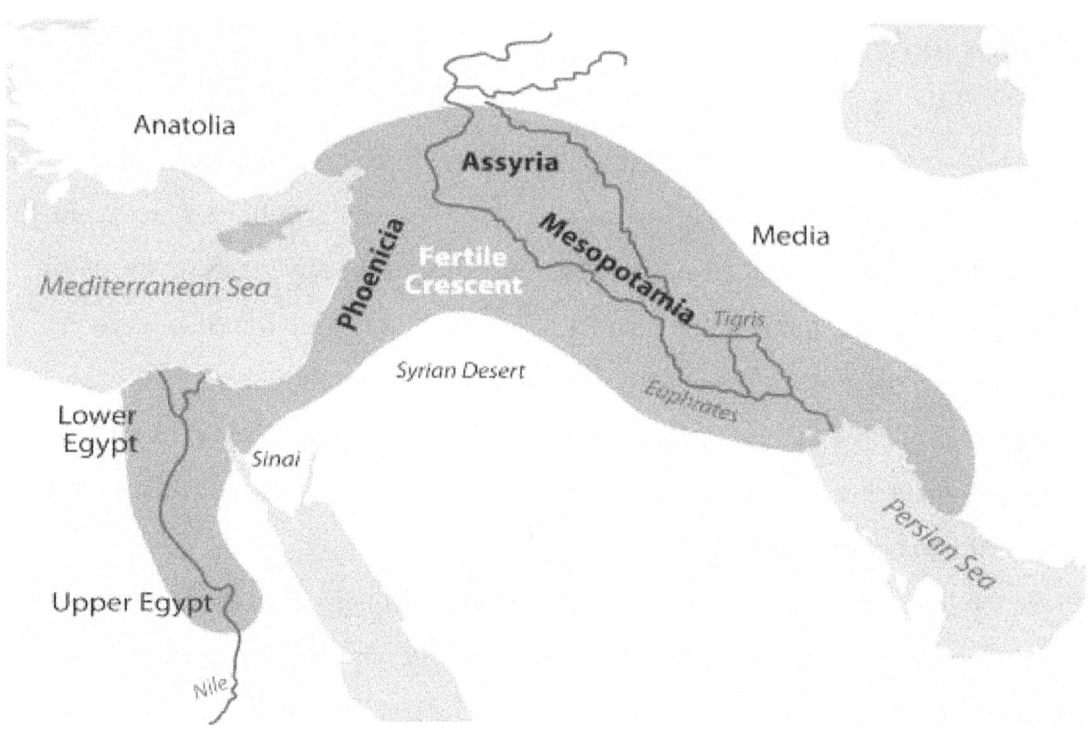

Yet, now, in this day and age, a lot of this same land is considered *arid*, at least not like it was before. Why? Could the climate have been a bit different back then? Could something have happened to forever change the course of how habitable these ancient lands would end up becoming? Whatever was in store for these pagan lands may have, indeed, begun to prompt a number of former residents to decide it was time for them to leave, and go somewhere else.

We get a hint to there being some kind of issue here in Scripture. Abraham's father, *Terah*, was a dignitary of Babylonia - he seemed to be a successful government official. Yet, for whatever reason, he felt a desire to leave:

And Terah took Abram his son, and Lot the son of Haran his son's son, and Sarai his daughter in law, his son Abram's wife; and **they went forth** *with them from Ur of the Chaldees, to go into the land of Canaan; and they came unto* **Haran***, and dwelt there.*   - *Gen.* 11:31 (KJV)

What could have made him leave? Yes, Terah was the father of that great patriarch Abraham - the "friend of God;" and his family was believed to have been located in the Babylonian city of *Ur* (at least for a while). Maybe the ravages of war were starting to take its toll here. Maybe it was something else. We're not quite sure. Yet, there are reasons we need to look at their migration (as we soon shall see).

While still up in the northern regions of Babylonia, they halted the progress of their travels, and temporarily began to settle in the area known as *Hanan* (as mentioned in the above verse).

> *Haran is almost universally identified with Harran, a city whose ruins lie within present-day* **Turkey**.
> ("Haran - Where & Who?", 2024, p. 1)[23]

Now, Haran seems to have been an ancient city about 300 miles northeast of Israel (in what we would now call eastern Turkey); and many of us would also know that Abraham would end up getting out of the area totally... eventually relocating into the Holy Land. Now, the question still burns: Could there have been some kind of negative event in this ancient land of Babylonia, which could have helped to prompt even a successful government official to leave the area?

Migrations Into Africa

We'll soon see how there could have been something to the migration of peoples, out of ancient Mesopotamia. To help get us there, let's go out on a limb a little, and assume that others could have been on the same trajectory as Terah, needing to move. If a good number of people were itching to get out of the area, it may have proved itself a little more difficult than one might think. The reason being was that there were neighboring communities, such as Canaan and Egypt, still holding onto their pagan roots, and may have been caught up in a lot of this same "cross-fire" (of Shem and his posse). Also, these nations may not have been very open to a lot of immigration, especially to a large number of migrating people (because they were, most probably, currently dealing with enough problems of their own).

What if a *large* number of people may have felt the need to relocate? What if they (now) felt the desire to relocate to another place, a place entirely *new* (because they couldn't easily access any other surrounding nation)? So, if a large number of people did feel the need to migrate here, why not try to head to a place that *is* entirely new, a place where no one else has settled yet, and a place that would be considered far enough away from being on the radar Shem's posse? This way, if they were able to go to some entirely *new* area, they would be out of most any conflict, and able to continue on with their former (pagan) ways of life. They could enjoy it all without interruption, and without all of the insecurities they once had.

And, yes, there *was* an area of our ancient world that, most probably, could have served as a suitable place for this mass migration - a place where a number of individuals may have already known about, a place where many knew was not occupied, and a place where they could all go to settle into (without many problems). As we also may recall (from previous volumes), Noah directed a number of the patriarchs underneath him just where to settle. He dictated that the sons of Shem were supposed to head into the Near East or Middle East, and the sons of Ham and Japheth into other areas. We also recall that *Canaan* (via Noah's direction) was supposed to settle his generations in the western corner of Africa. But, of course, any Bible reader probably knows that Canaan never really settled there. He and his kind stayed in the Middle East, and decided to plant themselves in the land that Noah planned out for Shem! Yes, that is why the land of *Israel* was once known as *Canaan* (and a reason why God commanded the Israelites to rid all people from the land)! It seems as though they weren't supposed to be there in the first place, so they had to be removed.

Well, just what may all of this mean to our discussion at hand? We'll now see that, if Canaan and his people assumed a land they weren't supposed to, then there would have been a vast area of land that was still unsettled. And, if a number of people knew what Canaan did what he did, wouldn't it make perfect sense for a number of those displaced people of Babylonia to figure they now had a place to go, if necessary? Wouldn't this have been a perfect place for them to live, and thrive, uncontested?

What if a number *did* decide to go westward, beyond the nation of Egypt and beyond Libya, then what could have been next for this crowd? Plenty.

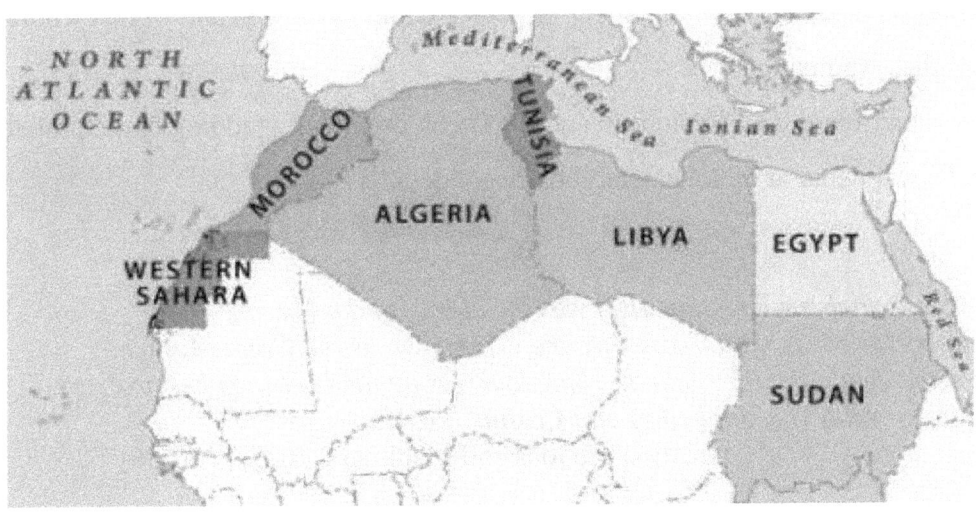

Let's suppose that a group of people *may* have decided to migrate away from the troubled Middle East, and into that westwardly direction (towards the Atlantic Ocean). Shem was busy purging their former homeland, as well as any lands settled by giants. What if *this* area could have been considered a *new* gateway to all of their (pagan) "progress?" And, if a vast number of people have already heard about this migration along the way, wouldn't that allow for a number of people to want to jump right in, and follow along? Imagine having a huge caravan by the time they ended up reaching their new "promised land."

If any of this was a distinct possibility, and a good number of people decided to travel towards Canaan's appointed land, just what could have this place have been called, and who would have been among the leadership of this whole caravan? Do we have any insights to all of this here, in ancient history? Apparently, there *may* have been a number of historical insights at our disposal here, and, on top of it, their migration *could* easily have been related to a number of Biblical characters, as well (believe it or not)! Let's see.

We already know how **Shem** was extremely righteous, and totally God-fearing. He also went around hunting and silencing major pagan leaders, as well as the giants. So, obviously, he probably wasn't a direct part of this. But, what about Shem's *other* brothers, or other major patriarchs of the Bible? Could a number of Noah's descendants have "crossed over"… into this pagan path? Could some of Shem's descendants, as well, have decided to go against this great patriarch, as well… following along these same pagan pathways? Assuredly, a number of people could have been part of this whole cabal, if they wanted to.

Here's an excerpt from a story in ancient Greek mythology (adding in the probable *Biblical* equivalents of their ancient gods or goddesses):

> *Basileia (Noah's wife **Naamah**?) was the eldest, and had reared her brothers (or sons), which was why she was known as the **Great Mother**... After the death of... Basileia, the kingdom was divided between her brothers (or sons), **Atlas** (i.e. Japheth?) and **Cronus** (i.e. Ham).*
> ("Creation of Gods and Mankind", 2022, p. 35-36)[24]

Of course, a number of these ancient stories might not always get the exact details of a story right, but it does seem to be interesting here. We already know how Cronus was another name for *Ham*, and Naamah was considered that "Great Mother" of so many in our post-Flood world. So, instead of being Ham's brother, we may be able to assume that she was, in actuality, Ham's mother. Sometimes, things can become a little blurred over time, but that's okay. Regardless of this one little tidbit, we may discover something very interesting, here: a number of Noah's immediate children (as well as his wife) may not have exactly end up on God's side. They, at least, were not very passionate, like Shem was.

A number of sources beyond this one state that Ham, and a number of his descendants, ended up quite contrary to God. A number of Japheth's descendents may have started out somewhat indifferent (in regards to their moral stance), but, over time, a number of them probably headed in the same moral direction as a number of Ham's descendants did. Shem, as well, was not able to keep a number of his descendents as passionate as he was, and a good number of his descendants also took the pagan "plunge." As a result, people of every branch of Noah's family were falling for this pagan temptation, and, most probably, a number of people from each ended up in this westwardly caravan, heading towards Canaan's appointed land.

Could **Atlas** (in the above) have been another son of Noah and Naamah, as well as a brother to Cronus (i.e. Ham)? It probably was not Shem. Could it have been Japheth, this other son of Noah? In another ancient text, we see that:

*After his (Cush's) beginning (at the Tower of Babel), Noah sent Ham to Egypt, and to Libya and Cyrene (a city in Libya) he sent **Triton** (i.e. **Shem**) and **the rest of Africa Japetus** (i.e. Japheth), the former **Atalaa**...*
(Asher, 1993, p. 203)[25]

Now we see that Japheth had some African lands reserved for him. So, if we begin to incorporate the above two texts together, we might be able to conclude that Japheth could have easily been one who would might know about this large migration. Could he have been the brother of Ham known as ***Atlas*** (or even *Atalaa*)?

Atlas was thought to be, by some ancients, a *son* of Iapetus (which, of course, was another name for Japheth). Either way, it seems that Japheth must have been related to Atlas here, in some way - either being the son of the patriarch or the patriarch himself. We also recall that Japheth wasn't exactly the epitome of what a God-follower was all about. And, being at such a high level of authority (and respect), it only makes sense to assume that he was famous to a number of his descendants (as well as others)… famous enough to be known by a name such as *Atlas*.

As we research, we see that there is more to this mythological title of *Atlas*. This god was supposedly able to "hold up" (or "push back") the heavens, restraining whatever's in the sky from having their own way. In other words, Japheth may have been given this title because *he* was considered the patriarch who was able to "hold back" the attempts of an "oppressive" God, as well as His influencers, to take them down. What if this implied that Japheth had, indeed, become a major patriarch here, assisting in the westwardly movement of this entire caravan? What if he was now accredited for helping the rest of his people to "push back" (or "overcome") those nasty "hunters" of God - the ones who went into their former lands, and tried to take them down.

Maybe, because of his leadership, Japheth was thought to be a **hero**, because of his "brave" decision to move a number of people out here, towards a "better" state of being.

The Title of "At-las"

Sometimes, as we may already know, pagan gods and Biblical personages may have been given a number of names, titles or epithets over time. Sometimes, the ancients wouldn't even call famous people by their proper names; it may have seemed more appropriate for dignitaries to be known as *pharaohs*, *gods*, what have you. The same probably applied here, with Japheth. What if he, or a close descendant of his, was known by the title of *Atlas*? What if he decided to lead a hoard of people to the western tip of Africa - "holding back" the "oppressive" God of Noah?

And, if we really think about it, anyone who might have been responsible for all this, assuredly, would have been celebrated by the people beneath him or her. They may have even had things named after them, in this western tip of Africa.

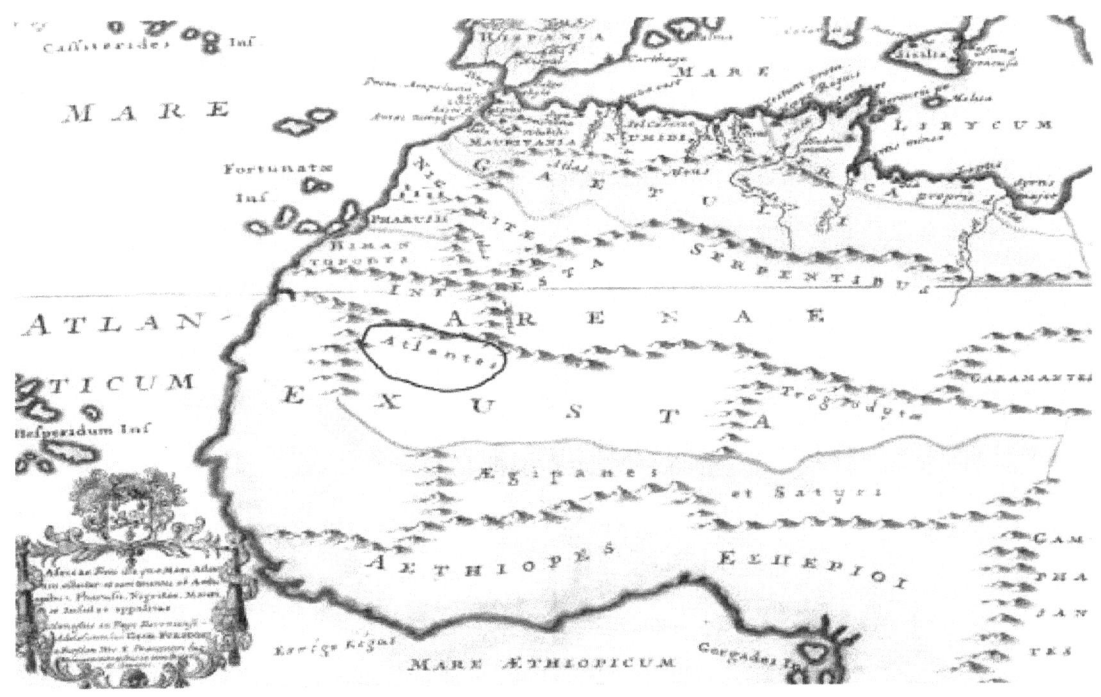

Interestingly, we do seem to find some evidence of this god Atlas in the region:

Atlas *became the ancestor of the **Atlantides**, the people in western Libya, giving the name to **Mount Atlas**.*
("Creation of Gods and Mankind", 2022, p. 36)[26]

We now see that his people - once they reached this extreme corner of Africa - were called the *Antlantes* (or ***Atlantides***). There also was a mountain chain, here, named in honor of him (in the above). Also, we see that, to the immediate west of this corner of Africa, there was also an ocean: the "***Atlantic*** Ocean." Fancy that. Yes, these references *do* seem to point towards some kind of civilization in this area, with a dignitary named Atlas.

Have we ever heard of some kind of advanced civilization in this general area, with a namesake that may have been close to the name *Atlas*? Actually, the answer might indeed be *yes*.

Chapter 5

The Real Story of "At-lantis"?

<u>Atlas</u> *n* (*strong, genitive* Atlas or Atlasses or **Atlanten**, *plural* **Atlanten**)
derived terms: **Atlantean**

("atlas", n. d., p. 1)[1]

The extreme western tip of Africa may not have ended up as exactly as people had hoped for, once the caravan began to arrive. The land may have had a few good qualities, but not everything. It may not have been the most fertile, especially for all of those people migrating over. But, what about the possibility of migrating just a little more westward, or even a little to the northwest? Maybe this area would have been a little more inviting to them all. And, assuredly, no one else would already be out that way, because this whole land mass, essentially, was considered the edge of the known world.

Today, this upper region of Africa seems to possess a number of mountainous areas, with a few deserts nearby- lands that aren't exactly habitable. Maybe the people decided to move on a bit, until they found a land where they really wanted to be. And, if they decided to go a little bit westward, or even northwestward, then what land could they have come across? Today, it would seem to be ocean; but, back then, could there have been some kind of arable land in this vicinity, for them to migrate into?

Before we look into the plausibility of a number of people establishing themselves in this area known as *Atlantis*, let's dissect the name of *Atlas* a bit further.

At, Ad, or Adad

If *Japheth* - or *Atlas* - was once a powerful leader, and, if he may have, possibly, had a large area of land named after him, let's take a deeper into his name, so that we can understand the whole situation a little better. If we look at the etymology of the word "Atlas," we may be able to separate the word into two distinct syllables: "At" and "las." And, with this, we may, then, be able to establish a connection between that syllable (*At*) and a few famous patriarchs of our past, or even some pagan "gods!" We actually do seem to have pagan gods with the title of *At*, as well as a few variants: *Ad*, *Adad* or *Hadad*. And, once we begin to decipher just "who's who" here, it might begin to help us broaden our overall understanding of this whole Atlantean possibility.

First, let's take a look at the variant *Ad*. We have some ancient information regarding a particular people, known as the "People of Ad" (or "Adites") in the Middle East:

> *In Islamic tradition, the **Adites** are believed to be among **the first** inhabitants of Arabia.*
> ("Ad", n. d., p. 2)[2]

Could these *Adites*, or *people of Ad*, have been a group of individuals believed to have been the "first" in a particular land? Could the variant *Ad*, then, stand for the "first of," or a "first nation" of sorts?

Maybe these *Ad* or *At* titles do represent some kind of *beginning*, or *first* group of peoples. Maybe Japheth could have been thought of as "the first" to reach a point of land, or even the "highest" or "most prominent" individual in the land? Surely, he would have been the oldest and most prominent patriarch of this whole migrating cause, because, first and foremost, he was a direct son of that great father Noah! Maybe there were a number of reasons why this particular title of "Atlas" was associated with him.

Of course, there are a number of famous "firsts" here, in regards to our ancient pagan world, such as Adam, the Serpent, etc. These two, as we may recall, were considered the "first" fathers of our ancient world (at least according to paganism). Adam was the *first* man to be thought of the viceroy of God; and the Serpent, of course, was given the title as the "first" or "most prominent" god - eventually becoming a "co-viceroy," with Adam.

What if Adam's name could be connected with these particular variants, as well?

Ad-am

Let's also look into the name *Adam* (or "Ad" and "am"). No matter how you look at it, he was surely considered the "first" leader of many, or viceroy of our current world. He was also considered the "highest" ranking manager of the Garden of Eden. In ancient Egypt, one of their top gods was known to be *Atum*. It's funny how close this name is to *Adam*, however. *Atum* was just another title for the Egyptian sun god (which only makes sense, because we also recall that Adam was considered to be a "sun" god in paganism as well). They all seem to be the same.

We also have the god *Ad*ad (or *Hadad*) in the Middle East, who may, actually, have been a couple of additional titles for the *Serpent* himself (in paganism)!

We also have *Athena* - one of the top goddesses of ancient Greece. And, of course, we may recall (from previous volumes) that *Athena* was another name for the Biblical *Eve*, the mother goddess of pagan lore. And yes, Eve was also considered the *first*, or *top*, matriarch of the pagan religion, so we have the same *At* in her title as well. Interestingly enough, we also see that - breaking down the word *Athena* into "**At**" and "hena" - the meaning of *Hena* could derive from the Hebrew word *hannāh*, or *chaanach*... another variation of the Hebrew word for *Eve*.[3] It's so obvious that *Athena* could have easily been considered the reincarnation of that "first," or "top," pagan goddess. And, as we now see, a number of alternate uses for *Ad* or *At* are out there, and could easily stand for the "first" of something, or some kind of "top," or "premier," individual.

Now, if we have an inkling of what this first part of the word *Atlantis* means, let's look more into the rest of the word. First, it makes total sense to believe that *Atlas* and

Atlantis could have been related, at least somewhat. And, we also know that the title of *At* is in both words. We now discover that the second half of the word *At-las* (i.e. the "las") could easily stand for the word "that."[4] Put the two words together and we have "that first one," "that top one," or even "that principle one." Now, what if Atlas was considered to be their "top dog," or their "highest" god, with the Atlantean continent also being named after him? What if this word *Atlantis* could easily be defined as "the **land of the *first* one**?"

Now, if this could indeed be what the name *Atlantis* means, then wasn't the "first one" or the "highest" god Japheth himself? Or, could this title have been utilized for some kind of *religious* significance, as well - dedicated to the *highest* pagan god of these migrating people? So, what if this new and exciting land was to be a celebration of their *first* or *highest* spiritual deity... a god already know to be the *Serpent*? This, also, could have been a possibility, here.

What if *Atlantis* was a nation dedicated to their major god - **the Serpent**, the one who first **"pushed back the heavens,"** and rebelled against God" (all the way back in the Garden of Eden)! Both Japheth and the Serpent could have been celebrated as the deities who were able to do this. Now, things may begin to make *a lot more* sense than it may have ever done before. Maybe Atlantis was celebrated as a place where an individual could be "free to worship" whatever god they chose (as long as it was pagan, of course) - the area now considered to be *the* place where the heavens (of God) would, officially, have been "held back."

Those Pillars of Hercules

It seems that the people who eventually would migrate here could have, indeed, come from the Middle East, because they definitely were worshiping the same pagan deities that originated there. Maybe Atlantis, then, was populated by a vast number of people who had ancestors from ancient Babylonia, Egypt, and the like, as well as from the Tower of Babel.

So, now that we may have established the type of people that ended up migrating to such a place, and *who* they may have really revered, we may begin to wonder about the physical *location* of this particular continent. And, if it was indeed a physical place, then why haven't any physical remnants been discovered? If it was such an overwhelming influence on the world to come (as Plato said it was), then why wasn't it able to last for a very long time? What if this whole concept was merely "shunned" over time - thrown into a dark, dusty corner somewhere? And, if this was so, then what could have been the *real* reason for "sweeping" this continent under that proverbial "rug," just as it was done for the probable existence of giants? Maybe there were a couple of reasons why our top educators, nowadays, work to displace the truth of this particular piece of land.

We, for example, *do* seem to have a precise location of Atlantis, given to us by Plato - one of the most popular philosophers of ancient times (and the one who wrote the most about this lost continent). He clearly stated that Atlantis was "beyond the Pillars of Hercules," which would have placed it a little to west, or even a little to the northwest, of this northwestern tip of Africa we were talking about. Fancy that.

Yes, those Pillars of Hercules lie at the extreme western tip of the Mediterranean Sea. One is located at the southwestern tip of Spain, with the other at the northwestern tip of Morocco (in Africa).

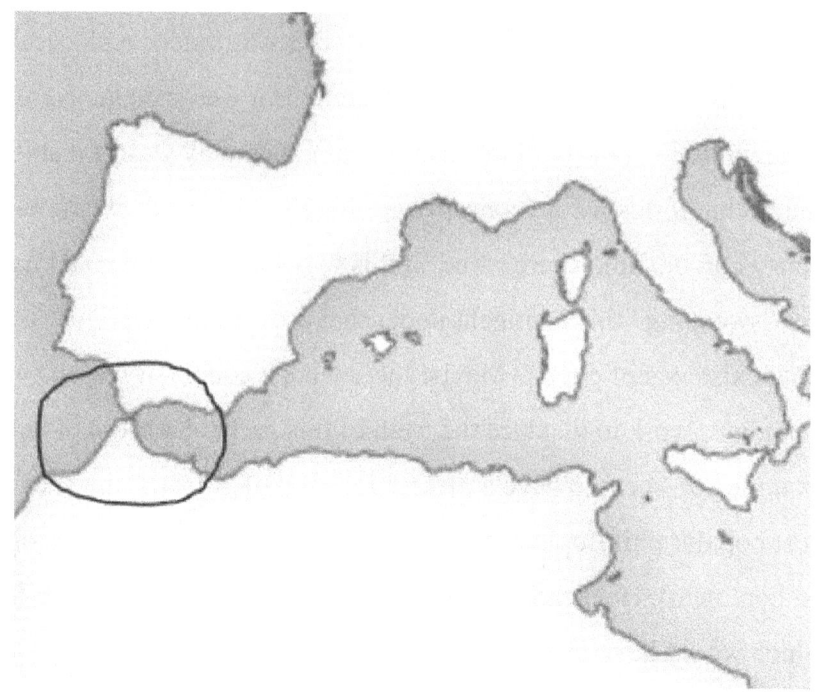

Of course, for some strange reason, many modern scholars often seem to gloss over this particular statement, or quickly find ways to propose a number of *different* places where Atlantis might have been situated. Why? It's as clear as day what Plato said; and, if anyone would have known something about this lost continent of Atlantis, *he* should have.

So, it also seems pretty clear that this particular location was, even in ancient times, a very famous landmark... a place where a lot of people already knew of. Yet, so many with knowledge on this particular subject may quickly begin to suggest looking elsewhere, such as near Greece, near the Bimini Islands, or even off the coast of Japan or India. Could all of these alternate theories be viable, or could there be a little *more* to the denial of what Plato claimed?

Interestingly enough, the Pillars of Hercules were also (by the ancients) considered the location that "marked the limit of civilization."[5] So, beyond this general location, there may have once lied a parcel of land, along with a number of ancient islands (inhabited by few barbarians), and even an ocean. The funny thing about all of this is: anything to the west of that northwestern tip of Africa, today, is clearly an ocean - the ***Atlantic*** Ocean. Was this ocean named after the continent that once sat there? Could there have been a parcel of land in the general location that, eventually, was submerged?

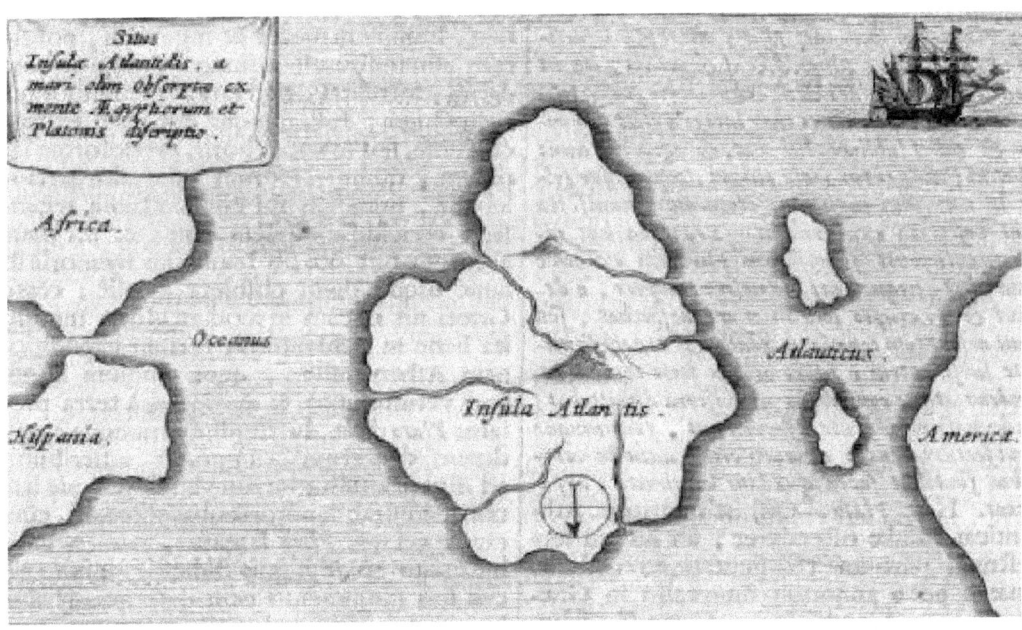

And, if this did happen, what would have happened to the survivors (as Plato said that there were)? Did a number of people migrate to other ancient lands, setting them up to be a number of ancient civilizations that we may already know about?

...The "Spirit" of Babylon?

As we move further, we now need to ask: What if those migrating individuals (from ancient Babylonia and beyond) began to enjoy their stay in this continent? What if they became very successful in all of what their pagan beliefs (as well as all of what their neighboring giants) had to offer them (at least for a little while)? Was the land good enough for a vast number of people to capitalize on all of their anti-God sentiments?

Many different kinds of people (as we've already discovered) may have united together, to form that early migration. And, the caravan could have united together once again, to form this early Atlantean continent. What if this combination was able to build a civilization unlike the world had ever seen... all unabated by those "mean" followers of God? Who would be able to stop their "advancements" now?

And, if we're to assume that this Atlantean land was large enough (and usable enough) to contain a whole number of pagan worshippers, along with a number of brilliant minds along with them (including those giants), then the land could easily have been a perfect location to fully capitalize on all things pagan - all of that advanced (and/or occult) knowledge of this fallen, lower world. What if Atlantis was able to take on the "spirit" of ancient Babylon, Egypt and a number of powerful ancient pagan nations, and bring it up another notch? Could this particular situation have allowed Atlantis to become a gigantic, *powerhouse* of a pagan force... able to pass on their anti-God elements into a vast number of succeeding nations (worldwide)?

And, if this was all so, then Atlantis would easily have become a problem for a number of modern historians. To them, mankind evolved slowly, and nations also evolved independently of one another. There wasn't an early, united front of paganism, like with the occurrence the Tower of Babel, or Atlantis! Of course, for one, they couldn't really say anything that actually supports the Bible, as well!

Now, they need to make it all look as though a bunch of hunters and gathers "just came across" a good deal of advanced knowledge over the years (somehow), and they received it all *on their own*... they wouldn't *dare* say that any of it may have come from the contributions of those early giants, or antediluvian Nephilim.

Now, if Atlantis was a source of so many ancient pagan contributions, spreading out into so many ancient subsequent nations, then some questions might arise: exactly where *they* may have received their advanced knowledge and technical information! Atlantis, then, becomes a huge "link" between the ancient past and the present... a link that, if played "right", could be "broken" (and no one would really become the wiser)!

So, a number of those with an *agenda*, today, would rather try to stress the ideas that **mankind** had slowly evolved, and did it all without the help from any ancient giants (of course), or any "gods," or beings from the "Other Side." Anything other than their agenda becomes a *thorn* in their side, assuredly:

*If the existence of the ancient **advanced civilization** were officially acknowledged, they assert, the current hypotheses concerning the history and development of humankind would have to be completely **revised**. Acceptance of a prehistoric supercivilization would make the **current understanding of history obsolete**. To find **irrefutable** evidence of a great… culture that thrived while the rest of humankind was struggling to exist on a primitive level would demolish conventional knowledge of the progress of civilization.*

(Steiger, 2006, p. 40)[6]

If anyone discovered Atlantis, and learned all of what it may have actually accomplished, and passed on, then it may all throw a big "monkey wrench" in a lot of what these societal "betters" have been pushing all along… and they can't have that.

Civilization and High "Teche"

One major reason to hide the possible existence of this continent involves its use of advanced (or even "otherworldly") knowledge. It has been said that there were incredible technological feats going on in the continent - from great advancements of building and architecture, to advanced engineering, to a number of early technologies. So, for our cultural "betters" to be able to keep their "slowly but surely" narrative going, there might need to be a few "breaks" in some of the historical "links" here… especially the links that may allow us to source the origins of all this to Babylon, to the Middle East, as well as to the offspring of these **fallen, terrestrial angels**!

Well, what about the *huge* advancements we see in our world of today? We've had some unbelievable discoveries in the past century (or two): *transistors*, *Kevlar*, *nuclear energy*, and so much more! What if a number of these things come from a few questionable sources (at best), or even *beyond* our world? It doesn't seem that we could have just come up with so much of this, in so little time - at *least* by comparing it all to the other centuries before us! Once again, we see civilization "taking off," way beyond normal.

What brought it about *this* time? No, we're not talking about a few people studying very hard (although it helps). We're not necessarily talking about space aliens either.

Every century had some of this. In this day and age, as we have seen it during the time of those ancient giants, many people may have actually engaged themselves in another round of spiritual *fornication* - people bartering with supernatural entities of the "Other Side," in order to facilitate a rise in personal knowledge or power. We know that these exchanges occurred in the antediluvian world; it assuredly happened after the Flood, with those exchanges between giants and humans. Assuredly, the same must be going on today. This time, it's not necessarily with physical giants, or fallen, terrestrial angels walking around, but more like the *communication* with fallen, demonic entities (of the supernatural world). Without a doubt, those extremely hungry for power and control have found ways to communicate with this "Other Side."

Of course, those with an anti-God agenda would find that these act would not settle very well with the many people of this world who believe in God, and want to follow Him. It just doesn't look good! And, once again, Christianity and Judeo-Christian values are the enemies, here, to a lot of their advancements. They actually hate exposure. They don't like Christians calling them out for the devilish deeds they are taking part of. Again, it's just one way or another, and that's why so much of this seems to be so secretive, or seems to be done "behind closed doors."

Cracks in their "Utopia"

We recall that: one major unifying trait that those migrating people wanted to have, in regards to the entire continent of Atlantis, was for them to be a **pagan**-centered civilization, without any restraints and without any binding elements of their time (such as Shem). There could have been a number of Egyptians who went there, a number of Canaanites, and even Semites (i.e. the sons of Shem). There could have been a number of Hamites there, and, almost assuredly, there were those from Japheth's family there as well, providing him all kinds of support… anyone who seemed to be discontent with the way God was working in our post-Fall world.

Although the continent may have been a good way to bring a vast number of different people together (as well as the giants) it all didn't last for very long. Through their strive for "unity," the population of Atlantis, most probably, had almost everything going for them… except for one thing: they did not want to have anything to do with the God who created them. And, this whole "independent" concept didn't really seem to work too well for them in the end. Why? Maybe it was because they could get away from the reaches of Shem and his entourage, but they couldn't get away from God… not *totally* away. He created the world, and He still holds all of the cards.

The Fall

This time, as we know, Shem and his entourage were not on their doorstep. He may not have even known where they ended up moving to, or even cared. Maybe their reconciliation was to come from *another* source, here. We may want to think that: if paganism was so right, and a number of these pagans - the best and brightest at the time - were placed in such a good place, and were unabated, then why *did* the whole continent collapse? And, no, it wasn't just because of the disaster that was to come – many people who know Plato's account realizes that their whole society was already failing apart, collapsing under its own weight, due to corruption. **Why**? Of course, so much of it had to do with a lack of morality. Go figure. There was no real reason why it shouldn't have been able to continue indefinitely… except if the way they led their lives wasn't exactly "kosher." Doesn't this entire situation, in a way, sound a lot like what happened at the Tower of Babel? This continent was destroyed, due to internal corruption, and most probably the people were scattered abroad. At the Tower of Babel, the people were corrupted as well (and hated God), with their organized effort being splintered apart, and the people scattered! It seems that: to those who do not want God in any way, things like this just "seem to happen."

With paganism, people seem to heavily concentrate on all of what the "father" and "son" of paganism (i.e. the Serpent and Cain) had for them. And, of course, the Bible hints to these two individuals as "perdition" and the "son of perdition." Cush, that leader of post-Flood paganism, was also known as the god of *Chaos*. Again, it seems as though: when people begin to follow certain individuals, things just seem to rub off on them, and take them over. In Atlantis, perdition and chaos, once again, followed those individuals who openly wanted to be against God, and caught up with them.

We also recall that these anti-God persons began to become highly supportive of *secular humanism* - believing that one's own reasoning (on moral things) becomes all that's really needed. Their moral code does not need to rely on an absolute moral code (such as what God might provide); it only needs to be subjective (to a person's own interpretation). Political correctness now becomes the norm. People then strive to "fit in" with the opinions of other people around them. In the case of Atlantis, it involved a nation of people who began to think according to their *own* rules (only), and began behaving in their *own* best interests. Yes, once again, this could not end up very well. Chaos, once again, would begin to raise its ugly head. With everybody running around, doing whatever they wanted to do, then the nation almost cannot help but to fall apart. With a number of people scrambling, trying to find ways to raise their *own* self-esteems, many cannot help but to step on other people's own toes. Other people usually become effected, negatively - *especially* when people begin to resort to what this lower, imperfect world (of darkness) has to offer. There always will be some causalities to this "war" of self-esteem (with people never feeling totally satisfied, or satisfied for very long). Again, the fight for individual self-actualization (without God, and without some kind of absolute moral code) usually turns a society more and more chaotic, as time progresses. It just seems to be a fact of our fallen, and imperfect, world.

A Recent "Pangea" Event?

Plato said that, next, a catastrophe was to be on their horizon. Internal corruption had already begun to take hold. Even though the continent was about to go down (literally), a number of individuals still had the time (and the ability) to do something about their futures, and flee. What would happen next, and where did a number of these survivors end up going? Now, with all of this information already in hand, let's continue on with our expose' of what could have happened next - what would have turned Atlantis into a "lost continent," and a springboard to so many new societies. Of course, this represents a "link" - a link from the ancient world to a world more recent. And, we'll also discover a few reasons why those "powers that be" may have felt that the information was much better left at the bottom of some "sea."

Of course, even the most casual reader of the Atlantean legend probably knows that the continent had succumbed to some environmental disaster, and was submerged under the sea. Now, *when* could this have probably occurred? There are a number of those who claim that this catastrophe should have taken place around 9,000 B.C. (according to an interpretation of Plato's works). But, as we already know, there is *politics* in most everything we face (nowadays), and this "9,000" figure would seem to fit a little better into some human evolutionary timeline (dictated by our societal "betters"). And, corruption is everywhere… things can be changed, or "reinterpreted," in order to help it "fit" into a scenario that may already be established.

Yet, there are a number of things that actually may point us in the direction of Atlantis' collapse as a more recent event. One thing that Plato said was: the Atlanteans were battling the ancient Athenians (from the area of Athens, Greece), a bit before the major catastrophe.[7] Now, if we pinpoint the collapse of Atlantis around 1600 B.C., rather than about 9,000 years earlier, then we see that this could be a possibility. The ancient Athenians, most probably, were not around 9,000 years before the time of Plato, but could have been more recently. Also, Plato states that he received his information from a man who talked to some Egyptian priests, a few hundred years prior. Now, if we think about it: Egypt must have also been already been in existence at the time of Atlantis for some individual to be able to go over there, and tell these priests the whole story. Who's going to wait, and sit on a story for 9,000 years, and then decide to go over and talk to a few Egyptian priests, as if it's a new story… unless it *was* a fairly new story, or an event of some kind of recent significance. Somebody may have made it back into Egypt, from Atlantis, and told the priests everything that just happened (in detail). Again, the story that Plato received probably would not have been very detailed at all - if there was a 9,000-year gap here.

Why do our educated "betters," so often, try to *expand* the origins of some kind of ancient event? Why make it seem like something is a lot *older* than what it may actually be? Of course, one thing that those educated, and ungodly, scientists may need to do is to, somehow, "mold" what they have in front of them with the chronological timeline of world history that they were given… simple. They usually need to "stretch" time out, not only to have it all "fit" with their theory of evolution, but also to allow for things to "just happen," or things to just "come about," all by themselves! If Atlantis existed right along with those ancient Athenians and Egyptians, then Plato's story seems to make a whole lot more sense, here. But, once again, this "link" could be a little more difficult to sever… if it was a much more recent event. See how this all works?

Regardless of what timeframe people may place the Atlantean civilization at, the question still remains about how this particular civilization had become so far advanced, so long ago. Also, the farther people try to place the existence of this lost civilization *back* in time, the harder it also is for them to explain where these people were able to learn such things, right? We're there just "hunters and gatherers" around this early time (i.e. 9,000 years ago)? Again, even keeping the concept of Atlantis alive, with this date, hurts them, and their causes.

Next, if the continent did sink a bit more recently, then how could it have all happened? What might have been the catastrophe that took out the whole thing? Plato said that: overnight, a catastrophe rained down upon Atlantis, and it sunk into the waters. But, what if a massive catastrophe did a lot more than just sink a continent into the newly-formed Atlantic ocean? What if there was a massive event going on at this time - something of such magnitude that it went on to affect a vast number of *other* areas in our ancient world? What if there was a catastrophe that even caused a massive shift in the earth's crust, allowing for a few continents to start drift apart from each other (sinking the Atlantean continent in the process)? There is a geological theory, regarding continental displacement, known as "Earth Crustal Displacement." This theory implies that the earth's crust could, at certain times, be able to *move* (over the liquid layers beneath it), effectively able to shift the geographic locations of entire continents (if something major was to happen on the surface of the world). Could something like this have happened, quite suddenly, to Atlantis? Could there have been some kind of crustal displacement going on at the time, underneath the surrounding continents, to allow them to be able to drift apart from the sinking Atlantean continent at the time? Could God have set up some kind of catastrophe, here?

If we look at a current map of the world, it seems very plausible that North and South America could have once been located a lot closer to the European and African continents than they do now.

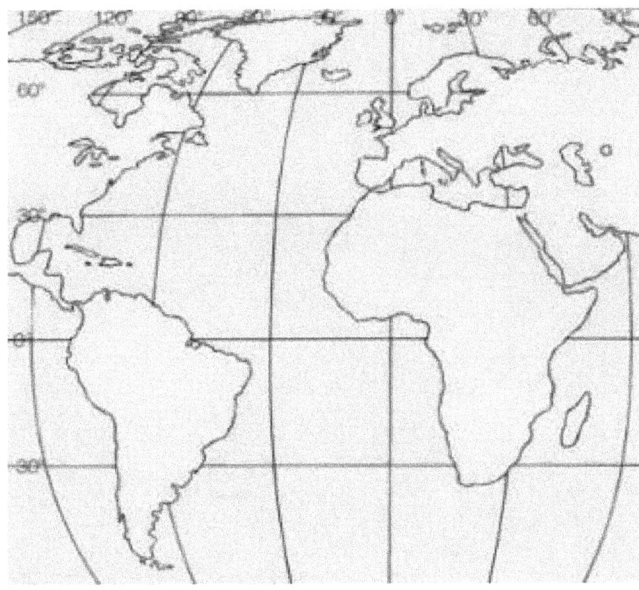

We see that the two sides of the world could have almost "fit" together (at least for a time), if we really think about it:

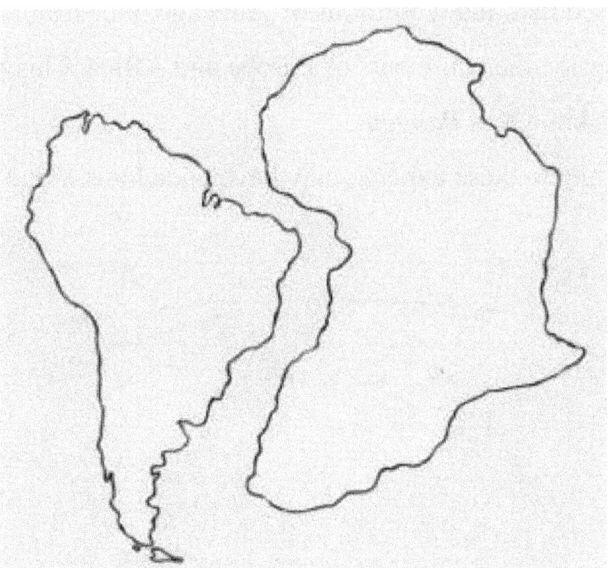

What if these continents were, indeed, together for a time, and were displaced, through a major catastrophic event (with Atlantis, once, smack dab in the middle of it all)?

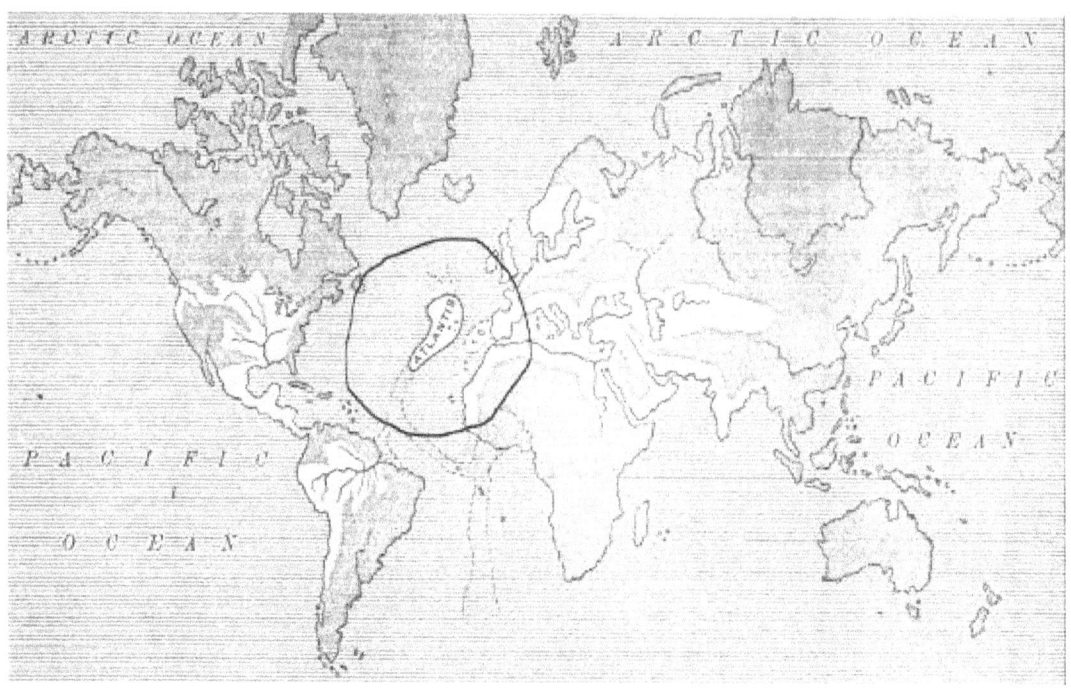

And, of course, if this was really the reality, then it all might not sit very well with those trying to push some kind of slowly-moving, evolutionary theory.

Some have proposed that: many millions of years ago, North and South America *were* positioned right alongside the continents of Europe and Africa. This once-unified "supercontinent" was known as **Pangea**.

The world, according to these experts, may have once looked like this:

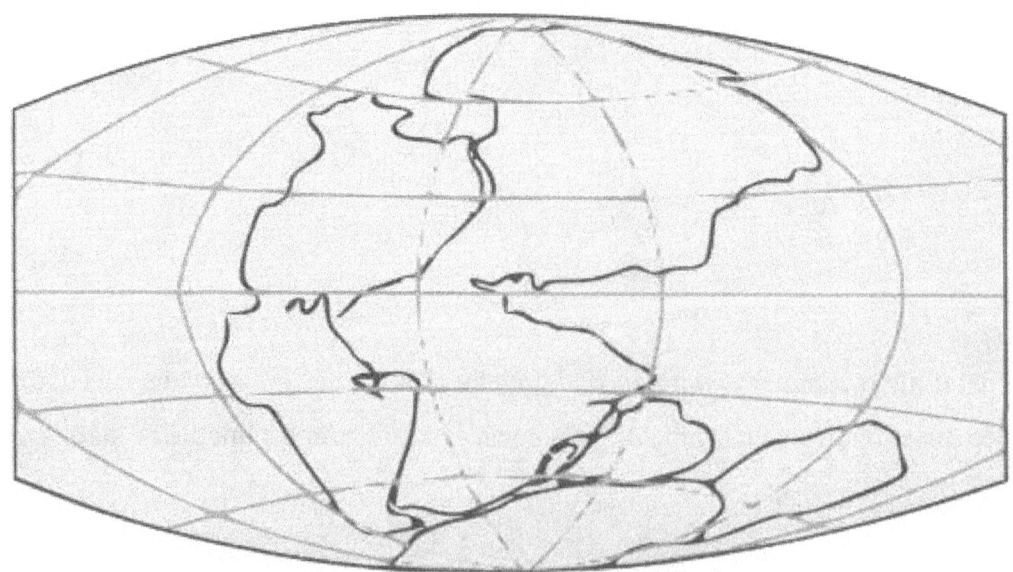

Again, for those who need this evolutionary process to work for them, the slower the better. But, what if this split did not occur millions of years ago, but only thousands? What if it could have happened around the same time that Atlantis was destroyed? Again, we are dealing with real people here, who need to make their intellectual interpretations based upon the politics that they may subscribe to, as well as according to who may be paying them. Quite often, people may need to claim that things occurred "millions" of years ago... because they're benefiting from saying this. Let's say, for example, that certain government authorities might want to front how the moon was really made out of Swiss Cheese. They, then, will want to push a number of scientists (of whom they are paying) to convince the populous to take this whole concept seriously. It works the same with Atlantis, and other *obscured* elements of our historical record. Yes, that is the power of money, and the funding of research at work here.

And, of course, many of those in the private and public sector - those who are not exactly on the side of God - would much rather push some *evolution* theory, or anything that seems to take God out of the picture... so, why not extend the amount of time to *millions*, here?

What if the continents were, indeed, a lot closer - around 4,000 years ago? Here is a quote from Plato:

> *This power came forth out of the Atlantic Ocean, for in those days **the Atlantic was navigable**; and there was an island situated in front of the straits which are by you called the Pillars of Heracles; the island was larger than Libya and Asia put together, and was the way to other islands, and from these you might pass to the whole of **the opposite continent** which surrounded the true ocean; for this sea which is within the Straits of Heracles is only a harbour, having a narrow entrance, but that other is a real sea, and the surrounding land may be most truly called a boundless continent.*
> — *Plato* Timaeus 360 B.C.[8]

Now, it seems that Atlantis would have been smack dab in the middle of four major continents (i.e. North America, South America, Europe and Africa); and the Atlantic Ocean, of course, was navigable... because it was not really an ocean at the time (but just a sequence of thin waterways). The only ocean at the time (according to Plato) was *beyond* (or, to the west of) those "opposite" continents - **North and South America**.

So, if we think about it, it truly seemed as through these five continents could have been *clumped* together in such a way, like Pangea - with the civilization of Atlantis located right in the middle of it. What if a horrendous catastrophe (i.e. a huge asteroid, possibly) was about to rain down upon this middle continent (Atlantis), destroying it completely and helping to send the rest of those land masses into opposing directions (eventually into the places where they are now situated)?

Also, what if these Atlantean survivors decided to head into the direction of either one group of opposing continents or the other?

Those Survivors

Possibly, the continents of America may have begun to drift to the west, with the continents of Africa and Europe to the east, and the waters of the new *Atlantic* Ocean collecting together, into the cavity of destruction that was once Atlantis.

Eventually, the two continental drifts reached as far as they were going to go, and we have the layout that we have today.

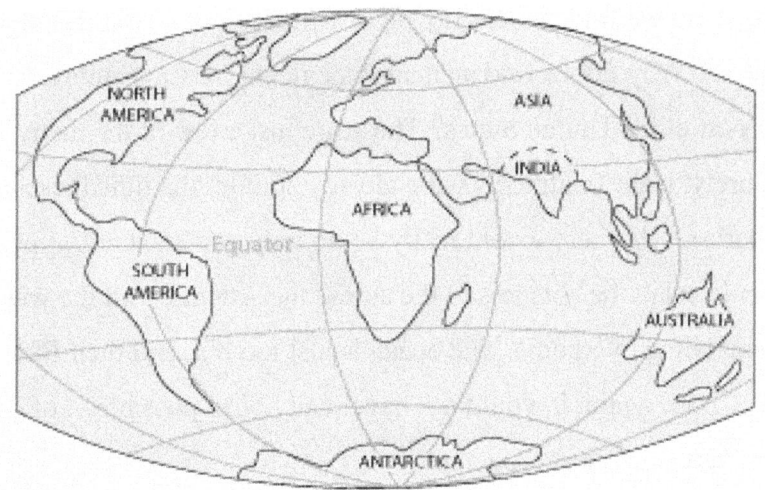

Now, the important thing that we may need to take away from this all is: where could those remnants of Atlantis have migrated to, if they did leave, and what elements of their former continent did they bring along with them (if any)?

Of course, the current explanation of how North and South America was populated, early on, stems from the modern theory that: migrating individuals would end up coming to the continent via northeastern Siberia, walking across a frozen strait of land (which, supposedly, happened around 11,000 years ago).

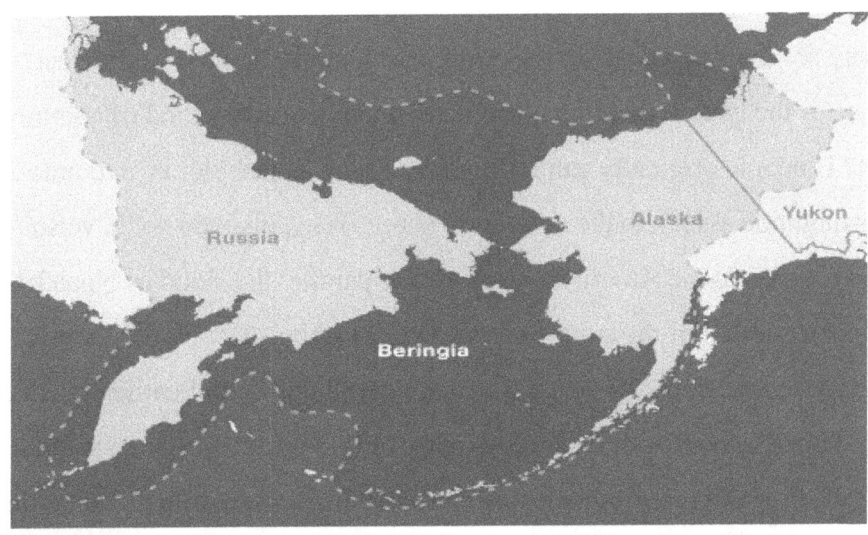

Yet, assuredly, to the dismay of a number of modern archaeologists out there, there seems to be a vast number of OOP (or "Out Of Place") artifacts in North and South Americas (for example), which may lead us to some answers *other* than what they tell us. Why, for example, do we find ancient Egyptian artifacts in the Grand Canyon, as well as in southern Illinois? Why do we find ancient Phoenician (or Canaanite) stone structures on the eastern coast of the United States? These are just a few of the many examples that are out there. Surely, if the continents were already split by the time these ancient people came (from Siberia), then there would really be **no way** that ancient Egyptians and Phoenicians would easily be able to sail the across the Atlantic - all the way across the Atlantic - without being overcome. The ocean is just too big, and their little boats were just too tiny. Yet, once again, it would not have really been possible… of course, unless the land masses were a lot closer together.

We have another scenario, here: a good number of *giant* bones, skeletons and other artifacts were actually discovered in the Americas. As well, there are a good deal of oral traditions regarding these giants - as the builders of, or powers behind, a number of ancient American mounds and stone structures. How could this have been possible, if the early inhabitants of the land were only these migrating peoples from Siberia? A number of "indigenous" or "first nation" peoples say (in their ancient lore and legends) that giants were around them, building things and teaching them a lot of advanced, or sacred, knowledge. *They* were the ones accredited for building a whole number of ancient structures and monuments. Again, how could this all be… if science says that only a few people migrated to America from Asia?

Also, why are there *pyramids* in the Americas, just like in the Middle East? It makes perfect sense, if the two civilizations who made them had some kind of common origin, wouldn't it? If people originally came from areas such as Babylonia, and onto Atlantis, then things might be able to make a lot more sense. Why, also, do we have so many ancient *flood* stories in the Americas - stories that parallel the flood of Noah? There's even an ancient parallel of the story of the Tower of Babel… in North America! Where did these things come from? If we assume that only "hunters and gatherers" decided to take a trek, across some frozen ice bridge (over 11,000 years ago), then we really have no answers. If we begin to insert *our* scenario into the mix - with Atlantis being the probable hub of so many future civilizations - then all of these (and other) questions find a sensible answer.

According to Plato:

*Now in this island of Atlantis there was a great and wonderful empire which had rule over the whole island **and several others**, and over parts of the continent, and, furthermore, the men of Atlantis had **subjected the parts of Libya** (in Africa) within the columns of Heracles **as far as Egypt**, and of **Europe** as far as Tyrrhenia.*
- *Plato* Timaeus 360 B.C.[9]

If Atlantis already expanded itself out, and had a number of colonies, this gives them even more options for escape. We also, for example, have the ancient **Minoan** civilization, located near modern-day Greece, which was thought to have possessed a lot of similarities to this Atlantean civilization. And, this island civilization was also destroyed by the eruption of a local volcano, known as *Thera* (in 1628 B.C.). Now, if this was an ancient outpost of Atlantis, could the Minoan civilization have been destroyed around the same time as Atlantis, due to a massive catastrophe which facilitated a number of geological upheavals, all around the area (including some major volcanic eruptions)?

Chapter 6

The Great Cover Up(s)

...and in a single day and night of misfortune all your warlike men in a body sank into the earth, and the island of Atlantis in like manner disappeared in the depths of the sea.
                              - *Plato* Timaeus 360 B.C.[1]

Atlantis - "First Nation" of the Post-Babylonian World?

If Atlantis could have truly been destroyed in the way we've already postulated here, then North, Central and South America, as well as western Europe and western Africa, could have been a number of destinations for all of those survivors to flee to (because the continents were still fairly close together at the time).

*Plato says that there was a "passage west from Atlantis to the rest of the islands, as well as from these islands to the **whole opposite continent** that surrounds that real sea..." how could he have **invented... the whole continent (of America)** enclosing that real sea? If we look at the map, we see that the continent of America does "surround" the (Pacific) ocean in a great half−circle. Could Plato have guessed all this?* (Donnelly, 1882, p. 78)[2]

It does not really make sense, here. How did Plato know this... if America was nowhere near to the shores of Africa and Europe? It, most probably, would not have been the way that Plato claimed... if there was a huge volume of water in the middle of all these continents. America would not have been "just around the corner" of the Pillars of Hercules - it would have been "way across the ocean."

Also, if these Atlantean survivors began to go in the direction of western Europe, western Africa and the Americas, then they would have, most probably, brought their forbidden, esoteric knowledge (of those antediluvian Nephilim) with them. People, now, had to start over in these new lands, departing Atlantis with individuals that they, most probably, felt the most comfortable traveling with, and forming their new (and distinct) civilizations with. But, either way, they all would have had tidbits of this esoteric knowledge and pagan belief.

And, once again, it seemed that practically all of this information originated in that huge caravan who left their former lands, such as Babylon, Egypt and etc. These are the "links" that, most probably, have been broken for us. This, most probably, is the reason why Atlantis has not been taken very seriously over the years, or just "cannot" be found.

And, if this all was the case, then those who fled into the Americas would have been considered the "first peoples" of so many areas of our New World. And, if those *giants* were also amongst the individuals who once lived in Atlantis, then they would have also ventured into these new lands, teaching anyone near them (or right behind them) the "tricks" of their occult trades. And, yes, there apparently was physical evidence for a lot of this early giant knowledge and influence… all over the areas of North, Central and South America (even though so much of it has been *downplayed* by many mainstream archaeologists). There seemed to have been numerous stone structures (in these continents) built by extremely knowledgeable persons, with advanced uses of mathematics, engineering, architecture, astrology and technology (to say the least). And, of course, we have the many elders of these same lands (today) bringing up ancient *giants* as the ones responsible for so much of it.

And, as we may already know, these migrating people may have already found themselves as a *collective* of like-minded individuals, with common knowledge of everything **pagan**, just diverting into their own civilizations now. A number of these people, most probably, had ancestors who were once at the Tower of Babel, or, at least, carried on the spirit of this **Babylonian** city! Yes, Atlantis may have truly been a "link" - between the Middle Eastern world of old and the American worlds of the new. It seems so obvious that the old world and the (American) new must have had a number of commonalities, or a common origin. They both worshiped the *sun* (i.e. the celestial symbol of the **Serpent**). They both venerated serpents, and had a serpent god of whom they highly venerated. They both built pyramids. They both knew astrology, advanced mathematics and a lot more. And, they both had the superior knowledge of the **giants**.

There were even pyramids build (in the New World) to show their reverence for their serpent god. The following pyramid is known as the *Castillo Pyramid* (in the ancient city of Chichen Itza), and a shadow of this serpent shows up at certain times of the year:

Go figure. No "expert" worth their salt can really say that these civilizations - on both sides of the earth - just "happened" to learn about these same pagan elements, and built their cities with a lot of the same intentions. Not many should be able to claim that people on both sides of the pond "just acquired" these same pagan elements organically... unless they're *willingly* trying to keep their eyes shut, in regards to this all.

It may be a brand new land, here, but it's still the same *old Serpent*.

The Name "America"

We also see that:

*The Kurgans (a.k.a. the Aryan giants) were a real people who lived in the steppes of Russia (near the Caucasus Mountains) between 5000-2000 b.c., thereafter apparently migrating from that region to settle practically every part of the world... even **to the Americas**.*
("Giants in the Earth Part II: Giants of the Americas", 2003, p.9)[3]

Now, if most of these American "first people" came from Atlantis - i.e. the "land of the first (or premier) one" - could there have been even *more* references to this "first one," or "highest one" of paganism... the *Serpent*? We already have the representations of the sun and the Serpent (seemingly) everywhere. And, we also see that the very name of *America* could stem from this early element of paganism:

*Welcome to Amaruca, the Land of the Serpent Gods... the chief god of the Mayan Indians in Central America was Quettzalcoatl / Kukulkan ("Plumed Serpent", "Feathered Serpent"). In Peru this god was called Amaru and the territory **known as Amaruca**.*
("America May Derive From Peruvian Name", n. d., p. 1)[4]

Also:

*These Children of the Sun adore the Plumed Serpent, who is the messenger of the Sun. He was the God Quetzalcoatl in Mexico, Gucumatz in Quiche; and in Peru he was called **Amaru**. From the latter name comes our word America. **Amaruca** is, literally translated, 'Land of **the Plumed Serpent**.'*
("America/Amaruca - Land of the Plumed Serpent", 2013, p. 1-2)[5]

Of course, this all fits perfectly with our scenario. Both sides seem to honor a *serpent* as a supreme being. And, from what we already assume about the Atlantean origins of these ancient Americans, it all makes **perfect sense**! This *spirit* of ancient Babylon, now, was able to manifest itself into the farthest regions of the earth, leaving bread crumbs of their former influence along the way.

"Fatherland" of the American Empires?

Let's take a look at a few more examples of possible Atlantean influence in America. One group of people considered one of the earliest civilizations of this New World were the *Toltecs*:

> *The Toltec culture is a pre-Columbian Mesoamerican culture that ruled a state centered in Tula, Hidalgo, Mexico in the early post-classic period of Mesoamerican chronology (ca. 900-1521 AD). The later **Aztec** culture saw the Toltecs as **their intellectual and cultural predecessors**...*
> ("Toltec", n. d., p. 1)[6]

Okay, if they influenced later civilizations, then where would the Toltecs have originated from? Interestingly enough, we do see that:

> *The Toltecs traced their migrations back to a starting-point called "Aztlan," or "**Atlan.**" This could be no other than Atlantis.*
> (Donnelly, 1882, p 105)[7]

Ignatius Donnelly, that famous politician who ended up authoring a book on Atlantis (in the late 1800s), said the very name of "Aztec" was derived from the word *Aztlan*, meaning "the original island."[8]

Wow, doesn't that sound like something very familiar to us - an area by the name of *Atlantis*, or "*land of the first one*?" Yes, they both seem to fit together, almost perfectly! Donnelly also said that: "All the races that settled Mexico, we are told, traced their origin back to an **'Aztlan'**, a 'most attractive land.'"[9]

Well, we have a little information on these early settlements of Central America. What about the other lands of North and South America? We have an ancient text in South America, known as the *Popol Vuh*, which was originally rendered to be all-but-extinct by a number of invading Catholic priests in the land (after the initial invasion of the Spanish Conquistadors). Of course, the document was considered "heretical" by early Catholics. Yet, it seems to have contained knowledge of the **original** area where their ancestors came from. According to the text, the original land was considered a land that was multicultural, and from the *east*… right in the direction of Atlantis:

> *The Popol Vuh, in which, after describing the creation of the first men 'in the region of **the rising sun**'… we are told, 'All seem to have spoken one language, and to have lived in great peace, "black men and white together"'… How did the red men of Central America know anything about 'black men and white men?' The conclusion seems inevitable that these legends of a primitive, peaceful, and happy land, an Aztlan in the East, inhabited by black and white men, to which all the civilized nations of America traced their origin, could only refer to Atlantis—that bridge of land where the **white, dark, and red races met**.*
> (Donnelly, 1882, p 175-176)[10]

This, once again, fits our scenario - with those migrating people into Atlantis consisting of many different cultures, or nations. Another researcher takes on this position:

*There are indications that some of Noah's family travelled from **Babylonia to Egypt** and **thence across to Africa to America**. The Encyclopaedia Britannica (ed.XI) says "that on account of those indications the first Spanish explorers of Mexico arrived at the curiously definite result that the Mexicans were descended from Naphtuhim, son of Mizraim and grandson of Noah **who left Egypt for Mexico**"...*
(Bristowe, 1927, p. 163)[11]

This, once again, seems to fit with our scenario. The only thing that wasn't mentioned in the above quote was that *Atlantis* might have served as a midpoint!

We also have some mysterious stone structures in Peru (out of many in South America), known as *Puma Punku*. Of course, we have the locals, here, claiming that those ancient *giants* were involved in the construction of a number of ancient sites:

Also, in North America, we have the American Indians echoing these same ancient accounts - of *giants*. They are thought to have been related to a number of mound-building projects in these areas, even the construction of the Serpent Mound (in Ohio):

Modern intellectuals, today, might quickly claim that the Indian tribes of the region were, naturally, the ones who built mounds such as these (and, in the case of this Serpent Mound, the local tribe would have been the *Shawnee*). Who *else* could it have really been? Yet, as we see, there could have already been some problems with these quick assumptions:

"...originally, the Shawnee said they never built this... (and they) really didn't have serpents in their iconography, of religion... (and) were never really known to be mound builders."
- *Fritz Zimmerman (Author)*[12]

We even have a modern elder of this Shawnee tribe, saying something completely different as well:

*"Although **we don't claim that we built** Serpent Mound, historically we respected and protected various mounds and earthworks."*
- *Chief Wallace (Shawnee Ttribe)*[13]

We've also mentioned how there were a good number of *giant* skeletons found in the United States (even in a number of those mounds, scattered about), as well as some huge stone tools and other giant remnants (i.e. giant sandals, giant footprints, etc.). There, supposedly, was some kind of giant connection to ancient *cities* in the land as well (such as in ancient *Cahokia*, in Illinois). Yes, it's all here, and the examples are almost endless... if they hadn't already been pushed in a dusty corner, or eliminated, that is.

*How completely does this agree with the statement of Plato that the kings of Atlantis **held dominion** over parts of "**the great opposite** continent!"*
(Donnelly, 1882, p. 106)[14]

Could those giants have been a part of the entourage that, at one time, escaped this failing Atlantic continent, traveling westward? Could those "mysterious" cultures, migrating into North and South America (after the destruction of Atlantis), be just a few extensions of that same old Babylonian "beast?"

Back Into Europe

We also begin to take a look at more of the same - on the other side of the pond. In the regions of western Europe and upper Africa, we may have also been a number of migrations from the failing continent as well - with individuals fleeing into an eastwardly direction, some in the direction of where they had once come.

We also seem to have the evidence of *giant* activity in parts in western Europe (especially), including France, England and Ireland. There is a good amount of evidence in the British Isles, for example. And, of course, the most famous one of them all is the stone monument of *Stonehenge* - allegedly being built by *giants* (once again). We also have ancient megalithic structures at *Avebury* and *Glastonbury* (in England). We have *Newgrange* and the *Poulnabrone Portal Tomb* in Ireland, as well as the *Poulnabrone Dolmen*. And, we also have the *Standing Stones of Carnac* in France, as well as the *Cromlech of the Almendres* in Central Portugal. Whenever we begin to research a number of these strange, standing monoliths, these stone circles, or these stone tombs, we only need to dig a little bit down (into their histories), and we most probably will discover something related to the handiwork of giants. It's that prevalent!

Wouldn't it seem natural for these *giants* to be a part of this all, anyway? The stones making up a number of these sites are huge, and they couldn't have been moved by just anybody. They were also placed together in ways that no human (of the time) could really do efficiently. For their time, ordinary human beings really needed some kind of help, in order to accomplish such things… it's plain and simple.

Into the Mediterranean

Along with the Americas, along with western Europe, maybe a number of former Atlanteans decided to head *back*, into the direction of where they came (via boat). Maybe they believed that they could sail, back through the Pillars of Hercules, and through the Mediterranean Sea. Maybe they thought they could return to the lands of Libya, Canaan, Egypt, and a number of other places that their ancestors originally came from. This, indeed, could have been how Plato was able to receive his information about Atlantis in the first place: He claimed that *Egyptian* priests, hundreds of years before him, knew about what had happened. Now, how could those Egyptian priests have found out about all of this? There were no phones, no internet. Could it have been because a number of people decided to head *back*, in that same direction, and told them?

We also seem to find evidence of ancient *giants* taking residence on a couple of Mediterranean islands, near the Italian Peninsula.

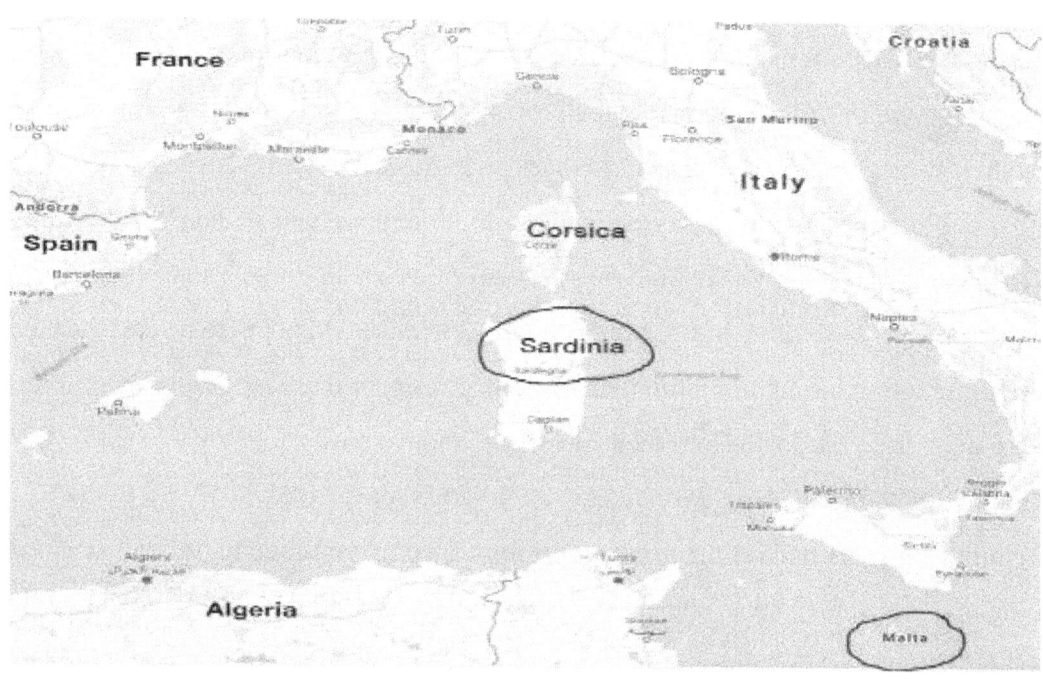

It seems to be a perfect place for giants, fleeing their former land of Atlantis, to pull ashore, and establish themselves. There does seem to be a number of ancient structures on these islands - known as the islands of **Sardinia** and **Malta** - which were, once again, thought to have been built by giants.

At the extreme westwardly tip of the sea, we have the land of Canaan (a.k.a. Israel). And, at this extreme shore, we also see that a number of "**sea people**" were thought to have landed here, and began to settle. And, we also see that a number of individuals who lived in these lands were reportedly *giants*. But, again, *where* did they originate from, and why did they end up traveling to these shores? Was it out of necessity, maybe? These question are rarely discussed, nowadays. And, yes, this is also where we get the Biblical

Philistines, and the most famous giant of them all: **Goliath**. Yes, this was the same pagan giant that the Biblical *David*, himself, had confronted (and killed)!

> *Other researchers think it likely that later-day* **Kurgans** *(or* **Aryans***) were the "Sea People" who laid waste to the Holy Land...*
> ("Giants in the Earth Part II: Giants of the Americas", 2003, p.9)[15]

With all of these giants arriving in a number of ancient Mediterranean shores, it seems quite possible that there could have been *some* manner of Atlantean retreat - something that a good number of modern, historical writers may also refuse to contend with. Even if all of these giants were not necessarily from Atlantis, modern historians still have to deal with the oral traditions of *giants* in so many of these ancient areas.

Their "Giant" Conundrum

There has to be something to this all. There's just too much out there. Without understanding these additional elements, a lot of history really does not come together properly. This additional information does **not** deserve to be placed in some vacuum, to be "edited out," or downgraded as a bunch of "coincidences," just because it doesn't seem to fit into their evolutionary timeline:

> *Look at it! An "Atlas" mountain on the shore of Africa; an "Atlan" town on the shore of America; the "Atlantes" living along the north and west coast of Africa; an Aztec people from Aztlan, in Central America; an ocean rolling between the two worlds called the "Atlantic;" a mythological deity called "Atlas" holding the world on his shoulders; and an immemorial tradition of an island of Atlantis. Can all these things be the result of accident?*
> (Donnelly, 1882, p. 172)[16]

Atlantis, then, becomes another "link" for them to break.

Once again, things that might really upset their humanistic and pagan "apple cart" are those numerous references to ancient giants, migrating into a number of different areas -

the same thing that the ancient survivors of Atlantis would have most probably done. Fancy that.

We may really need to understand that: according to our modern societal "betters," everything is about *control* (ultimately)... working over the minds of others, and getting as many people as possible on their side, and along with *their* ways of thinking. Any evidence to the contrary, of course, hurts their cause, and must be dealt with. Being able to bring as many people as they could "on board" to what they are presently pushing allows them feel a little bit better about *themselves*, and gives their self-esteems a boost, undoubtedly. A lot of psychology is going on here, assuredly; and, that's why a number of these authoritarians end up, for example, using *other* people to achieve their own ends.

One strategy that a number of "elites" might begin to use would be the attempt to push this concept of "first peoples": that the people who firstly arrived in a number of ancient areas around the world (usually under the authority of *their selves*, in some way) would be the ones entitled to a majority of the fringe benefits allotted. Since they were the first in the land, then (naturally) *they* should be the ones allowed to make a good number of decisions regarding that land. How convenient! Yes, it sounds noble and compassionate, of course, on the surface; but, in regards to our entire scenario here, it may pose a whole number of problems for those searching for some kind of truth.

What if some kind of ancient, archaeological evidence was discovered on one of these lands (controlled by these "first peoples") which pointed towards something *other* than what this ruling elite was now shoveling? With the stance of these "first peoples," the elite powers that be could easily claim that: there will be no more digging, because the "first people" claim that land is "sacred." Or, they may even feel the need to *confiscate* whatever might have been initially found, because it was their right. See how this all works? Under that cloak of compassion, with respect for indigenous tribes, we have the attempt to *stifle* any evidence of anything contrary to what the agendas (of a chosen few) might be. Sneaky, eh?

Don't be fooled. Governing authorities do not really care *that* much about a people that they, once, needed to battle with, to take over the land. To the victor goes the spoils, of course; and, if they need to use the conquered for their own bidding, it may have to be done… it's as simple as that. As long as they could control these people and their situation, they'll make it seem as though they *care*, immensely.

But, now, either in the lands that the government already has control over (such as the numerous national parks), as well as the lands that have already been designated as those of the "first peoples," could all be "off limits"… stopping any unsanctioned diggings (which might end up providing any new evidence of giant activity). Once again… sneaky.

Governments could also work to weasel their way into privately owned land, to pressure the owners in a number of the same ways. They want to control the flow of information, and what physical evidence is out there.

(OOP) Out Of Place

Yet, they still haven't been able to work their magic with every piece of physical evidence we see… at least *not yet*. How could they *deflect* a number of things that we already understand as commonplace, such as stone structures or mounds which are "too big" to move, or ancient structures too popular to "disappear" (such as Stonehenge)? There are even a number of "Out Of Place" artifacts out there, which do not seem to align with their agenda. What to do?

In one piece of evidence, here, we have the ancient *Olmecs*, living in Central America, who represented a people of clearly *African* features!

Of course, this shouldn't have been even possible (with their agenda). According to them, a number of Asians migrated over the frozen Bering Strait (near Alaska) around 11,000 years ago.

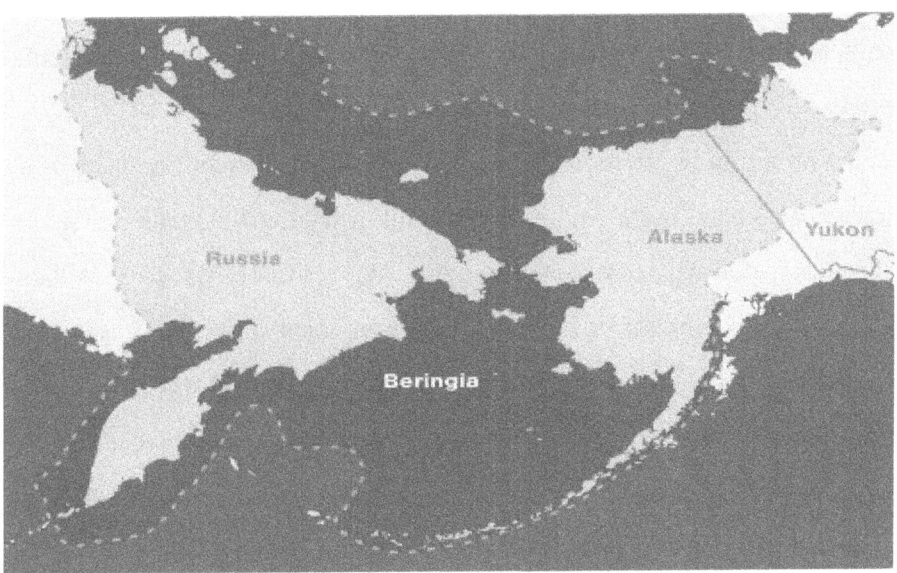

Yet, we once had people - with African features - living on the *eastern* coast of Central America! Africa was *believed* to have been totally inaccessible (according to their theory), because it was far across the Atlantic Ocean. Yet, if we go with *our* scenario, with a sinking continent that wasn't too far away from the eastern coast of Central America, then this, indeed, could have been an option!

Those who speak out against the possibilities of certain occurrences, such as Atlantis, may want to have all those historical anomalies (such as OOPs) to just "go away." Some may even try to claim that extraterrestrials, or space aliens, had a part in some of these anomalies. Again, assuredly, these are *diversions*. In reality, we'll eventually see that it is either *one way or another* - with those "aliens," once again, acting as agents of this "Other Side." Of course, these elites will push almost anything, anything, of course, **except** the possibility of fallen, terrestrial angels walking the earth, as well as their giant, hybrid offspring, teaching the people arts and sciences often forbidden by God. Anything but that! Anything but the Bible! See how it all works?

How could our ideological "betters" keep hiding all of those *other* possibilities? How can they keep claiming that *their* ways are "settled science," without any serious challenges to their ideas? To add fuel to their "bag of tricks," we also discover that they do seem to have another ideological weapon at their disposal: whether something seems "politically correct" or no! A lot of people, indeed, have fallen into this present method of manipulation, and have chosen to side with whatever may *sound* better to them, rather than what may be a real truth.

Now, one who might begin to hold onto this politically correct mindset (or a secular humanistic mindset) may, then, begin to speak out or try to sway someone *away* from anything that really doesn't seem very "humane," or "altruistic" (at least to them). Below is a typical quote from someone who may have already subscribed to these same rationales. They, essentially, were trying to say that: there **could not** have been a group of ancient individuals out there (such as giants) who originated the advanced knowledge and technological wisdom necessary to build a number of these ancient structures, or figure out certain things… *other* than the "indigenous" human beings of the area:

> *"I don't believe there is any solid evidence for a 'race' of such people in North America or anywhere else that descend from the nephilim. Nephilim descendants and races in North America is, of course, part of the modern Moundbuilder **myth**. It is a **<u>fact of history</u>** that the Moundbuilder myth **was created to deny** the indigenous native North American races **the ability and credit** for such creations."*
> ("The Myth of Double Row Teeth and Elongated-Skull Nephilim", 2017, p. 2)[17]

We've already referenced this above quote. And, yes, it seems as though there's a lot to chew on, in this case. First, they claim that their opinion was based on a "fact of history." Yet, we've already mentioned that: how could we call *anything* a "fact of history," when there is no one alive (today) who could recall it? Today, we only have what we are *told*, and what was written about it. We, now, only have words, and a bit of physical evidence, to support any particular theory. No one could be *that* secure with history to claim "facts" on the history of these moundbuilders, however, because, as we know, **politics** were, and are, inserted into almost everything. *Politics* and political deceptions are everywhere; and what one may call a "fact of history" is, in actuality, a claim subjected to some kind of collective interpretation, or individual conclusion.

In the end, maybe the individual who uttered the above quote had nothing but good intentions, attempting to push something that may have sounded *good* to a whole number of people (as well as to his or her own self). All of this is understandable. Maybe the individual wanted to show how compassionate or caring they were to other people around them. Again, it's all understandable. **But**, of course, intertwined in the efforts to make something to sound good on paper, we may some negative elements to the process. Should we really be given the green light to (quite often) manipulate, or allow for the manipulation, of *real* history to come to the surface? Is it a good thing to try to *stifle* all information, for the sake of "equality," "inclusion" and "compassion?" What takes precedence here: real, possible history, or one's own take on what might sound good?

Trying to *force* a narrative, in some cases - by injecting political elements into a specific argument - may sound humane and just (at least on the surface); but that does not really help out those who are seeking real *truths* out there, or anything *different* than what they may have been taught as right.

We also see that, in the above quote: anyone who might begin to disagree with the aforementioned stance, now, could be considered a bit biased, or even "hateful" to other people. Believing anything else - such as the suggestion that these early Nephilim (and their hybrid offspring) could have had a stake in all of this - does not really promote an atmosphere of *equality* in all people. It gives these giants credit for most everything. And, that wouldn't appear to be very complimentary to the intelligences of the human beings involved here. Again, with political correctness at the helm, any other thought could have become a bit *insensitive*, or even "unfair." Yet, once again, what are we *really* trying to achieve, here, with certain assumptions - a possible *truth*, or something that might sound a bit more sensitive? Do we see how *political correctness* could come into almost conversations, and distort everything? See how the direction of almost any argument could begin to go "off course," because of these politically correct insertions? If the ancient giants *did* have that advanced knowledge, and represented the force behind so many early human developments, then it shouldn't be taken *down*, as something that might sound a little *negative* towards another human being. Those aren't the original parameters... but, they seem to be *now*.

Yes, watch out for those (and other) "tricks of the political trade" here, used to stifle the possibility of examining the possibility of historical *giants*. Don't be fooled with these attempts to *stifle* independent thought, as well as critical thinking.

Here's another quote from the same work:

*"While I don't believe modern nephilim enthusiasts **intentionally seek** to **denigrate** the non-white European people in ancient North America, that's **actually where this idea leads** - because that was the milieu in which it arose."*
("The Myth of Double Row Teeth and Elongated-Skull Nephilim", 2017, p. 2)[18]

Again, as we now see: the main topic of conversation seems to have shifted - onto another (political) lens. Now, the original topic of conversation needs to be able to pass some "smell test," or it may not be considered viable. See how this works? See how - through secular humanism and politically correct assumptions - anything deemed "not up to par" becomes unwanted information, or something that may be too "offensive" to even bring up?

Government-Sponsored Cover-Ups?

Now, if we have anyone trying out there, trying to understand some of these *other* possible scenarios of our past, contemporary elitists work to get people around them to adopt these modems of thinking - to *immediately* greet anything new and different with laughter, scorn and even contempt. They need foot soldiers to speak out for them - those who will not allow anything to compete with *their* accepted thoughts of the day. And, yes, a majority of the elites who push these humanistic, and political correct, stands probably have (and still have) some kind of ***pagan*** lean to them... they sure wouldn't be out there pushing God. And, yes, these are individuals who have weaseled their way into the highest positions of power and governance over us.

Today, these political "safeguards" seem to be *everywhere*, halting conversations about practically everything different that what may be "socially acceptable." Yes, these elites, for the most part, have control over academia. They have the news media, and a whole lot more. Their attempts to rid our modern world of anything that might even *remotely* compete with them began, in earnest, around the late 19th century… and it continues, in earnest, to this day.

So, now, let's continue, by looking a little more into the history of this all. It was around the same time (i.e. the late 19th century) that a number of governmental elites began to devise that "indigenous people" narrative. Way back in the late 1800s, the so-called "Powell Doctrine" was established, by a few members of the U.S. government. And, yes, this doctrine was supposedly set into place for a very *noble* cause. But, as we'll soon see, the motivations behind this particular doctrine may have been hijacked… for some *other* particular reasons:

> *The cover-up and alleged suppression of archaeological evidence began in late 1881 when John Wesley Powell, the geologist famous for exploring the Grand Canyon, appointed Cyrus Thomas as the director of the Eastern Mound Division of the Smithsonian Institution's Bureau of Ethnology. When Thomas came to the Bureau of Ethnology he was a "pronounced **believer in the existence of a race of Mound Builders, <u>distinct</u>** from the American Indians."*
> ("The Smithsonian cover-ups", 2011, p. 1)[19]

Uh oh. Here we go again! How dare someone start to drift away from the narratives they were now establishing. If someone began to utilize critical, independent thought, it may begin to lead them in the direction of *other* possibilities… and that can no longer be allowed!

The late 1800s, however, was a tough time for the implementation of this agenda. The elites just couldn't hide this existence of giants that easily… because there were so many new archaeological finds out there (as well as simple finds by common folk, as well). Giant bones and skeletons were being discovered in a number of ancient burial mounds, which suggests that those ancient "moundbuilders" (for example) could have, at least in part, associated themselves with more than just the human beings of the area.

With anyone starting to believe anything a little bit different than what those ruling elites now wanted to usher onto the scene, a 19th century version of "political correctness" was, also, being ushered in:

> *However, John Wesley Powell, the director of the Bureau of Ethnology, a very **sympathetic** man toward the American Indians, had lived with the peaceful Winnebago Indians of Wisconsin for many years as a youth and felt that American Indians were **unfairly thought of as primitive and savage.***
> ("The Smithsonian cover-ups", 2011, p. 1)[20]

Powell, now, was starting to become influenced by *another* way of thinking. Political correctness, if we really think about it, could easily be perceived as something a person might "catch" (if you will). Once a person begins to go down those politically correct pathways of thinking, their new ways may begin to "overtake" them, and infect almost everything they think about next... twisting the original reason for their thought, and turning it into a political argument. These diversions, of course, help to destroy a person's rationality, their common sense, and their ultimate ability to see things *as they really might be*... all for the sake of focusing on an outcome that other people may believe is right, or aesthetically pleasing. Everything else, such as objectivity, goes out the proverbial window.

Again, we now see that, at this time, the political tides were really beginning to change. And, of course, what Powell was now starting to think *could* have sounded a lot better, or even more compassionate; but, when the dust all begins to settle, any *new* attempt to discover the true origins of these moundbuilders were now subjected to a *new* set of rules, and critiqued accordingly.

Indeed, we see that a number of early **pagan** practices, by these American Indians, could have (quite easily) been thought of as a bit **savage**. Take *scalping*, for example, a practice that often seemed to have taken place after an enemy of those pagan American Indians were killed.

Again, it wasn't implying that *every* American Indian out there was evil, or savage at heart, but this practice didn't sound like something a typical *American* (of the time) might do to their conquered dead. It just didn't seem like anything a typical Christian might do, either; and that's why it was thought to be something a bit unsavory. Simple.

And, if we really think about it, the *focus* should center around the ceremonial or *religious* practices that these Indians were participating in… the *pagan* things that they were doing (and not the people themselves). This, of course, points to *paganism* as the problem… and those powers that be need to stop people from possibly thinking *these* particular things, so more and more political correctness needs to be inserted.

Of course, we already know how paganism and pagan practices (throughout the ages) were not very civilized at times: people had their hearts ripped out of their cavities, fed alive to lions, and even burned up in wicker baskets (alive). What would have represented the **"savage"** element here: the people or their pagan practices? We already know… but, of course, we can't be allowed to start going down *this* particular pathway, as well.

Sometimes, their attempts to cover up things makes it even harder for them… unless they become more and more militaristic, and more and more controlling. Again, it's all a game here… to stifle *all* of what may actually be out there, rearing their ugly heads.

In another example of how things were continually being covered up, we have a huge, government-sponsored entity, known as the *Smithsonian Institution*. It was (and is) an organization that, seemingly, has accomplished a great amount of *damage* to almost every new postulation regarding ancient giants:

> *The Smithsonian began to **promote** the idea that Native Americans, at that time being exterminated in the Indian Wars, were descended from <u>advanced civilisations</u> and were worthy of **respect and protection.***
> ("The Smithsonian cover-ups", 2011, p. 1)[21]

Of course, there's nothing wrong with giving people respect and protection, and the outward drives of a number of these people may sound good, fair and compassionate. And, of course, there's nothing wrong with an official allowing *full credit* to be given to those American Indians out there, as those early moundbuilders. There's nothing wrong with it, of course, if it all was true.

Of course, does that mean that we should "throw in the towel," and allow everything that those members of our governing authorities may want out there... as the only dogma out there? Of course, if they, now, want to sell the theory that native American Indians came from that migration of early people from *Asia* (through the Bering Strait), thousands of years earlier, they still cannot tell us where their ancestors ultimately received **their** advanced knowledge from. Their "hole" just keeps getting deeper and deeper, if they try to take some "pieces" out of the story, or cut a few "links." Yes, so many things will still remain a mystery... if we look at everything *their* way, of course.

Because of these attempts, we see, as time went on, their "suppression tools" (of the Powell Doctrine, as one example) had to work a little bit *harder* here, to assure that things are still going to be obscured "properly":

> *...(They began by) suppressing and denying **any** archaeological evidence that could indicate the presence of **other** ancient peoples in the Americas **or contact with ancient cultures from across the oceans**.*
> ("The Smithsonian Cover Up", 2014, p. 7)[22]

> *...**suppressing any archaeological evidence... lent credence** to the school of thought known as **Diffusionism**, a school which believes that throughout history there has been widespread dispersion of culture and civilization... **via contact by ship and major trade routes.***
> ("The Smithsonian cover-ups", 2011, p. 1)[23]

Eventually, those higher ups began to only perpetuate *their own* take on history, and only allow the digs that may be able to help their causes. It was starting to work:

> *The Smithsonian opted for the **opposite** school, known as Isolationism. **Isolationism** holds that most civilizations are isolated from each other and that there has been very little contact between them, especially those that are separated by bodies of water.*
> ("The Smithsonian cover-ups", 2011, p. 1)[24]

Saying that almost every ancient civilization was able to do it "on their own" is not insulting, nor is it racist, nor is it "supremacist" in any way... yet, on top of this all (and, most importantly for *them*) this ended up working for their agenda! It's a good way to change the topic of conversation, and eliminate any undesirable talk. Time for them to keep it up, and expand upon their new modem of thinking about things!

A dignified man of the time, named *Cyrus Thomas*, was "accredited for creating the paradigm, which still exists today, that native Americans built the mounds, **but they had forgotten** they had done so."[25] Talk about trying to force a meaning, here! Do we really believe that a nation of people may have "just forgotten" that *they*, themselves, were the ones who built a number of these great earthen works of the past… on their *own* lands?

Once again, we see that it's, actually, all politics. We recall a great quote about this whole thing, from earlier on:

> "…what's happening now is, with the implementation of NAGPRA (the National American Grave Protection & Repatriation Act)… if you find skeletons, if you find remains, if you find artifacts, or whatever, it's protected by the federal government, and the tribe who's assigned to that region takes custody of those items… what better way to keep people from going into the mounds, and finding seven, eight, nine foot tall skeletons, then that to have a standing force of Native Americans that are going to come, and they're going to protest, and they're going to stop anything like that from happening."
> - *Chief Joseph Riverwind* (Author, Lecturer)[26]

Now that they've established a number of diversions in place (which would hurt conversations regarding almost any *giant* discovery in the future), what about those giant discoveries that might have already been on record? What about those relics and bones that were already found, up to this present time? What about any new finds, from any of those "small potatoes" out there? They, of course, would need to "step up" a few things, over time. And, yes, an "intellectual war" was actually starting to take up steam, for them to be able to handle new problems, such as this:

> *When the contents of many ancient mounds and pyramids of the Midwest were examined, it was shown that the history of the Mississippi River Valleys was that of an ancient and sophisticated culture that had been in contact* **with Europe and other area**s. *Not only that, the contents of many mounds revealed burials of* **huge men**, *sometimes seven or eight feet tall…*
> ("The Smithsonian cover-ups", 2011, p. 2)[27]

Uh oh! Again, discoveries such as this (to them) seems a lot like showing a vampire the cross. A little *more* might need to be done here, with all of what's already out there… in order to slow the flow of everything opposing them:

> *…when Spiro Mound in Oklahoma was excavated in the 1930's, a **tall** man in full armour was discovered along with a pot of thousands of pearls and other artefacts, the largest such treasure so far documented. The whereabouts of the man in armour is unknown and it is **quite likely that it eventually was taken to the Smithsonian Institution**.*
> ("The Smithsonian cover-ups", 2011, p. 2)[28]

Yes, when the government began to "step it up," they began to confiscate a number of new artifacts (in order to "properly" study them, of course). A lot of these things were never to see the light of day anymore. Or, they just began to be "lost" in the fray. Oops. What a surprise. Now, it seems as though, when the Smithsonian desires to step in - and tries to make *their* contributions to humankind - a number of strange things just "seem" to happen. What a surprise.

Yes, the above author seems to expand on things a little bit, and tells us what might have *really* happened to a lot of this contradictory evidence:

> *In a private conversation with a well-known historical researcher (who shall remain nameless), I was told that a former employee of the Smithsonian, who was dismissed for defending the view of diffusionism in the Americas (i.e. the heresy that other ancient civilisations may have visited the shores of North and South America during the many millenia before Columbus), alleged that the Smithsonian at one time had actually taken a **barge full of unusual artefacts out into the Atlantic and dumped them in the ocean.***
> ("The Smithsonian cover-ups", 2011, p. 2)[29]

Of course, so much of this evidence was, over the years, probably confiscated in this way, or even "disappeared," all for the sake of their new take on things. Almost all of it was now designated to inhabit some dusty museum shelf, or was to be removed altogether! Of course, these things are all good… for *their* version of history!

Working to "Erase the Threats"

Of course, we might recall (from previous volumes) that this same type of censorship may have occurred with the story of the Lost 10 Tribes of Israel. Certain ruling elites may not have really desired for anyone to have a real understanding of what could have happened to the Lost 10 Tribes of Israel, over the years… as being scattered throughout modern Europe, and other areas. Also, as far as the role of ancient *Atlantis* in the history of mankind, we've already seen how much this has been twisted, and essentially downplayed… into, for the most part, just a *mythological story*. Both of these things were, seemingly, downplayed… for politically correct reasons. Eventually, we'll also see that the same thing happened to the nation of *Tartaria* (in what would be modern-day Russia). The powers that be, once again, had to make sure that this nation was removed from the history books. How corrupt would these elites need to be, form them to delete certain nations off the face of the earth, or push only *certain* agendas (such as isolationism or evolution).

The elites don't want us to understand that the people Israel *still* exist, and in good number, beyond those two tribes that we already know about. Those same elites do not want anyone to connect the ancient (and pagan) nations of Babylon, Egypt, and other empires of the Middle East to Atlantis… and, ultimately, to the "first peoples" of North, South and Central America (and other areas). Of course, if a number of these things existed, and were *true*, then it may be a little *too easy* for us to understand a lot of what we see around us originated in those fallen, terrestrial angels, Cain, as well as the Serpent himself.

Of course, we also know the deeper reasons for all of these cover-ups: the elites want to **ultimately** destroy the major threat to their own "fronts" - their fronts being secular humanism, paganism, and politically-controlled science. And, of course, their biggest threats are **Judeo-Christian ideologies**, the **Bible** as well as **God Himself**. This represents the *true* battle of the ages, and was a big part of the reason why that *White Horse* came about in the first place, and was transformed into what it is today.

And, for those White Horse elites to be more and more powerful over time, they had to find a way cut a number of those crucial "links" to our natural flow of human history, especially those which may expose them (which they did). Don't be fooled. All of this manipulation works to lead the average seeker into confusion, doubt and a general misunderstanding of what, indeed, could be the *real* truths of our world. The harder it is for *us* to understand things, the better it is for them, overall (of course)!

Chapter 7

Archetypal Pagans Fleeing… To Godly Areas?

Pagans fleeing into Godly areas, and famous ones at that? There couldn't have been a lot of good coming out of those amalgamations, assuredly! What *really* might have been going on here? We've already learned something about the migrations of so many ancient people, ancient giants (as well as the ancient *Owph*), as well as how Shem formed a posse of like-minded Godly warriors, traveling around and trying to corral a number of pagan lands back onto the pathways of sanity.

We also know how a vast number of people - pagan and Godly alike - took it upon themselves to chase away (or even kill) their neighboring *giants*, whenever they found it necessary. We've also discovered how ancient, post-Flood paganism, regardless of all these other things going on, was *still* able to spread throughout much of our ancient world (and, seemingly, gain their followers a lot easier than anything Godly). And, we also understand how most of it had originated from those early, centralized pagan "hotspots" (such as Babylon, Egypt… and, also, **Atlantis**).

Next, we'll need to return our focus *back* to the Middle East (at least, for a little while), to the world soon after the Flood. There was so much *more* going on here, besides a number of early migrations. We'll, now, see how the conflicts - between those early Godly patriarchs and their formidable pagan adversaries - would begin to form the skeletal structure of this up-and-coming *White Horse*. And, we'll also begin to see how this all would begin to take shape, and get off of the ground. This is oh, so important, if we really want to understand what the *Antichrist* is all about, and how these systems of *antichrist* might work in our world. So, now, let's begin by diving into another section of our early post-Flood history. We'll also take a look at a few obscured ancient texts as well, to help us learn more about the post-Flood story of Noah, his sons (i.e. Shem, Ham and Japheth) and *their* sons. With this, we'll begin to discover a few more "missing links" in this overall chain of *Mystery Babylon*! Let's "connect" these "dots" a bit further!

Birth of the "White Horse"

First, we need to recall those two "atrocities" that were attributed to the White Horse early on (according to the Bible): ***hunger*** and ***famine***, by which we've already postulated that these are more about *spiritual* starvation than anything else. It's not that most people under the spell of this White Horse would *physically* be starving (even though a number of them might), it would be more about how a person would *not* be receiving the correct "nourishment" of God's way, leaving their lives extremely "hungry" for some spiritual fulfillment.

And, as we're already beginning to discover, the agents of the White Horse will, quite often, claim that they are *like* Christ in a whole number of ways. They try to give out good information, and provide proper ways to live - but, it's not exactly the way one would have thought of as Godly in the past. The *end results* of what they are now saying will just seem to fall a little *short*, or even fall apart. Things may end up being quite *different* than what a typical seeker might have originally wanted. Call it the old "bait and switch" approach if you will - the "infusion" of Christian values with something that might not exactly seem very Christian (such as the addition of pagan or humanist elements).

Often, the ideology becomes compromised - to be able to "fit in" with what may be going on in the rest of the world. It would be those *adulterated* bits of theology that ends up leaving the subjects of this White Horse spiritually *starving*. Now, we will begin to see how these compromised systems would find their way into everything Godly.

A Couple of "World Tours"

First, in order to begin our discovery of just how this *adulteration* process began to take shape, we'll need to return to a few patriarchs who existed a few hundred years after the Flood. We, first, must return to the patriarch *Noah*, and discover more of his desire to go into the Italian Peninsula, and retire there. As we might recall (from previous volumes), the area that once sent Noah's heart aflutter was also the approximate piece of land where ***Rome*** now lies. Italy, eventually, was probably one of the last (and greatest) bastions of Godliness and moral purity of the post-Flood world (at least for a long while), with Noah leading the charge, here.

Now, if this could have all been true, then we really might need to ask ourselves: if the area where modern Rome is now situated had such a history of righteousness and Godliness, then what would it have to do with this up-and-coming White Horse of deception (if anything)? We shall soon see.

Now, if we accept a popular take on the timing of Noah's Flood, many thought that it all occurred around 2348 B.C. And, around 100 years after this particular event, the whole northern section of the Middle East (around the land of *Armenia*) was becoming a little overpopulated. The people of the post-Flood world were living near where the ark came to rest; but things were no longer working (with so many people being born). Noah, then, decided that a new way was needed - to divide up the people, and dictate where a large number of individual groups would be asked to relocate into.[1]

After Noah began to direct people on where to go, a number of them did depart in the direction of where he pointed. For a while, a number of people tried to live a Godly existence, but Nimrod, Cush and Semiramis - those famous pagans of the era - were attempting the opposite: to bring the people together once again (in rebellion to God), at the Tower of Babel! Now, there were two conflicting edicts out there, pagan and Godly (under Noah's direction).

This was probably the moment when Noah decided, as "father" of the post-Flood world, to go abroad, and do something about "righting" a ship that was already beginning to go wrong. On his first "world tour" (if you will), Noah attempted to visit a number of people in their new lands, and help them to "set up shop" properly, and Godly.[2] He already dictated where a number of people should go, and how to reach it. But, as these migrations were officially underway, Nimrod and Cush were beginning to throw "monkey wrenches" into this whole separation process, encouraging a vast number of people to come back, and unite with them (in the area now known as *Babylon*).

Beginning in his homeland of Armenia, Noah, first, set out in the direction of Africa. Next, he began to travel into a few areas of the European continent, such as Spain and (possibly) France. After instructing these people in the proper ways of working and living, he eventually end up on the Italian Peninsula. He did this all with good intentions, with the hopes of "making a difference."

But, first off, how did things seem to go in such a *pagan* direction, in regards to Cush, Nimrod and Semiramis? According to a few ancient sources, it was around the year 2217 B.C. (or, 131 years after the Flood) that Noah asked his grandson **Cush** (and his people) to go to the land of Shinar (where Babylon was once located). Noah, of course, had the best of intentions here. He didn't think that Cush and his followers would begin to go down the *pagan* path… but they did. Cush was the one, as most of us know, who went on to start the construction of that original *Tower of Babel*, so we *know* that he didn't exactly follow Noah's original instruction.

Regardless of what Noah was trying to accomplish here, his entire effort - thanks to Cush and his son Nimrod - was, slowly, beginning to take a turn for the worse. A vast number of *giants* were also beginning to slide down that slippery-slope of pagan ideology and corruption; and worked to take a number of people along with them, as well. Through these efforts, the everyday lives of so many were beginning to head right back - into the same moral direction as what occurred in the antediluvian world. It was not going well.

So, approximately 131 years after the Flood, Cush began, in earnest, the construction of this tower (along with his son Nimrod). They both began to work together, to "pull the rug out" from all of Noah's original intentions, bringing people under *their* ultimate rule. They begin to unite them all, in some kind of "revival" of **Cain's** original powerhouse - Babylon (of course).[3] And Noah, most probably, found out about all of what was beginning to transpire here, and it may have also prompted his son *Shem* to want to take action, and raid those areas now infected (once again) by that same old Serpent religion.

And, we'll now discover how Noah, eventually, would have to embark on another "world tour" (about a hundred and fifty years later). ***Each*** time he departed, however, he would go on to entrust his Armenian homeland to *one* particular individual, a person he may have been fairly close to. Yet, the person of whom he had left in charge, here, would actually end up *hurting* his overall efforts, in the long run. Why? What was he doing by commissioning such an individual… twice? And, just *who* was this particular individual anyhow, and why would this individual end up doing this?

Yes, the leadership over Armenia would be dictated to one mysterious individual, known as **Sabatius Saga**. And, now, we'll be able to discover just *who* this ;particular individual was, what he did, and *why* he ended up betraying Noah in such a way.

The Mysterious "Sabatius Saga"

> *Noe... and many multitudes of people besides, began his voyage...*
> *- An Historical Treatise of the Travels of Noah Into Europe* 11[4]

> *...(and) upon Noes **first** departure out of Armenia, he constituted and established... **Sabatius Saga**, surnamed **Saturn**, to rule as King and Patriarch over that country; wherein he afterward reigned peaceably...*
> *- An Historical Treatise of the Travels of Noah Into Europe* 15[5]

This character, in actuality, was probably an **extremely** famous person of his day, a powerful player in all that was going on (at the time). And Noah, for some reason, surely believed in him. And, if this was really so, we may need to ask ourselves: what's the big deal here? What importance would this particular person have on our whole story, as well as the establishment of that whole, up-and-coming *White Horse* system? We'll soon understand how everything, here, seems to be related.

There are not a lot of ancient sources that mention his name. And, when we look deeper into this character, it seems fairly obvious that *Sabatius Saga* could have actually been an *epithet*, or a *title*, rather than someone's proper name. Now, in order to dig a little deeper into it all, we'll need to figure out just *what* this particular title may have meant.

As we discover this, we, first, need to understand that there could have been a backstory to this all: Noah, as we know, appointed this Sabatius Saga to rule his homeland of Armenia, and for two separate tours.[6] Yet, the second time would be a little different than the first. In this second time around, Noah didn't seem like he was planning on returning. He was going for good. And, if he really was leaving forever, he assuredly must have wanted to choose someone that he immensely trusted (and felt comfortable with), to take on such a responsibility!

Yet, assuming the reins of this area (twice) didn't mean that Sabatius Saga was the best individual for the job however. In fact, we'll soon see that he was actually one of the *worst* choices out there, and one who was not really able to hold onto this "top spot" for a very long time. Why? What happened? And, what could have been the reason why he had stepped down? All of these questions will be answered soon enough, and it all should be pretty fascinating, because there is a great, unexpected twist to come.

Beyond discovering just who this Sabatius Saga was, we'll also begin to see how there were other patriarchs of the past (beyond Noah) who felt that this Sabatius Saga was **not** a very good choice to run this nation, or any other… and wanted him out. In fact, they didn't even think that Sabatius Saga was good enough to be around at all. They wanted him *dead*!

So, in order to continue, let's begin by dissecting this mysterious title, or epithet.

Sabatius = Saba-tius?

As we delve into what makes up the first word, *Sabatius*, we'll see that it could actually have been a conglomerate of *two* different words. In one ancient (i.e. Greek) pronunciation, we have a similar title: *Saba-zios*.[7]

> *Sabazios… is the horseman and sky **father god** of the Phrygians and Thracians. In Indo-European languages… the -**zios** element in his name derives from dyeus, the common precursor of Latin deus ('god') and Greek **Zeus**.*
> ("Sabazios", n. d., p. 1)[8]

The two seem to be practically the same (just varied slightly). And, now, we've just seen that the word *zios* (in *Saba-zios*) stands for the father god **Zeus**.[9] And, as we recall from previous volumes, there was an *original* pagan deity out there, by which pagans considered to be the "original" *Zeus*. And, we know that the original *Zeus* ancestor god was, in pagan thought, none other than **Adam** himself. Also, of course, there ended up being a number of "reincarnated" *Zeus* gods out there, after his time. So, this particular (and "reincarnated") *Zeus* god - now believed to be *Sabatius Saga* - was, most probably, one of those many "paganized" avatars of that great "father" god, *Adam*!

Next, we need to look at a couple of ancient meanings of *Saba*, the first part of this word *Sabatius*: it's either "old" or "ancient."[10] Now, if we put these two definitions back together, we at least have the meaning of *Sabatius* itself: a figure believed to be an "**Old**" or "**Ancient Zeus**," or a "**Zeus of Old**." Now, we see that it's beginning to make a little more sense: Sabatius Saga was considered a kind of "reincarnation" of that older, paganized "father" god... Adam.

Now, what about the meaning of the second part of his title: *Saga* (in *Sabatius Saga*)?

The Word "Saga"

As we look into this other half, we already can find other ancient individuals who were given this same title. From this, we may be able to get a pretty good idea of what this other half of the title meant:

> *Noah was called Ogyges* **Saga***, which means Scythian,* **Great** *Patriarch,* **Sovereign** *Priest, and* **Mighty** *Sacrificer. Berosus (the historian) affirms it saying "Primium itaque dixerunt Ogygam Sagam, id est, illustrem sacrorum pontificem Noam".*
> ("The Travels of Noah into Europe", 2002, p. 2)[11]

From the above quote (and other definitions), we can grasp the meaning:

- "great"
- "sovereign"
- "mighty"
- "sage"
- "teacher, or teller of oral tales"
- "priest, priestly"
- "sacrificer"
- "high" "priest, sacrificing priest, or pontiff"[12]

Now, if we put the two words together, this title (or epithet) of *Sabatius Saga* essentially translates into: "**the learned sage and Father-god Zeus**" or "**the learned**

sage who served as the reincarnation of the father god Zeus." Either way, it should get us closer to understanding just *who* this famous character really was.

Which famous individual, around these earliest of times, could have been considered a very learned sage, or high priest of paganism? Who would have also been considered a great "father" god, a reincarnation of that early "father" god Adam? Well, we know that it wasn't Noah, because Noah was the one who wanted him to help him out. He wasn't the infamous *Nimrod* either, because Nimrod was a well-known "son" god (not a "father"). He wasn't Semiramis (for obvious reasons). And, he probably was not Noah's son Ham, because Ham (as we may recall from previous volumes) lived in Egypt for a long time (being sent there by Noah). Yet, this particular individual was famous, and ready and willing to go into Armenia, and rule the nation. Just who was he?

There *was*, in actuality, one particular individual considered very knowledgeable in the supernatural (or occult) arts. He was also a "father" figure to **so many** - he held great sway and majesty over a vast number of post-Flood people (at least for a while). And, yes, the reason was: this individual was one of those responsible for the construction of the infamous *Tower of Babel*. What? Yes. This title, as we'll now see, fits perfectly with that "father" god of early paganism - **Cush**.

Wait! Cush - the patriarch who helped to lead so many *away* from God - as Noah's primary choice of a leader? Could it really be? This totally sounds wrong. And yes, if it really *was* him, then why would Noah stick his neck out here, and invest so much trust into this man… a man who, essentially, double-crossed everyone striving to follow the proper ways of God? Why give Cush control over his own Armenian homeland, considering his reputation… and do it *twice*? Makes no sense really, or *does* it?

Why Not?

From previous volumes, we already have a good idea of what may have happened to a couple of famous pagans in post-Flood Babylon, including Nimrod. Shem caught Nimrod in some kind of ambush, and ended up taking him out. We also had a good idea of what Semiramis did in response all of this: she now claimed that her newborn child was actually a reincarnation of this martyred Nimrod - one who came *back*, into our world, in order to "save" it. Yet, in all of this, we really never had much of an understanding of what may have really happened to *Cush*, throughout the ages, after the tower's fall. We know that he was shamed, but we don't really know where he may have ended up after this all… until now.

Still, can we be sure that this Sabatius Saga was, indeed, that (infamous) Cush? If we dig a little deeper into a few of these ancient texts, we'll discover a bit more about this individual. We recall that:

> *…(and) upon Noes **first** departure out of Armenia, he constituted and established… **Sabatius Saga**, surnamed **Saturn**, to rule as King and Patriarch over that country; wherein he afterward reigned peaceably…*
> - An Historical Treatise of the Travels of Noah into Europe 15[13]

So, now, we see that there could have even been *another* title for this same individual: *Saturn*. And, as we recall from previous volumes, the branding of someone as a *Saturn* god was, once again, to just be a *title*, rather than a person's proper name. The title of *Saturn* stood for a famous and knowledgeable "father," a "senior" god in pagan mythology.[14] We may also recall that, in paganism, Noah was considered a *Saturn* god, as well as Ham, because they *both* were considered to be famous "father" gods.

And, if we go a step deeper here, we'll see that there may have been a good reason why these ancient (pagan) "father" gods were given this particular title: it was, most probably, because these *Saturn* gods had famous *sons*, as well… sons who walked in their same footsteps. And, as these sons would grow up to be like their fathers, their worshipers, quite often, needed some way to tell the two apart. And, through these titles, it was just a little easier for pagans to give those "son" gods *another* title, other than Saturn - such as "Jupiter." Now, Nimrod indeed walked in his father's footsteps. Ham, also, had a son named Canaan, who acted in a lot of the same ways he did. So, in order to reduce any confusion surrounding these deities, it became much easier to just give *titles* to certain family members, here.

When one famous *Saturn* god sires a son (who follows him in word and deed), the "son" god, often, gets the title of **Jupiter**. When this particular "son" god decides to sire a child (one who follows him as well), this third "son" ends up receiving the title of

Hercules. It's a lot like how we, in today's world, give a father the title of "Sr.," his son the title of "Jr.," and the third son (in succession) the title of "the 3rd." Yes, if it wasn't done in these ways, things, over time, could easily have become blurred, and misunderstood.

With this understanding, however, we can now see that, in the case of Sabatius Saga (or Saturn):

(Saturn)... taught the ceremonies of religion.
(Simpson, 2009, p. 14)[15]

And, yes, **Cush** was also thought to have been famous for his vast understanding of occult knowledge, and pagan religious practices. He was also a learned *sage*. Everything seems to fit here, once again.

Now, here's a couple more pieces of information for us to dwell upon, as revealed by a couple of ancient sources, that might help us to be confident in our choice:

*...he (Saturn) marked out the city (of Babylon) and laid the foundations of a very **great tower**... as a sign and monument to the fact that the Babylonian people is first in the world and it should be called the kingdom of kingdoms... And in fact he **built the tower** but did not finish it...*
(Asher, 1993, p. 203)[16]

*Saturn therefore seeing himself in those dangers and casualties, to be deprived of all dignity and command for succour and refuge fled unto **his grandfather Noe (i.e. Noah)**...*
- *An Historical Treatise of the Travels of Noah into Europe* 15[17]

Wow! This narrows things down... to practically *one* person. Yes, there *does* seem to be another "Saturn" out there, another "father" god, and very knowledgeable sage (or teacher of religion). This particular individual was also a grandson of Noah, *and* the one who began the construction of the Tower of Babel! With all of these credentials, who else *could* it be?

Yes, it, most probably, had to have been Cush. And, if this was so, then we may need to ask ourselves: just **why** would Noah want to bring Cush on board for anything like this? Why would Noah - a Godly man - want to obtain services from an individual considered to be the instigator of a post-Flood **pagan** rebellion? Why trust him to rule in your stead? It makes absolutely no sense here, that is, until we begin to think of what kind of man Noah most probably was.

There are reasons for almost everything; and, in this case, the reason was probably because Noah was such a caring and sensitive person (as well as a loving father). He was someone who assuredly wanted the best for everyone in his family, even under negative circumstances. What kind of decent father wouldn't want this for the members of his family? So, if we begin to think about things along these same lines, it makes sense that Noah might have wanted to give Cush another chance.

Now, if Cush really was this *Sabatius Saga*, then how could things have begun to pan out, over time (knowing what we already know)?

Forced to Depart

As we might recall (from previous volumes), a "Saturn" god could have also been thought of as a "hidden god" (of sorts). There may have been a number of reasons for this, however. In a few examples, we see that Noah was considered a "hidden" god because he was believed to have been *hidden away* aboard his own ark (for a long period of time). Cush, as we recall, was also considered a *hidden* god because Ham may have *hid* the pregnancy of his wife (and Cush's mother) away from Noah, while they were aboard the ark. Why do we mention these connections? It's because this element of the title *Saturn* may also have a place here, strengthening our ability to link Cush with Sabatius Saga once again.

We recall the quote above, in regards to Sabatius Saga:

...he marked out the city (of Babylon) and laid the foundations of a very great tower... And in fact he built the tower but did not finish it...
(Asher, 1993, p. 203)[18]

Yet, the rest of the sentence reads:

*...because after fifty-six years **suddenly he disappeared**...*
(Asher, 1993, p. 203)[19]

So, if this Sabatius Saga (or *Cush*) needed to *hide* himself, away from everyone around him (once again), we see how this could possibly be another connection between him and the title of "Saturn" - the *Hidden God*.

Well, if this was all so, then just what may have happened to Cush here, at the time of his disappearance, and why did he have to hide away? Well, we already know how Cush was put to shame, because of the fall of Babel's tower. We know that his contemporaries referred to him as "Chaos," because they blamed him for this dispersion of tongues. After stepping down as chief administrator of this famous tower building project, he must have gone *somewhere*, and did something.

His son Nimrod seemed to have the desire to please the dispossessed (and angry) people of the area, and, somehow, lead them out of their shame; so he may have begun to speak out openly against his father, as well as all that would have been his legacy... with the hopes that it all would just "disappear." And, maybe because the times were slowly beginning to change in Nimrod's favor, Cush, his sympathizers, and a whole number of his descendants, probably felt the need to **relocate** out of Babylon, and get out of the possible crosshairs of a number of angry people.

Could it have all really gone down in this way? Well, we do seem to have a few ancient maps that show some probable settlements of Cush (and his fellow travelers). They moved away - but not too far away - from ancient Babylon.

Below, we see that there was an area, slightly to the east of Babylon, known as *Sabatis* (which, interestingly enough, is extremely close to Cush's own title of *Sabatius*).

Could this have been one area of Cush, or his fellow travelers?

Also, if we look a little to the southeast of this area (in the map above), we notice another piece of land, known as *Susiana*. In a different map (below) we see how this very name could also be translated as the name *Cush*.

Wow. It seems as though these lands could have actually been amongst the areas that Cush and his colonies felt the need to relocate to, after being pressured out of Babylon. Cush, obviously, had a large following, or, probably, a number of descendant on his side, because entire lands were named after this particular patriarch.

*...(Noah appointed Cush as) the first Saturn of Babylon, to build there first
with his colonies*. (Asher, 1993, p. 203)[20]

Yet, to Nimrod, these groups - living so close to Babylon - may have still been a problem for his image. Eager to dissociate himself from his father's failures, Nimrod may have eventually decided to do all he could to make sure that Cush was not heard from again, or at least chased far enough away. Time to forget the past.

Nimrod, then, may have decided to get all of this behind him, and push his father farther and farther away from the hub of Babylon. He may have even began to issue a siren call for action - Cush, and all he once stood for, needed to be "taken out." So, yet again, Cush had to sneak out of his new land.[21] And, yet again, there does seem to other areas, even *farther* away from Babylon, that could have been associated with this same patriarch.

In a number of historical maps, we also see, to the south of *Egypt*, a nation known as *Ethiopia* - an area that has, quite often, been associated with the name *Cush*.

Also, in the map below, we discover yet another land of *Cush*, just to the northeast of Noah's homeland of Armenia. How convenient.

Maybe Cush and some of his followers felt the need to move north, to get farther and further away from Nimrod's rage. And, of course, Noah would have gotten wind of Cush's proximity. And, regardless of what may have happened in Babylon, Noah was probably a forgiving father, and cared a lot about his grandson. Noah may have believed in second chances... even if Cush had such of a falling out with God.

Maybe it was around this time that Noah asked Cush to lead his Armenian homeland, hoping that he may begin to see the error of his ways. And, maybe Cush (through the association of a number of *good* people around him) would now want to begin the trek *back*, in a Godly direction. Noah could only hope.

Could Cush have really gone "back and forth" here, leading a pagan life, and then leading the people of Noah for a period of time? Or, could Nimrod have ended up pushing Cush into Noah's arms, blaming *him* for everything that happened at the tower's fall?[22] What if Nimrod also began to interpret Cush's migration near (and into) the land of Noah as some kind of **betrayal** - to his former pagan cause? Maybe, after seeing Cush coddle up to Noah, Nimrod ended up considering his father a "heathen," or a "traitor." Maybe he decided that it would be better to turn the *death* of Cush into some kind of "trophy," or a symbol of Nimrod's devotion to his pagan cause. Who knows?

> *...he (Sabatius Saga, Saturn, Cush) reigned peaceably, even until the time of the reign of Iupiter Belus (i.e. Nimrod)... the second King of Babylon: who yielding unto his disobedient desires, and coveting to command as sole Monarch of the whole world, was the first violator & infringer of the ordinances appointed in those days, and by whose means the golden age afterward lost such her title... for before such his over haughty humours, all things were peacable, common, & free. This Iupiter endeavoured by all devices possible to **overturn the greatness of Sabatius Saga, surnamed Saturn**... (and eventually) to undertake all means how to bring him and his family to **death and destruction**...*
> - An Historical Treatise of the Travels of Noah into Europe 15[23]

> *But Jupiter Belus (a.k.a. Nimrod), since he could not subjugate the others unless Sabatius... was **conquered and killed**, secretly strove to destroy him... Jupiter Belus had prepared countless ambushes for him...*
> (Asher, 1993, p. 207)[24]

Most probably, Nimrod wanted to make it clear that *he* (and he alone) was the one who was now carrying on the proper torch of paganism. Anyone who was considered "wishy washy" was now to be treated as a turncoat, and even taken out.[25]

Regardless, Cush may still have had *some* power and influence over a number of people (at least those who chose to go along with him, as well as a number of his descendants). He still seemed to have been able to maintain a reign over a number of nation-states. He could have even expanded his influences in the region somewhat, after filling Noah's shoes.

> *And this Sabatius Saga (called Saturn) had all the country even unto the land of **Bactria** (i.e. where Iran, Afghanistan and Pakistan are now located), lying towards India (at this day called Tartaria) under his rule and authority.*
> *- An Historical Treatise of the Travels of Noah into Europe* 11[26]

Cush was quite the complex individual - holding sway over Godly people and pagans alike. We also know that he had a vast understanding of medicines, divination, magic, and other (previously forbidden) occult sciences. Through these things, Cush could have easily been able to gather more and more curious people - as well as more and more physical land - under his ultimate authority (while living up north). We see that *Bactria*, in the above quote, was once an ancient nation located to the slight west of China and India and a little south of modern-day Russia. Was Cush's influences (and his occult knowledge) able to spread as far east as China or India, and even up into Russia, and the surrounding areas? How about the ability of Cush to push his *religious* knowledge into these areas, helping to help establish pagan religions such as *Hinduism*? Being lord over a number of these ancient lands could have really helped Cush to spread out his **pagan footprint** into a good number of eastern nations - eventually allowing paganism to establish itself as a "world religion" (and, as a *Black Horse*).

Regardless of Nimrod's anger against him, Cush was still able to prosper (at least for a little while). Would he continue to be successful, with these "bulls eyes" on his back? Would Nimrod need to do more, in order to prove his point... even, possibly, going up there, and *personally* taking his father out? What twists and turns would this story end up taking on next?

Ham - The "Reluctant" Pagan?

> *...Chem (i.e. Ham)... was allotted the name Chem Esenua, that is, Chem the shameless and lewd, propagator of devilry.*
> (Asher, 1993, p. 201)[27]

For the sake of chronology, we'll need to change gears here, just a little bit, and move onto a parallel story. We'll soon return to these struggles of Cush, Nimrod, and all of what was going on to the north of Babylonia. But, first, we need to head into another ancient pagan stronghold: **Egypt**. And, apparently, we now discover how there was a few struggles going on in this land as well (at about the same time). So, let's begin by shifting gears here a bit, to discover what might have been going on in this Egyptian stronghold. The reasons why we need to do this will become apparent, soon enough.

From previous volumes, we may have already discovered a number of things about the patriarch **Ham**, the third son of Noah, and what his contributions were to post-Flood paganism. We also know a little about his attitude (early on), such as how he really wasn't totally "on board" with the pagan cause, at least for a while. Yet, later on, he would find himself becoming one of paganism's most prominent and proficient patriarchs.

Ham, assuredly, would end up as a very *sneaky* character over time, seizing almost every available opportunity he came across. Through these ways of trickery, Ham, slowly, was beginning to go down a number of very *dark* paths, finding himself dabbling in a number of dark pagan rituals, such as black magic. Speaking of this sneakiness, we also recall (from the Bible) how Ham defiled Noah's nakedness. He either sexually violated his own mother, or violated his father sexually (or both), all for the sake of some kind of personal gain. He even could have castrated Noah. Whatever Ham did, he seemed to already be progressing - slowly - into the world of the "Other Side."

Yet, for a while, he *still* was a little reluctant to be totally "on board" with the entire pagan cause. Today, he would have been thought of as being a bit "wishy washy" - sometimes wanting to follow the Godly ways of Noah and sometimes being seduced by those occult ways of the Serpent.

Ultimately, Ham would end up going in the wrong direction, becoming known as the one who would *resurface* a lot of those dark, pagan rituals after the Flood (the things that were supposed to be destroyed at this time)! And, just *how* was he able to do that? Ancient sources tell us that he went and inscribed most of this occult information on a couple of large, stone tablets, just before the Flood - the information that a number of fallen, terrestrial angels used to barter with (in order to achieve their need for sexual fulfillment with human beings). After the Flood, Ham would go back to this same general area, and retrieve it all. And, of course, this is what helped to bring about so much antediluvian *sacrilege* back into the hands of the post-Flood pagan populous. Again, it was very *sneaky* of him.

What this did do, over time and circumstance, was to allow *Ham* to, eventually, turn himself into a huge stakeholder in all that's dark, and occultish.[28] He probably passed a lot of this onto Cush, who took full advantage of that situation (as we already know). Ham would eventually become so powerful, over time, that he naturally began to be propped up by other people around him, elevated into some kind of "god-like" status. And, because he became so knowledgeable on those elements of the "Other Side," he eventually would stay on the same, *pagan* pathways for the rest of his life, continuing on, as a troublesome force to all who would rather follow other ways, such as the ways of God.

Here's what a few ancient sources said about Ham, a number of his immediate descendants, as well as his sympathizers:

...he was hostile to his father on account of his own vices.
(Asher, 1993, p. 201)[29]

Some also say, That he only in the world came out of his mother's womb laughing and with a smiling countenance, which is an uncouth thing, and (as most hold) **prognosticating no good***.*
- An Historical Treatise of the Travels of Noah into Europe 24[30]

The Irish annals speak of the Formorians as a warlike race, who...were... descended from Cham (a.k.a. Ham), the son of Noah, and lived by pyracie **(piracy)** *and* **spoile** *of other nations, and were in those days* **'very troublesome to the whole world'***.* (Donnelly, 1882, p. 174)[31]

In previous volumes, we recall how *Egypt* was to be the land that Noah dictated to Ham and his descendants.[32] The Bible even calls Egypt the "land of Ham" (in *Psa.* 105:23, *Psa.* 106:22, etc.). So, now, let's begin to understand Ham's role in the development of this *White Horse*, by understanding all of what he began to do with his advanced knowledge, power and influence.

> *Cham was **out of favour** with his father, but he had his heritage allowed to him, the other third part of the world.*
> ("The Travels of Noah into Europe", 2002, p. 3)[33]

> *...father Janus (i.e. Noah) sent Chemesenuous (i.e. **Ham**) to Egypt with colonies: and to Libya and Cyrene he sent Triton (i.e. Shem), and to the whole of the rest of Africa Japetus (i.e. Japheth)...*
> (Asher, 1993, p. 203)[34]

Ham, obviously, was to have a gain of connections, all over the place. His son *Mizraim* was considered the individual who "united the upper and lower Nile river," which helped to turn Egypt into the powerful nation-state it once was. Because of this presence, Ham became a major figure inside of ancient Egypt.

> *Among men, the Egyptians have followed him in this doctrine: they have made him comparatively young their own Saturn among the gods...*
> (Asher, 1993, p. 201)[35]

> *...they called him by the name of Ham Esenus, which signifies their famous god Pan. And thus, he **ruled in Egypt** (for a) long time...*
> (Simpson, 2009, p. 20)[36]

His presence, as well, helped to solidify a *pagan* way of life, and of worship.

> *...the young man, Chem (i.e. Ham), who, always studying magic and poison, had acquired the name Zorast (i.e. the Zoroaster).*
> (Asher, 1993, p. 201)[37]

To show their love unto him (Ham), they (pagans around him) lived in an impious and ungracious manner, perpetrating the most odious villainies.
(Simpson, 2009, p. 20)[38]

And, because of this, a number of prominent pagan areas - including *this* one - could have easily been invaded by Shem and his posse later on. Ham, naturally, would have been a target of these individuals. And, there actually does seem to be ancient references to a certain group of people - known as the "Shepherd Kings" - who ended up invading Ham's Egypt for a time. These foreigners felt the need to come into this particular country, and dominate it (at least, for a little while). Well, just *who* were these mysterious foreigners, and why did they feel the need to do what they did?

Shem and his son *Asshur* could have easily become a couple of major candidates for these "shepherds" - those who tried to usurp paganism's hold over the land.[39] And, interestingly enough, the famous historian *Josephus* actually referred to these "Shepherd Kings" (or, ancient *Hyksos*) as **Hebrews** (or *Israelites*). He also said that they were the same Hebrews who, after they eventually left the land, would go on to found the city of *Jerusalem*.[40] And, yes, we've already discovered (a few chapters ago) how *Shem* was the one thought to be *Melchizedek* - the person accredited for building this same, great city! Indeed, Shem could have been a major part of this whole Egyptian invasion, working on the side of God.

And, as one may be able to conclude: the hopes of those living in these areas - continuing on with this same pagan "utopia" - were being jeopardized, and fast. We recall that there were a few other regions in the Middle East (such as in Babylonia) that were going through this same thing, becoming a little unstable as well - all due to either those invasions of Shem or some other kind of societal or environmental upheaval. This time, *Egypt* would be primed for a lot of the same *instability*.

Shem's raids may have indeed inspired Ham to desire to leave, at least for a bit. Things were becoming just a little too "hot." It wasn't that easy for Ham (and others) to practice certain elements of their pagan faith (such as black magic) out in the open… at least without looking over their shoulders.

Now, if Ham felt as though he needed to leave the area, *where* would he have ended up going, and *why*? *What* would have made him feel a bit safer? *Who* would have naturally been there for him… in his time of need? Could it have been the same person who attempted to help *Cush* out, during the time that *he* was in a similar situation?

Back to Father Noah

The giant of Babylonian paganism - Nimrod (a.k.a. *Jupiter, Belus, Nin*, etc.) - began to rule Babylon in approximately **2161** B.C. (after this initial ousting of Cush). And, as we've seen in a former quote (above), Ham would dominate Egypt around the same timeframe, until, at least, around the 56th year of Nimrod's reign. This would have taken us to, approximately, the year 2105 B.C. Now, we come to a point in time when something may have happened to Ham's homeland, and he had to leave.

> *…he (Ham) ruled Egypt…to the 56th year of Jupiter Belus (i.e. Nimrod)… In that year, he began to travel and came into* **Italy***…*
> (Simpson, 2009, p. 20)[41]

It was time for Ham to leave. Yet, out of all the places for the particular patriarch to go, we see (in the above quote) that Ham might have decided to go back to the area where Noah, his own father, retired to - **Italy**. How convenient. Migrating back to his own father? Surely. Makes sense. Maybe Ham believed that he would find Noah there, and he would be welcomed, because Noah was the type who, usually, would welcome any close family members "with open arms."

Yet, we recall how sneaky Ham was, and how he abused Noah's trust before. Why not go over there, and try to con his father once again? Why not work his way through this "land of innocence," and sneak his way to the top (somehow)? Ham probably believed that softie Noah would *surely* take his own son back, and forgive all of the past.

Yet, during this time, Noah was not even in the area. Before Ham made the decision to go into the land of Italy, Noah was already on his "second tour," and had left the Italian Peninsula in the hands of a son of Japheth, named *Gomer* (i.e. "Comerus Gallus").

> *Gomer, the eldest son of Japheth, otherwise known as "Comerus Gallus", was the **first king of Italy and** the country was called **"Kytim**."*
> ("From Noah to Dardanus (according to Annius)", 2002, p. 3)[42]

For a while, Gomer's rule over the land seemed quite positive, and it, probably, continued to be Godly in nature. Gomer may have strived to maintain Italy as the same quality plot of land that Noah intended. But, sadly, Gomer ended up dying just before Noah was to return. And, in the meantime, Ham came, and discovered that there seemed to be a *vacuum* there - with the subsequent leadership being extremely weak. And, because of this, Ham quickly assumed authority. People must have respected Ham a lot, not only because he was a direct son of Noah, but also because he had access to occult power and that forbidden, esoteric knowledge… and he wasn't afraid to show it off in any way.

Ancient sources stated that Ham arrived only a few years before Noah was able to return. Yet, during this time, Ham was able to *slither* his way into turning *paganism* into a major religion of the land, causing it to go (totally) mainstream. He, then, was able to slowly degrade the sanctity of the land, and the people became corrupt.

> *Chemesenuus (i.e. Ham) came to Italy… (and) began to rule and corrupt the colonies with his own impiety and evil.*
> (Asher, 1993, p. 207)[43]

Ham, once again, took advantage of a situation at hand… twisting things around, and manipulating it all in his *own* favor.

Noah's Second Tour

In regards to his "second tour," Noah would begin to wonder how the people of this new world were really managing their lands. He desired to "know of their estates." Hopefully, a second tour may allow him the opportunity to see how people are going, and keep them in the direction of God. He, at least, wanted to give *everyone* hope for a better tomorrow (and win any wayward souls back in the process).[44] So, he left.[45] He tried to help out a lot of people, but paganism was slowly taking hold… and this became difficult for Noah.

Upon arriving back in Italy, Noah probably believed that Gomer was still alive. He probably strolled into the area, exhausted, with the belief that (at least) this land would be untainted - still being a beacon of Godly living and hopeful aspirations. Ham, of course, was already bringing the land into the *opposite* moral direction, into something more like his former land of Egypt. He, reportedly, even brought a number of people from some other impious regions, to help him facilitate these detrimental changes![46] There may have even been **giants** in the area, now, wielding their own influences to the population at large. This takedown of a once-Godly Italy was quickly becoming a reality.

Noah, finding the country in such a pitiful state of disarray and immorality, was extremely disappointed - to say the least. He gave an ultimatum to Ham:

> …*father Janus (i.e. Noah), coming to Italy when he discovered that Camesenuus (i.e. Ham) was corrupting the youth **beyond belief**, endured him calmly for **three years**. Then, having assigned several colonies to him, he ordered him to leave Italy.* (Asher, 1993, p. 209)[47]

Softie Noah even tried to look the other direction (from all that was going on), and put up with Ham's shenanigans for three *long* years. Of course, he hoped that Ham would change it all back, and things would begin to work out. But (of course), it didn't. Eventually, Noah couldn't take it anymore, and "banished Ham from the kingdom and began to govern it himself, setting things in order."[48] Ham was then forced to go to the south of Italy, to the neighboring island of *Sicily*.[49]

Noah tried to revive the area. In one instance, he set up an establishment - on a plot of land known as the *Vaticanum* (right around the area of where the city of Rome now stands, interestingly enough)!

> *Noah… caused to be built… a marvelous and great city… which he then called Janiculum. Afterward, it was called Vaticanum…*
> (Simpson, 2009, p. 12)[50]

"The **Vaticanum**?" Doesn't this area sound like it could have been (eventually) renamed as another area - the precursor to the *Vatican City*, perhaps?[51] Yes, this very well could have been the story. And, if this all was so, then how telling it all really could have been! More on all of this, later.

At first, it seemed as though Noah was beginning to turn things around. But, pagan assaults on that particular area would not seem to end there. In fact, the time would soon be ripe for *another* blood relative (with very strong pagan beliefs, as well) to come back to Noah, because he felt a need to escape persecution in *his* former area. Now, just *who* could this character have been, and what changes could have taken place on the Italian area because of *his* influences? Would he end up doing "more of the same?"

The Killing of Nimrod

We'll return to Ham, and what happened to him as a result of this banishment from Noah (soon enough). But, for now, in order to get into this other invading character (and, also, for the sake of continuity) we need to return to the area of Babylon, and what was going on with Nimrod and his father **Cush**. We remember the strife that went on, between the two. It has not let up since. But, there would be an event that end up shaking up this feud a little but… but, not too much.

From previous volumes, we recall that Shem, with his periodic raids, was at least successful in killing Nimrod - that major dignitary of Babylon (and cut his body into little pieces). It became quite a blow to their current pagan belief… a belief that facilitated the concept that their leaders were, in fact, "gods." Now, A death and dismemberment would, assuredly, not sit very well with this concept. Many quickly began to question the thought of a living "god." Nimrod *did* die, and killed by one of those pesky "hunters" of God, nonetheless! Shem, reportedly, sent a piece of Nimrod's body to different pagan areas, as a **warning** to the people… to stop their pagan ways.

This left Queen Semiramis (the mother of Nimrod) to take over the reins of Babylon, and become the new face of contemporary paganism. And, we also recall (from previous volumes): if there would have been any good "prototype" for a member of the upper echelons of this "White Horse," it probably would have been **Semiramis**. We recall that, after Nimrod was killed, she would go around, convincing the populations that she had a *new* style of paganism in the works - something a little bit different, and a little more "righteous" (if you will).

Assuredly, the queen was in a pickle. After Shem took out her "god-like" husband (and son), the people were left doubting the veracity of what they were practicing. An immortal god was chopped up into pieces, with parts of his body scattered almost everywhere. Semiramis, then, knew that a lot of those militant, God-followers were not buying a number of these "harsher," pagan elements, so she had to change the belief a bit. Paganism, now, began to look as though it could have been a "wholesome" belief too, just like the ways of God… with "good" elements to it. It was now marketed as an innocent, nature-worshiping religion, with a number of elements that didn't seem too far away from what a Godly follower might accept as "close enough" to their own beliefs. Parts of the religion were even morph into something that looked, somewhat, "Christ-like." Maybe the Godly were just "misunderstanding" the whole pagan cause, because it now seemed a little more humane, or even "sanitized."

Maybe the people who formerly jumped on Shem's bandwagon would, now, begin to believe that this *revised* form of paganism wasn't really that bad… overall. The great propagator of these *old* ways was dead. Maybe, things would now become a little different. Maybe her new facade would, over time, help to take some of the "fight" out of anyone trying to take it all down. And, yes… that, indeed, **did** seem to be the case, over time (with a good number of Godly individuals)! Their attitudes of people, in regards to what Shem was doing, *did* seem to soften.

And, if we also think about it, **these same techniques** would end up sounding a lot like what a number of those who ended up fronting the *White Horse* would do in the future. Go figure!

Solidifying their Power Structure?

Still, those onslaughts of Shem and his posse were not over. A number of Godly people still would not fall for these phony pagan "changes." And, as we'll now see, there could have been yet ***another*** patriarch out there who, over time, felt the need to continue on with Nimrod's original legacy - of wiping out Cush. He didn't care much for Cush as well. But, unlike Nimrod, this particular character seemed to have also ended up fighting alongside of Shem and Asshur… against the pagan way. The funny part about this all was: this particular character was actually, once, a ruler of **Babylon** himself! What? How could this be? Let's see.

The year is approximately 2099 B.C., or 249 years after the Flood. Nimrod is not yet dead. He is still in charge of the Babylonian empire. And, it's been about 62 years since he took over the reins. Shem and his son Asshur were out there, stalking major pagan patriarchs (such as Nimrod himself). But, at least this time, Shem would be successful… in a major way! An ambush did occur, and Shem was now able to take out Nimrod. Yet, we also recall that Semiramis, after the incident, took it upon herself to claim that she was now pregnant, and her child was to become (none other than) the "reincarnation" of this former pagan "god," Nimrod (or course)! Yes, this immortal "god" wasn't really dead forever. He just needed to be "swooped away" into the heavens for a while, to live amongst the gods, to be a martyr for the faith. He *needed* to be killed (as Abel did), in order to be able to come back, and show the world how strong paganism really was! It was to show how this "god" was able to defeat death (through reincarnation). What a guy! Now, with these accolades, wouldn't that be able to give paganism another (desperately needed) "spiritual" boost, as well?

If Semiramis was now able to get away with her claims, it might become a good way for her to "prove" how her new pagan ways were "right" and "just," and how reincarnation really "works" in the world. It also "proves" that Nimrod died to become the new "savior" of the world, providing a perfect example of how one is able to achieve everlasting life - just follow what the "goddess" mother now has to say. Yes, doesn't this sound *very* similar to what Jesus would need do, so many years in the future?

All the pagans now needed to do was to "believe," and accept these new ways of the post-Flood "goddess." Of course, all of this was done because Semiramis really needed to *save* face, and change the belief a bit… in order to survive. Yet, regardless of how phony it all was, the people were slowly beginning to buy it… and Semiramis *was* now pregnant.

So, if Semiramis was able to make things work out perfectly, she needed to play her cards right. Her newborn son had to be looked upon as "reincarnated" Nimrod. Yet, there was one "monkey wrench" in the whole works here - something (or someone) that would threaten to expose all of this sacrilege as fraud. Interestingly enough, that particular "monkey wrench" would be manifested as *one* particular person of the time: that "savior" child of Semiramis **herself**! Let's explain.

Although it all may begin to look good, at first, Semiramis needed to keep the charade of this "god-like" child going. Yet, things were not about to end up as "peachy clean" as Semiramis originally tried to present it all. Her attempt to "duck, dodge and hide" the ramifications of Nimrod's death would, eventually, leave a number of pagan individuals scratching their heads. Even though she *did* become pregnant, it all wasn't exactly a "virgin birth" (as she may have originally claimed). She, at first, claimed that the deceased "god" (i.e. Nimrod) impregnated her, and that's how he would come into the world. Of course, that sounds so familiar (to most Christians out there). And, to so many contemporary pagan individuals of the time, the early father was *still* considered "nonexistent," because he was the son of a "god"… but, he wasn't "nonexistent" to everybody! As much as Semiramis may have tried to claim that her child (like Jesus) was "immaculately conceived," there *still* was an earthly father in this case… and,. he was, in actuality, a very **famous** father indeed!

Let's see just *who* this father was.

Nynus - (Righteous) Son of Asshur

Regardless of a father, actually, being in the picture, a number of people would still would end up falling for this claim of a "virgin birth"… just enough to allow Semiramis to maintain this throne of Babylon. But, how long would she able to, pull it off?

There, actually, may have been an early group of dissidents out there, around the area of ancient Babylonia, known as the *Assyrians*. And yes, these early Assyrians were, most probably, not of the same spirit as the later Assyrians we may have heard about… but, the *original* members of this ancient nation. These early people could easily have been descended from a famous patriarch (of the same name): *Asshur* (or *Assyr*). And, as we've already realized, *Asshur* was actually a son of Shem, that main hunter of pagans! Could it be? These early *Assyrians* may have been righteous. And, if so, what does *Asshur* have to do with our story, here? Could Asshur have, actually, been the father of Semiramis' "miracle child." And, if this was so, then *how* did this all really come about?

The whole idea seems a bit fantastic... at first. Yet, if we think about it, it could have indeed been a very good possibility. We already know how Asshur was considered a patriarch of *Godly* intention... fighting right alongside his father Shem. Yet, we also know that Semiramis was extremely beautiful, and a top matriarch of the **pagan** cause. What could have happened between the two, to get Semiramis pregnant in this way?

Man leader and woman leader - both on opposite sides here, with a gorgeous woman leader desperate to get out of a predicament. Could something have happened, here, to allow Semiramis a way out of her "pickle?" Could there have been a "quid pro quo" here, or some kind of sexual exchange, to allow each dignitary to be able to get something out of it all? If Asshur had her on the ropes - either by the death of her husband, or because he was also able to take her out, as well (if he wanted to) - could there have been some kind of "compromise" here, in the works (in order to save Semiramis)? What if she decided to barter a few things, namely her *body*, behind the scenes? What if she was able to seduce Asshur enough to leave her be? And, of course, it could also work well for her plan. Asshur, assuredly, would not want to make the fact that he was "sleeping with the enemy" very public... it just didn't sound good. It might actually work out, for both parties: Asshur could have sex with one of the most beautiful people of the era, and Semiramis could now have a "silent partner" in her scheme - to have a child that was "fathered by no man." Why not attempt something, if both parties were able to get away with what they may have wanted?

Yes, apparently, this *did* happen. Semiramis may have batted her eyes, put on some makeup, and talked Asshur into some kind of deal - a kind of "peace treaty," if you will. Call it "friends with benefits." Asshur, apparently, did not really handle this situation very well (being a child of God). Yet, not only would he get to spend an opportunity to spend an evening with one of the most beautiful women in the world, he knew that it would have to be withheld from the public, and for **good** reason... so, why not?

If we think about it, the "crossing over" of political power seemed to have occurred a number of times throughout history - with one leader of a nation *intermarrying* with the leader of another, establishing a "working relationship" between the two nation-states. Think of **Cleopatra** here. She did this exact same thing with Mark Anthony - an Egyptian dignitary involving herself with a Roman dignitary! Semiramis may have believed that it was in her best interests to propose a scheme such as this, as well.

So, if she was actually able to pull this all off, and maintain the phony narrative, then she (with Asshur looking the other way) would also be able to remain *on top* of the ruling hierarchy. To her, everything seemed to have hinged on keeping this child under her thumb, and going in the *same* pagan moral direction. No "reincarnated" god of paganism would ever want to betray this faith, of course!

Yet, the child was born. And time began to pass. Most pagans were accepting this whole thing: a "miracle" had actually taken place, and her child was, "truly," something special. Semiramis was winning. And, the people of the land just had to continue on, believing the whole thing, so she could continue on. The interesting thing about this whole process was, however: the child *did* grow up, and became a great warrior; but, he didn't exactly **remain** a warrior in his mother's image, or, for the pagan cause. He would, eventually, end up going into the opposite direction - the direction of his real, biological *father*! Yes, that's right, her son - **Nynus** - would (more or less) become a fighter for those who were on the side of **God**, and not Nimrod! Uh oh. Talk about upsetting the apple cart! Maybe this young successor began to have a few *internal* struggles (being Asshur's son). Maybe, as he began to grow up, just felt more attracted to the moral directions of his father, rather than his mother… and began fighting for the side of God. Both sides were calling out to the child, This time, Asshur was winning.

That "miracle" son of Semiramis (and Asshur) was, as we've just discovered, *Ninus, Nynus* or even *Nynus* **the Young**. Now, why would he have been referred to as "the Young" here? Well, if we think about it, the people around Semiramis, soon after the birth, may have started taking her at her word, and began to pressure her to let this "god-child" rule as soon as possible, so she conceded. He may have begun his reign, then, at a very tender age - **almost 10 years old**! Ancient sources stated that, around 259 years after the flood, Nynus may have begun his reign (which was only ten years after his birth).

And, after this, Nynus would continue on, ruling areas inside of Babylonia for almost 52 more years.[52]

Semiramis, of course, hoped that Nynus would continue to follow *her*, and *her* own footsteps. Yet, we'll now see that this would not tot-ally come to pass. For her, things were starting to slowly slip away. It was only a matter of time until the child went full circle, and was exposed… as the God-follower he really was. What else could have been brought out into the open here, if given enough time?

As Nynus continued on into manhood, he may have begun to develop his own ideas on how to "clean up" Babylonia. It seemed as though he wanted to do more of what was *right* (by God), rather than what was right by his peers. He, at least in one respect, may have begun to go down this same path as Nimrod… as far as wanting to take out **Cush**! Nynus, also, probably began to believe that Cush was still a corrupter of the people, and would remain a corrupter as long as he was in charge of any nation/state, so, he wanted him removed (no matter where he was now located). So, Nynus may have begun to accept this as his *duty* - as a Godly leader of Babylon. He probably felt the need to head up to where Cush was, someday soon, and *take him out*.

The Year "299"

Great shakeups were now on the horizon, in regards to a good number of pagan areas. Approximately 300 years after the Flood (or 2049 B.C.), a number of shakeups seemed to happen at once. A number of these *did* seem to be in development for a while now. All it took was a few "sparks" to blow everything up. In one example, we've just discovered how Nynus spoke out against the evil practices of Cush and his entourage. And, as we'll now see, he also began to speak out against a number of those troublesome *giants* in the area (for they were continually corrupting the people around them (morally), and being very troublesome, as a whole). So, now, this became the year that Nynus would start to put all of his threats into action.

Now, he decided to take things to another level, and do some damage. *Cush* was number one on his list. By the time he turned 50, he had already been reigning for about 40 years. Sparing his mother Semiramis (of course), he began to head up north, with a number of his followers, and focus on his goals. When Nynus made his decision, Semiramis may have either took over the reins of Babylon (in his absence), or was encouraged to go into Egypt, and set up shop there. We're not exactly sure what the immediate results of these shake ups were, but, apparently, there did seem to be some shifts in pagan leadership, as a result. It's quite possible, however, that: after Shem and Asshur left the region, Asshur (Nynus' father) could have easily entrusted Nynus with control over both lands (i.e. Egypt and Babylon)… because he knew his heart was in the right place. And, Nynus may have entrusted Semiramis to maintain some kind of control over one of these regions (or even both), while Nynus headed up north.

Either way, one could guess that things were about to change in both lands. After the raids of Shem and his posse, things were really beginning to take their toll (as far as the lands). As we already recall, there may have even been a vast migration of peoples, out of these lands, and towards Atlantis.

The interesting element to this all is: at the very time that things seemed to have become hard for the pagans of the land, a *very famous* dignity of Egyptian lore was about to be born (as we'll discover soon enough)! This figure, along with his sister, would go on to be one of the most powerful rulers of ancient Egypt... and his name would be none other than **Osiris**! And yes, believe it or not, this Osiris would also begin to be on God's side, at least somewhat (just like Nynus had been). We'll soon see.

And, in response to a number of these initial changes, it would be around this same time that **another famous patriarch** would make the decision to gather up all of his belongings, and leave his former abode. Can we guess who this individual was?

In the Direction of Noah, Once Again!

Yes, of course, **Cush** - realizing that Nynus had decided to do more than just talk about taking him out - probably felt that it was time to leave… forever. No longer would he be able to get away with just hiding out, or moving from one area to another. He had to get out of the Middle East, and figured that Nynus was wholly determined to get him if he stayed. So, the pressure was on.

He now had a major decision to make: where to go?

> *In the forty-third year of Nynus, when Sabatius realized that he could not by any means be king… he withdrew to the Sarmatian shore of the sea.*
> (Asher, 1993, p. 211)[53]

About 59 years after Ham had left Egypt, and decided to go back to Noah, *Cush* realized he was in a similar situation, and took it upon himself to do the same.

> *…as hardly escaped he (i.e. Saturn, Cush) the snares and subtleties laid to entrap him. Saturn therefore seeing himself in those dangers and casualties, to be deprived of all dignity and command for succour and refuge fled unto **his grandfather Noe**, there hoping to be protected, safeguarded, and defended…*
> - An Historical Treatise of the Travels of Noah into Europe 15[54]

Of course, he went off to see his grandfather *Noah* as well, hoping to receive the same welcome that Ham had.[55] It only made sense, though, judging from what we already know about this gracious father Noah. Cush was now on his way.

After looking unsuccessfully for Cush in the regions around Armenia, **Nynus**, after a good period of time, was said to have eventually went up, into Europe, possibly even following in his own father's footsteps (for, as we know, Shem and Asshur may have already went into Europe, after their purge of the Middle East). Could Nynus *still* have subtly been looking for Cush, after he found out that Cush may have also fled into Europe, looking for Noah? It's entirely possible, because Italy, of course, is a nation on the European continent. Regardless of the reason Nynus also decided to ventured up there, our plot continues to thicken… a lot more.

Once Cush began to arrive on the Italian Peninsula, he met up with Noah; and Noah, once again, felt that Cush may have needed *another* shot at some kind of governing position. Ham, as we know, had already been banished to Sicily (because of his pagan lean), and Noah was *still* trying to run everything on his own, even though he was getting much older. Noah probably could use a leader to help him out, because of his advanced age. How about giving Cush a try, one more time?

> *He (Noah) was then joined by Sabatius Saga, surnamed Saturn… (the one) who had fled from Armenia because of a threatened assassination attempt…*

*Noah and Saturn **reigned together** in Italy...*
    ("From Noah to Dardanus (according to Annius)", 2002, p. 3)[56]

As we know, Noah seemed to have bent over backwards for the people that he loved, no matter *what* they may have done after the Flood, and no matter what they may have done to him personally. Now, once again, Noah decided to welcome *another* famous **pagan** patriarch to his Italian abode... hoping for the best.

*...Sabatius Saga (i.e. Cush) sailed by sea to **Italy to father Janus (i.e. Noah)**, who welcomed Sabatius hospitably...*
    (Asher, 1993, p. 213)[57]

Twelve years after Cush first stepped foot on the Italian Peninsula (i.e. around 312 after the Flood), Cush "began to reign" with Noah.

Noe acceding to the expectation of Saturn, friendly entertained him & gave him many gracious signs of his welcome & and [wished] arrival: and for to honour him the more, and to show the effects of his friendship and good will towards him, created him the Commander, King and Patriarch of the Aborigines (i.e. locals of the Italian Peninsula)...
    - An Historical Treatise of the Travels of Noah into Europe 15[58]

Noah had high hopes for a righteous outcome (this time). He was, probably, getting sick of everything not working in the direction of God, and was feeling too old to really involve himself in any more "back and forth." And, for a while, it seemed that Cush did act justly, and the land of Italy remained chaste.

...Sabatius Saga taught agriculture and something of religion.
    (Asher, 1993, p. 213)[59]

Saturn likewise very painfully instructed to the people in the tillage, and in the nature of soils, wherein he had great skill and knowledge, as also in the ceremonies of religion...
    - An Historical Treatise of the Travels of Noah into Europe 15[60]

And, as we may recall from a previous volume, Cush was very knowledgeable - not only in the occult arts and pagan religious practices, but also in the understanding of a vast number of scientific disciplines (medicine, agriculture, engineering, astronomy, and a number of others). Noah, apparently, became proud of his progress, and felt good that Cush was teaching the people a number of (somewhat) "positive" things. And, because of it all, Noah decided to do one more thing... something in Cush's honor:

> ...and (Noah) there caused him also to build a **city**, which he called after his (Cush's) own name **Saturnia**... in which very place at this day **one part of Rome**, which lieth on the other side of the river Tybre...
> - An Historical Treatise of the Travels of Noah into Europe 15[61]

Wow! Once again, we see how the city of **Rome** came into play. We now begin to see how it was (slowly) being constructed, and (quite probably) connected with the **spirit of Babylon**. First, we have Noah's city of *Vaticanum* (i.e. the *Vatican*?), and now we see Noah beginning to allow for the construction of Rome. And, if we think about it: we also have once had (in the area) a supreme leader of pagan Egypt, and now of pagan Babylon... both with influence. Could there have been a chance that the spirit of *Babylon* could have also been passed on here, with these particular characters!

We now see that *Cush* had a city being built in his honor, and *he* was also the one who helped to launch the Tower of Babel! Go figure. And, we're not just talking about hyperbole or ancient symbolism, here. We have an **actual leader** of the Serpent's post-Flood paganism. You can't get much closer to *Mystery Babylon* than that!

Now, the question that may remain: we see that Cush had a part in the development of ancient **Rome**, parts of it even being named in honor of him. As we see in the above, we have the city originally being named "Saturnia" or the "City of Saturn" - after one of the most infamous pagan patriarchs of the post-Flood world, Cush. What could have been the potential for this city to, slowly, fall into corruption (if paganism would ever become a bit stronger in the area)? What was Noah thinking?

In modern-day Rome, we do, interestingly enough, still see the remains of a temple that was once dedicated to this very same individual!

Yes, as we can clearly see here, there was (and still is) a temple - a temple of **Saturn** - situation right in the middle of Rome. It's right there. And, yes, some of this all may, at first, seem to be a little frightening, especially when we see actual evidence of what may have once happened there, so long ago. But, if anything, it helps to prove (to us) how all of this, indeed, could have been a reality! The gavel of post-Flood paganism, indeed, could have been passed on here, over time - from ancient Atlantis, Egypt and *Babylon* to Cush's new city of the future: **Rome**.

Would the good people of this area - now partially under Cush's influences - be able to maintain this land as something God-following, or not? Would it remain the powerhouse that Noah once intended it to be, or would things begin to, slowly, change… for the worse?

If anything, it's very interesting to see how those **actual** patriarchs of the post-Flood pagan movement found their ways to slither back into Noah's life, and into his land… just how the *White Horse* would, eventually, be able to do a lot the same (to a vast number of pious individuals out there, as well).

The Reversal

After about 25 years in this position, Cush was getting quite old, and his health was not as good. Noah wasn't exactly full of pep himself, because he was Cush's grandfather. So, the time had now come for Cush to pass away:

> *...he (Cush) died, in the three hundred and forty fourth year after the inundation of the world (i.e. the Flood). In the very same year also, Noe Ianus finding & perceiving his end to approach, and that now his lustiness and vigour of spirits began to shrink and decrease, created one of his sons, called Cranus the King and Patriarch...*
> *- An Historical Treatise of the Travels of Noah into Europe 15*[62]

Noah had a backup plan, however: he may have asked a son of his old age, *Cranus*, to take over the responsibilities that Cush once had. And, not so long after this time, Noah began to have the feeling that it would soon be *his* time to pass on.

> *...and the **sixth year** after (Noah did this) departed this life, and gave up to his maker, his noble and heroic spirit which was after he had reigned in Italy fourscore and two years...*
> *- An Historical Treatise of the Travels of Noah into Europe 15*[63]

Noah, assuredly, wanted the best for this land, and held steadfast in his hopes that the close members of his family would, somehow, keep the same ship sailing as it was. But, as history shows us, intentions don't always pan out in the ways that one might hope; and the land, once again, was soon to be up for grabs, for a number of other influences to come in, and take over.

What might have happened next... *if* a few immoral patriarchs were able to move in, and begin to work their magic over the populous?

> *Italy fell into disarray again after Noah's death, and came under the tyranny of **giants who continued to rule** the country...*
> ("From Noah to Dardanus (according to Annius)", 2002, p. 3)[64]

Apparently, around this time, a number of *giants* were thinking about usurping the land, and wielding their influences in the area, as well. Once more, things in the area would start to go downhill. And, as we'll continue to see, the post-Flood ideological battle over this particular piece of land would never seem to end.

Friends of Shem… or Enemies of Canaan

First, to discover a little more on what may have happened after this time, we'll need to take a look at a couple *more* patriarchs of this early day and age - those who didn't seem to be finished with this spiritual feud (at least, not yet).

It's fascinating to look at these "forgotten" (or, even *forbidden*) elements of our ancient history. It's interesting to see how there could *still* be a lot more to this whole conflict, over the soul of Noah's favorite land mass. We already understood how Noah established a city known as the *Vaticanum* (i.e. the *Vatican City*?), in that general area of Rome. And, we also see that Noah helped to establish a city known as *Saturnalia*, in this same area (in honor of Cush). Will there be more? What would happen as these areas began to expand, and if they became subjected to *pagan* rule, once again?

Apparently, **Rome** would find itself thrust back in the spotlight, soon enough! But, first, we'll need to return, once again, to that person who was banished from this particular area, early on (just to the south). Of course, the character would have been none other than that pagan patriarch, and one-time leader of Egypt: *Ham*.

The long and short of all that may have happened next was: around 249 years after the Flood (or, approximately 2099 B.C.), another individual would come onto the scene. And, this particular individual's name was *Hammon*. Hammon was, in actuality, a great, great grandson of Ham himself; and this man was also the person who assumed leadership over a land adjacent to the Egyptian nation, named *Libya*. He was also married to a woman named *Rhea* - a direct sister of Ham. And, yes, we have a great, great grandson of Ham marrying Ham's own sister! Go figure. What a world they must have had back then.

Nonetheless, Rhea ended up becoming extremely angry at her husband, because he, supposedly, had an affair with a young woman named Almanthea, and the two ended up having a son, named *Dionysus*.⁶⁵ Rhea, then, quarreled with Hammon, quite a lot, and wanted revenge.⁶⁶

And, although their union already seemed to have started out a little strange, things were about to get worse. A few years after their divorce, Rhea wanted the baby Dionysus *dead*… literally dead. And, to help her out with this, she ended up traveling up north, towards Sicily… to the island where her famous brother Ham was now at. And, to top everything off, Rhea did a little more, beyond asking Ham to help her out. She did the unthinkable: she ended up marrying *Ham*, as well (her own brother)! But, as we'll now see, there was, seemingly, a strategic reason for this act:

> *Cham (i.e. Ham) had a sister called Rhea… she (then)… went to her brother Cham, who was in Sicily, and they were married… After the marriage of Cham and Rhea, they left Sicily and went to Libya. They (Ham and Rhea) raised an army… (to fight Rhea's ex-husband, and his army)…*
> ("The Travels of Noah into Europe", 2002, p. 3)⁶⁷

She worked on her new husband (in a number of ways) in order to help her get rid of the old. She desperately wanted to get back at Hammon, and destroy his illegitimate son.⁶⁸ After pleading a long time to Ham, he ended up agreeing to help her out; and, after that, they both began to head south, with a sizeable army on top of it, to confront Hammon, in his home nation.

With all of this help, Ham and Rhea swiftly declared war on this Libyan leader, and ended up defeating him.

> *…when Camesenuus (i.e. Ham) had left Italy, Rhea came to him, and, married to him, they both proceeded with the Titans against Hammon… and there when war had been joined they expelled Hammon from his kingdom…*
> (Asher, 1993, p. 211)⁶⁹

Around the timeframe of 2049 B.C. (299 years after the Flood) they, not only, were able to expel Hammon from the land, but they also began to look for his child - to kill him.

Even though her act of revenge seemed to have been a success, there was another huge twist in this whole story - one that could have been totally **God-inspired**! Let's explain it all a bit: after their victory, Ham and Rhea ended up traveling into Egypt, and soon found out that they, themselves, were about to have a son, of whom they would name *Osiris*.[70] Yes, this Osiris would eventually go on to become one of the most prominent, and most famous, individuals of the Egyptian area (without a doubt). He was, most probably, that son of Ham (in the Bible) known as *Mizraim*.[71]

Things were not over, just yet. Yes, that illegitimate son of Hammon - *Dionysus* - was not found and killed. He, in actuality, was growing up fast... and vowed his *own* revenge. He would eventually come back into the land of Egypt, heading an army of his own... looking for Ham and Rhea the whole time. When he eventually met up with them, Dionysus, relentlessly, forced the pair to leave their high abode (of government), and "head for the hills." In the whole process, Dionysus actually ended up capturing their son **Osiris**, however; and, instead of killing him, he began to show mercy upon him! It's almost like something out of a Hollywood movie. Dionysus ended up showing so much mercy on Osiris that, over time, he would move to *adopt* him as his own son!

> *...Dionysius, son of Hammon, took up arms and **drove** Rhea and Camesenuus (i.e. Ham) out of his father's kingdom: **keeping Osiris** with him and adopting him as a son... and handed on to him (i.e. Osiris) the kingdom of all Egypt.*
> (Asher, 1993, p. 211)[72]

> *After that Cham and his wife and sister Rhea were thus disconfirmed and overthrown by Dionysus the new king of Libya, and now retired with such disgrace into the furthermost and obscurest corners of Egypt,*
> *- An Historical Treatise of the Travels of Noah into Europe* 23[73]

My, how things change! Dionysus also ended up making a dent in any of the "accomplishments" of Ham and Rhea in Egypt. He was totally changing it around. As well, his son *Osiris* (or *Mizraim*) would eventually go on to become a major part of his military cabinet. What a reversal!

Osiris, after this time, would eventually end up making a name for himself, becoming a "father" to so many of those ancient Egyptians around him (just as Adam was considered a "father" to many people around him, in the past). Osiris, also, was considered the person who helped to "unite the upper and lower Nile river," which helped to launch Egypt into a strong nation. The people absolutely began to love him for all of what he was doing (unlike his father Ham). Things were going good, and former pagans were beginning to enjoy life under his rule.

> *...Chem (i.e. Ham) openly corrupted the human race... But the descendants have **neglected** this depraved dogma...*
> (Asher, 1993, p. 201)[74]

One thing seemed to be sure about Osiris: he operated with the *opposite* moral code that Ham possessed, and this tells us quite a lot. Osiris may have even ended up siding along the side of *God*, in a number of ways... just like Shem, Asshur, Nynus and other famous ancient warriors of the faith once had. At least, Osiris lived by a critically thinking mind, and followed common sense rules.

> *...Rhea had a son of her husband Cham, called Osyris, afterwards surnamed Iupiter Iustus, who proved a most noble and gallant prince, **far differing** from the wicked humours and dispositions of his father (Ham).*
> *- An Historical Treatise of the Travels of Noah into Europe* 22[75]

In a similar manner, however, Osiris ended up marrying his sister - *Isis* - the same way his father and mother had. But, this time, the two would both seem to go down the pathway that Osiris was already going down - being good to everyone and fighting against immoral people like Ham.

> *They excelled in goodness and virtue, as their father Cham (or Ham) had excelled to the **contrary**.*
> ("The Travels of Noah into Europe", 2002, p. 4)[76]

In his new government, Osiris also took it upon himself to make sure that his father was to *remain* in some dusty corner of Egypt, without being allowed to stir up any more waves. With this, he was able to continue on with his tenure - instructing his subjects in positive, harmonious ways. He was teaching the average person things that one could actually benefit from (such as elements of "agriculture, victuals and justice").[77]

> *(Osyris and Isis)… began to apply themselves to the study of the nature of herbs, and to the finding out of planting, tilling, and sowing of corn, **which afterwards they instructed their people**…*
> *- An Historical Treatise of the Travels of Noah into Europe* 24[78]

Interestingly enough, Osiris and Isis seemed to have been communicating with *another* individual, in order to gather themselves a lot of that helpful information:

> *…and (after this Osiris and Isis) showed the use to their neighbours dwelling in **Palestine**, of which ruled king and governor **Sem** (i.e. Shem), surnamed Melchisedech, who was the first that ever offered bread and wine to **God**.*
> *- An Historical Treatise of the Travels of Noah into Europe* 24[79]

Yes, this shows us that they, most probably, were on *the side* of Shem, at least to a degree, because they actively went over to Shem's Palestine, and over to his people, to get their intellectual help! Wow. Once again, it seems that we have a couple of famous patriarchs, here (in pagan mythology), who actually headed in this same **Godly** direction. Now, that's something that most of us, almost assuredly, will **not** find in modern history books (at least not anymore)!

Osiris and Isis even ended up going into other areas in the world, instructing people on positive ways to live and work. As well, they worked to dispel a number of giants from these same lands, just as Shem would have, most probably, wanted.

> *Afterward he (Osyris) travelled into many other countries, always learning them… in the knowledge of such his new inventions; and by these gentle and mild courses he gained the **love of all people**, and by that means almost possessed himself of all the world, with the regalities and principalities thereof (the Empire of Babylon only excepted).*
> *- An Historical Treatise of the Travels of Noah into Europe* 25[80]

There definitely seems to have been an *split* here, in regards to the moralities of those ancient patriarchs! Now, this Osiris became, not only a hero to the Egyptians, but a hero to a number of those nations around him! He taught them so many different things; and, probably, most of it wasn't exactly something *pagan*. No wonder why, in Egyptian mythology, Osiris was considered the great "god of fertility, agriculture, the afterlife, the dead, resurrection, life, and vegetation."[81]

Along with his teachings, it seemed that Osiris was also successful in taking out a number of sacrilegious individuals in the process, either dispelling them or killing them outright. Yes, he truly ended up being a powerhouse for the ways of God, whether he consciously strived to have these as his goals early on or not.

The Big Betrayal

When Osiris eventually ended up back in his homeland (of Egypt), he soon was about to face another major opponent: an important, and very powerful, pagan of his time, with the title of **Typhon**. But, just who was this major opponent? Was he in the Bible? Why would they be at such odds? And, most importantly, what significance would this Typhon have had to our study of the up-and-coming White Horse?

Believe it or not, **Canaan** - that devious son of Ham in the Bible (and son that Noah eventually ended up cursing out) - may have had more to do with these ancient squabbles than we may have ever thought. Christianity and the Bible may not remember him. History books might not really care about him, but ancient mythology sure seems to have something to say about him!

As we recall, ancient sources close to the Bible state that Canaan, most probably, was sired by the incestuous act between Ham and his mother (Naamah), with Noah being extremely angry about the entire situation. It seemed that Noah ended up becoming so upset that he put a *curse* on Canaan, as well as his entire existence. Why? What did *Canaan* do so bad? He was just a baby at the time - the problem being the sexual choices of one (or more) parent(s). Or, what *would* Canaan possibly do *in the future* (with Noah sensing something about him)? Could Noah have already sensed something about this child, believing that he would be worthy of some kind of terrible curse, later on in life? Let's see.

We may also remember (from previous volumes) that Canaan and his descendants did not exactly want to go to the lands that they were apportioned to (by Noah). They did not want to travel to the areas around northwestern Africa. Many of these individuals may have stayed in the land where Shem and his descendents were supposedly allotted (i.e. ancient Palestine or Israel). And, even though Canaan might represent a small fraction of our overall story of *Mystery Babylon*, it seems that one of his actions could have been monumental (at least in regards to our chronology here, as well as in ancient mythology). Let's see what he may have actually did, here.

To explain it all, let's first discover why Canaan could have been given the title of *Typhon* (or, even *Set*). Now, if we think about it, the namesake of *Typhon* - a *typhoon* - represents a massive, hurricane-like storm... something of monumental (as well as negative) proportions. It's a storm that predicates a lot of death and destruction. Now, why would Canaan be given such a title? Ancient sources say that this god Typhon was also a son of *Ham*, and a brother to Osiris (i.e. Mizraim):

> *Cham (i.e. Ham)... got many children, as Cus (i.e. Cush) the father of... (Nimrod)... the giant the first king of Babylon, **Typhon** the giant, and also many others.*
> - *An Historical Treatise of the Travels of Noah into Europe* 21[82]

This totally fits Canaan (and, not a lot of others)! We also may discover how a number of ancient sources proclaim how *malicious* and *evil* this son really was, out of the rest of Ham's children - and, we also seem to discover the same thing about Typhon:

> *Unto this Cham (i.e. Ham), **Tiphon**... **was heir**, and also **succeeded him in humours and malicious dispositions**, who was brought up in Egypt, & there continued.*
> - *An Historical Treatise of the Travels of Noah into Europe* 24[83]

There was no other child - out of the children of Ham - who has been amplified in this same way.

Anyone who regularly reads the Bible may know about the Canaanites, and how malicious they were to the children of Israel. Could Canaan have done something to make him so infamous here - to start this whole "ball rolling" if you will? Only Canaan, it seemed, was able to achieve the same level of dissidence and depravity as Ham himself. So, just what did he do, here?

One could easily guess that Canaan may have had some ill feelings for Osiris, because of what he was doing. He, assuredly, wasn't happy about what was happening to his Egyptian land. He could have even considered Osiris (and Isis) "turncoats" to the pagan cause, and took it upon himself to do something about it.

*The Egyptian Typhon, with the full knowledge of all the giants of the world, destroyed his own **brother**, Osiris, the just Jupiter of Egypt, and himself assumed tyrannical power in Egypt…*
(Asher, 1993, p. 221)[84]

Osyris…was most treacherously and vilely murdered by his brother Typhonas Egiptus (i.e. Typhon, or Canaan).
- An Historical Treatise of the Travels of Noah into Europe 58[85]

And, yes, it happened again… some more "back and forth." Maybe *this* was the reason why Noah cursed Canaan early on - he was to kill one of Noah's grandsons! It's a little fascinating, once we begin to take it all in.

We also notice, in the quote above, how Typhon began to collaborate with a number of those malicious *giants* in the area - the same giants that Osiris was hunting for a time:

*When Osyris returned to his kingdom of Egypt, his brother Typhon went into a **conspiracy with many other malicious giants**, and by subtlety and craft they entrapped and murdered him. They divided his body into 26 pieces and distributed them among themselves, one for each giant. Some time later, his wife Isis found the parts and gathered them together and buried them, with due solemnity and honour.*
("The Travels of Noah into Europe", 2002, p. 5)[86]

This practice of cutting someone "into pieces" may have become some kind of "harsh" tradition of the day. We saw it with Shem, and now we see it with Canaan. This, ultimately, must have been an extremely tumultuous blow to those ancient Egyptians, and all of the people who benefited from Osiris' goodness. They seemed to have loved him so much, and now he was dead. So much infighting. So much bloodshed, here. And, now, their greatest leader was dead, causing the story to become infamous throughout ancient Egyptian lore.

But, there were a number of individuals in Osiris' camp who were not exactly about to take this lying down... no way!

Mighty "Hercules" Makes His Move

Many of us may have heard of another god in ancient mythology: *Hercules*. Many might think that this particular title refers to an individual who was strong, domineering - a *powerhouse* of a god. One such powerhouse "god," referred to as Hercules, may have actually been a member of Osiris' immediate household! And, we'll now see how a few children of the slain Osiris' did not exactly approve of what happened him, and did something about it:

> *Osiris had **many other children**, from Isis and from other women, and when they were grown up he assembled an army and went around the world overthrowing giants.*
> ("From Noah to Dardanus (according to Annius)", 2002, p. 2)[87]

Well, if there were a number of people now on the move, acting on the same side of God, once again, then just *who* was the one given that title of *Hercules*?

As we recall, any grandson of a famous *Saturn* "god" could have been known by this title (in ancient mythology). And, yes, there may have been one child of Osiris out there, up for the challenge of being a *Hercules*. This one became very strong - in his desire to avenge the death of his father, as well as "right" a number of Canaan's "wrongs" here.

Assembling a large army of individuals, this prominent figure became obsessed with usurping the new course that his Egyptian nation was now taking.

> *The children of Isis followed her instruction, and went into battle against* **Typhon** *and his associates…*
> ("The Travels of Noah into Europe", 2002, p. 5)[88]

If Semiramis was still in the land, she probably would no longer be as welcome as she may have been before, and may even have went back to Babylon. Apparently, this son of Osiris was serious, and didn't want to see Egypt go down any proverbial "toilet" (i.e. to become a pagan stronghold, once again), so he set out - first, seeking out Typhon (i.e. Canaan), and then all of those who may have accompanied him.

> *…***Hercules***… instantly took up arms, and scoured almost all the countries of the world,* **until he had found** *out the [author] of the murder of his father Osyris, upon whose body, his angry and wrathful mind took in the end direfull and cruel revenge…*
> - An Historical Treatise of the Travels of Noah into Europe 58[89]

> *Hercules, assisted by some of his brothers, avenged the death* **of his father by killing Typhon (i.e. Canaan)***, then* **he went around killing other giants as his father had done***…*
> ("From Noah to Dardanus (according to Annius)", 2002, p. 2)[90]

Soon, Canaan - that evil patriarch - was taken out. And, in the same manner of Shem, Asshur, Nynus and Osiris, Hercules began to leave his land of his origin, and do some good for a whole number of nations around him (and, all the while, hunting down a number of prominent deviants everywhere, including those malicious giants)!

Interestingly enough, we also see that this Hercules of old may have had *this* in common with Osiris, as well:

> *Throughout the world's history, the life stories of the supreme Spiritual teachers, or Saviours of mankind, have been so **identical** in incident that a thoughtful comparison of them leads inevitably to the conclusion that to be "**a priest forever after the order of Melchizedek**" is to fill a definite office and to perform a predetermined work in the transmission of spiritual force for the liberation of human souls. For example, the parallelism between the lives of **Hercules** and of Christ is so close that orthodox writers admit Hercules **to have been a typ**e of that which the Christ was to accomplish and to endure.*
> — *The Conte de Gabalis* Hercules[91]

In other words, Hercules (according to a number of ancient orthodox writers) followed along this same pathway as other Godly patriarchs of his day, such as **Shem** (who was also thought to have been the above **Melchizedek**) as well as Osiris (his father) - he tried to be on this "same side" as Christ, plain and simple.

And, through this, it seemed as though the wind was truly at his back, as it was with Osiris. Quite probably, God was on his side! Hercules, then, was able to swoop down, and go into a number of nations, taking out a number of bad elements in the process (including a number of those ancient giants). After this, he, then, began to assume command over the nation… corralling a number of people back onto the "straight and narrow" path.

> *…at which time also (**he** (i.e. Hercules) being in the pride and fullness of fury and choler) **searched out** all corners and places of abode, where any such like bloody and impious giants, rulers, and commanders, kept their tyrannical and uncivil governments…*
> — *An Historical Treatise of the Travels of Noah into Europe* 58[92]

After these victories, Hercules seemed to have become the "final say" in a vast number of nation/states. When Hercules arrived in France, for example, he "was welcomed because of his many exploits around Europe… and became their king."[93] He also went to Spain, and the welcome was much of the same. The people in Spain actually built a temple in his honor, after his eventual death.

*In solemn remembrance of whose generally deplored death, the people of
Spain erected many most sumptuous and costly monuments, and bestowed upon
him a wonderful, rich and stately tomb, which as some hold, was built hard by that
place, which as we now call them, the Gades, pillars, or columns of Hercules are
seated upon, being not far from the famous straits of Gibraltar. Unto him also
after his death they attributed very godlike honours, and terms of veneration and
reverence; so was he possessed while he lived among mortals, with the love and
opinion of all those people thereabouts, and wheresoever else he had governed
and commanded.*
      - *An Historical Treatise of the Travels of Noah into Europe* 60[94]

And, yes, this could have been the *same* Hercules by which the Spaniards would name those two mountains after, near the mouth of the Mediterranean - those "Pillars of Hercules" (near the continent of Atlantis)! Wow. Go figure. It's so interesting to see how things just begin to "take shape" here, once when we begin to discover all of the information that may have been left out of our contemporary, historical narrative!

And, in all of this, we'll now discover that his efforts were not yet over. He wasn't dead, not yet. He still had a lot of living and conquering to do! Yes, Hercules truly became known for making waves, all around the world - "fighting the good fight"... and winning! He wasn't taking very many prisoners.

Yet, on top of all of these victories, there seemed to be *one* more obstacle that Hercules would have his eye on - one more area that was in need of a massive purge.

Hercules, son of Osiris, whose name is Lybius... turned to the tyrants of **Italy**...
*In Italy he made war for ten years and expelled the Laestrygonians, and for
twenty years after that he reigned among them peacefully...*
      (Asher, 1993, p. 221)[95]

Another reversal, here! After the time that Italy had, once again, begun to fall into a bit of disarray (after Noah's death), it was Hercules who would, eventually, be able overcome this negative situation, and take it all over.[96] Now, this mighty individual would go over to the land of Italy, and "clean house," one more time, directing the people of Italy (most probably) *back*, in the direction of Noah's earlier vision.

...after all tumults quieted, and the resistants subdued, he fell to peaceable laws to the people and to instruct them very carefully in matters of civil association & orderly living...
   - An Historical Treatise of the Travels of Noah into Europe 36[97]

...he appointed his son Tuscus as their king.
("From Noah to Dardanus", 2002, p. 2, 5)[98]

Hercules had a son, Tuscus, who was now appointed to be king of the land. Hopefully, he would be able to keep the area on the right side of history, for a long, long time.

As we have begun to see here, a good number of the Ham's descendants, as well as a number of other people (in these formerly-pagan nations), didn't *always* have their heart set on adopting these pagan way… a lot of times, they had a lot of pressure to do so (by peers and leaders alike). A number of these people may have even been in God's corner, *subtly* (even though a number of their rulers may have been among those pagan patriarchs). And, yes, we see that: even if all of these other patriarchs were not *totally* on board with everything Shem fought for, a number of them at least wanted to run things the way he would have run it, and went after common sense values.

Still, at the height of all these Godly conversions, there was still *one* more major patriarch around - one who still could have inflicted some kind of damage to the direction this ship was now sailing. Top pagan patriarchs, as well as a number of giants, were being handed defeat after *defeat*. Would *Ham* still be able to do something about this Godly trend? Would he be able to take back some of the momentum that Hercules (and some of his other freedom fighters) were now enjoying, reviving the pagan cause (at least somewhat)? What was about to happen next?

Ham's "Last Stand"

From previous volumes, we may also recall that Shem, Ham, Japheth and even Noah - those born before the Flood - could have been able to live a lot *longer* than those born after. And, yes, Ham was probably still alive while all of this was going on. He may have even been going strong when a number of his descendants were starting to grow old. Even people like *Nynus* were beginning to feel their age by now. But, Ham, even though he was getting a bit old, may might have had a little gusto left in him… enough for one last "hurrah."

Hercules did a great deal of damage to pagans everywhere, killing giants left and right; and this, assuredly, angered Ham. While in Egypt, and under banishment, Ham could have easily gotten wind of how Nynus - that "miracle" son of Semiramis and Asshur - did a lot of damage to pagan Babylonia as well. This could have indeed been the last straw for him. The sanctity of the ways he remembered, in the lands that he most favored, were all in question. He probably felt that it was time for *something* to be done, by someone… so, he probably concluded that *he* was one of the only ones left who could actually make some kind of difference.

Now, in an attempt to change this balance of power, Ham decided to set out, to make another stand for his pagan cause. He, as we may recall, did have a number of things going for him, however. We already know that he retained a lot of that forbidden, antediluvian knowledge of the occult, as well as dark rituals and magic. And, he probably figured that *now* might be the perfect time to capitalize on some of it. And, with a number of people he was able to bring on board, another battle would soon be underway:

…Camesenuus (i.e. Ham), driven out by almost the whole world, had taken himself off to the Bactrians: and he **had bound them** *to himself with* **magical trickery**, *to such an extent that he ruled with very great power.*
(Asher, 1993, p. 215)[99]

…he (Ham) subjugated and brought under all those people thereabouts, insomuch as he there reigned in great puissance, pride and mightiness…
- An Historical Treatise of the Travels of Noah into Europe 23[100]

Ham's ideologies, once again, were beginning to take hold, and spread like wildfire with a number of people.

…those factions that Ham had embittered by his (Noah's) example felt suddenly unfettered to do as they pleased. They were no longer constrained to stay in their homeland, but instead they seized power in as many lands as they chose. They enslaved and oppressed their hapless subjects.
(Simpson, 2009, p. 19)[101]

At first, Ham had a few victories, and felt a bit of *pride*, once again. It has been said that he even ended up battling Semiramis, causing her to flee from battle. This, in turn, severely damaged her control over the lands that she was once presiding over.[102]

Next, he began to direct his efforts in the direction of that great warrior *Nynus*, attempting to see how he would be able to do with this fight.

> ...(Ham) yet not with this satisfied, gathereth great troops and armies of men, and invadeth the Assyrians, against whom marcheth their king called Nynus, the young, the son of the before mentioned Semyramis...
> - An Historical Treatise of the Travels of Noah into Europe 23[103]

In actuality, the time had finally come for this era of history to come to a close - all of those militaristic "back and forths" would soon find themselves at an end. Unbeknownst to Ham, Nynus was superior, in regards to his battle tactics - even with Ham's use of magic and the occult sciences![104]

> ...whose fortune was such, as he (Nynus) victoriously triumphed over his enemy Cham (i.e. Ham), suppressing his glory, rule, and haughtiness, he himself being in that battle **slain**, and all the army shamefully discomfited.
> - An Historical Treatise of the Travels of Noah into Europe 23[105]

Yes, Ham was finally taken out, being one of the last major patriarchs of this immediate post-Flood world. Yes, times were changing; and there were not very many players really left in the game, here. Sadly, even Nynus' victory would also be a bit short-lived here, because he was about to die, as well.

> ...but Nynus was superior to fighting him, and slew Camesenuus (i.e. Ham): then shortly afterwards he himself died.
> (Asher, 1993, p. 215)[106]

We're not sure why he died... possibly of old age himself. Regardless of how all of these things went down, this chapter of the world, and all of the "back and forth" that went on, was now at a close, with the righteous people of God holding a slight edge over their pagan adversaries.

The Incredible "Back and Forth"

As we look into it all, and discover how the many dignitaries of the Bible had such a sway over a lot of what happened in this post-Flood world, what a number of us might want to think is: "Wow! What a lot of information to digest, here!" What a lot of irony for us to sort out, as well.

We have, for example, that son of **righteous** Asshur and pagan Semiramis going *full circle*, now acting on behalf of Godly ways, as well as ending the tyranny of that last, infamous patriarch of the post-Flood world (Ham). Go figure. So many strokes of irony, here: he was the one of whom Semiramis claimed to be the "miracle baby" of the pagan cause, and look what he did. This "reincarnation" of Nimrod himself actually turned out to be the one who stopped a lot more damage from coming back into these ancient areas. Who would have ever conceived of endings such as this?

A lot of these stories have amazing endings. Yet (of course), humanists and pagan-leaning historians would probably feel a little embarrassed by a lot of this information, and wouldn't want it to come to the surface, if possible - *especially* anything that may show the proper names of these individuals as being those from the Bible! They also would not want to admit that the one individual - declared their (pagan) "savior" - would actually turn on them, and their entire cause. Nynus, now, left the area once considered the most powerful stronghold of the Serpent's paganism (i.e. *Babylon*) into something that almost wasn't recognizable (to a number of pagans). Nynus also traveled around, reducing giant populations on top of it.

We also had that great pagan god *Osiris* who, in actuality, fought for human decency, common sense rules, and Godly values - all the while colluding with that destructive "God-lover" of the Middle East, **Shem**. Again, this kind of information would not sit very well with a number of modern archaeologists and educators today… so it, as well, had to have been subtly *disappeared*, or even "laughed off!"

We also had a direct son of Osiris, *Hercules*, taking out the evil patriarch Canaan (of the Bible), all the while realigning a number of wayward nations back in the direction of something right, or something Godly... or at least something *other* than these pagan ways of old. That, also, wound not sit very well with a number of these people.

Again, it's so interesting to see how a number of those early pagan "gods" - even their acclaimed "savior" - found themselves as a warriors for the causes of God, or, at least for something different (and better) than what paganism was currently feeding them! It has even been stated that Nynus could have returned to ancient Babylon (a bit before his death) and destroyed the authority of his *own* twisted mother - Semiramis. Some sources stated that he, or another son of Semiramis, could have (eventually) become disgusted by his mother's actions, and her rule, and cut off her head![107] Talk about an "about face!"

Yes, in one way or another, these particular warriors seemed to have "woken up" to what was really going on around them, and began to see things for what they really were. They, at least, saw how messed up the world was becoming, because of paganism as a whole, and decided to act on their own consciences, or their own common sense, to do something about it. We also see a number of Godly people enlightening them to what was truly right (such as **Shem**). Talk about God working in mysterious ways! Here we have it for sure.

No wonder "paganized" historians may have wanted a lot of this information to just "slip way," referring to it as ludicrous, or some kind of forgery. At least, they want to turn it into something that's *against* their archaeological mainstream, so, as a result, it really needs to be promptly discarded. History and legends have, almost always, been subjected to some kind of twists, or manipulations... in order to get everything to fit into some kind of *"paganized"* narrative. We, now, need to accept the ways that *they* might have wanted to shape the past. And, of course, there surely cannot be anything in there that might support the ways of God, or the Bible. Yes, this battle hasn't ended, nor will it... until the "end times" are over.

In today's world, they are, subtly, doing the same type of "book burnings" that once happened in Nazi Germany... just digitally, and just through the manipulation of public opinion. Don't be fooled. Both sides have tried to silence the other, in a number of ways. The Serpent's paganism is very seductive, and easy to adopt... that's what makes it so dangerous. And, yes, this "back and forth" fight has been going on for a number of millennia.

In fact, we also find one of these early patriarchs of the "good fight" trying to remove the forbidden, occult information of those antediluvian Nephilim (i.e. the knowledge that Ham brought through the Flood) from the hands of a number of contemporary pagans:

> *Many writers have affirmed, That this Cham (i.e. Ham) was a man of singular ingenuity and sharp capacity, and that he first found out the seven liberal Sciences, and had wrote many books of* **great worth**, *among which, his chiefest were of Necromancy (i.e. communicating with the dead), of which* **most part of them** **were** **burned** *by the before said* **Nynus**.
> - An Historical Treatise of the Travels of Noah into Europe 24[108]

And, yes, not only do we have *Shem* as the major patriarch of this "good fight," we also have a number of patriarchs after him, doing a lot of the same. We have Asshur and Nynus, as well as Osiris and Hercules - all participating (either directly or indirectly) in fronting the ways of that *true* Father of our universe… and not the father of this lower, darkened world of the fallen, the *Serpent*!

All (Pagan) Roads Lead to Rome?

Now, once we begin to discover just "who" was once "who," and "who" may have actually went "where" (and did "what"), a good amount of this may begin to give us some answers… even answers to a number of lingering questions from those previous two volumes! Yes, we also see how a number of Biblical characters may, actually, have been linked to a whole number of pagan, mythological character - those who were transformed into a number of pagan "gods." And, most importantly, we are beginning to understand the background behind all that would go into the formation of the White Horse. With all of this, we're really starting to unravel a number of those tightly-wound "bundles" of world deception.

This additional knowledge could give us even *more* reasons why people may have eventually wanted to leave ancient Babylon and Egypt (such as the situation with

Abraham's father, Terah), and had the desire to move somewhere else (such as Atlantis). Things might all seem to come together, once we are supplied with a lot of this missing or suppressed information.

Well, where do we go next, then? We've seen a number of these *open* battles. In our next chapter, we will see that: conflicts would begin to manifest themselves in a slightly *different* way. Sure, there would be confrontations, but, this time, the battles would not be so "out in the open," as they were before. This time, the war wouldn't be as clearly defined, with as many "hunters" out there - openly proclaiming their causes with a big army behind them.. We'll soon begin to see how things would become a lot more *subtle* - almost "underground" if you will. The next chapter will also begin to show us the links between this *old* world (and those *old* ways of the Serpent) and what would become the *new* ways of this world - the ways of this White Horse.

But, what exactly would become these *new* ways of confrontation? How can you battle an enemy without really looking as though you are actually fighting them? How will one side end up "toppling," for the most part, the other?

We, soon, will see how subtle that **White Horse** would be able to come onto the scene, over the years; and, we'll also begin to see some of the early "tricks" of its trade. We'll also see how this horse would end up being able to use a number of *systems* to help it along the way - subtly, take over all things *Godly*.

Chapter 8

More Corruption… in Rome and in Judaism

But, again: *how* could this all begin to work? Well, to begin, we may really need to understand just how important the control of the *Italian Peninsula* was, to those on both sides of this religious "coin." We'll also begun to discover how the development of ancient *Rome* was, once again, very important to the establishment of this White Horse.

We've already discovered how a number of pagans seemed to have had the desire to go into a particular Godly area (such as Italy), and conquer it - setting up shop there for a good, long time (under the pagan "flag," if you will). In the future , we'll eventually see that the new "flag" of dominance wound not be something *overtly* pagan (or something "out in the open"), but, rather, something that might look, more or less, a bit **Godly**! Yes, *this* would become the new "battle plan" - their new way of attacking their enemy! We already recall what Semiramis did, after Nimrod was cut into pieces… and, it worked (at least for a little while) This technique seemed to have been the enemy would begin to perpetuate itself, and penetrate the moral foundations of those who follow God. This, of course, would give rise to a number of those *White Horse* systems. Simple.

No more outward battles of good versus evil, Godly verses pagan. The next set of battles would be something on the *inside*, for the **soul** of a city, nation, and its people. As we'll now see, there would, eventually, be more than *one* "Godly" option for people to choose - things wouldn't be as "cut and dry" anymore! Now, a number of these other "ways to God" might, at first, sound quite wholesome, and even "Christ-like"… but, in the end, they all won't really seem to pan out (overall)! Yes, this represent the *core* of how the next fight would proceed.

The New (& Roman) Pathway

And now, we'll begin to see how a few succeeding rulers of *Rome* began to manipulate a good number of people already living there, using some of those same stealth tactics (and twisted dogmas) we've just mentioned, in the above. Sadly, over time, the Italian Peninsula would, once again, begin to fall under some kind of pagan "umbrella;" and, this time, their "flag" would end up *staying* there... for a long, long time!

In previous volumes, we also delved into the city of *Rome*, and how a number of people stemming from it would, eventually, begin to adopt the influences of a very famous character of the Bible: Jacob's brother **Esau**. We discovered how this entire area, through his descendants, would eventually be turned into a pagan stronghold. Yes, those sons of Esau - the **Edomites** - would eventually have their fingerprints all over what would become of Rome next, and a lot of what they would end up conquering.

In one example of this, we'll see that the major struggle of this area would be between those Edomites of Esau and another son of Esau's father Isaac: *Jacob*. Of course, most of us know how this particular patriarch would have been the one who would go on to sire those **12 tribes of Israel**. Wow, this sounds like it could be a major battle brewing... and, yes, it was. Once this particular confrontation would begin to get off the ground, the war between these two brothers (and their descendants) would, seemingly, *never* end.

The following quote will give us a good idea of the new battle that was about to emerge, here:

> *He (Shem) said to her (Rebekah, mother of Esau and Jacob): "My daughter, I confide a secret to thee. See to it that none finds it out. Two nations are in thy womb, and how should thy body contain them, seeing that **the whole world** will **not** be large enough for them to exist in it together peaceably?"*
> (S. Baring-Gould, 1881, p. 217)[1]

Yes, these conflicts are yet to come, and are just over the horizon. But, for now, we need to see how Rome was about to be prepped for such a battle. We recall, from the last chapter, how there was a lot of *stiff competition* between the patriarchal followers of

Godly ways and the ways of the post-Flood, pagan peddlers… it was all-out *physical* combat! We had a few good men out there, such as Shem and Asshur, towing the line for God. We were also introduced to the strategic importance of this Italian Peninsula, and how the city of **Rome** was starting to become symbol of a good many things… most importantly, the spiritual battle between all that was Godly and all that was *not so* Godly. There was a lot of "back and forth" here, and whomever was able to "raise their flag" above this particular stronghold seemed to have been considered the people with the "upper hand."

We also remember that (in the past): there were valiant attempts of Godly people to go after a number of those sacrilegious patriarchs, as well as exterminate a number of those deviant giants. The influences of these same individuals (as we know) helped to influence a vast number of people into the same mindset as Cain and the Serpent. Yet, even though these Godly patriarchs were able to cleanse a whole number of ancient areas (at least somewhat), a number of them would, eventually, end up going back, into the same direction. And, as we've also recall, the battles that were openly waged would no longer be considered as "out in the open," but a lot more subtle. Let's see what would begin to go down now.

Enter a few *new* celebrities of God's choosing: the famous *Abraham*, for example, and his son *Isaac*. We'll also begin to delve into Abraham's grandsons *Jacob* (a.k.a. *Israel*) and his twin brother *Esau*. It will be through these two brothers that the *next* generational battle would take place… and Rome, once again, would be a *major* hub of influence and spiritual exploitation (believe it or not)!

There's so much more that will go on, in regards to this struggle (as we shall soon see). The Babylonian mantle, and spirit of Cain's ancient *Babylon*, would continue to be passed on, beyond the world just after the Flood. It would now morph into something of "new ownership."

That Trend Downward, Once Again

We recall from the previous chapter that Hercules' son Tuscus ended up ruling Italy after his father "cleansed" the area, at least for a while. As he ruled, he tried to keep it away from corruption and pagan domination. But, eventually, his government began to falter some, and the land began to go right back in a pagan direction. The funny thing about this all is: this deviation may have begun to take place right around the *same* time the "friend of God" - Abraham - was born! Yes, it seemed that: even though Rome was beginning to go down, once again, a new **powerhouse** of God was about to come on the scene, gearing up the world for whatever would come next!

Also, with the development of these new characters, we'll begin to understand how a lot of this White Horse corruption would come about. There wouldn't be that many physical battles. There wouldn't be a lot of valiant warriors, fronting Godly principles. No. The top pagan brass would, in actuality, begin to fight their enemy by subtly *usurping* those the Godly faith - destroying them *from within*. They would begin their deeds slowly and stealthily, and right out from under the noses of all who may want to oppose them. It will, eventually, be able to work that well! Those up-and-coming Children of Israel (i.e. Jacob), and a number of other God-followers (in spirit), were about to be "sized up" by this new method of their warfare.

The New, "Spiritual" War

Now, there would be a "slow-but-sure" manipulation of Godly principles and theology, twisting around things into a new, and *warped*, vision of what (formerly) was considered right. Man, eventually, would be thought of as the new "measurer of all things," not God. Pagan ideals would also seep into almost everything that was once pure and Godly. These additional "pieces of the pie" would truly become a vital part of the next pagan strategy - to infiltrate whatever made up these Judeo-Christian elements, and adulterate them at their cores, They, soon, would be able to just change a few things around (just a little), which would *still* allow something to *seem* Godly, with just a few differences now It's almost like a *generic* version of a popular drug - they may look the same, and also may seem to work the same (almost), but is not the original. And, yes, this all epitomizes the White Horse to a tee! This will be directly related to how the *antichrist* system would rise in power, in the future, and be able to fool so many. This modus operandi actually originated way back in time, in these earliest of eras.

So, now, in order to advance into this *next* step of manipulation, we'll need to recall those two "atrocities" of the White Horse (in the Bible): **hunger** and **famine**. We already know how they, most probably, refer to one's own *spiritual* hunger, or *starvation*, more than anything else, really. It's not that *every* person who begins to practice under the White Horse would become *financially* poor (even though a good number may); most, in actuality, will end up becoming quite poor in *mind* and *soul* - lacking the proper *spiritual* nutrition.

Again, why would those heading this White Horse want to do this? It's simple: in order to take the people of God down *now*, they need to cause a person to feel spiritually *hungry*, *unfulfilled*, even starving.

Those aristocrats representing the White Horse may still look pure, or as *white* as snow, on the outside, but, after a while, their entire experience would begin to usher in an era of misdoubt or confusion. Their hybrid messages would, eventually, be able to draw millions of people in (because of its "politically correct" exterior, or it "Godly shell"); yet (as we recall from previous volumes), we will now see why God would end up "hating" Esau - the founder of the people who would end up pushing this sacrilegious way of thinking and doing things onto the people. God actually *hated* him (in *Mal.* 3:1 and *Rom.* 9:13)! He does not like people who *act* in the ways He may want them to act, or speak in the ways He may want them to speak - only to turn a lot of individuals into *another* deviant direction, away from Him. These people become the worst of the worst.

Eventually, these methods of the White Horse would go on to became the *pinnacle* of all ungodly attempts to take over the righteousness of people, as well as their foundations… in order to bring it all *down*. Sad but true.

A Lot Like "Those of the Cloth"

As we also recall (from a previous section), there would eventually be a number of religious "**predators**" or "**whores**" out there, acting righteous on the surface; but, in the end, working to defraud people left and right. Some may consciously know what they're doing, and that they are hurting seekers in the process (or, even that they are doing something for the sake of the Serpent's paganism). Others may not consciously know;

they may just be doing what they are doing in order to *get something* out of it (materialistically). Regardless, both will end up hurting people, and both will end up behaving like wolves in sheep's clothing.

We may recall verses such as the following:

Beware of false prophets, which come to you in **sheep's** *clothing, but inwardly they are ravening wolves.* - *Mat.* 7:15 (KJV)

Even so ye also outwardly appear righteous unto men, but within ye are full of **hypocrisy** *and* **iniquity**. - *Mat.* 23:28 (KJV)

If we really think about it, some of the *worst* examples of people out there are those who end up becoming so hypocritical - or, those who come off as so good, or holy, or as "shepherds;" but, in actuality, they are quite the opposite. This will be what we will see coming out of *Edom*, quite a lot.

Jesus, so often, called out these religious hypocrites, and exposed them - even back in *his* day! Yes, the White Horse has been forming into what it was for a long time! In Jesus' time, the elites of the White Horse would go around, touting themselves as "shepherds of righteousness." Many would come off as only out for a "good," humanitarian cause... helping people from themselves. But, of course, deep down inside, a number of them were only filled with "dead men's bones" (Mat. 23:27).

The Priestly-Cainite Conglomerate - A Redux

And the families ***of the scribes*** *which dwelt at Jabez; the Tirathites, the Shimeathites, and Suchathites.* ***These*** *are* ***the Kenites****...*
- *1 Chr.* 2:55 (KJV)

Now, in order to get a little background into what may have worked to corrupt the sons of Jacob (i.e. Israel) a long time ago, we need to recall a bit of information from previous volumes. As we may already recall, there were *two* fronts working on the ancient Israelis, corrupting them and trying to take them over: the descendants of *Cain* and the descendants of *Esau*.

First, the Kenites (or, post-Flood Cainites) were already beginning to darken the faith of Judaism via the priestly route (as we see in the verse above). They began their apostasy by assimilating themselves into the early priesthood, as **scribes** - mere assistants. But, over time, they would become more and more powerful - doing their best to gather more and more control (and, ultimately, corrupt the faith more and more, over time).

In the New Testament, we see Jesus speaking to a group of fellow Jews, as well as some religious scribes and Pharisees:

<u>John 8</u>:
38 *I speak that which I have seen with my Father: and ye do that which ye have seen with **your father**.*
39 *They answered and said unto him, Abraham is our father. Jesus saith unto them, If ye were Abraham's children, ye would do the works of Abraham.*
40 *(Jesus continuing) But now ye seek to kill me, a man that hath told you the truth...*
41 *Ye do the deeds of your father. Then said they to him, We... have one Father, even God.*
42 *Jesus said unto them, If God were your Father, ye would love me...*
43 *(Jesus continuing) Why do ye not understand my speech? even because ye cannot hear my word.*
44 *Ye are of your father (Cain) the **devil** (i.e. an all-around, moral deviant), and the lusts of your father (Cain) ye will do. He was a murderer from the beginning...*
45 *And because I tell you the truth, ye believe me not.*
47 *He that is of God heareth God's words: **ye therefore hear them not**, because ye are **not of God**.*

Wow, what was he saying here... *really* saying? He was clearly saying that these people were not of God, in a couple of ways - morally, as well as **physically**! Really, we see that they were probably of Cain and his ways - morally, as well as physically! This entire exchange does seem to mirror almost *all* of what we're been talking about previously... this time, it comes straight out of Jesus' mouth!

We also recall that the title of *devil* could relate to any kind of deviant being, or immoral fallen angel (and not only the Serpent) And, we may also recall how the Kenites were considered the post-Flood descendants of Cain. What Jesus was saying seemed so easy to understand. Things couldn't have been much more clear, here... except if someone is purposely trying to "look the other way."

Slowly but surely those Kenites would begin to inject themselves further and further into the faith, and elevate themselves more and more, into prominent positions over time. Especially when the Jews were exiled by the Babylonians of Nebuchadnezzar (in 586 B.C.), these same scribes "took on important duties and filled powerful roles."[2] Yes, beyond just being copyists, they, eventually, would become educated teachers and experts of the law - elevated to the same professional level as one might view a lawyer, today.

Yet, so many of them were actually impostors... *not* Godly dignitaries at the core, but *Kenites*, or at least Kenites at heart. They were not looking out for the Messiah, but looking for ways to hold onto their *own* power. They did not care about doing what was right by their constituents, but selfishly looked to hold onto oral traditions (and traditions that were able to do right by *them*). They truly were, for the most part, hypocrites of their day... pressuring the people into conformity by the inherent fears in religion. Simple as that.

Another thing that we may need to remember about this whole scenario is: the problem with early Judaism, once again, is in regards to those *at the top* - those whores and predators of the faith - not everyone. The rest of the people following them were, for the most part, trying to do what they were told. The problem was the upper crust, or the top 1-3%... back then (as well as today).

Jesus had a lot more to say to these individuals, which was much of the same:

Mat. 23:
33 Ye **serpents**, ye **generation of vipers**, *how can ye escape the damnation of hell?*
34 *Wherefore, behold, I send unto you prophets, and wise men, and scribes: and some of them ye shall kill and crucify; and* some *of them shall ye scourge in your synagogues, and persecute* them *from city to city:*
35 *That upon you may come **all the righteous blood shed upon the earth, from the blood of righteous <u>Abel</u>** unto the blood of Zacharias son of Barachias, whom <u>**ye slew**</u> between the temple and the altar.*

Mat. 12:
> 34 *O **generation of vipers**, how can ye, being evil, speak good things? for out of the abundance of the heart the mouth speaketh.*

Here we go again! The religious authority of Jesus' time were actually represented by those who, in one way or another, came from a ***serpent***, and were from the one who actually shed the righteous blood of **Abel**! Now, who could that have been? Who *else* could that have been?

We notice how Jesus wasn't exactly trying to say things in a figurative sense, here; he was talking about their *generations*. Again, so much of this begins to unravel… once we begin to understand the whole *rest of the story*, and entire background of what we've been missing, here.

Jacob the Israeli Vs. Esau the Edomite

> *When Rebekah passed before a synagogue **Jacob** made great efforts to escape into the world, when she passed near an **idol Esau** became excited and desired to come forth.*
> (S. Baring-Gould, 1881, p. 217)³

Beyond the early corruption of this priesthood, people set out to make things worse - a lot worse. As we look into our next level of deception (of the Jews), we'll begin to see that, even in the womb (in the above phrase) there would be unborn **Jacob**, already bursting with the desires to learn more about the ways of God. And there would be the other baby, Esau, bursting with the desire to learn more about the ways of the "Other Side." Their destinies seemed to have be upon them, even before birth. And, the latter would, of course, help to push the corruption of the *Kenite* even further and further into the minds of the *true* Jewish people - actually inscribing it all on a much deeper (and even more *spiritual*) level, as we'll soon see. We actually have the twin brother of Israel himself, trying to twist things around a bit - you can't get much closer to true Israel than that! How could the Jews stop this onslaught? Would they even be able to? What damages could this twin brother (and his descendants) end up doing to the wholesome Israeli people, over the years?

The following information will become **extremely important**, in order to help us understand - not only the further corruption of the Israeli people - but a link to the development of this White Horse, as well. And, of course, most of this information may not sound too good to a lot of those already corrupted by this subtle onslaught, but, we really need to carry on here… for the sake of those *true* sons of Jacob who were already affected, and taken over. They need to have a voice.

After that initial corruption of the (ancient) Israeli religious aristocracy (by those early Kenites), we'll now begin to see all of what damage **Esau** (and his descendants) would be able to do. We may already recall (from previous volumes) how **10** out of the original 12 Israeli tribes were already taken away by the ancient Assyrians. And, we also know what may have (most probably) happened to them after this - they escaped, and ended up traveling north (through the Caucasus Mountains), never again to be officially thought of by their aforementioned tribal names. This leaves us with two tribes left- the tribes of Judah and Benjamin (i.e. the *Jews*). And, as we'll soon see, a number of these ancient Edomites once resided in close proximity to these last two tribes; and some would go on, to live a lot farther away. But, *both*, however, had set out for this same end-result (against their Jewish brethren) - eventual *domination*.

"Israeli" and "Anti-Israeli"

The descendants of these two brothers, as one might guess, would continue on, with their animosity towards each other. They, assuredly, had no love loss, over time. Why? What's behind all of this anger and vengeance? Well, once again, we see that (in the Bible) Esau actually had lost his birthright to his brother - that valuable piece of human privilege - by selling it for a pot of **beans**. This birthright enables the son to become a "special protégé" of God, if you will, with a number of privileges given to him - something of immense, intangible importance to the people of ancient times.

And, ever since this early time, the battle between these two would become the battle over *which* son would have been considered the "children of promise," or those chosen to be under "God's covenant" - it's a simple as that. And, ever since their patriarch Esau gave it all away, those **Edomite** descendants began to strive after getting it all back. And, if those ancient Israelites were to be the ones of whom God would call to follow Him from now on, then the goal of these Edomites, of course, would be to *usurp*, this mandate, in any way possible… and, somehow, take over. And **that's** what, in actuality, had happened… many, many years ago.

Assuredly, there was a lot of scorn for the current birthright-holder here. And, because those Edomites held onto such negativity here, the ancient Israelites really needed to be able to "watch their backs" at all time… because an attempted disruption, and assimilation, would be ever-present. Sadly, the Edomites would never give up… until they began to overthrow all of what God might have originally planned for the Jews to represent.

As we'll soon see:

"…the counterfeit always wants to kill the real thing…"
　　　　　　　The Alex Jones Radio Program (12/7/16)[4]

Yes, the Edomites would, slowly, begin to have more and more skin in the game, in their attempts to "counterfeit" the original. All it would take would be a few opportunities for them to enter in the Jewish fold, and begin to "take over." This was serious stuff, and the Edomites played for keeps, and wouldn't let up until they got what they wanted.

With this drive, things would, eventually, become pretty bad that most of the Jews, over time… if they allowed these Edomites a way "in." Ultimately, they would slowly begin to lose their own identities in this entire process, if they began to fall to this corruption, over time.

Eventually, the Edomites would work to be able to call *themselves* the "chosen nation." And, if we think about it: who really wouldn't mind moving themselves into a better situation? Who wouldn't mind being able to call *themselves* the "blessed" people of God… if they could get away with it? And, yes: that is, most probably, what happened here, to the last two tribes, over time. Sad to say.

Don't be fooled by so much of the flowery rhetoric we hear nowadays. Don't be fooled with the attempts of people to stifle the exposure of these elements of their history and faith. There was a dark history of Jewish subversion here, over time... and, as we'll soon see, their own works even admit this! Be careful of those who always try to hush" up any independent research, here, in regards to this all. Of course, there would be a number of people out there - in our ancient past (and present) - who would have been more than happy to try to hide all of this.

Also, many contemporary Jews, most probably, do not really understand the veracity of *what* may had slowly overtaken them, over time. They may not understand just how *bad* this counterfeit wanted to assimilate them, and ultimately destroy them. Sometimes, things take time. And, yes, this slow assimilation took over two thousand years... so, it's almost as though the very mention of these things might sound absurd today, and totally out of sorts... but, as we'll soon see, history seems to be telling us something *otherwise*.

So, with all of this information at hand, our task now is to discover just *how* those ancient Edomites began to ready themselves for their next "plateau," and how they were slowly able to do it.

...They Said They Were!

Eventually, to be able to masquerade themselves off as Jews, and ascend themselves, once again, into the position where they "thought" they should have originally been, they'll need to do a few manipulations, and a few subtle assimilations. They would need to slither *their* own ways into the entire Jewish process, as well as even the Jewish people, over time... until their take over was near completion.

As we'll also see, the Edomites would also end up using **White Horse** tactics to achieve their assimilation, and ultimate domination. As we may recall, these same techniques could be used for the subtle systems of *antichrist*. **Both** may act in ways that seem something like Christ might want to do. Both would pass themselves off as followers of all things Christ-like, or Godly; but, a number ways that they go about things, and what they seem to really be about (in the end), are not really typical (as they had been before). They take down the real thing with a slightly-twisted version of the former truths! They're chameleons. They are counterfeits... only out for themselves, and their deeper cause. They represent the classic definition of what an *imposter* is.

As we also recall, in the book of Revelation, we discover:

*...I know the blasphemy of them which **say they are** Jews, and are not, but are the synagogue of Satan.*
- Rev. 2:9 (KJV)

*...(they) **say they are** Jews, and are not, but do **lie**...*
- Rev. 3:9 (KJV)

Someone apparently knew that there would be some kind of corruption within the Jewish ranks, as well as the people, over time. Why would some people eventually want to lie about being Jews? No one would really need to lie about being *themselves*, right? We will understand about these two verses soon enough; but, for now, let's just begin to identify these phony individuals by a name: the "**EJC**s," or *Edomites in **J**ewish **C**lothing*. Yes, the problem with the Jewish world would now be these *Edomite* impostors - those who now want to step into their former shoes, and claim themselves as the real thing. And, in the upcoming material, we will begin to use this acronym quite a bit. It will make things a lot easier, and also differentiate those supplanters of the true Jews (and all of what they might stand for) from the real thing.

We may be able to compare this title to a number of those so-called "Republicans" out there (in U.S. politics), known as "RINOs," or "**R**epublicans **I**n **N**ame **O**nly." This, once again, is practically the same thing. A number of these politicians *claim* to be on the Republican side, but really don't stand for the values that the republican party holds, and usually votes for. In fact, they usually end up siding with opposing (i.e. Democrat) party! It's a lot of the same, here: the "EJCs" (or Edomite Impostors) often "talk a good talk" within the Jewish community. They may seem as though they are the same as every other Jew. They may even *look* the same part, doing practically the same things as a typical Jewish person may have once did; but, deep down inside, they are **not** of the same blood, nor would a lot of what they practice be what God may have wanted the Jewish people to participate in, ultimately. Ideological "cracks" would, slowly, begin to show up. Their "true colors" would eventually begin to show through, over time. They will begin to *sway* their Jewish peers in a number of alternate, or even opposing, moral directions - things that, overall, do not really seem to be of God (as they were before).

Much like the theological invasion of those Kenites into the Israeli priesthood, the invasion of the Jewish people *themselves* was a long, long process! And now, we've also can see why Jesus had so many theological issues with, not only the religious aristocracy of the time, but also a large number of people around him... the corruption of the **people** was already underway! There were reasons why people on both extremes - the religious and the **political** - wanted him dead... even as an infant!

Because of this all, we find ourselves in a bit of a dilemma, today: just *how* may we begin to identify the two elements of this Jewish faith (and the people) - the original and the **imposter**... especially when there has been almost a near-perfect assimilation? Again, the best way to really understand just "who was who" (and "who" still is "who") is to look at their *thoughts*, their *deeds* and their *actions* - their "fruits." Jesus, once again, was the thorn in the side of this total assimilation, by saying: "ye shall know them **by their fruits**" (Mat 7:16). This, essentially, tells it all. That is the answer; so, don't be fooled. What they preach, and in what *direction* they end up trying to take you, could indeed be two different things. And, this is a good way to spot how much the "wheat" has been infiltrated by the "tares" - another plant that may stand right alongside them, but are different. This was also, of course, why so many of the Jews around Jesus wanted him dead, overall. Jesus was exposing them... doing his Father's work.

*(God speaking)... I have made Esau bare, I have uncovered his **secret** places.*
- Jer. 49:10 (KJV)

Zepho's Revenge

To discover more of this assimilation, let's begin by looking a bit more into those early Edomites, and how they were able to start their whole "transformation" process. We, once again, return to the history of *Rome*, and re-examine another ancient character of the Bible (as well as his fellow constituents), who began to get the whole assimilation process off the ground.

Some time had passed since the decline of those great warrior patriarchs (of the previous chapter). Things seemed to settle down in Italy also, quite a lot. But, instability would soon raise its ugly head, once again. In previous volumes, we may recall the story of **Zepho** the Edomite, and his rise to power in the Italian Peninsula. Yes, those Edomites were even able to end up migrating into areas around ancient Rome, to manipulate things in the area once again! Esau's descendant *Zepho* would, eventually, be known as a major player in one more attempt to recapture the entire area (for the pagan cause). And, this time, there's a bit more to the story that needs to be told, so let's begin.

Most of the following story comes from the ancient *Book of Jasher*, which tells us so much about how Rome would end up developing into the militaristic powerhouse it once was. This text also gives us the *Edomite* connection to this all, and how *they* were the ones who, eventually, would be were able to infuse enough power, majesty, and overall military *might* into this early city… in order for it to "take off."

Let's begin our venture, by discovering how much Zepho and his fellow Edomites hated the children of Israel, and how they were planning to "take them out" (if the opportunity would ever arise). The Edomite attack on those last two (Jewish) tribes would, eventually, be coming from *two* fronts: one would be the Edomites who began to infiltrate ancient **Rome** and the other would be those Edomites who lived right next door to the last two tribes (in the Holy Land). First, let's get into the little-known story of how a number of Edomites would go on to eventually transform Rome, into the great enemy of the Jewish people - through *Zepho*. This will give us our *first* reveal.

As we might already recall (from previous volumes), a number of Edomites would end up leaving the areas around the Holy Land, and expanding outward (into different directions). Some of them would end up going north, or northwestward. Some would end up settling near a mountain known as *Seir* (at the southern end of the Holy Land). Still others ended up just to the immediate south of where a vast majority of the Jews were currently staying. From all of this, the possibility may even exist for a number of Edomites to migrate farther and farther away, and into the vicinity of Noah's *Italy*… all led by this famous grandson of Esau, *Zepho*.

We'll soon see how, in a whole number of ways, this Zepho would have begun to "take over the reins" of all that represents government on this Italian Peninsula… taking over where Cush, Ham and the rest of those ancient giants had left off! Yes, even though these incoming Edomites might not have *directly* moved into this land in mass numbers, and displaced everyone already there, they may have used their authority to manipulate the people at large… causing *them* do their bidding. They may have begun to teach these natives how to *fight*, assembling them into an early, militaristic force.

Of course, some of these Edomite invaders may have interbred with the locals as well. And, as we'll also see, *they* would have ended up becoming the "puppeteers" over all the land, after on. They would become the ones *indirectly* behind the many transformations of this entire Roman city, over time.

> …'[True,] you have not stolen, [but tell us] who was your partner in the theft; you have not killed, but **who was your accomplice** in the murder.' (Midrash Rabbah - Bereishit 37:2)
>
> ("Nimrod", n. d., p. 4)[5]

As we see (in the above quote), a person could be considered guilty of a crime, even though they weren't directly responsible for the crime themselves. It is the same here, with these Edomites. They were, not entirely, the Roman people at large - they were just the ones who ended up providing a majority of the anti-Jewish influence, as well as militaristic backing. Yes, their additions helped to set Rome into motion, as a major militaristic power. In this way, they became the *new* spirit behind Rome's eventual transformation into a great force of their time… one of the greatest of the ancient world.

Let's look a bit more into that famous descendant of Esau, and how he began to transform this city into that antithesis of Israel it had once become:

> …*These are the children of* **Esau** *who were born to him in the land of Canaan; and the sons of Eliphaz the son of Esau were Teman, Omar,* **Zepho**…"
> - *Book of Jasher* 36:23[6]

Zepho - the grandson of Esau - was also mentioned in the Bible (in Gen. 36:11). And, as we now will see: constant warfare would exist, between the sons of Jacob and the sons of Esau early on. It had already become the *norm*, with a great deal of animosity emanating from the two peoples. Zepho began his militaristic campaign by feeling a little outraged with a few sons of Jacob (i.e. Israel) early on! Let's discover what happened.

Taken into Egypt

Many of us may already know about the story of *Joseph* in the Bible: Joseph, a direct son of Israel himself, was sold into slavery by his eleven (tribal) brothers. And, because of this, he eventually ended up as a slave in Egypt. We may also remember that, while Joseph was in Egypt, the pharaoh began to realize how special this man seemed to have been. He sensed that Joseph had God on his side, and ended up elevating Joseph into his own cabinet, to hold one of the highest positions in the land.

Apparently, sometime after Joseph's eleven brothers decided to go into Egypt as well (because of a famine), there were also a number of *Edomites* who apparently did a lot of the same. Now, there were both Israelites and Edomites in this same land, living right alongside one another. But, the land - most all of it - was still under the control of the pharaoh's friend Joseph (to a degree), and Joseph didn't exactly agree to the Edomites living right next door to his people.

Once again, scuffles began to break out between the two groups:

> *And the battle was heavy between them, and the sons of Esau were smitten before the sons of Jacob, and the sons of Jacob slew of the sons of Esau eighty men, and not one died of the people of the sons of Jacob; and the hand of Joseph prevailed over all the people of the sons of Esau, and* **he (Jacob) took Zepho**, *the son of Eliphaz, the son of Esau, and fifty of his men captive, and he bound them with chains of iron, and gave them into the hand of his servants to bring them to Egypt.*
> - Book of Jasher 57:2[7]

Talk about bad blood! These sons of Jacob were, at first, able to subdue a number of those neighboring Edomites, and made their lives a lot harder. Even Zepho was in that same position.⁸ And, with the clout that Joseph retained over the land, as well as the overall likability of those sons of Jacob by the Egyptian elite, the children of Esau were no longer able to fare there... very well at all.

There was more:

> *Joseph (Yuya) saw that Esau's descendents were prospering in their slavery and he decided to put them **in iron shackles** to tire them as they worked...*
> ("Zepho, Balaam, Jannes & Jambres pt 1", 2015, p. 3)⁹

Maybe the Israelites feared that their angry brethren were always (at least on a subliminal level) "out to get them;" so, maybe they felt that a few "preemptive strikes" here were a good way to stop any of them from being usurped, and took over. Maybe they were right about their fears and assumptions. Nevertheless, these Edomites began to be beat down - *hard* - as an entire group. And Joseph, with all of the clout he had over the Egyptian people, probably found it a bit easy to pull something like this off.

We also have this:

> *(Chapter 57:3...) And it came to pass when the **sons of Jacob had taken Zepho** and his people captive, all those that remained were **greatly afraid** of their lives from the house of Esau, lest they should also be taken captive, and they all fled with Eliphaz the son of Esau and his people, with Esau's body, and they went on their road to Mount Seir." Here we see that Jacob (Acrisius) and his sons actually defeated and enslaved Zepho with fifty of the descendents of Esau (Proetus). The remaining Edomites fled to Mount Seir led by Eliphaz, taking the dead body of Esau. Zepho and... fifty men were sold into slavery in Egypt.*
> ("Zepho, Balaam, Jannes & Jambres pt 1", 2015, p. 1-3)¹⁰

It also seems as though the Edomites who were not taken away, here, and made captive, were able to flee, and head up towards a mountain named Mount Seir. Yet, Zepho was not able to escape; and, obviously, was not thinking very highly about the ancient Israelites around him by this time. He, most probably, had become very distraught about situation that he (and his fellow brethren) were now in... and wanted revenge.

His Escape

And it came to pass at the end of many days and years, when the children of Esau were dwelling quietly in their land with **Bela** *their king, that the children of Esau were fruitful and multiplied in the land, and they resolved to go and fight with the sons of Jacob and all Egypt, and to deliver their brother Zepho, the son of Eliphaz, and his men, for they were yet in those days slaves to Joseph.*
- Book of Jasher 58:14[11]

Tensions seemed to have remained high, especially as far as how a certain number of Edomites may have felt about the situations that they were in. Eventually, the time had come for Joseph to die; and, now, things were about to change:

After Joseph's death Zepho escaped Egypt and went to Africa, to Aegneus king of Carthage.
("Esau, Edom, Rome, and the Christians", 2016, p. 2)[12]

So, it seems that, after Zepho was able to flee to Africa, he (and a number of Edomite bretheren) came across a leader called Aegneus. Aegneus took them in, and began to feel highly of Zepho. He even made him captain of his host. After getting along with him for a long while, Zepho had the idea to go back to Egypt, and carry out some sort of revenge against the people of Israel, and the leadership that Joseph once belonged to. Aegneus, however, did not want any part of it, but, rather, had Zepho go and invade the Italian peninsula instead - the land of Chittim/Kittim (a.k.a. Italy).[13]

It's interesting to see how this African leader tried to send his new comrade Zepho into Italy, to allow him to be able to move onto bigger and better things. Yet, Zepho still had the past on his mind:

*And Zepho enticed Angeas king of Africa to collect all his army to go and fight with the Egyptians, and with the sons of Jacob, and to avenge of them the cause of their bretheren. But Angeas would **not listen** to Zepho to do this thing, for Angeas knew the strength of **the sons of Jacob**, and what they had done to **his** army in their warfare with the children of Esau... and he (Zepho) continually enticed them to make war against Egypt, but **they would not**."*
- Book of Jasher 60:4-6[14]

For a while, it seemed that, even though Zepho was stuck where he was at, he was able to turn the land of Italy (i.e. Kittim) into something fairly significant (on the world's stage). When we look at Rome today, we could easily guess that it had a long, involved history. Would Zepho, once again, turn Rome into something that would, in the end, be advancing paganism, or would it still stay on a Godly plane? Would he be satisfied with having control over this region, or would he begin to work on the *other* cause in the back of his mind?

Adding in those Doctrines of Balaam

Our story continues with another interesting piece of character plot development.

In Chapter 61, we find that **Balaam the Magus (i.e. a witch, magician, etc.)** *is 15 years old and in the service of Angeas, the king of Africa. Zepho then betrayed Angeas because he would not go to war with the sons of Jacob in Egypt based on the prophecy of the young Balaam.*
("Zepho, Balaam, Jannes & Jambres pt 1", 2015, p. 4)[15]

Yes, for those who may be a bit familiar with the Bible, we see that this might have very well been that same (infamous) *Balaam* mentioned in the Old Testament (e.g. Num. 24:1). He was an individual that God didn't particularly like. In fact, He openly *despised* this individual... on the same level as He would despise Cain and Esau.

Woe unto them! for they have gone in the way of Cain, and ran greedily after the **error of Balaam** *for reward...*   - *Jude* 1:11 (KJV)

Wow. Now, why would God be so harsh to him? What did he do? Well, this Balaam must have done something very sacrilegious to God, or undermining to the people who wanted to follow God.

Now, just *who* was this Balaam, and why would Zepho end up valuing *his* input on things, here? And, most importantly why would Balaam end up on the same **par** as Cain (as far as Godly disfavor)? That really would have been a tall order for someone to fill;

but, Balaam was able to do it. The answer to this, in actuality, is fairly straightforward: it was all about his *deceptions*, or the ways he worked to (spiritually) "manipulate" people around him.

On top of all this information on Zepho, we'll also begin to see how his particular individual, and his "way of working" over people, would stand out as something the propagators of this White Horse would end up utilizing - on a grand scale! It's a very fascinating topic, when we begin to connect the dots... and link it all to a number of things we see around us today.

So, without further ado, let's look more into this whole process of human manipulation, beginning with one of the early masters of it himself: Balaam.

> *Although Balaam lived among idolaters, he professed great knowledge of God. So, when the Israelites encroached on the plains of Moab, the king of the Moabites, Balak, summoned Balaam. He feared the Israelites would attack, and he wanted Balaam to put a curse on them... God tells Balaam not to put a curse on the Israelites because they are blessed. Because of this, Balaam tells Balak's officials that the Lord will not allow him to go with them. So Balak sweetens the offer, tempting Balaam with, "Do not let anything keep you from coming to me, because I will **reward you handsomely** and do whatever you say. Come and put a curse on these people for me" Num 22 16-7. Then Balaam, in what I believe is the revealing moment, goes back to God. He sees Balaam's heart. It's possible that God knew Balaam wanted **the prize money** more than God.*
> ("The Error of Balaam", 2005, p. 1)[16]

We see that: although Balaam was tempted to curse the Israelites a number of times, God, ultimately, stepped in, and would not allow him to do so. Yet, Balaam was able to pull off something *just as bad* (if not worse), in order to hurt the people:

*Balaam could have helped the Moabites and their neighbours to "turn to God from idols, to serve the living God" (1Thessalonians 1:9). However Balaam let God down badly. Balaam was to**o easily led away from God's truth int**o error, and he **in turn led many others astray** (Numbers 31:8,16, Revelation 2:14). Instead of giving the counsel of God, **he taught people to practice idolatry and to commit fornication** (Revelation 2:14) It was **his (twisted ideological) counsel that caused the children of Israel to sin** and to suffer a terrible plague (Numbers 25:1-9, Numbers 31:14-16). (He) **Loved money more than truth**… Balaam "loved the wages of unrighteousness" (2Peter 2:15-16). Balaam knew **what pleased the Lord, but what pleased the Lord did not please Balaam**.*

("Important Reminders From the Story of Balaam and His Talking Donkey", 2023, p. 1)[17]

Yes, he helped to destroy the people (of Israel) from *within*! He would begin doing it though deceptive words and ideological twists (of the true ways of God)! He would be able to do it though *verbal* trickery, as well as theological manipulations - something that White Horse advocates would, seemingly, find useful later on.

*Balaam had the power God gave him, but **twisted it for his own** means. He messed up Israel because he "slept with the enemy," as well. He advised an enemy of Israel at the time - the Moabites - on **how to <u>entice</u> the people of Israel with prostitutes and idolatry**. Assumingly, God would not allow him to curse Israel directly, so he came up with a plan for Israel to bring a **curse upon themselves**. Eventually Israel harkened to his advice, and fell into sin…*

("Who was Balaam in the Bible", 2002, p. 4)[18]

Balaam twisted the ways of God around, clearly, which confused the people; and, he, subtly, brought them to think about the possibility of heading towards the "Other Side." And Balaam did it all for the sake of his *own* personal gain. This is all simple; but, wow, doesn't this sound familiar? Doesn't it sound a lot like those *whores* and *predators* of the White Horse?

Yes, this is what made God so **angry** with Balaam (as well as the family of **Esau**)… they *both* ended up using those same tactics - tactics that would (eventually) take out the Israelites, in a whole number of ways.

And, yes, if we think about things in this same way, Satan, as well, wasn't allowed to *directly* curse Eve, but he **was** able to *lead her on*, in a number of different ways. And, as a consequence, she was able to lead Adam on, as well. They *both* ended up going down the pathway of disobedience… not by direct command, but deciding to go down a pathway of deception. They ended up walking down this particular pathway *by their selves*. This is the definition of that **error of Balaam**!

Yes, this is the type of "error" that entices the minds of people, filling them with "alternative" information - information that, after a while, begins to confuse the individual, at deep levels. It, also, allows the individual to question their Godly resolve - giving them the "green light" to go off, on their own… making *their own errors*. What a racket.

> *Although he was a wicked prophet, Balaam was not a false prophet. In other words, Balaam did hear from God, and God did give him some **true** prophecies to speak. But, Balaam's heart **was not right** with God, and, he eventually he showed **his true colors** by **betraying Israel and leading them astray**.*
> ("Who was Balaam in the Bible", 2002, p. 1)[19]

Balaam (and other seducers of the faith) would, over time, begin to show their *true colors* over time. It almost reminds us of what Jesus said, as far as identifying an impostor in our midst: we know them *by their fruits*. And, yes, this above betrayal seems to be spelled out in the Bible, as well:

> *But I have a few things against thee, because thou hast there them that **hold the doctrine of Balaam**, who taught Balac (a king of Moab) to cast a stumblingblock before the children of Israel, to **eat things sacrificed unto idols, and to commit fornication**.* - Rev. 2:14 (KJV)

So, in order for us to securely link **Esau** (and his descendants) with this next level of Godly sacrilege, let's go back to our story of Zepho, and see what Balaam might have done early on, to churn the whole pot.

In the Jewish Encyclopedia, we have this information about Balaam, and what he eventually became:

> *He (Balaam) has been identified with **Bela**, the son of Beor, and first **king** of **Edom**…*
> ("BALAAM (*The Jewish Encyclopedia*)", 1906, p. 11)[20]

Wow, we have Balaam - as an early king of ***Edom***! Here, it seems, we have yet another connection. Once again, it seems that another "torch" has been passed on here, from *old* Babylon to the *new*. And we've also seemed to have discovered the origins of one major sacrilegious protocol of those Edomites, and how it all came to be. Truly, these actions were a force of evil, and of deception…. going all the way back to the Serpent of Eden.

Let's, now, go a little more in what happened after Zepho came back onto the whole scene. As one might assume, Zepho would follow Balaam's advice, and began to work this particular form of magic on the Chittim (i.e. the early Romans), as well.

> *In Chapter 61, we find that Balaam the Magus (witch) is 15 years old and in the service of Angeas. Zepho then betrayed Angeas because he would not go to war with the sons of Jacob in Egypt **based on the prophecy** of the young **Balaam**. Zepho went to work **for the Chittim**.*
> ("Zepho, Balaam, Jannes & Jambres pt 1", 2015, p. 4)[21]

So, now, we see that: under the advice of this prophet, Zepho began "sleeping with the enemy" - working over the people who occupied Rome, influencing them, manipulating their resolve, as well as showing them some good ways they could use to defeat their enemies.

> *From Africa he (Zepho) went to the land of Chittim (i.e. Rome). Due to his bravery he was given dominion over all the land of Chittim and throughout Italy. His sons reigned after him, and that is why the **Romans are Edomites**.*
> ("Esau, Edom, Rome, and the Christians", 2016, p. 2)[22]

It wasn't *just* the bravery of Zepho that made him so noteworthy here; it was also the use of this particular prophet - that twisted prophet of God - to assist him in "ramping up" Rome, and giving the people their "military edge." Either way (with or without the help of Balaam the prophet), Zepho would soon end up on top of this Roman "heap," as a major military leader (and major influencer).

Angeas, Zepho's mentor, wanted him to stay in Kittim (i.e. Italy); but, as one might guess, Zepho still had the desire the take down Jacob's people, back in his former land of Egypt! And, if Angeas wasn't going to help him out here, then Zepho may have to turn his back on the whole partnership, and use the people he had right in front of him… to pull it all off.

Because of his particular position, not only would Zepho be able to dominate this land of Kittim, but he would, eventually, be able to stoke the powers of warfare across neighboring lands. First, he was able to convince the Roman people to declare war on Angeas, in order to get him out of the way. Of course, there was a reason for all of this: to assist him in his warped desire to, eventually, get back into Egypt, and wage war against Israel. Everything seemed to be about his revenge. Go figure.

King Angeas, however, was able to counter some of those attacks by traitor Zepho; but, in the end, he would eventually **lose**. The battle seemed to have been fairly lopsided at first, with Angeas holding the upper hand. But, interestingly enough, it seems that we may even find *God* stepping into this situation, and *helping* Zepho to stop Angeas! Wow. Maybe it was because of those earlier acts of Joseph, and his Israeli brethren - being a bit hard on their Edomite brethren. Maybe God wanted to help out Zepho, because of what Israel did to him. Or, it may have even been for the fulfillment of some kind of prophecy. We're not sure. But, regardless, with this newfound victory, Zepho seemed to have accepted God's help (even though he really didn't acknowledge Him for it). No matter what, it seemed as though Zepho had a dark heart - a heart bent on vengeance and hate, and would never really not want to go out, and see things God's way.

<ins>Jasher 64</ins>:
> 5 *But Zepho remembered not the Lord and considered not that the Lord **had helped him** in battle, and that he had delivered him and his people from the hand of the king of Africa, but **still walked in the ways of the children of Chittim and the wicked children of Esau, to serve other gods which his brethren the children of Esau had taught him; it is therefore said, From the wicked goes forth wickedness.***
> 6 ***And Zepho reigned over all the children of Chittim securely**, but knew not the Lord who had delivered him and all his people from the hand of the king of Africa…*
> - Book of Jasher 64:5-6[23]

Balaam's error must have also brewed into *Zepho's* error. It also seemed that the moral capacities of the Romans were also beginning to go south, and in Zepho's favor. Zepho loved what was now going on, assuredly.

And, if we really think about all of this, we must remember that *all* human beings have flaws - no matter if they were thought of as special protégées of God (via Jacob) or those losers of the birthright (via Esau). *Both* brothers, over the years, did some questionable things, or didn't exactly do things in the "kosher" way. And, we can't really say that God was too partial… at least as far as sin was concerned. At least at first, He seemed to be merciful to *both* descendants of Isaac, and wanted the best for them. Yet, it seems that Esau, and a number of his early descendents, did not want a lot to do with the God of their fathers (Isaac and Abraham). Both descendants would ended up *choosing* the side they wanted to be on, over time.

And, on top of this all, we see that a young Balaam would help Zepho to "work over" the people of Rome, bringing them onto some of the same darkened pathways that Zepho was already on (in his mind). Well, as they say: "like attracts like."

<ins>Jasher 64</ins>:
> 1 *And **Balaam** the son of Beor was at that time with Angeas in the battle, and when he saw that Zepho prevailed over Angeas, **he fled from there and came to Chittim**.*
> 2 *And Zepho and the children of Chittim **received him with great honor**, for Zepho **knew Balaam's wisdom**, and **Zepho gave unto Balaam many gifts and he remained with him**…*
> - Book of Jasher 64:1-2[24]

Everything that was going on in Zepho's *Rome* may have helped to solidify the beginning of this long-lasting feud between Israel and Edom. It also helped to solidify *Rome* as a major symbol of Edom's great counteroffensive here, as well! Zepho was well on his way towards the fulfillment of Balaam's *spiritual* error, here… hoisting a lot of it onto the people of Rome, as well as his fellow Edomites.

This also seems to represent the "links" between those *old* antagonists of the post-Flood world (i.e. Ham, Cush and Canaan) and the *new*. Once again, these "links" - between old Babylon and the up-and-coming Rome - were now solidified. The pagan torch was slowly passed along, down a pathway of continued manipulation… eventually ending up as the systems of this White Horse.

What About Romulus and Remus?

Certainly, a number of modern historians will tell us that Rome went through some slow, "evolutionary" process over time - until it became a major city of our ancient world. There were also a number of legends about this early birth of Rome. The most popular legend is based upon two major mythological characters: *Romulus* and *Remus*. To simplify the story, let's take a look at it - with a slightly *different* interpretation of those two major characters. At the founding of Rome, one of the two characters (of whom are brothers) - *Remus* - has just died. Romulus, then, was given the credit for founding the city. And, since the founding of Rome seemed, quite often, to have been associated with this legend, a particular *image* had become associated with Rome's founding - an image of the two brothers suckling off the teats of a mother "she-wolf."

And, interestingly enough, we actually might have *Zepho*, and his influences, intertwined into this whole legend, here! One particular author (Ken Johnson) gives us an interesting take on that whole "Romulus and Remus" story:

> *In Roman myth, Rome was founded by Remus and Romulus, who as children were nursed by a she-wolf. This is a good example of real history being reinterpreted by pagans. As we have learned, Zepho, grandson of Esau, pulled together the city states and founded the first* **united Italy**. *He then trained and handed over the government to the first Latin king. In ancient Latin "Zepho" can be translated* **"she-wolf."** *So the she-wolf myth is an ancient memory corrupted by pagans and a testimony to the accuracy of ancient Hebrew history. The first kings of the Roman Empire (not the city of Rome) were nursed (trained by) the she-wolf (Zepho).*
> (Johnson, 2010, p. 81)[25]

Possibly, this "she-wolf" was actually a "paganized" symbol of Zepho, and his influence over the land. This time, it would be the natives of the region suckling off of Zepho's "teat"… his "teat" of knowledge and influence!

It only makes sense, here, to associate the native, aboriginal people as being "programmed" by Zepho, here, into becoming a more and more militaristic, as well as more and more *viscous* (as a mother wolf may be)! Zepho (with Balaam's help) began to turn the entire area into a *powerhouse* of "animal-like" pagan prowess - much like how a young wolf (through the suckling of its mother) would become a major hunting and killing force, as well!

> *…since Zepho went to Italy carrying the enmity against Jacob, there is no question that* **he bequeathed this enmity** *to his descendants, the* **Romans**.
> ("Esau, Edom, Rome, and the Christians", 2016, p. 2)[26]

This time, those (symbolic) "wolves" would be out there, actively seeking any of those tasty "lambs" of God (i.e. the Israelites).

Once we dig deeper, elements of our ancient actually seem to make a bit more sense… again, once we add in a number of the missing pieces. Rome always seemed to be a mighty, majestic force. It all had to have begun somewhere! And, we've also noticed that the people of this area have seemed to "have it out" for the children of Israel for a very, very long time. **Now** we have some good, solid reasons *why* this all could have been so.

And, now, we'll begin to discover a little more about why there (almost always) was a good deal of *enmity* between these ancient Romans and the ancient Israelites (or, ancient Jews). The missing piece of this puzzle seems to have been the ***Edomites***. They, as we know, had it out for ancient Israel since the very beginning; and (as we've just seen), a member of their same group was (for the most part) responsible for setting up the entire area into becoming that vast, "military machine" it would eventually turn into.

More On this "Majestic" City

There may have been a couple of other interesting elements that may relate to this whole above scenario - elements that seemed to have made *Rome* unique to the world's stage. Let's, first, begin by looking at a couple more early meanings of the name *Rome*:

> *Attempts have been made to find a linguistic root for the name Rome. Possibilities include derivation from (a Greek word)… meaning **bravery**, **courage**; possibly the connection is with a root rum-, "**teat**", with a theoretical reference to the totem wolf that adopted and suckled the cognately-named twins (a.k.a. Zepho's knowledge?)… Jean-Jacques Rousseau and his "The Social Contract", Book IV, Chapter IV, written in 1762, where he writes in a footnote that the word for Rome is Greek in origin and means **force**. "There are writers who say that the name 'Rome' is derived from 'Romulus'. It is in fact Greek and means **force**."*
> ("History of Rome", n. d., p. 2, 32)[27]

Now, we've seen (in the above) how the name *Rome* could have been associated with words such as *bravery*, *courage* or even *force*. And, we've also seen how the name could have been associated with a *teat*. They all seem to make sense, based on our earlier discussions. Yet, when we look at Rome **today**, so many of us might begin to associate it with some kind of *majestic or holy* city - like Jerusalem - because of its association with the Roman Catholic Church. With this, we'll also discover that:

*Zepho's grandson, **Latinus**, is the one who gave the Romans their language and their alphabet.*
      ("Esau, Edom, Rome, and the Christians", 2016, p. 2)[28]

Wow. It's interesting to see how we could, possibly, discover a namesake of the language to a son of Zepho - the language of *Latin*! And, as we may also notice, a lot of Catholic dogma, openly spoken in church proceedings, still use this language. Go figure. Should we wonder why, or what may have brought on all of this? There is more, much more.

One may also need to recall that Jesus, himself, was crucified on a **Roman** cross. It all seems to fit, once again. There, truly, was a lot of animosity between those ancient Edomites and the ancient Israelites... *as well as* there was similar animosity between the ancient Romans and Israelites. If we think about it, could there have been some manner of commonalities here, between those ancient Edomite and Roman groups?

With all of this, maybe we could begin to start *reevaluating* a lot of what a number of contemporary experts might say about the ancient history of these areas, and *why*, in actuality, things may have turned out the way they have. Adding a lot of this information, assuredly, would help us to look at things a bit differently, and, quite possibly, allow for us to believe that there could have been *Edomites* in the works, somewhere - manipulating world events. They may have, indeed, been that missing "key" - the ones fueling a great deal of *enmity* between people... especially the ancient Israelites.

In the next chapter, we'll begin to see just how these Edomites would, once again, strike out, against their neighboring Jewish brethren... from *another* strategic position that they held. We'll begin to look at another faction of Edomites, in another part of the ancient world, who were just as intent on corrupting (and eventually destroying) the ancient Jewish people as Zepho was!

Chapter 9

A Second Group of Edomites

Edom… the great destroyer, guilty of the ruin of Israel…
("Esau, Edom, Rome, and the Christians", 2016, p. 2)[1]

We recall, in the last chapter, how the Edomites - those children of Esau - had divided themselves up in the past, and went off to live in a number of different areas. We've discovered how some of them would have become the *force* behind the powers of ancient Rome, as well as that (up-and-coming) Roman Empire. We've also seen how some of them could have settled near Mt. Seir, as mentioned in the Bible (in Gen. 33:16, 36:8, etc.). But, there seemed to have been one more group of them - living fairly *close* to those remaining two tribes of Israel (i.e. Judah and Benjamin) - who were about to make waves… some **major** waves. Yes, large a number of Esau's descendants also lived just south of some Jewish territory n the Holy Land, in a land that was called *Idumea*.

From previous volumes, we may recall that, around the time of 720 B.C., those other ten tribes of Israel were captured by the Assyrians, and taken away to their home land. These would be the tribes who, eventually, would become known as those **Lost 10 Tribes**. At least, these tribes would no longer be subjected to the corruption of these early Kenites, as well as the influences of Zepho's Rome. They would not be subjected to any of these Edomites, living nearby them. But, the other two tribes, on the other hand, were still targets of all of this corruption - ripe for the "slaughter of identity."

The remaining two would still be subjected to the remnants of those early Kenites (in the priesthood). They would still be subjected to those militant Romans (under the Edomite *Zepho*), attacking and taking over Israel whenever possible. *Now*, we'll begin to see *another* faction of those Edomites, slithering their way onto the world's scene, here - attempting to drive the final "nail" in the proverbial "coffin" of Godly purity that He originally wanted for this Israeli group. Let's see how the remaining attempt to take down all things Godly would have begun.

Before we get into these details, we'll need to take a look at one more group of **pagans** - the *Neo-Babylonians* - and what their role was in the "softening up" of the remaining two tribes for the takedown, as well as the *assimilation*.

Abducted By Neo-Babylonians

The Jews of the day had an enemy - the *Babylonian* Empire (under the current ruler Nebuchadnezzar). Once again, we have ancient *Babylon* in the picture. How fitting! When Babylon's king, Nebuchadnezzar, decided to gather an army and attack the Holy Land (in approximately 609 B.C.), he was set on totally taking over the area, and bringing *back* the last two tribes to his homeland as slaves (the same as the ancient Assyrians had done). After he was successful in doing this, he, also, ended up taking a vast number of those ancient *Edomites* in the land, who were, once, living just south of the Jews. For a while, the two groups were in a similar situation.

And, because of their captivity in Babylon, it only makes sense to assume that a majority of Israeli leaders of the time (religious or otherwise) would have become a lot more "paganized" as time went on, because of how their Babylonian overlords instructed them. It only makes sense to assume that these Babylonians would have inserted their *own* politics and religious doctrine into the Jewish people, because they were now slaves!

Yet, after living in Babylon for a number of years (and being influenced by a lot of those ungodly, pagan ways), change was in the air. This exile would formally end, about 70 years after they were abducted (in approximately 539 B.C.). Around this time, a Persian conqueror named *Cyrus the Great* would end up conquering Babylonia, and he would go on to allow the ancient Jews and Edomites to *both* return to their previous areas inside of the Holy Land, if they so desired.

Yet, if we think about it: it's interesting to contemplate that, because the two groups went through this *same* horrible abduction then maybe some feelings of empathy and comradery would exist between the two former slave nations. Maybe, after this, they wouldn't be at each other's throats as much, because they were once in the same boat, side by side. Maybe there was a little; but, assuredly, is was not totally gone.

But, things did seem a bit different between the two, at least in some respects:

Many years later, when Cyrus the Great allowed Judah to return to Jerusalem and rebuild the city (cir. 522 B.C.), many descendants of Esau went with them and continued **to mix with** *those of the tribe of Judah and settled with them in Judea (Jer. 40:11-12)...*

("The People of Mt. Seir", 2009, p. 5)[2]

Now, it seems as though the children of Esau would begin to associate a little more with the Jews; they even began to *mix* with them, in a number of ways. The open enmity and separation may have (apparently) been dissipating some... or *has* it?

In this chapter, we will begin to concentrate on those neighboring Edomites - the ones who left Babylon, along with a number of Jews, now resettling a bit to the south (just as they had done before). The interaction between these two groups would turn into quite a tumultuous story, loaded with twists and turns. And, as we'll eventually see, it will also take us into *another* story, a story that a lot of people, today, might not particularly want out there, for the world to see. It will truly become eye-opening, even a little scary... because it will show *more* corruption within the Jewish faith. In fact, this time, it will get to the point where those ancient Jews, in large part, would be taken over, **practically**... absorbed by those envious, Edomite neighbors of theirs. It was sad moment in history, assuredly; and, for the most part, it was an *untold* story.

After Their Return From Babylon

We may wonder why the ancient Israelites, over a number of times, were conquered by other nations, and, often, treated so horribly. Weren't they supposed to be the nation blessed by God? Well, according to the Bible: a good deal of Israel's historical problems seemed to rest upon the *moral* decisions that they often made, just before a particular tragedy came over them. They were human, just like the rest of us. And, of course, we all make mistakes and incorrect judgments. It appears that: when the ancient Israelites wanted to follow God they were blessed; when they did not, and went in the opposite direction, the *opposite* end-result seemed to have fallen upon them. This was, so often, the case in the Bible. And, this time, their antagonists would be their very brethren - trying to take down their nation... not militarily, but from *within*.

If we really stop, to look a little bit deeper into why all of this animosity began in the first place, we need to understand that Esau, at one time, was considered "the older" brother (because he was the first out of the womb), and Jacob was "the younger" brother, obviously, and not given the birthright. Yet, interestingly enough, we have this quote (supposedly given by God Himself, to the mother of the two boys):

> *"The older of the two will serve the younger, provided this one (Jacob)* ***is pure of heart****, otherwise the younger will be enslaved by the older."*
> (Ginzberg, 1909, p. 314)[3]

Wow, what a stipulation here! As we see, it appears that the Jews would remain on top of this "brotherly battle," and hold onto the special privileges of the birthright, as well as continue being blessed, as the special protégés of God, **as long as** they continued to follow Him, and stay on the straight and moral path. Sounds simple enough. But, once again, the stipulation on this seemed to have been: they had to have remained *moral*. No idolatry, and no other pagan influences allowed!

Yet, as most might easily guess, all of the twelve tribes did not exactly keep their hearts overflowing with Godly purity. They may have tried it for a little while, but failed (as most human beings would). Temptations from the outside, a lot of the times, were just too tempting. And, since these "breakaways" were often the case, the Jews were allowed to suffer a number of heart-wrenching experiences over time (such as being taken over by other invading empires). That seems to be our answer, sadly.

Now, with these neighboring Edomites, something deeper, and a bit *darker*, was on their agenda. It wasn't just about conquering another nation, like with the Assyrians or Babylonians… it seemed to have been a lot more *personal*.

The Kenites have already punctured the religious aristocracy, causing a lot of corruption … even by the time of Jesus (as we might recall). The ancient Babylonians, as well, introduced the rest of the Jewish people to their pagan world, by taking them off to live in Babylon. Now, it seemed as though the Edomites wanted *their* turn.

Maybe, because the Jewish population was fed so many negative (and pagan) elements by the (corrupted) Pharisees, Sadducees and scribes, and didn't do anything to really counter it, a massive downswing of the entire group was to be in order next... for a good number of years to come. Maybe, because the people went on to follow these religious authorities, and did not really question the inconsistencies enough over time, it was time for God to make good on what He said earlier. It wasn't that God didn't warn these people that they were slipping away - through the number of Old Testament prophets! No, the religious authorities, as well as the general public, ended up either scoffing these prophets, jailing them or killing them. Something, now, was in the air... to take up where these prophets left off.

The sad part about it all was: just how could a number of these people get out of what was in store for them next, when their **own** peers and religious authorities were continually working to keep their "ship sailing" in the same, general direction?

So, as far as the battle between the two brothers was concerned, change *did* seem to be nigh for the common people. Jacob's descendants *must* have really been going out of God's favor by this time (through the fault of those at the top, for the most part), because the "older" brother was indeed taking steps to, ultimately, relinquish the control of the "younger"... in ways that most of us may have never even thought of.

Only a Boarder Separated the Two

Now comes the second "wave" of Jewish infiltration - and corruption - by their Edomite brethren. And, from now on, we'll begin to see the "birth" of what one might be able to call the "Edomite Jews," the "Edomite Impostors" or those "Edomites in Jewish Clothing." Now, for simplicity's sake, let's begin by giving these imposters a specific moniker: the "**EJCs**" - or "**E**domites in **J**ewish **C**lothing." It's just a way for us to identify, and somewhat separate, those infiltrators from the *true* Jewish people out there (at heart).

Of course, we're not intentionally trying to put *any* person down, especially the true Jews of the world. We are just, in actuality, trying to point out the corruption that began to go on back then, in the Jewish ranks of years past. We are trying to identify those particular individuals who seem to have this *other* trait - the trait of the Edomite. We're trying to point out those who - on a *deeper* level - might want to go around, calling themselves "Jews," or "self-styling" this Jewish experience as their own… but, in reality, they *are* really *not* the same thing.

Some of these individuals might look the part, they may look as though they stem from a long line of Jewish individuals… those who have closely followed the faith. We may not be able to tell the difference on the outside… but, inside, they're not *exactly*. Some may, visually, look like a Jewish person - even *exactly* like what a typical Jewish person might look like… but, inside, they're not exactly. Some may (seemingly) have *all* it takes to qualify as a member of the Jewish congregation… but, in reality, they're either from an Edomite background, or they will sure act as though they could have been!

Looks can be very deceiving. And, doing certain behaviors, or participating in certain rituals, do not necessarily make a person what they claim. A number of people, throughout history, might not even know (consciously) that they are of Edomite blood, or have "married" into is, somewhere down the line! Yes, there has been assimilations out there here. And, yes, that is the tricky thing we face now - trying to talking about this, when it doesn't appear so (at least, on the surface)!

We shall see that, indeed, blood has been so compromised (over the years), so much so that we, for the most part, can no longer really distinguish any differences between what would have been the two brethren. Yet, there are still a number of things we can utilize here, in this world,, to help us identify just "who's who," or "who" may be truly acting like "who" (as we soon shall see).

But, for now, in order for us to understand just how this entire assimilation process began (and how it began to take hold), let's, once again, go back in time - to a hundred-or-so years before the time of Jesus himself.

John Hyrcanus

As a person who may be able to add some dark *ink* into a glass of crystal clear water, the Edomites would end up doing much of the same, hypothetically - through the *additions* they would soon be in the position to bring. And they (eventually) would end up *darkening* practically the entire Jewish population over time, as well as the entire Jewish experience. Sad.

Well, just what would help to spring all of this into motion? First, we find that, over two thousand years ago, a particular Jewish leader (with a little help of the Roman Empire) would do something that, in reality, was *not* in the best interest of the Jewish people overall. Let's see.

John Hyrcanus

The assimilation process of these Edomites was initiated, and accelerated *unintentionally*, by a powerful Jewish ruler named *John Hyrcanus* (as pictured in the above). Once their standing leader, he was considered to be a "a wise and just ruler and a skillful warrior," as well as the "high priest" over a number of early Jews.[4] After ruling Judea for a good while, he decided to take on one more project:

*The Encyclopedia Judaica states: "John Hyrcanus conquered the whole of Edom and undertook **the forced conversion of its inhabitants to Judaism."** (Joseph., Ant. XIII, 9, 1.) "Thenceforth the **Edomites** became a <u>section</u> of the Jewish people." (Encyclopedia Judaica, (1971) 6:378). And The New Standard Jewish Encyclopedia, (1977) p. 589, says the same thing. From what the Jewish Encyclopedia says, the* **Jews admit that they incorporated their eternal enemy, the Edomites, into their own religion to become part of their people**.
("The People of Mt. Seir", 2009, p. 5)[5]

Could this be? What could have been the ramifications of an act such as this? Incorporating your generations-long, mortal enemy into your own fold *by force*, and then hoping that it would all work out? Could this have really been possible (then *or* now)? Maybe there were some good intentions to it all, somewhere down the line. Maybe John Hyrcanus **did** want to do some good for his people, here. Maybe, he thought that this would absorb the enmity between the two feuding brothers. Maybe, he ended up hoping that, in *some* way, these subjected Edomites would now want to view themselves as the conquered tribe, the "second fiddle" if you would… those who, now, would understand their place on this earth: beneath their fellow Jews. Maybe he hoped that these Edomites would begin to see the "error of their ways," and realize the hate they held against their own brethren… and be *happy* with what they were now forced to do.

Just how long would this type of subjection last in a person (if at all)? How much did he understand human nature? Did he really think that these subjected Edomites would end up *wanting* to accept their positions - as *subjects*… with the former holders of *their* own birthright asking them to voluntarily submit to them, and their ways of life? It's entirely possible, but not very probably (in this particular situation).

There's not a lot of people in this world who would, voluntarily, want to sit back, and humble themselves to their captors for the rest of their lives (just as John Hyrcanus may have wanted). Yet, he still made the two groups come together (at least in a number of ways), directing them on how to live similar lives, practicing the same kind of religious rituals, etc. Now, the only thing that really separated the two was a thin, physical boarder (between their two lands)… and, even that would be in jeopardy, as we soon shall see.

In some ways, Hyrcanus may have believed it made some sense to allow these conquered Edomites a chance to live like Jews, in their own plot of land… **as long as** both knew, and continued to understand, just "who" was "who" on the outside, as long as they did not *physically* mix too much, or live *too* close together. It may have made sense to John, as long as these Edomites were forced to understand that they were the ones who needed to remain in the "number two" spot (under their birthright holders). But, of course, *who* would want to think in these ways… for long, and how long would this "two-tiered" existence be able to hold up (especially when there was so much **enmity** between the two brothers already)?

We must not forget about human nature, in cases such as this, and that the deeper desires of people in these types of situations were, most likely, something of the opposite extreme! No one would really want to stay at that "second" rung for very long. And, if this was going to be the new protocol for the two brethren, then the kings of the hill had better watch out, because the "number twos" would, most probably, be continually thinking of ways to usurp their subduers authority, and drag them down. Of course, this whole pecking order would, probably, not stand as firmly as when it was first set up… not for very long. A lot of people just don't forget the things that may have been a part of them in the past, not very easily.

*As generations progressed, the Edomites continued to play an **antagonistic** role in the destiny of Israel.*
(Sanger, 2020, p. 191)[6]

Now, a majority of those "second-place" Edomites would, most probably, end up trying to make the best of their forced merger, in whatever ways they could get away with. Their end goal, in this new, particular situation, would probably be to wipe out the other brother's existence, in whatever ways they could. It was their destiny, now… no matter how long it took, and no matter *what* they had to do to accomplish it, *even* if it meant they had to take over the identity of some Jews *themselves*! Wow. Yes, maybe, through this attempt at removing subversion, an assimilation was not to be in order. Maybe they could get out of their "second class" status by assimilating into the people over them. As well, they might be able to, once again, be considered the holders of the birthright (by actually *becoming* a member of these *protégés* of God)! Wow, both things accomplished… in one swoop!

*At this time the descendants of Esau were forced to convert to Judaism, along with conformity to all Jewish laws, customs, and government. Hence, the Edomites became assimilated as part of the Jewish nation, their country being in Judea, or southern Palestine**, but they stayed idolaters.***
("The People of Mt. Seir", 2009, p. 6)[7]

Their forced adherence to Jewish law wound not really seem to pan out. Yes, deep down inside, bitter human hearts do not change, not too often... especially when the hearts of one particular group is, for the most part, *void* of a Godly moral code at the start. Esau was openly against the God of Abraham and Isaac (his father). He really didn't care about the birthright... until it was too late, and he'd lost it. A vast number of his Edomite descendants, deep down inside, still would rather choose to worship idols, and would continue on, (subtly) promoting the ideological elements of *their* ways of life, and their theological (and pagan) beliefs. There wasn't really a very good chance for this amalgamation to work, given those particular circumstances.

Their new struggle was upon them. And, because it really did not have a chance at working very well, things would not end up faring too well for the ancient **Jews**, as well. They, of course, would soon find themselves on a *receiving* end of all this negativity. Not the best of moves by John Hyrcanus, here.

Yet, some still may want to ask: does the above information actually reflect the *real* story, or is it just the opinion of some? Could this information have only come from a few obscured, or even *questionable*, websites? Apparently not. As we'll now see, even a few of the more *modern* - and accredited - Jewish works of history seem to reflect this same thing. And, as we'll soon discover (in the quotes below), there seems to be a number of references to this same story - coming right from "the horse's mouth" if you will. It comes right out of a modern Jewish encyclopedia!

> *They were... subdued by John Hyrcanus (c. 125 B.C.), by whom they were forced to observe Jewish rites and laws... (and were)* **incorporated with** *the Jewish nation...* ("EDOX, IDUMEA (*The Jewish Encyclopedia*)", 1906, p. 8)[8]

> *...the [non-Israelite] Edomites* **became a section of** *the Jewish people.* ("EDOM" (*Encyclopaedia Judaica*), 1971, p. 378)[9]

Interestingly enough, this same story seems to have come from the ancient, non-Biblical historian *Josephus* (who was also a Jew). He wrote, many years ago, that John Hyrcanus did the same as was mentioned above. He also stated that: not only were the ancient Edomites of the area subdued, and brought **into their new Jewish fold**, but there were some ramifications to it all… onto the backs of the Jewish people *themselves*:

> *Hyrcanus took also…(the) cities of Idumea (i.e. the ancient Edomites), and subdued all the Idumeans; and permitted them to stay in that country, if they would circumcise their genitals, and make use of the laws of the Jews… (and utilize) the rest of the Jewish ways of living; at which time therefore this befell them, that* **they were hereafter no other than** *Jews.*
> - *Flavius Josephus* Jewish Antiquities, Book 13.9.1[10]

This last sentence seems to have said it all: "they were hereafter **no other than** Jews." Another translation has Josephus stating: "And from that time on they have **continued** to be Jews."[11] In other words, these Edomites ended up absorbing themselves into the Jewish population, acting the same as Jews themselves! What else could it mean… other than they began to *assimilate* themselves as members of the current Jewish experience? Could it have really meant that they were trying to better themselves, in regards to their current situations, stealing back their own birthright in the process?

It would have been quite a feat, if they could pull it off, over the years. Once again, we see a very famous Jewish historian (of the time) saying this exact thing! And, once again, we've seen that this information comes out of their own mouths… so we're not just making this all up. The Edomites, now, were beginning to turn themselves into Jews… *literally* (for a number of reasons that we now understand). This assimilation process (and eventual dilution process) of the Jewish people had now begun!

We may need to remember that there, most probably, was *no love lost* between these two particular nations. And, frighteningly, we see Biblical evidence that these Edomites, over time, would do or say almost anything they could, in order to mess up the Jews:

> *Throughout history, the Edomite repeatedly seized opportunities to take advantage of Israel's calamities. True to form, on the day that Jerusalem fell to the Babylonians in 586 B.C., the Edomites* **chanted**…
> (Sanger, 2020, p. 258)[12]

Well, what exactly did they chant, here? Were they watching in horror… lamenting over the destruction of the city of their brethren, or were they chanting something else? We actually find out the answer in our Bibles:

> *Psa.* 137:
> 7 *Remember, LORD, what the Edomites did on the day Jerusalem fell. "Tear it down," they cried, "tear it down to its foundations!"*
> 8 **Daughter Babylon**, *doomed to destruction, happy is the one who repays you according to what you have done to us.*[13]

Please notate the *other* city that Edom was compared to, here… another "daughter" of Babylon? Yes, a number of things seems to be interrelated - with Edom, once again, becoming the spiritual remnant of pagan *Babylon*. Don't be fooled, today. Why would these Edomites really want to chant anything different here, especially under their particular circumstances? And, if they were made to behave like Jews, why would they *ever* stop their plight to rise above their current situation, and work on destroying the Jews, once again?

Zepho's Rome… Now, Back in the Picture

And, on top of this all, and, to add more insult to injury, we seem to have Edomite *Rome* coming back into the picture once again, supplying its own "two-cents worth" into this Jewish takedown equation. Something else was taking place in Jewish history, right along with John Hyrcanus' takeover of the Edomite people. Josephus even expands upon this additional element a bit, and continues on (right after mentioning that Hyrcanus made the decision to amalgamate the two):

> *…And from that time on they (the Edomites) have continued to be Jews. Now as the high priest Hyrcanus wished to **renew the friendship with the Romans**, he sent an embassy to them. And the Senate received his letter, and made an **alliance of friendship** with him…*
> - *Flavius Josephus* Jewish Antiquities, Vol. 7, p. 256-260[14]

Wow. What's really going on here, in the entire, global picture? Now, we see John Hyrcanus setting out to form a **friendship** with Zepho's pagan Rome! Smell a rat here? Yes, he, first, begins by assimilating the neighboring Edomites into his own Jewish fold; next, he begins to make deals with the *Edomite* Romans (of Zepho). Can we sense something a bit *nefarious* going on, in regards to the whole process? Can we sense *two* fronts, about to be working together (because they are of the same brotherhood)? Could the two have felt the same way about their enemy - the Jews - and wouldn't mind working in tandem to overwhelm any and all of those remnants of Jacob himself? It's entirely possible.

Edom - Now Known as "Idumea"

> **Edom** is mentioned in the cuneiform inscriptions in the form "**Udumi**"... They were again subdued by John Hyrcanus (c. 125 B.C.), by whom they were forced to observe Jewish rites and laws... They were **incorporated with** the Jewish nation, and their country **was called by the Greeks and Romans "Idumea"**... ("EDOX, IDUMEA (The *Jewish Encyclopedia*)", 1906, p. 8)[15]

Again, in the Jewish Encyclopedia, we see that the land that those Edomites once called home was known by another name: *Idumea*. This name, simply, seems to be the Greek word for *Edom*. So, either way we stack it here, it's all the same.

The Roman Empire - a former Edomite stronghold in its own right - was now on the scene, subtly working to manipulate things here a bit more. And, as we'll now see, it already appears that the Idumeans (or Edomites) were starting to take over a few positions of *power* (throughout the Holy Land). They were, slowly, supplanting the Jews... in more ways than one.

Even according to the Jewish Encyclopedia (below), we discover that the power grid was changing, for the worse. Before Rome even came onto the scene, the ancient Greeks (under Alexander the Great) swooped into the Holy Land, and took it over. Interestingly enough, the (pagan and) Greek leadership already seemed to have given the *Edomites* the upper hand in the land, early on:

> *With Antipater (the Greek leader) began the **Idumean** dynasty **that ruled over Judea** till its conquest by the Romans.*
> ("EDOX, IDUMEA (The *Jewish Encyclopedia*)", 1906, p. 8)[16]

Soon enough, the Romans would step in, and take hold of the situation:

> *The first intervention of Rome in the region dates from 63 BCE, following the end of the Third Mithridatic War, when Rome established the province of Syria. After the defeat of Mithridates VI of Pontus, Pompey (Pompey the Great) sacked **Jerusalem**...*
> ("Judea (Roman province)", n. d., p. 1)[17]

And, of course: the apple would, once again, not fall too far from the tree. Secondary rule would, assuredly, shift from only one Edomite clan to another, because of who the Romans were!

And, if we really think about this whole takeover, it, actually, had become the fulfillment of Zepho's earlier dream - to have the **Romans get back** at Jacob, and dominate his entire nation! Any way he could get it to work, he would have done it. And, now, with the help of the powerful Roman Empire, the Jews of the Holy Land were completely under the thumb of their mortal enemies.

Of course, those Edomite Romans probably felt that things would fare a lot better if they put *their own* "puppet" government over the lands that they conquered, like the Greeks did. And, of course, by the time of Jesus' birth, we already see a famous *Idumean* in charge of the Holy Land (under Roman care, of course) - and this person's name was *Herod*.

King Herod - An Edomite

> *...from then on [the Edomites] constituted **a part of** the Jewish people, **Herod** being one of their descendants.*
> ("Edomites (The *Standard Jewish Encyclopedia*)", 1966, p. 593)[18]

Again, we have a Jewish Encyclopedia stating that, not only were these Edomites absorbing themselves into the Jewish nation, but they were ruling over a number of them. Yes, we know of him: the famous *Herod* of the Bible, the leader who held onto the reins power during Jesus' birth. And, yes, he was actually an *Edomite*, a person of Idumea… the one who gave the order to slaughter of vast number of Jewish infants in Bethlehem (go figure).

Many of us may recall this story of Jesus' birth, and how the leaders of the day tried to kill him as a baby. This was, quite possibly, because he was showing "his fruits" (because he was an Edomite)! We recall that it was Jesus himself who said that we would be able to identify certain people *by their fruits*.

What a treacherous act of this Edomite person, here! It surely doesn't sound like something a follower of God might want to do, right? *True* Jews of God do not go around, killing their own babies. No way. But, of course, to these Edomites, it was probably something that *they* felt was good for them (deep down *inside*), and was necessary. They wouldn't want any Jew (no matter who he was) to come into their world, and usurp all of the progress that they've been making (i.e. all of the power they were now accumulating, and starting to enjoy)! No way.

> *Hyrcanus converted the Idumeans to Judaism by forcing them to submit to Jewish law if they wanted to stay in the beloved land of their ancestors. We can only presume that for most of the Idumeans, their conversion to follow Yahweh (i.e. God)* **was not genuine**. *Even though during this period of history, the Idumeans appeared to be joined with the Jews, there were* **still underlying tensions**.
> (Sanger, 2020, p. 192)[19]

Yes, things were changing in the Holy Land, both politically and religiously; and it all may not have ended up the way that John Hyrcanus (at least *initially*) wanted for his people. Sad.

Judas Iscariot

In the New Testament, we may have another (possible) Edomite infraction, one who may not have appeared to have been that way… at least at first. We know that Jesus had disciples, twelve of them in fact. We have Peter, Thomas and John, to name just a few. And, interestingly enough, most of the these disciples were originally from the Sea of Galilee area, on the northern side of Israel. And, interestingly enough, they all were (usually) referred to by *one* name, not two. Yet, we have one disciple who was a little different than the others. This one, most probably, was *not* originally from the same place as the rest of them were, nor was he usually referred to by only one name. This disciple was *Judas Iscariot*

Now, if we think about it, the different way by which he was usually mentioned - as an "*Iscariot*" - may, actually, be a little suspect. What was this extra title? Was it a surname; or (quite probably) was it the *town* of his origin? And, if this was the case, then *why* would his town need to mentioned, along with his name?

There seems to be so many "tells" in our world - "tells" that give us valuable information… if we seek it out. Sometimes, if we're not really looking for them (consciously), we might just glaze over it all, or even forget it. But, in this case, things may be very relevant. And, judging from what we already know about this particular disciple (and how he was the betrayer of Jesus), it may be of some value for us to take a deeper look at him, assuredly.

Let's look at a few possible "*tells*" about Judas Iscariot, through this extra title.

*All of the apostles, except Judas, were from Galilee. His name, Judas Iscariot, indicates that he was "Judas from Kerioth." Iscariot is not a word in any known language. It is believed to be a corruption of the Hebrew word Ish Kerioth (man of Kerioth). Kerioth was a small village on the **southwestern extremity** of the territory of Judea… This territory was occupied by **Edomites**.…*
 ("What Do We Know about Judas? This Might Surprise You", n. d., p. 2)[20]

KERIOTH **kĕr' ĭ ŏth**. *The name of two cities mentioned in Scripture.*
*1. A city of Judah in the extreme S toward **Edom**.*
 ("Kerioth ", n. d., p. 1)[21]

Wow. Not really too much of a surprise here. Doesn't that make a lot of sense, understanding the circumstances of our previous discussion (as well as recalling what he did to Jesus himself)?

During this time, there indeed seemed to have been some succinct boundaries, in regards to the areas where the Jews lived and the areas where those Edomites lived. Most probably, the people still felt the need to be separated, at least in a physical sense. This may have even been apparent with Jesus' ministry:

*...most of Jesus' three and half year public ministry took place in the northern regions. Only toward the end of that time did He go to Jerusalem, but He did not go to the far **southern** regions of Judah.*
("What Do We Know about Judas? This Might Surprise You", n. d., p. 3)[22]

*...all the disciples/apostles are from the tribe of Benjamin, including Paul, with the exception of Judas. Guess what he is? An Edomite mixture. How do we know? He is from the town of Iscariot. If one reads the Gospels very carefully, Jesus has been careful **not to venture into their territory**.*
("I Know The Blasphemy of Them Which Say They are Jews", n. d., p. 1)[23]

If Judas indeed had some *Edomite* blood to him, this may help to explain quite a lot, especially in regards to the enigma of why he was continually referred to by the town of his origin – it was as if those mentioning his name wanted to *make sure* that everyone knew where this particular individual was from, and just *who* he was - an **Edomite**.

Once again, his Edomite past could have been allowed him to become a "third wheel" in Jesus' life. It could have also helped Judas to make that decision to want to betray him, without really a second thought.

*Furthermore, we might note that an Edomite (Herod) opposed the birth of Christ and tried to kill him and that **Judas**, an Edomite, opposed Jesus and conspired to bring about His death.*
("What Do We Know about Judas? This Might Surprise You", n. d., p. 3)[24]

Now, we've already mentioned a way to identify a possible *Edomite* earlier on: with Judas' "kiss of death," here, we may have had another example. He could have easily been another individual who ended up showing his *true* "fruits" over time, by doing this to the future savior of the world... all for 30 pieces of silver.

Continuing... After the Time of Jesus

Of course, Herod failed to carry out his deed, and the infant Jesus was still be able to have grown up. We also have Judas - possibly of the same blood - and his (successful) attempt to betray Jesus, which allowed him to be railroaded into his end. One conclusion that we could surmise out of the two is: it seems as though these Edomites - deep down inside - felt **no love loss** for anything, or anyone, of a Jewish nature.

After Jesus' death, burial and resurrection, their attempts to continue on with their assimilation, and eventual corruption of the entire Jewish way of life continued, and still seemed to have been "on track." Those corrupted Pharisees, Sadducees and scribes - the ones that Jesus openly spoke out against - were also continuing on with their *own* interpretations of what the current practices of Judaism should be. Beyond Jesus' existence, those infiltrators both tried to keep their corruptions going, as long as they possibly could.

For the most part, the corruption of the Jewish people would continue. Yet, there was one major caveat on the horizon, something that was about to give them a bit of competition, here - a new, *Christian* movement! Yes, a major "thorn" was about to pierce their own, sovereign sides. And, unbeknown to a number of the EJCs (at the time), the Christian movement would actually begin to take off, on a massive, massive, *upward* trajectory. Now what. It was disrupting their "silent takeover"... especially when a number of their targeted individuals now began to seek after Jesus Christ. What to do?

In regards to this new faith of Christianity, we may already recall how Jesus told his disciples to go *abroad*, and look for new converts, as well as look for his "lost sheep!" Well, just *who* might they be? What it, most probably, means is: he wanted all of the people of the earth (of every nation or creed) to come into God's fold, and be grafted onto this faith... no matter who you were. You just had to believe, and accept him. As well, he wanted to get the "lost sheep" of the House of Israel back into the fold as well - those Lost 10 Tribes of Israel. Yes, they were called the "House of Israel" before they were taken by the Assyrians; and, Jesus refers to this House of Israel as the "lost sheep" - indicating that they were scattered, somewhere. Who else could these be?

Yes, it only makes sense that *he* was the Messiah - the one who was able to unite the present two (Jewish) tribes with those Lost 10 Tribes… through the Christian faith! Now, this new faith of Jesus' doing was able to bring *so* many people back to God. And, as a consequence, there would be a huge upheaval in the old pagan systems of authority - even usurping the progress of Edomite assimilation. It was, obviously, beginning to turn the faiths of a number of contemporary Jews in the *opposite* direction - of where these Edomites wanted them!

Now, all that the Edomite imposters could do was to double-down on what they already had, and were doing, in order to make the best of it… bashing Jesus, and his message, in any way possible. Yet, sadly, the new Christian faith would not bring as many Jews back into God's fold as it would people outside the Jewish experience, because these current ruling authorities attempted to clamp down *hard*. Sadly, a lot of the same would still go on in the Jewish world, a lot of this same assimilation. And, with that, the number of days that the Edomite people (as a whole) would, probably, be able to live out their lives as a *separate* people, away from the Jewish people, would soon be numbered. Let's see what had transpired next.

To Squash Them… Permanently!

> *…Edom **is no longer** a people and the Edomite kingdom has **been lost to history**. The sovereignty of Edom/Idumea was destroyed, but its people remained and **mostly converted to Judaism**.*
> ("Have the prophecies about Edom been fulfilled?", 2022, p. 3-4)[25]

Jesus, already, had been resurrected, and ended up going back to God (through the transfiguration). The Christian faith was well underway, with the current establishment in the Holy Land was all up in arms… scrambling to still keep *their* people under control. But, something would now happen, thanks largely to the Roman Empire, which would manipulate things even further for the Jews. Apparently, the Romans were now beginning to feel the need to *stifle* a number of religious practices of these Jews (and their corresponding EJCs). At least, they wanted to begin to slow everything down.

We must recall that the current population of Edomite Rome was *still* pagan; and, assuredly, Christianity was starting to inflict pain on their belief system. So, with any Roman attempt to stifle any competing faiths out there, it, naturally, was met with resistance... especially with those inhabitants of the Holy Land.

Around forty years after Jesus' resurrection, the Romans began to feel a resistance. And, to show evidence of their "iron-fisted" authority, they began to clamp down on any of these Jewish/Edomite efforts. This, in turn, would prompt a massive Jewish/Edomite uprising - a revolt that eventually ended up dissolving any delicate "partnership" that those Jewish/EJC leaders and Romans might have once had.

The Jews and Edomites began to fight back... and, actually ended up working together in the process. And, around the year of 70 A.D., the Roman government tried to *squash* the rebellious ones once and for all... hunting them all down, killing them and even burning down the holy **temple** in Jerusalem (on the temple mount)!

An interesting thing also may have transpired during this time, however: although the religious practices of these early Jewish and Edomite communities were slowly intertwining, the unification of the two people *on a personal level* was about to get a quick (and unsuspected) "boost." Before this time, there *still* seemed to have been a *physical* separation of the people, through land boundaries and through separate living arrangements. A number of these individuals *still* lived apart, and enjoyed their sovereignty. They still felt it was better to have it this way, to maintain their own separate lives, and stay with those of their own kind. But, no longer anymore. No longer would this all be a reality with the Roman clamp down. The Romans were after them - all of them. And now, with these uprisings, a number of these individuals would began to join forces, fighting right alongside one another. The Edomites of the land were now being considered **so close** to their Jewish neighbors that, for the most part, they may have begun to be thought of as one in the *same*!

Yes, at this time, something interesting was about to happen (and, yes, we discover this information coming right out of the mouths of certain Jewish historians *themselves*):

> *From this time the Idumeans **ceased to be a separate people**...*
> ("EDOX, IDUMEA (The *Jewish Encyclopedia*)", 1906, p. 8)[26]

Wow. Once again, we recall the Jewish Encyclopedia stating that these early Edomites (i.e. Idumeans) were **once** a separated people, but ***now*** they appear to have vanished off of the face of the earth, while fighting alongside of the Jews. Well, what happened to them? They were fighting alongside the Jews, and the Romans were chasing both of them. Just *where* might they have went, here? It doesn't take a rocket scientist to figure out the probable answer.

Just like the Lost 10 Tribes, these people did not just 'disappear." If they had ceased to be a *separate* people, and were fighting alongside of the Jews during the last time they were accounted for, then logic tells us the probable answer: they fled together. Of course, it's seems to be easy to just put "two and two" together here, because the Edomites were no longer viewed as a separate people. It's because that maybe they were no longer were! Maybe, because of their current situation, they were now thought of as *one in the same*. Simple.

> *Because of rebellion, Rome finally got fed up with Jerusalem, and Titus laid siege to Jerusalem about 66-70 A.D. The Edomites participated in the defense of Jerusalem against Rome. The Jewish Encyclopedia again says, "Immediately before the siege of Jerusalem 20,000 Idumeans [Edomites] appeared before Jerusalem to fight in behalf of the Zealots who were besieged in the Temple." (Vol. 5:41.) When Rome was successful in subduing Jerusalem, the descendants of Esau **were dispersed off the land <u>with the Jews</u>**. In history, **this is the last we hear of the Edomites as a people.***
> ("The People of Mt. Seir", 2009, p. 6)[27]

So, from this point on, it's easy to assume (and important to understand) that the Idumeans "ceased to be a separate people," and ended up right alongside their fleeing Jewish neighbors. And, of course, why wouldn't they have been thought of as the same? They were involving themselves in the same religious practices (by this time). They lived right alongside one another for a long time. They were also fighting against this *same*, common enemy. Yes, this occurrence probably helped to solidify that transformation process - now, bringing the people *physically* together as well, to start living life as a single group of people. No more boundary lines anymore - the Edomites were now (one way or another) able to reach a tipping point, the point of a *forced* assimilation… physically!

And, if they had began to come together in such a way, then, the new question we might ask is: just *how* would we be able to know just "who" was "who," or just "who" is "who" today? The answer is: we **can't** know for sure. That is the beauty of their whole assimilation process. we can't really diagnose anything by just *looking* on the outside. We can't even *guess* accurately, because this assimilation process has been going on for over two thousand years, with one side working hard to merge into the other. Regardless of how unsettling this all might sound, at first… that doesn't mean that none of this didn't happen. Perhaps, the only way for us to get **an** *idea* of just "who" might be "who," or at least give us an idea of just *what* they may all may be trying to front to us, here, is to remember what Jesus himself had said: "Ye shall know them by their *fruits* (Mat 7:16)!"

It only makes sense to assume that those subjected Edomites, so long ago, would *not* want to remain under the thumb of their detested brethren for very long. It's only natural! As in any subjugated group, they would not be very content by just playing "second fiddle" here. No. They, naturally, would want to begin to have *their own* ways to shine through, somehow. They, eventually, would want *their* life choices to come back out, to the surface, or even take control of their restricted situations… and, that's what probably happened to this conglomerated group over time.

So, now, if we begin to see something in a person that might begin to seem a little *nefarious* to a typical God-follower, then this gives us some ammunition. Maybe there could be something else going on here, *inside* a particular individual. The *Edomite* side of the person may be coming out, and, so often, they almost can't help but show this off. It's human nature; and, *this* is also their "tell." *This* is what becomes our route to further understand what kind of person we may be facing, what they may really be all about, and *why* they may be directing us in the particular direction they are heading us into.

The Truth Hurts... Somewhat

As we've now see (from ancient history): all that glitters - in the case of these early Jewish community - is not necessarily **gold**. The *real* Jews, in all respects, were slowly being taken over by this Edomite force, and compromised to a horrible, horrible degree... until the integrity of a number of their descendents, later on, could have been all but assimilated. Eventually, the physical and moral purity of these Jewish survivors were slowly turning into something that, on the surface, might sound Jewish, or might look like something that is God-like, but, it's *not exactly* the same as what it was once before, or, it doesn't look the same as what these early books of the Bible may want them to look like before. There's definitely additions and alterations now... an early *success* story of this White Horse.

This, once again, seems to give us justification to a couple of verses in the Bible. We recall the following quotes from a previous chapter:

*Behold, I will make them of the synagogue of Satan, which **say** they are Jews, and are not, but do **lie**...*
- *Rev.* 3:9 (KJV)

...and I know the blasphemy of them which say they are Jews, and are not, but are the synagogue of Satan.
- *Rev.* 2:9 (KJV)

The Bible unequivocally states that there will be *phonies* out there - impostors, fakes, or pseudo-Jews - who would rather pass themselves off as the real thing. Wow. Who else could this have been? Who else could have been in the position to accomplish this (and who would have had such a desire to)? We already recall how this group definitely had the desire to take down those pure, ancient Jews in the past, and they wanted to usurp the brethren responsible for stealing the birthright of their patriarch. It seems so obvious. The Bible also tells us, definitively, that God was *extremely disfavored* by Cain, Balaam, and Esau (or Edom). They were the *real* progenitors of all of this phoniness out there, all of these deceptions, and were also considered the propagators of most everything that would end up going into the formation of the White Horse! Sad.

And, as we recall from previous volumes, Shem (Noah's son) told the mother of both Esau and Jacob about the future existences of their children, and how they would eventually go on to affect the entire world:

> *He (Shem) said to her: "My daughter, I confide a secret to thee. See to it that none finds it out. Two nations are in thy womb, and how should thy body contain them, seeing that **the whole world will not be large enough for them to exist in it together peaceably?"*   (S. Baring-Gould, 1881, p. 217)[28]

And, yes, we are **now** seeing some early evidence of this huge struggle. Of course, it's not the *true* Jews - the pure-blooded Jewish remnants of those tribes of Judah and Benjamin - that are the problem. And, it's also not necessarily anyone of any other bloodline who may want to *graft* themselves onto God's way… it's about fraud; it's about infiltration; it's about these manipulations.

Let's, now, begin to look into some *more* missing elements of our distant past, and what could have happened to our world… since the further **amalgamation** of these early Edomite and Jewish peoples.

"Palestine" - An Edomite-Roman Name

First, we recall that: it was these ancient *Romans* who tried to squash the remaining Edomites and Jews from the Holy Land. Next, we find that a number of these people did survive the Roman onslaught, and were able to migrate to a number of surrounding areas, even far, far away. And, in one final attempt to eliminate the presence of these people (in the area) *forever*, the Romans tried to do *one* more thing. After their initial push, they tried to *erase* the recorded history of these Jews and Edomites from the entire world… once and for all.

Wow. Doesn't that sound familiar? As we recall from previous volumes, the same happened with those Lost 10 Tribes of Israel, via the Assyrians. Assuredly, there were a number of oppressive regimes in our not-so-distant past which have attempted to do this same thing. These Romans strived to make sure that even **the *name*** of this land was no longer reflective of the people who once lived in it. So, in an attempt to numb their entire existence, this whole area was renamed.

Today, when many of us hear some news about the Holy Land, we may hear of the area being known as "Israel." But, also, we quite often hear of the word "Palestine" being used. Now, what is the story behind the use of this *alternate* name here?

> *In the 2nd century (AD)… the Romans crushed the revolt of Shimon Bar Kokhba (132 AD)… during which Jerusalem and Judea were regained and* **the area of Judea was renamed Palestina** *in an attempt to* **minimize Jewish identification with the land of Israel.**
> ("Origins of the Name 'Palestine' and Palestinian Nationalism", n. d., p. 2)[29]

Some, today, have said that this word relates to the ancient *Philistines*, who once lived in the land. Makes sense, at first. And, it is understandable to try and link this particular people (because they once resided in the area). But, these Philistines disappeared from off the map around 600 B.C. Now, why - in the first century A.D. - would the ancient Romans really want to do it this way? It makes no sense. But, if we look at a couple of the *other* possible meanings of that word *Palestine* (or *Palestina*), we discover that it could also stand for "migratory," a "land of strangers," or even a "land without people."[30] Could this have been because, even though there might have been a number of people migrating into the area, ever since the Jews were forced to depart, there wasn't exactly an established nation coming into the area, all at once, to take over. And, of course, the name makes a lot more sense now, if we think about it under these terms.

The Romans may have wanted that area to, now, be totally *uninhabited*, or without a nation to inhabit it (only a few migrating individuals) - with the Jewish people erased from that land forever, so they may have named it in such a way to reflect this dispersion, and elimination. If we think about it, it may have been meant to *insult* the Jewish people in such a way - proclaiming that "there's none of them left there anymore!"

It seems that a number of contemporary Jewish sources do share this same interpretation:

> *It (Palestine) has never been the name of a nation or state. It is a geographical term, used to designate the region at those times in history when there is no nation or state there... In the First Century CE, the Romans crushed the independent kingdom of Judea. After the failed rebellion of Bar Kokhba in the Second Century CE, the Roman Emperor Hadrian determined* **to wipe out the identity** *of Israel-Judah-Judea. Therefore, he took the name Palestina and imposed it on all the Land of Israel. At the same time, he changed the name of Jerusalem to* **Aelia Capitolina**.
> ("The History and Meaning of 'Palestine' and "Palestinians'", n. d., p. 2)[31]

Yes, even the name of their capital city, here - the world-famous *Jerusalem* - was apparently renamed, to "drive their point home" if you will. Go figure. Now, the next time we hear of the word "Palestine," spoken in casual conversation, we might be getting an inkling of exactly *why* the land was once named that. It wasn't really meant to be sound too complementary to the Jewish inhabitants who once resided there, that's for sure.

Next, we'll have to return, once again, to Zepho's Edomite stronghold - *Rome* - and see how their attempts at silencing anything and anyone *non-pagan* could have come back to bite them… in a major way! We'll also see what they may have had to do next, in order to continue on (with their stranglehold over a huge number of human souls).

Chapter 10

From the "Old" World to the "New"

The old (and pagan) Roman Empire was, over time, definitely beginning to develop an image problem. The attractiveness of Christianity was beginning to sink the attractiveness of these "same old pagan ways." The proverbial "rug" was, slowly, being pulled out from underneath them... now more than ever. Other religions were *nothing* compared to this up-and-coming Christian movement. Now, what were they going to do about all of this? Of course, the vast majority of the world's population was *still* under some kind of pagan domination; and their leaders, most naturally, would have felt an overwhelming desire to keep the power that they once had. What to do?

Even that former Edomite-Jewish conglomeration - slowly set up to replace (and utterly destroy) those Jewish individuals at the core - wouldn't really help out the Roman's cause, here. That one *Jew* named Jesus had delivered a major blow to those *Edomite attempts* to **totally** steal back their own birthright (as we soon shall see). What a coincidence, here... that Jesus was of the exact nation that the Edomites really despised. Go figure. Maybe this represents another *piece* of that whole, eternal battle between the two brethren. And, true, the Edomites were still be able to continue on, with their supplantation of those two tribes of Judah and Benjamin. But, as we may also recall, there are *still* ten more tribes out there. What if Jesus actually did what the Messiah was supposed to do - to unify the 12 tribes of Israel, once again (through Christianity)? We recall that Jesus actually asked his followers to "go rather to the lost sheep of the house of Israel (in Mat. 10:6)," and bring them back to his fold. Of course, if these Lost 10 Tribes were the nations that may have, for the most part, relocated into the areas of Western Asia and Europe (as we've surmised in a previous volume), then this unification could have, very well, happened.

Jesus, of course, was winning over a number of these Israelis from the tribes of Judah and Benjamin as well (i.e. the Jews). And, since so many Protestants and Catholics were located in and around the continent of Europe, then, this, in actuality, fits with our model perfectly - Christian and Catholic Europe, indeed, may have been the area that housed those Lost 10 Tribes, and a vast number of them *did* come back to God (through Jesus).

Yes, the people were reuniting - Gentile and Jew. From all walks of life, people were, once again, coming back to God. Regardless, those Edomite influencers of old were not about to give up the gains that they'd accumulated thus far (assimilating into the houses of Judah and Benjamin). They needed to do something to counter this great Christian revolution. Now, that great, worldwide battle between the two brethren - as prophesied by Shem - was about to continue on, and expand! The Edomites would have a few more "aces up their sleeve," however. Plans would soon be in the works to halt this whole "reunification" process, and twist it around a bit… at least enough to slow it down considerably.

Let's begin, by seeing how (Edomite) *Rome* was about to add their own "two cents worth" into the picture here, and do some assimilation of their own! Yes, this was the time the *other* Edomite faction - those following after the pattern of *Zepho* - were about to initiate their own infiltration into the Christian way of life, and, hopefully for them, change things in the same way that their Edomite brethren were able to do with the two tribes of Jews. Another battle would be on.

Of course, those contemporary pagan leaders of Rome would not want to just sit back, and allow this Christian movement to expand so much, as to overtake them. No way would they go down that easily:

*Emphasising the idea, Roman civilisation was extinguished suddenly and brutally: "Roman civilization did not pass peacefully. It was **assassinated**."*
- Andrae Trajannio[1]

The only way to take down a massive, political force, such as Rome, would be to *drag* it down, kicking and screaming. And, no matter how popular this Christian movement was to become (and it was about to become very large), **Rome** was still majestic *Rome*, and the leaders would *never* want to just sit there and allow themselves to be *totally* taken down! They were not about to lose out on all of that control they had over the masses (as we soon shall see). Any "assassination" attempts on Rome wouldn't truly work… at least not *totally*. The empire just had to make a few changes, or even had to work on getting a new *identity*, in order to continue on with their same role… as a world-influencer.

Decline of a Political Empire

This former Edomite stronghold would, now, have do things a bit *stealthily*, in order to keep their power and control. Zepho's Rome, now, would have to be open for a little "face-lift." Their politics needed to change; their image had to change; things had to be transformed into something that looked a bit more like the Christian belief. Why not take advantage of this upward trend? And, as many famously say: "if you can't beat 'em, join 'em."

We probably recall that, after the Flood, Noah wanted to maintain the *Italian Peninsula* as a piece of land that was *truly* pure, and God-following. It was to be the parcel of land where Godliness would reign supreme, hands down. Yet, as we also know, this area would become a battle ground, over time, seemingly because of this particular stance. It was to become a prime target for pagans trying to usurp whatever Godliness may have residing there. It was a battle. And, over the years, things still have not changed very much with this land. The fight would continue, on and on.

We might also remember that there existed pagan patriarchs (such as Ham and Cush) who eventually followed Noah up to the area, and slowly began to degrade it. Thanks to them (as well as a number of giants who began to migrate to the area), the *mystery* systems of Babylon would eventually be able to take hold, and do some damage.

Of course, Zepho would also come in, and continue to transform this "paganized" region into a militaristic (and political) powerhouse. In the end, this ancient land would have enough force behind it to, not only manipulate people in their immediate areas, but also manipulate things in their entire known world!

This time, things were not about to swing back in the direction of God, nor would everything turn out blatantly pagan. No. This time, it would be somewhere "in the middle." It would become close to God in some respects, and close to the other way as well! Oh my, now doesn't that sound familiar! Yes, all that was about to glitter, here - in this newly-refurbished Rome - was not necessarily gold... things were, in actuality, beginning to move in the direction of a *White Horse* system. Let's explain this all.

Rise of a Religious... Constantine?

We first begin by focusing on Zepho's Roman Empire, a couple of hundred years after the Roman authority had chased away a majority of Jews and Edomites from the Holy Land. This, as well, was the period where the Roman Empire was pursuing early Christians, trying to take them out. But, of course, Christianity was still on an upswing - rising a lot faster than they could keep up with. Their once-majestic pagan empire was, quickly, losing ground to this other faith. They tried to treat it as "just another religion," but the practitioners weren't having their input. The Christians were totally devoted to Jesus' message, as well as totally devoted to depart from any pagan theology.

Things were no longer working for the Romans. After taking a couple of Christians and throwing them into a lion's den, a couple more would step up, ready to take their places. They were dying for their faith. It, soon, became the time that things needed to change... it had to (for their own sakes).

Around the fourth century A.D., the leaders of Rome made a huge decision: it was about time to give up on their political ventures (such as an empire), and adopt a new outer look. Maybe, they thought: if they were able to turn this political force it into something of a *religion*, or something more of what these Christians might have been seeking after, then they could adopt a bit of this Christian momentum. Also, if they could begin to incorporate Christian elements into this new religion - *as well as* the paganism that their current Roman populous already *knew*, then maybe they would be able to keep things under control... still. Maybe they could begin to do the same as what those Edomites of the Holy Land were able to do to the Jews of the area (and their practices) - "weave" your way in, which may, eventually, allow you to take over. In the case of Rome, here, it meant that a formerly *political* empire, as well as a their formerly pagan religion, may both have to begin to *look* a little more *Christian.*

As we may recall from previous volumes: legend has it that a sudden, "miraculous" vision of a *cross* appeared in the sky, right in front of one of Rome's highest military leaders, on the eve of a massive battle that he was about to undertake. And, this vision came to a man named *Constantine*. The man, of course, won the battle, and took the sign as something (supposedly) that would have prompted him to *end* this persecution of Christians, and turn his entire pagan empire into something a lot more like it. What an abrupt change!

"In this sign conqueror" (manifesting as a *cross*) was the vision that Constantine apparently saw:

After claiming victory, Constantine was, not only the political leader of everyone around him, but, also, had now become their *religious* dignitary. A new world was being opened up. And, what may have been the best way for Constantine to "repay" this divine intervention - to set up the entire Roman Empire as a (Christian) religious empire.

Of course, the stage was being set for something new and big. It may have all sounded good and wholesome, at least on the surface, and it defiantly would have looked good for all of those persecuted Christians out there; but, there could have been a little *more* to all of this "great" change. Could there have been some *self-serving* elements initiated here, by the empire?

We may also recall (from previous volumes) that pagan Rome, before this, actually tried to see *itself* as the meeting place by which all of the different (pagan) religions could come together, and unite (even Christianity)! They even constructed a building - known as the *Pantheon* - by which people of all faiths could come together, and bring a godly representation (i.e. an idol) of their *own* into it (to be worshiped). Yes, Rome intended itself to become a "hub" of universal religious, and this invitation was also given to those of the Christian faith. They refused, however, claiming that their God was not an idol, and never would be.

And yes, this ancient building still exists today. And, it all sounded wonderful… if you were pagan. What if Rome was able to accomplish a "compromised" religion (in a way)? What if, like the Edomites before, they were able to take on more and more of their "enemy," manipulating it, and absorbing themselves into it - as something close to the original, but *not exactly the same*? It's interesting that: now, this same building would eventually become "repurposed" - as a *Christian* building!

If Rome did begin to adopt a number of these Christian elements, and form their own version of a Christian religion, then maybe they could have begun to claim "spiritual authority" over those presently in the Christian faith… at least a number of them. Maybe they wouldn't lose out as much control as they had once thought. If the combination was good enough (and, if they could have found a way *not* to lose their former pagan constitutes), then maybe they could remain in power, and *stay* there for a while.

There would have been perks to taking this route, assuredly, for the former Roman Empire. The advantages of having *religious* authority over the people, rather than just a political authority, allows one's innate fear of religious reprisals to help these Romans retain control... even over a distance. Unlike a political empire, the top leaders would no longer have to continually micromanage their subject's every actions and whereabouts. Now, they could use *religious* fears, in order to turn their new faith into a "self-restraining" psyop! Wow. The people would end up keeping *themselves* in line. How convenient.

Now, Rome could force the people to monitor *themselves* - as long as they are always the ones to call the short, and dictate what any new religious parameters might be. They'll *still* have control over the masses, in a number of ways (even though their political dominance was continuing to wane).

Now, to help them in this transition process, they felt a need to look to a few of those people that they once hated, and ran out of the Holy Land (for help). Yes, they needed the assistance of Jewish (or EJC) intellectuals to help get their belief *system* off of the ground. And, if we think about it: there already was an *Edomite* infestation into a lot of the top Jewish brass already - maybe some of their long-lost brethren could help them infuse *their* own empire into something of the same.

The EJCs and Rome - Once Again

As some may (correctly) say, "the enemy of my enemy is my friend!" And, yes, they may have now felt they needed to "join forces," one more time, with their former enemies, to take on this monumental new task. Whatever they felt it would take to get the job done - to bring Christianity down to their *own* level - they would now do it.

What if they were able to *merge* their current Roman authority with this up-and-coming Christian force, in a number of ways, to become a valid contender for a number of new Christian prospects? It would not only be good for *them*, to control that rise of Christian ideologues, but *also* help them gain control of any new converts into the faith.

We may also recall that the Romans, before this time, tried to unite the whole world (religiously) under them, by the use of the Pantheon. Maybe this was their "post-

Christian" way of attempting this, once again. Maybe this was their way of trying to become the new, universal church of the world (which would have *included* Christian values this time)!

To begin, Rome set out to ask a number of educated *Jewish* religious leaders to help them out (with their new religion). Maybe, the top brass could mend things, at least for a bit, in order to find ways to make this kind of conglomerate work for them.

Nicaea - "Partnering With the Enemy"

Around the 4th century A.D., and with the help of Constantine (the current emperor), a transformation was to be undertaken... at the Council of Nicaea. Constantine would do his best to assemble a number of the top learned minds of the time, together in one place... and this would include a number of Edomite/Jewish elites. He and his new religious authority would also begin to assemble a number of sacred Christian works, in order to have a holy book put together. The canonized a number of ancient texts, and the Bible emerged. It all sounded really good, right?

With the learned people under this Roman emperor, as well as with the learned Jews (or EJCs) of the time, the *Bible* came together (with both the Old and the New Testaments). What an undertaking this all must have been. And, on the surface, this all sounds like it would have been a **great** undertaking for the sake of Christianity, and the Christian movement, right? And, in a number ways, it may have been! But, as one could also guess, the people at the top of this intricate partnership - a large number of them - might not have exactly had the best interests of Christianity at heart.

Regardless, even if they were able to achieve this assembly of the Bible, then that would have been a great thing! But, wait a minute: isn't there some kind of conflict here (if we really think about it)? How could something as wonderful and perfect as the Bible come out of this meeting - pulled off by a number of individuals who, in the end, might have other end goals in mind? Could God have worked their plans to, eventually, be something of a benefit to the *true* Christians of their day (and beyond)?

Sometimes, God Uses Evil For Good

True Christians surely would have wanted to keep these texts of Paul, John and other Godly influencers, after the introduction of Christianity. And this "conversion" of Constantine's pagan empire into something more and more Christian may have opened up some doors for this. What's really going on here, in the whole scheme of things?

As mentioned in the Bible, God may, sometimes, use the most unlikely of sources (or even characters) to get His points across. In one example, we see that He used an enemy to Israel (i.e. Rahab the harlot) to help the Jews to conquer the Holy Land. In another example, He used a stubborn donkey. In another, He had a number of bad things happen to the prophet Job. In yet another, He used jealous brethren to assist the descendants of Israel from starving to death. As we see in this particular story, we find the righteous *Joseph* being accosted by his jealous brothers, and then sold into slavery. Joseph, a direct son of Jacob (or Israel) himself, was well favored by God (because he acted righteously), but not by his brothers. They wanted him gone.

After his brothers ended selling him into slavery (in Egypt), God seemed to have worked through these Egyptians, as well as the pharaoh himself. The pharaoh noticed something about Joseph, and how he seemed to be a gifted individual (or protégé of God). He liked him so much that he ended up *elevating* Joseph into one of the highest position of the land!

A famine, as the Bible tells us, would eventually come into the Middle East, and Joseph's brothers would end up finding themselves migrating to the same land that they once sold Joseph to. Seeking asylum in this land, and looking for mercy, they came across Joseph. What a shock for them. Joseph, however, said something very interesting to them:

> ...*as for you, ye thought evil against me;* **but God meant it unto good**, *to bring to pass, as it is this day, to* **save** *much people alive.*
> - *Gen.* 50:20 (KJV)

Wow. What a reckoning. What a way for God to utilize something that seemed (on the outside) to be totally negative (i.e. Joseph being sold into slavery)... but, it ended up as something *good* in the end. Once again, we see how He used certain people and certain circumstances to help Him fulfill His goals, or prophecy, or push things into a certain direction.

Many of us recall what the Bible also says:

*And we know that all things **work together for good** to them that love God...*
- Rom. 8:28 (KJV)

Even *nefarious* attempts might end up in this same direction. Things that may not have started out very good, or had begun with the best of intentions, have ended up being something of God's ultimate design.

A New, "Universal" Conglomerate

Regardless of who might ultimately benefit from the creation of this Bible (the most), those educated elites under Constantine began to look for other ways to make their new believe system seem legitimate. Constantine, then, set out to gather as many ancient Christian relics as one could, to help take this new Christian conglomerate off the ground. Hopefully (for them), this would begin to get people on board, very quickly. And, also, hopefully it would help to transform their former *pagan* empire into a new, and respected, religious force.

That Pagan-Christian "Hybrid"

For things to fully "take off" (for *everybody* that they presided over), the powers that be could make it sound like a good plan for everyone, even the many pagans out there (all over the land). What if they were able to find a way to market this religion as some kind of "mother," or "universal" religion - with elements of Christianly in it, along with a few of the same pagan elements that so a number of people in the empire were already used to. Time to bring back this Pantheon, and market it in a slightly *different* way?

And, for this all to work, there *had* to (absolutely) have been a number of concrete elements of the Christian belief in the religion… yet, the belief also needed to have a number of those "old" religious ways (in order to keep those pagan "hardliners" happy). Yes, their new faith would, surely, have to become known as a "conglomerated" faith.

And, in a number of ways, it might even be a "good" thing for people (according to them, of course): now, Christians would no longer be tortured, and people all over the land would be treated a lot better than they were before. What's wrong with unifying the people, right? Of course, one meaning of "Catholicism" is "universal," and it all seems to fit. The Roman authority wanted to create a "universal" church, with Christian elements, as well as with the pagan elements of their current population… and that's what seemed to have happened.

Well, if this was the truth, then just what were a few of those *pagan* elements inserted into this new faith? First off: the insertion of Jesus' mother *Mary* - as "co-savior" and "co-redeemer" of the entire world - was a prime example. There was nothing like this in the Bible, nor in the original Christian faith. It was the Father, the son, and the Holy Spirit. But, of course, in an attempt to *merge* a couple of belief systems, adding this element seems to have become a necessary part of their new religious dogma. Actually, Mary seems to have been modeled after that famous pagan mother "goddess" (or Eve, Naamah, Semiramis, etc.). And, of course, this is so telling: just why would the new Roman church have a need for a *female* deity - one that easily seems to parallels the female "mother" deities of early paganism?

There was more: we now have their new churches being built on top of former *pagan* sites and holy places. Why, once again? Would this be to keep their pagan constituents happy (being able to, essentially, return to their same place of worship)? We also have this new Catholic church utilizing charms, chants, and other things the pagan may have once utilized. We have new "Holy Days" of the Christian paralleling, in part, a number of *older* pagan holidays. As well, we have the installation of *images* or *icons* into these churches… similar to the pagan *idols* of the past. There is a lot more.

And, through this (of course), the new religious leadership really had to do this, to in order to keep their hybrid religion strong (and attractive).

"Holy Mother" Over Them All

As a mother may be considered the matriarch of her children, this new Catholic church began to view itself as much of the same - as "Holy Mother" over their religious children (all of them).

Yet, we've still seen those ancient *Kenite* scribes assimilating themselves into the ancient Jewish religious aristocracy. We've seen the ancient Babylonian pagans instructing their captured Jewish leaders on how to run their faith, as well as how to run their people. We've also seen those Edomites (or Idumeans) inserting themselves into the Jewish way of life, as well as with the people (genetically). Now, we have the pagan Romans about to do the same, in a way - assimilating Christianity and Christian values into their current (and pagan) fold. The Catholic church was now formed, as the new, universal "mother" over a vast number of people, bringing together a number of different faiths. The pagan Pantheon was now updated, and converted into a Catholic holy place! How convenient. An "ecumenical" way of doing religion was now under way.

Not Just The Bible...

Even though the Bible would have been the ultimate source of Christian reference (and still is, in a number of cases), those early Roman religious authorities wanted to have things work a little differently here… to allow them to have a better "say so" in the whole religious process.

Still, as far as true Christianity is concerned, the Bible (as it was assembled) continues to prove itself as the inspired Word of God, and it remains as <u>the</u> source of spiritual reference and guidance for the true Christian believer. And, as we'll now see, those who continue to hold onto this particular modem of thought may actually be following the concept of *Sola scriptura*:

Sola scriptura (Latin: by Scripture alone): *a Christian theological doctrine which holds that the Christian Scriptures are the supreme authority in all matters of <u>doctrine</u> and <u>practice</u>.*[2]

It all sounds pretty straightforward, and has been the way a vast number of Protestant peoples - from the past to the present - have lived out their lives. Yet, the early rulers of this new religious conglomerate wanted to make sure that *they* were able to hold onto enough power to keep them relevant (so they wouldn't just have to leave it all up to the interpretations of Scripture), so, they decided to put a few protocols in their new church, *above* the Bible.

Curiously enough, in the Catholic faith, we now have *three* pillars of authority:

1. Church **Magisterium** (the teaching authority of the Catholic institution)
2. Catholic **Tradition**
3. and (lastly) the **Bible**

Wow, talk about having the "say-so" here. The "Holy Mother" has inserted herself into the mix… turning the foundations of this entire Christian belief (i.e. the Holy Scriptures) into a living, breathing "document" - giving *them* the options to slice and dice dogma in any way they seemed to fit. Even their traditions may outweigh any old religious document.

"Paganized" Dignitaries

Speaking of the conglomeration of Christian and pagan theologies, there seems to have been another *infusion* here, which may be of some importance (to our discussion). As many of us might recall, the first two commandments (out of those famous *Ten Commandments*) have to do with the utilization of other "gods," rather than the worship of the one true God. And, obviously, since these two commandments were placed on top of all the rest, they may have been important to the Heavenly Father. God, as many of us might already know, is a jealous God, and He does not want to share any human worship here... with nothing, or no other entity of this lower world.

Yet, paganism, as we might recall from previous volumes, has a lot of polytheistic (or multi-god) elements infused in it. It usually calls for their people to worship a variety of different gods and goddesses. Now, what could the church do, here, in this particular situation? How would they be able merge the two elements effectively?

It seems they were *subtly* able to do it. In one example, we notice how the Catholic Church elevates Jesus' mother into another "goddess-like" position - on the same level as Jesus no doubt! Now, it seems as though we have both a male and female object of worship here. Christianity, before, just had a Father, Son and Holy Spirit. There seems to be more.

The Catholic Church also seems to strive to push patrons into praying to, or calling out to, "minor dignitaries" (such as "patron saints") for their help, similar to how pagans would need to call out to "minor" gods around them, for their help. Coming a little short of proclaiming that these patron saints are actually "little gods," they do seem to be utilized in much the same way pagans would. People venerate them. They pray to them. They ask them for favors. The same goes on with these patron saints of the Catholic world. What else would we call it?

The Bible, on the other hand, tells us **not** to reach out to, or worship, any human ancestors, nor does it tell us to petition any angels of God, as well.

Let no man beguile you of your reward in a voluntarly humility and **worshipping of angels**...   - *Col.* 2:18 (KJV)

The petitioning of those who came before us is clearly pagan, and is considered ancestor worship (no matter what "level" the church may have decided to elevate them to). Angels, as well, are only supposed to be *ministers* of God... not entities that we can reach out to, for help.

> *While there is no verse which explicitly states, "You shall not pray to angels," it is abundantly clear that we are not to pray to angels. Ultimately, prayer is an act of worship. And, just as angels reject our worship (Revelation 22:8-9), so they would also reject our prayers. Offering our worship or prayer to anyone but God is **idolatry**.*
> ("Does the Bible promote or prohibit praying to angels?", 2022, p. 1)[3]

This seems to be a lot more *right* than it is possibly wrong! If any angel intends on communicating with members of the human race, *they* will come to the individual, and God would have been the one to send them! We are **not** to elect people into an "angel-like" state of *sainthood* either. As the above quote seems to suggest, by doing this, we, most likely, would be connecting ourselves with the fallen entities of this world, who may try to fool us into thinking we are making some kind of supernatural progress. Watch out.

Angelic Changes For the 4th Century

Speaking of angels here, we'll also see that: in order for those early Romans to make their conglomeration of faiths a success, there may *still* need to be a bit a more "tweaking," here, to be done (for reasons that we shall soon see).

Soon, it would become time for them to start putting this conglomerated religious faith into practice. Their new church, for the most part, would soon be off and running. It's also interesting to see that, around this same time, a few changes in public perception and opinion may have been enacted. As we may recall (from previous volumes), a number of women in the antediluvian world could have had sexual exchanges with a number of fallen, terrestrial angels… both committing fornication with one another. This, in turn, would allowed for a number of women to be very knowledgeable and powerful (through the information that they gained from their exchanges). As well, a number of these same women ended up becoming pregnant, and giving birth to giant, hybrid offspring. Through the years since, it almost became common knowledge that these exchanges, indeed, did happen; and a lot of forbidden knowledge, indeed, was being supplied to the human race. It was a widely accepted part of our ancient history… at least until *this* particular time!

These exchanges, as we may know, gave people a great deal of previously-forbidden (i.e. occult) information… things that God really didn't want the human race to have, at least they way they had it. And *now*, with these attempts to merge Christianity with elements of polytheistic paganism, a lot of this forbidden knowledge would, naturally, begin to flow into this process, from *somewhere*. It's almost unavoidable. Once a person has the desire to know the *deeper* elements of their faith, they'll want to dive more and more into the *esoteric*. What if a number of people would begin to dive into this conglomerated belief system, and start to figure out how this combination wasn't *entirely* something of God (or, from a Godly source)? Then what? Things wouldn't shine a positive light down on this conglomerated belief system, that's for sure!

Maybe certain historical elements, such as fallen angels being able to mate with human women, or anything that may shed light on people gathering divine information from any some other obscure source of this world (such as with divination), would, now, have to be twisted, downplayed, or even "disappeared." Why? Or course… it's all about exposure, here. After this time, the sources of a number of "questionable" (or "eyebrow-raising") elements of esoteric information out there may need to be silenced. You just can't allow anything ungodly (or, seemingly ungodly) to become an essential part of Christian dogma. Surely, a conglomerated faith (as with what happened to the faith of corrupted Judaism, earlier on) needs to still appear "holy" to the current practitioners - without any pagan taint. There can be no fallen angels, no giants, and no information from any of those so-called "questionable" sources (at least, it can't *seem that way*)!

Now, as a result of this need to make things look a bit more "kosher," the time had arrived for a number of these religious authorities to "change history" a bit, and downplay anything that might expose them, and their sources - such as those fallen, terrestrial angels being able to communicate with human beings, and their giant, hybrid offspring doing a lot of the same. Of course, if these beings "do not exist," then the potential for any *impurities* emerging into their new and conglomerated faith would also be reduced, or even negated.

Changes in Perception

Now, how would one go about changing public opinion? There were a number of ancient tales about giants. There also seemed to have been a lot of physical evidence of these giants as well, such as giant skeletons, mounds being built, and monumental structures attributed to their own handiwork. How could these religious leaders be able to twist so many things around, and even conceal things once considered *commonplace*?

First off, they would begin to erase any and all literature about the existence of these terrestrial beings, or at least find ways to downplay it. Also, they would began to dilute or downplay the number of oral traditions about them. Any talk of those Anakim, the Refaim, or even the Fowl of the Air (i.e. those fairies, elves, etc.) would have to be put on a dusty shelf, or into the category of "fairy lore," or a "fairy tale." They, also, would have to begin to eliminate as many pieces of physical evidence as they possibly could, over time - stopping any new digs, disappearing existing bones, etc. My, doesn't this sound pretty familiar - like what the *Smithsonian* was said to have done, a number of years later?

Either way they would go about it, most of it would, most probably, have to take a while. I wouldn't just be overnight. Regardless, the desire to cover up almost anything *nefarious* to their conglomerated faith would, now, become quite important - in order to maintain that "Godly" image.

In fact, if we really think about it: any thought of those ancient Kenites corrupting the Jewish faith could have been affected by these changes, as well as any thought of there actually being Serpent Seeds out there, trying to control and corrupt humanity. These new ways of thinking would also be able to eliminate the understanding that Eve could have mated with an angelic *Serpent*, inside of the Garden of Eden, ending up with an hybrid offspring named **Cain**. If these concepts were not really real, then none of this would have really existed as well.

Again, pulling the proverbial "rug" out from all of this would also help to downplay **the entire origins of paganism** (i.e. as being from Cain and the Serpent), as well as what paganism was *really* all about. How could it be **so** bad, if the Serpent wasn't really a fallen, terrestrial angel, and did not sire evil human hybrids, such as Cain? If this Serpent was not a fallen angel, and if those other influential terrestrial angels of the day (i.e. the Nephilim) did not exist as well, then *how* could anyone associate *them* as being so contrary to God, or as the ones who may have be able to dispense a lot of questionable material? No Serpent; no hybrid son Cain - no "evil paganism." See how it all works?

Now, the "mystical" information that might end up coming to a number of these religious "higher ups" could not really be considered as *nefarious*… if their supposed *sources* no longer exist! What a scam here.

And, even if there *was* some paganism intertwined in this religious conglomeration, it still might not necessarily be thought of as all that bad - if the pagan faith was **not** what the people previously knew it as! Maybe, since there were no fallen, terrestrial angels and no Serpent, the belief system may have actually started out *on its own*, as a "neutral," or "nature loving" religion… by people "of the country." This "home grown" approach sounds innocent enough. And now, if some of it would have ever crept up into a Christian religious practice, then it really wouldn't have, necessarily, been viewed as something coming from the "Other side," or something demonic. There's a chance it might just be incidental, or some "extra filler."

Erasing these elements would open the doors for so much. It's like how Satan works so hard to convince people that he does not exist as well. No evil one… no real evil in this world, right? Now, a person could even, quite possibly, be allowed to communicate with a few of those "neutral" spirits of the world (through necromancy), because, for all practical purposes, they may not even be something to watch out for. Some spirits of this lower world are not necessarily evil (according to them). See how it works?

Removing the "Evidence"

Along these same lines, we find out that: certain revealing texts, such as *The Book of Enoch*, are discounted, and even silenced. They do not really need to have been read anymore, or even taken seriously… even though the book was found right **alongside** a number of canonical books (in the Dead Sea Scrolls).

In one interesting internet article, entitled *Why is the Book of Enoch not regarded as canonical*, we have an example of how certain ancient texts were "written off," because they had evidence of fallen, terrestrial angels in them. Apparently, before Constantine ever gathered a bunch of learned Jewish intellectuals together, in order to finalize the Bible (at the council of Nicaea), we, apparently, had a number of Jewish scholars coming together, around the time of 90 A.D., to work on some "finalizations" of their own. They wanted to unite a number of Hebrew books together, and form their own *canon* (in response to the ever-expanding movement of Christianity). Their results would have been known as the "Old Testament" by Christians later on. Yes, the interesting thing about this particular meeting was: they were already beginning to toss out a number of ancient texts that they didn't like... including the *Book of Enoch*. Since this time, there would be a number of intellectuals who would:

> ...***only accept*** *canon of scripture approved by Jews at the council of Jamnia in the late 1st century.*
> ("Why is the Book of Enoch not regarded as canonical?", 2012, p. 9)[4]

Again, we seem to have some corruption brewing. Of course, a number of these religious leaders (at the Council of Jamnia) may have already been infiltrated - theologically or even genetically - by the *Kenite* scribes of the past... those who came from Cain. Of course, they may have already begun to look for ways to downplay, or even eliminate, any talk of fallen, terrestrial angels mating with human women... including the Serpent himself. No angelic *Serpent* means no Cain *as his seed*. Simple - it was a way for them to - theologically and otherwise - save *their own skins*! If Cain wasn't a seed of the Serpent, then he was just another human being who may have had some hard times in life, and went a little *astray* at times (as we all might do). No big deal, here. Nothing to raise an eyebrow over.

And, as well, this fact wouldn't have really allowed for any of his Kenite descendents to appear as though they were doing the work of the devil, now would it? So, now, that Kenite invasion into the Jewish faith wouldn't have *really* been considered too nefarious, or too impure... since they were just "another group of post-Flood people." So, what's the real problem? Nothing to see, and *to expose*, here. Once again, do we see how this works? It all makes total sense, here, when we begin to discover just how a number of ancient (and corrupted) religious authorities may have felt about being exposed. They probably felt in much the same way as those Roman dignitaries would have begun to feel, later on. Both, assuredly, would have also been *more than willing* to start censoring a number of things, to save their own skin.

Over time, certain "questionable" elements have flowed into the Jewish faith (such as the number of traditions leading up to the Kabbalah). These "mystical" elements of the faith do seem to issue an extreme scent of the arcane and mysterious - assuredly, not on the same par as something typically from the Bible. Now, if this was so, then just where could these particular elements have had their origins? It's a mystery. And, if these ancient religious leaders were, somehow, able to stifle the possibility of any *other* ungodly influences (such as these fallen, terrestrial angels), then it may quickly call into question *any* talk of their religious elements as being anything other than "holy." That's the reason why certain books - such as the Book of Enoch - had to find its way into the shelves of oblivion.

In fact, we also find the Catholic church, for eons since this early time, have attempted to *totally* remove the existence of this particular book… their attempts at subversion even lasted up to the 18th century! Why do this? What's behind this continual denial of parishioner access? What had they seemed so intimidated about an ancient book such as this? Of course, the Book of Enoch is a book full of things that they may have *not* have wanted the general public to find out about, or contemplate!

True, there is also *some* angelic information in the Bible (of which they, once again, would have tried to deflect in some way). They could accomplish this in the Bible (because the references to angelic information is few and far between), but *not* in a book like the Book of Enoch. This book is "saturated" with a lot of information on fallen, terrestrial angels… which wouldn't be good at all for their agenda(s).

Although they may have been able to suppress the Book of Enoch (for a great long while), they surely couldn't have been able to suppress all of what's already in the Bible… at least not very easily. There were a few verses in there which seem to still expose a lot of what they were trying to hide… some very cumbersome verses (such as those in Genesis, Chapter 6):

*It was in the 5th century a.d. that the "angel" interpretation of Genesis 6 was increasingly viewed as an **embarrassment** when attacked by critics. (Furthermore, **the worship of angels** had begun within the church. Also, celibacy had also become an institution of the church. The "angel" view of Genesis 6 was feared as **impacting these views**.)*
("Michevious Angels or Sethites?", 1997, p. 2)[5]

Wow. Could political correctness have been slowly coming onto the scene? Notice how we see the *worshiping of angels* being mentioned here, as well. Could one belief be inversely working against the other, here? Could a person's belief in fallen angels have been *downplayed*, more and more (over the years), while the petitionings of Catholic *saints* have begun to arise?

In one prime example of Biblical manipulation, we now see how much people would have begun to attack this sixth chapter of Genesis (ever since this time):

There were giants in the earth in those day, and also after that, when the sons of God came in unto the daughters of men, and they bare children to them...
- Gen. 6:4 (KJV)

Eventually, people would begin to claim that those "sons of God" and the "daughters of men" were both human beings - the "sons of God" were merely "good" human beings... followers after God's heart. It sounds logical, but why would it be notated this way, in Genesis, if it were all so "simple?" And, of course, Genesis could not really be taken out of the Bible - it's far too important. So, they'll have to find *some* way to reinterpret these words. So often, they cannot allow these phrases to actually point towards something that might be taken *literally* - it must be something figuratively or *allegorical* in nature. Now, many will begin to believe that these "sons of God" actually stand for those righteous sons of *Seth*, Adam's son - even though the phrase, in the Old Testament, was almost *always* used in reference to angels! Regardless, the descendents of Seth - the "sons of God" - were now considered the ones who ended up marrying the Cainite "daughters of men." See how the twist goes? They *all* have to be human. No room for anything else.

Interestingly enough, a number of early "church fathers," and other apologists for the newfound Roman Catholic Church, seemed to have helped to set this all in motion:

> *Only when Augustine (an early Catholic theologian) began reinterpreting the Old Testament **allegorically**, so that he could reinterpret the literal promises made to Israel and apply them to the church, did the **sons of Seth** explanation take root.*
> ("Part Six: The Sons of God According to Ancient Sources", 2011, p. 7)[6]

Yes, there were a number of manipulations going on - inside and outside of the Bible - in order to allow for their new belief system to seem legitimate and viable.

It also seems that those corrupt EJCs (in Judaism) were beginning to downplay any talk of the same, because of its exposing nature. We even see some going to *the extremes* in order to downplay it:

> *Nor did the rabbis deign to give credence to the book's teaching about angels. Rabbi Simeon ben Jochai in the second century A.D. pronounced a **curse** upon those who believed it.*
> (Clare Prophet, 2000, p. 16)[7]

Wow... a curse. So much for allowing a person the freedom to find out things on their own! It seems that some religious leaders may be so intent on getting rid of a lot of this "old" information that they were willing to *put a curse* on anyone who even thought about believing in it. Wow.

But, *why* would they go to such a degree? Again, once we begin to understand just how much *exposure* this might bring to those in charge, it begins to make more and more sense. These religious leaders may, now, have to do one more thing: to lean their congregations in the direction of only accepting that only *they* - the *priests*, *rabbis* and *pastors* of the church - would be the ones to be able to gather this "divine" information, and also be the interpreters of any and all Scripture. Wow. Of course, this gives them the "keys to the kingdom" if you will. And, of course, if we have to trust in these people for, pretty much, all of what they tell us is "holy," then we also need to believe that all of their information would have come from a *legitimate* source - as from some kind of *divine* intervention from God, or from one of His holy messengers (i.e. a Godly spirit, or an angel). Again, no room for any fallen, terrestrial angels here, and their giant sons.

Getting their mystical or esoteric information from any other source, now, wouldn't even be considered *plausible* anymore, really… if they do not exist, of course (right)? Also, it's now okay for a person to petition their favorite "patron saints," to gather for themselves whatever divine information or assistance that these particular entities may have to offer (just like the pagans do). It's all "good" now.

We also, now, discover the "can of worms" that may actually result from a person researching these early tidbits of "unapproved" information. Of course, it seemed to be much easier for a number of these early (and corrupted) church leaders to just *erase* it all from our collective consciousness, rather than have to debate it, or allow for any type of *exposure* to come into their midst. There's a method to their madness here, truly.

Turning On Their "Allies," Once Again

After the establishment of this conglomerated (Roman) church was well underway, the partnership they may have once had - with those Edomite-Jewish religious leaders who were once helping them - was not to last very long. Why? Of course, it was probably because there was bad blood between these two groups already - they probably did not think too highly about each other to begin with. Disagreements would have easily flowed (especially after the Romans decided to get into the religious game). Religious "competition," as well as the gathering of land and relics sacred to both sides, was beginning to grow. Yes, as both began to promote their own faiths, squabbles would naturally break out - with each side wanting things that they believed were rightly *theirs*, such as specific plots of land (in the Holy Land), holy sites within these areas, certain relics, etc.

The land of Israel had now become *very* important to both religious parties (between Judaism and Catholicism) here, And, because of this, it was soon to be time for a number those EJCs, or Edomite Jews, to do a little subtle and manipulative "work" of their own. They were about to use whatever clout they had, at the time, to go on the offensive.

In one subtle "attack," for example, those on the side of Judaism would begin to point out that these historical Romans actually had *Edomites* within their own history - which, of course, would not look very good to any true Jew or Christian out there. They were already beginning to expose the corruption within the Roman Catholic Church:

Once the Roman empire became the Christian (actually, the Catholic) empire and Christianity (that is, in this case, Roman Catholicism) took the place of idolatry as the religion of Rome, the name of **Edom was transferred to the Christians (i.e. Catholics)**...
                       ("Esau, Edom, Rome, and the Christians", 2016, p. 2)[8]

We also discover how one particular writer on the subject may have interpreted it all:

I will quote a summary of this issue from the "Between Jews and Christians," Open University unit, pg 11-121: After the destruction of the Second Temple, Edom became a soubriquet for **Rome**. *Thus the new villain has taken on the name and fate of the old villain. Leading to this, it seems, is the prophetic image of Edom as the* **great destroyer, guilty of the ruin of Israel**...
                       ("Esau, Edom, Rome, and the Christians", 2016, p. 2)[9]

Now, with information such as this, those ancient EJCs were beginning to work on bringing these Romans *down*, accusing *them* as the *real* enemy of their ancestor Jacob (even though a number of *them* might have also been corrupted by the same ancient Edomites (ideologically, as well as genetically).

Regardless, this new "battle" for the Holy Land, and all of what would end up going along with this, was now beginning to "heat up." Assuredly, both of these Edomite groups were, not only out to manipulate the *true* elements of both the Jewish and Christian faiths, but were also starting to go after *each other*, in the process.

Chapter 11

Where They May Have Went

We need to, once again, go back to our chronological timeline, and continue with this *other side* of that Edomite conspiracy: the Edomite Jews, those EJCs or pseudo-Jews - whatever one might want to call this Edomite "infusion." We'll now begin to discover what they were about to do next, to "make a few moves" against the Roman Catholic Church. They were not about to allow themselves to be continually beaten down by this new (and "Christian-like") conglomerate, nor any other Christian-like faith out there, if they could help it.

Of course, most of us may not have heard much more on this particular group (of Jews and their EJC infiltrators) after this dispersion in the 1st century. And, of course, with that former Roman Empire - now self-identifying as the Roman Catholic Church - still being able to "call a lot of the shots," very little information about these people, and where they may have went to next, was probably going to be leaked. They were a true enemy of this Roman establishment, already "written off" of the world's stage.

But, as we'll eventually see, these EJCs leaders would **not** be written off of the world's stage, not for very long. They would, eventually, begin to work alongside *another* group of individuals out there - a strong group of individuals who would end up defecting from this same Roman Catholic authority. And, the *new* conglomerate that would end up forming here would be able to, over time, help these Edomite Jews turn into becoming a very powerful force (as we shall soon see). Yes, let's begin to see how a lot of this would have come about, and just *who* this additional group may have been. It's quite fascinating, once we begin to dig a bit deeper into it all.

As we've discovered in a previous chapter, there emerged a formidable enemy to the Edomite Jews, or EJCs out there: and that would be this up-and-coming Catholic powerhouse! Because of their new stake in the Christian ethos, this particular group of Roman Edomites (now turned Catholic) now wanted to begin staking their *own* claims on sacred sites of Christianity, as well as any relics. The claim to Jerusalem and the Holy

Land were now in their crosshairs... all in order to "validate" their own stand as a major religious movement of God.

And, soon, there would be militaristic campaigns to control Jerusalem - that ancient Jewish and Christian "hot spot." But, as time would roll on, another faith - Islam - would also begin to stake a claim over this land, claiming it as being sacred to their religion as well. As number of faiths would be brewing at this time, as well as a number of battles (over *control* of this part of the world).

We, next, begin by looking at where a number of those influential Jewish and Idumean people might have ended up, after being dispersed from this ancient Holy Land (and *who* they may have eventually been associated with). And, please recall: the issue of this whole expose' is to understand the corruption that may have taken place within the numbers of **true** Jews and Christians out there. Our concern, here, is to point out the *infiltrators*, and how they had brought a pure bloodline and ideology to corruption and adulteration... how they brought it in the direction of what a typical *Edomite* may have wanted for his belief system, or for his way of life. The problem with this type of expose,' so often, lies with this: for the most part, it's not the individual practitioners who are the real problem here (i.e. someone just trying to be a good follower of Judaism), but a small percentage of those corrupt ones at the top (usually, or in some kind of powerful positions)! They are the ones who, subtly, are working to subvert the entire faith, and Jewish ways of life... all to their own gain. *That* is the major problem with this Edomite infiltration.

Now, with that understanding in tow, let's understand what may have happened with a good number of those Edomite Jews, or EJCs, after they were driven out of this Holy Land. Of course, as with the Lost 10 Tribes of Israel, the nation did not just *disappear* (like a puff of smoke)... they had to have went *somewhere*.

Back to Babylon?

It seems that a vast number of this mixed faction may have headed right back into the same direction of where many of their ancestors had been *taken* before (believe it or not): yes, Babylon! Yes, pagan *Babylon* (out of all the places for them to go)! Well, once again, we may need to ask ourselves: just *why* would they have wanted to go back there? Why would any *true* followers of God want to go back to the hub of **pagan** theology and ideology... unless there could have been a number of individuals within their religious ranks (such as those EJCs) who may have felt a little more *at home* there, or felt a little more welcomed *ideologically*? It makes a lot more sense, once we begin to start believing that there was corruption within these Jewish ranks. It makes sense, once we start to believe that, by this time, **EJC** contamination had begun to manifest itself, overwhelmingly, within the Jewish people.

A quote from an actual website on Jewish history has this as:

*After the Jews were sent into exile in 70 CE, the **main Jewish community**... was (in) **Babylonia**. It was the **only place in the world** where Christianity (mainly this Christian conglomerate of Roman Catholicism) did not take over, and therefore, the **Jews thrived there**.*
("The Origins of Sephardim and Ashkenazim", n. d., p. 1-2)[1]

In other words, it seems as though these EJCs may have even preferred that particular pagan hub to **any** kind of Christian affiliation (Catholic or not)! Wow. It really seems as though these EJC leaders may have had a strong disliking against the *true* children of Israel, whether they be of those last two tribes, the Lost 10 Tribes, or the Jew that started that whole Christian movement - *Jesus*. Why wouldn't a number of them want to go there... *especially* if they were *Edomites* at heart? It makes perfect sense to understand how the city of Babylon - that original powerhouse of **Cain's pagan** belief - wouldn't exactly mind the migration of people who **weren't** exactly Christian, or Godly. It fits.

And (of course), if a number of these Edomite Jews decided to migrate into Babylon, one more time, wouldn't this open the doorway to many *more* darkened paths of pagan corruption? It's like walking into a lion's den of the "Other Side." The longer they stayed in this area, the greater the chance of these individuals to come across something *contrary* to God... something out to *change* them, theologically and ideologically.

The Downfall of Babylon

Yet, even this safe-haven of *Babylon* would only be temporary. In the 9th century A.D., it seemed that this Edomite-Jewish community (in Babylon) was on the decline. Babylon was continually being attacked by advancing Muslims, set on taking over the entire area (of which we will discussing more, in greater detail, later on). A number of those displaced Edomite Jews of EJCs would soon be discovering that they needed to leave this area, and move on towards something else.

The people began to split up, and would head (at least) in two different directions. Some went to the west, far away (possibly by boat). Most may have migrated to another area, not too far away. It, now, had become a time of dissention, and a time where we begin to see a number of *modern* takes on it all: saying one thing, while our research says another.

Let's now take a look at those two possible directions that a number of these people may have ended up migrating towards.

Towards Spain, as the "Sephardic" Jews

> *There are two main types of Jews today, the* **Sephardic Jew** *(i.e. the "Spanish" or "Moroccan" Jews)... makes up a small percentage of the Jews in the world...*
> ("The People of Mt. Seir", 2009, p. 6)[2]

> <u>**Sephardic:**</u> *a member of the occidental (or Western) branch of European Jews settling in Spain and Portugal and later in the Balkans, the Levant, England, the Netherlands, and the Americas...*[3]

As we've already mentioned, a small number of these individuals may have decided to migrate to the west, and eventually to the north, into the continents of Africa and Europe. It's been estimated that about 5% of those Edomite Jews may have went up, into this direction (after they had left Babylon).

In the 9th century, the Jewish community in Babylonia began to decline, so many Jews went to North Africa, which was populated by two Moslem tribes: the Berbers and the Moors… and by the time the Moors were emigrating from North Africa into Spain, they brought along the Jews…
    ("The Origins of Sephardim and Ashkenazim", n. d., p. 2)[4]

They were considered the "Western" branch of European Jews (and, in regards to most of our discussion, we will not be getting too much into this branch).

Edomite Corruption Followed

Yet, regardless of how little we will be discussing this particular group (in the future), Edomite blood and intellectual graft assuredly would have ended up coming along with these people, as well. And, of course, there's still another 95% out there, migrating away… and, most probably, carrying on this same Edomite baggage as well.

Eventually, a vast majority of these individuals would no longer really know, nor *care*, about the ramifications of this infusion, or what it would have meant to them in the present day. They already had enough on their plates… leaving Babylon, finding a new home to settle to, etc.

And now, with all of this said and done, let's begin to concentrate on that *other* migration of people, where the 95% percent of those Edomite Jews ended up going. We'll need to take a detailed look at what *their* history may have been, after they took to the road once more, and how their invisible Edomite "underbelly" would continue to follow along with them as well, inside of their ranks, hoping to eventually *overtake* them all as a people.

Towards the Turkish Area of Ishkenaz - As "Ashkenazis"?

According to most modern historians, we are told that this 95% majority would end up being referred to as the Ashkenazi Jews. Well, what does this word mean, and why had they become known by it?

A common definition of *Ashkenazi* is:

> Ashkenazi - *a member of one of the two great divisions of Jews comprising the **eastern European Yiddish-speaking** Jews.*[5]

Now, as we see from the above definition, this particular group of individuals seemed to have had a lot more in common with those people living in *eastern* Europe (rather than one the western part). Why? What would have happened to them, over time, and how would they have eventually ended up reaching this side of the earth? And, are there telltale signs that point to the spirit of *Edom* being with them, along the way, and trying to work them over? These seem to be a couple of serious questions that we might need to address at this time.

A number of Jewish scholars (ancient and modern) may want to lead us in the direction of those *Ashkenazi* originating from an area around (what would have been) modern-day **Germany** (near the Rhineland), known as *Askenaz* (or *Loter*). But, if we *really* think about things logically here, this location is nearer to the northwestern edge of *Europe* - not in the Middle East, or even close to it (or, to Eastern Europe)! Are we to assume that they migrated, all the way from the city of Babylon, almost three thousand miles away, to somewhere in the modern country of Germany… just because there was situated a village with a similar name? Couldn't there have been another explanation out there that may have sounded a bit simpler, and even more practical? Apparently, the answer is a solid *yes*.

In a land *adjacent* to Babylonia, we have an ancient area - known as the land of *Ashkenaz*. As well, we have a few ancient villages within this land, known by names such as *Iskenaz* - located in an area that would have (now) been considered modern-day **Turkey**. Yes, this land of Turkey, indeed, would have been a lot closer to ancient Babylon (about a third of the distance, in fact). It does seem to be a lot more *logical* for a group of people, wanting to leave Babylon, to migrate to, rather than running all the way up to Germany. Also, it seems more logical for a nation of people to want to migrate to an area where they wouldn't necessarily have to travel over any type of water (as they would have, if they decided to migrate all the way to the German Rhineland).

Now, if there was indeed another possibility out there, then let's begin to gather some more information on just how *close* this ancient Turkish region would have been to

Babylon, and if it really would have been considered a better option for a group of people wanting - or even needing - to travel.

A verse in the Bible has:

*Blow the trumpet among the nations, prepare the nations against her [i.e. Babylon], call together **against her** the kingdoms of **Ararat**, Minni, and **Ashkenaz**.*   - Jer. 51:27 (KJV)

Wow. We see, here, that there was indeed an parcel of land known as *Ashkenaz*, and it was not too far from ancient Babylon. In fact, this area seemed to have been close enough for the entire city of Babylon to be attacked, so it mustn't have been too far away!

Yes, the Bible seems to give us even more on this area of *Ashkenaz*: Just after the Flood, a son of Japheth - *Gomer* - was said to have fathered a person called *Ashkenaz*; and this son (along with a few more of his brethren) could have been the ones who eventually settled into this same region of Asia Minor (giving the land its name):

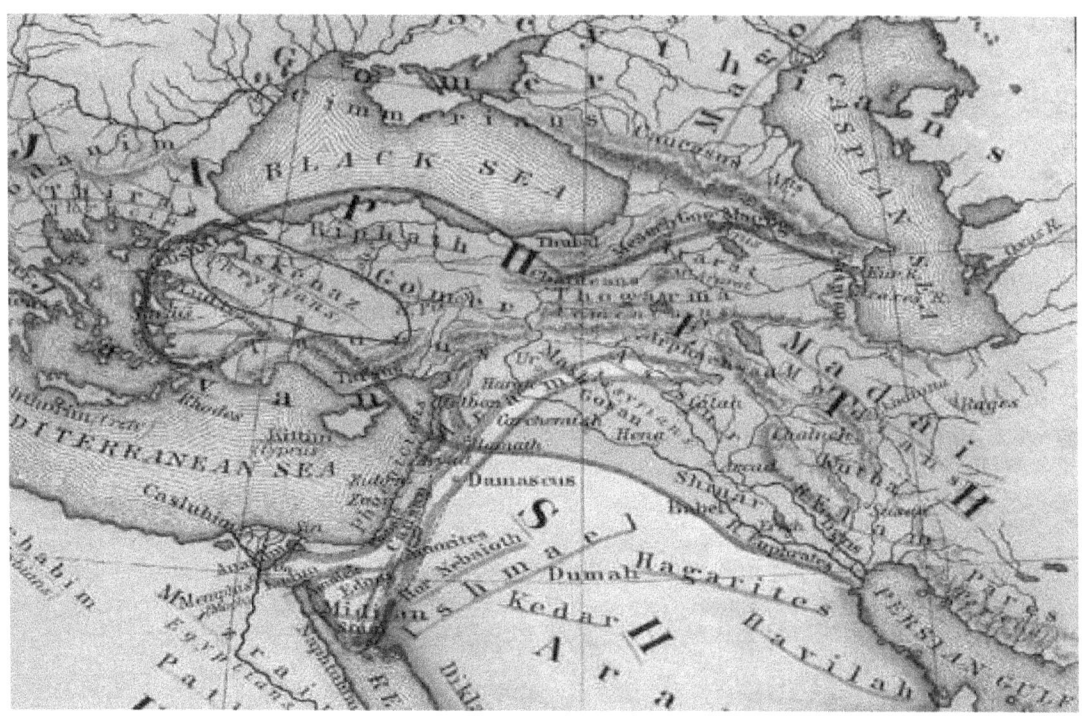

So, what if these Edomite Jews decided to migrate a bit to the north, and also a little bit to the west… to make a better life for themselves? This, of course, seems to make a lot more sense.

Yet, once again, we see that: if someone might want to break a "link," here, in regards to the *real* story of this Jewish migration, they would begin to promote a theory - such as how the Edomite Jews traveled over three thousand miles, and "just happened" to end up in a particular area which was known for having a village with a similar name. Come on now!

Along these same lines, it's funny to see some modern historians, and authors, say things such as the following:

> **Outside** *of their origins in ancient Israel, the history of Ashkenazim* **is shrouded in mystery.**
> ("Ashkenazi Jews", n. d., p. 1)[6]

Of course it is a "mystery," in their world. In actuality, it could have served as another "easy way out" for a number of people, here… if their desire was to stop others from putting all of the "pieces" of this historical "puzzle" together. It's humorous to note (in the above quote) how the author has no real information on what may have happened to those Ashkenazis *before* they became the *Ashkenazis*; but, they (for *sure*) *do* seem to know that these same people **must** have once been in Israel at one time, or originated there! Really, now? Talk about trying to push a narrative.

As we've just seen, if a certain number of scholars, or "people of influence," want to deem certain information as "non-complementary" to their own particular plight, or their own agenda, then it might become beneficial for a number of them to accept a few breaks in their "links," or even break a few "links" on their own. It's all about diverting something for the sake of not raising any eyebrows! If it hurts them, no one should know the whole history of something - claim something like these ancient Edomite Jews must have traveled over three thousand miles (and all the way up into southwestern Germany), just because the village had a similar name.

. Logic does tell us one thing though: these people must have went somewhere after leaving Babylon. Assuredly, if there were a vast number of people in their caravan (with them travelling on foot), they probably would have rather wanted to travel to a place closer... maybe an adjacent area named after one of those sons of Gomer: *Ashkenaz*.

In reality, there were said to be a number of ancient *villages* in this same part of Asia Minor, which all sound eerily similar to that title of *Ashkenaz*.

> *...our GPS homed in on north-east Turkey, where we found four primeval villages, one of which was abandoned in the mid-7th century AD. These ancient villages identified by the GPS tool are clustered close to the Silk Road - the ancient network of trade routes - and are named* **Iskenaz, Eskenaz, Ashanaz, and Ashkuz**. *And it is likely that these are the villages that mark the location of the lost lands of* **Ashkenaz**.
>
> ("Uncovering ancient Ashkenaz - the birthplace of Yiddish speakers", 2016, p. 2)[7]

> *Our continued research revealed that the ancestry of nearly all Ashkenazic Jews could be traced to four ancient villages with remarkable names: Iskenaz (or Eskenaz), Eskenez (or Eskens), Ashanas, and Aschuz (30BCE-640CE). These names might be derived from the word 'Ashkenaz', and are* **unique** *to northeastern* **Turkey**.
>
> ("How DNA traced the Ashkenazic Jews to northeastern Turkey", 2024, p. 1-2)[8]

Again, this is so much closer. Could they have actually ended up in *this* land, originally settled by a son of Japheth?

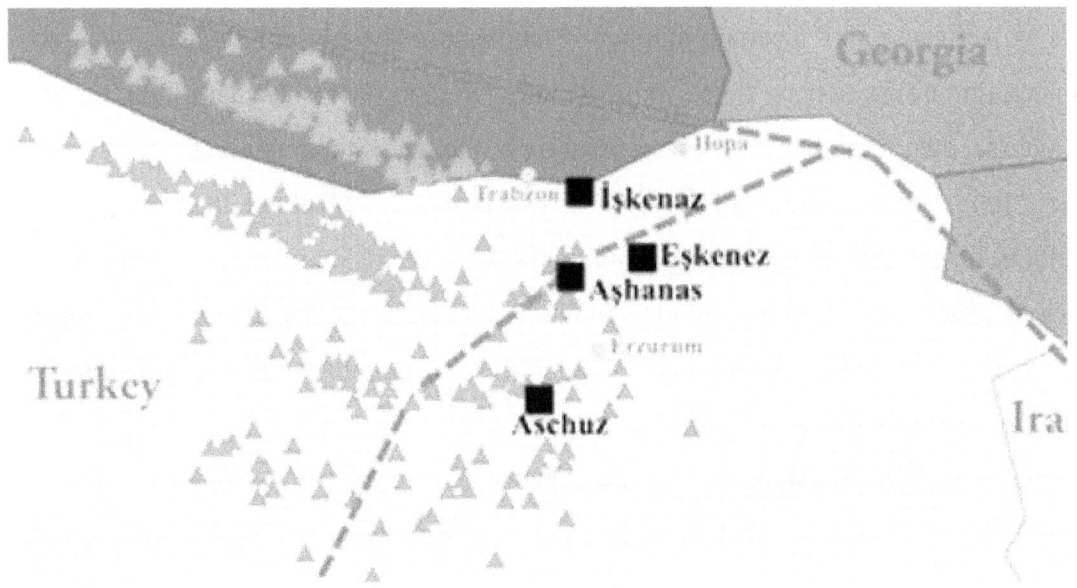

*Dr Elhaik said he believed that that three still-surviving Turkish villages - Iskenaz, Eskenaz and Ashanaz - located in north-eastern Turkey made up part of the original Ashkenazi homeland and formed the nucleus that developed the modern Jewish language of Yiddish… The three villages all derive from the word "**Ashkenaz**", which is the root of the word "Ashkenazi". Elhaik… (stated) that north-east Turkey is the **<u>only</u> place where the four place names exist**.*
("Ashkenazi Jews descended from ancient Turkey: New research", 2016, p. 2)[9]

The above seems to have said it all. It doesn't need to be a small village, all the way up in Germany.[10] Yes, we see that: a whole number of things could make a ton of sense… if we begin to use a little logic, and if we begin to look *around*, to some other bits of suppressed (or even disregarded) information. Things make sense, once we begin to look "outside of the box," and discover what the "modern consensus" may have been trying to pull over our eyes. These may be the attempts - by either those *Edomites* or a number of *Edomite sympathizers* out there - to try and twist our entire Judeo-Christian history around… very slowly, but surely!

Let's continue on, by discovering just *where* they may have ended up migrating to, after they felt the need to leave this Turkish land of *Ashkenaz*, or those ancient villages of Iskenaz, Eskenaz and Ashanaz... and just *who* they may have ended up running into next.

The Khazars (or Chazars)

Another hotly-debated topic, in regards to this migration of early Edomites and Jews, has to do with their relationship with the ancient *Khazarian* civilization. Now that we, possibly, have those Ashkenazi (Edomites and Jews) feeling a need to migrate out of their former lands in Asia Minor, just what could have happened to them next? And, *where* exactly could they have gone, to settle peacefully?

If a number of people retained the common knowledge of where those ancient giants had once migrated (after they had to leave the Middle East), then they may have had a plan of action. If they had the common knowledge of just where those Lost 10 Tribes - their brethren - may have had to migrate towards (once they needed to leave the Middle East as well), then this may have given them a viable place to go. Yes, maybe *they*, also, ended up going in the direction of that famous "escape route" - through the Caucasus Mountains (to do like others had done before them). Maybe they decided that this was the best way to get out of the entire Middle East, "Scott free"... allowing themselves to be able to travel in the direction of the continent of Europe.

Now, if they would have continued on, through the Caucasian Mountains, there would have eventually been a nation-state directly ahead of them… one that, indeed, may have had some connections to their history (as we'll son see). So much of our "known" Jewish history, however, remains curiously silent about the possibility of *this* nation-state being part of their past… and, maybe, for good reason (as we soon shall see). Yes, this particular area was once known as the nation of *Khazaria*.

The Khazarian nation was once thought to have been founded by a whole number of different and independent peoples, all coming from a number of different directions. They ended up in one area - Khazaria - which would, at this present day, been located a little to the south of modern-day Russia (between the Black and Caspian Seas).

And, the timeframe for this meeting may have began somewhere around the neighborhood of the seventh to the tenth century A.D.

*The kingdom of the Khazars vanished from the map of the world many centuries ago. Today **many people have never even heard** of it yet in its day the Khazar kingdom [Khazaria] **was** a very **major** power, indeed **holding sway** over a large empire of subjugated peoples.*
("The Khazars", n. d., p. 1)[11]

Because of its centralized location (in certain respects), Khazaria seemed to have been thought of as a "crossroad" of migrating (and trading) peoples:

*History records that the Khazars were derived from a mixture of Mongols, **Turks** and Finns.*
("Khazars", n. d., p. 1)[12]

With a number of different people deciding to form one huge country, while still holding onto a number of their former cultural influences in the process, one could easily make the case for this Khazarian nation turning a little complex, over time. Because of all this multiculturalism, people were trending to do things in a whole number of different ways… to each his own. So, there may have indeed been a variety of different practices going on, here, which complicated things in the area somewhat. Yet, one thing seemed to have remained consistent, however: their *religious* take on their world. Almost all of these individuals seemed to have retained some kind of **pagan** affiliation, however, which unified them in this one important way.

Yet, even with all of the different ways a person could express their own *take* on the pagan religion, the doors to conflict were open, and would seem to open further and further. A number of improprieties and deviant behaviors began to spring up, because every person truly did what was right in his or her own eyes, or did what was self-serving enough to them. A number of these negative practices would, then, begin to give the Khazarian people, as a whole, a bit of a reputation. Yet, it would be this reputation that would have, in a number of ways, actually helped out their nation… to become more powerful and more influential over time:

*The Khazars were a **Pagan** civilization, and in a short period in history, became the **largest and most powerful kingdom in Europe**, and possibly the wealthiest also. They brought with them their religious worship that was a mix of **phallic worship and other forms of idolatrous worship practiced in Asia by other Pagan nations**. This form of Pagan worship continued into the seventh century with **vile forms of sexual excesses and lewdness** indulged in by the Khazars as part of their religious beliefs.*
("The Khazarian Empire", 2019, p. 1)[13]

They... would prey on travellers, steal from them, murder them, and then assume their identity... (and they) were idolaters and phallic worshippers who worshipped many false gods. It was their religion the way it was the religion of many other Pagans or Barbarians...
("The History of the Khazars Part One", 2020, p. 3)[14]

The Khazars were so violent they quickly amassed nearly 1,000,000 square miles by conquering the agrarian societies in the Caucasus region. The Khazarian kingdom encompassed what is now... parts of Eastern Europe.
("Khazaria Rothschild Dynasty, New World Order Ukraine and Implementation Of The Nephilim Agenda", 2022, p. 1)[15]

One way or another, they were turning into a massive force in the area. And now, with all of this, let's begin to take a deeper look into these people as a whole, and the possibility of those Edomite Jews migrating up into there, and, even doing a little mixing of their own.

But, before we go deeper into all of this, let's take a quick look into *another* group of individuals who may have *already* migrated into this area, before any Ashkenazi Edomite or Jew made the decision to head up, into that way (believe it or not).

Edomites... As Those Early "Turks"?

As we've already seen (in a quote, above) the people of this early Khazarian nation were very different, with one group being those migrating *Turks* from the southwest. And, yes, if Khazaria had *already* been inhabited Turkish individuals from the *south*, then why couldn't there have been *more* migrating people, coming up from this same area... such of those migrating Ashkenazi?

We'll now present another scenario, here: what if a number of these earlier founders of the Khazarian nation - those from the Turkish south - were *already* thought to have had **Edomite** blood in them? What? Could it be? Apparently, that was the thought.

Yes, according to a number of historical scholars, there *were* ancient Edomites who, for a period of time, once lived near a mountain range, called *Seir*:

> *...the Seir was a mountain range south of the Dead Sea, the "Seir Mountains" being none other than the original **land of Esau**. "Thus dwelt Esau in mount Seir: Esau is Edom" (Gen. 36:8.).*
> ("The People of Mt. Seir", 2009, p. 7)[16]

As we may recall (from an earlier chapter), a number of Edomites could have already been chased out of their former abode in the Holy Land, by the children of Jacob (i.e. Israel), a long time before this. This was right around the time when Zepho and his fellow Edomites were taken captive. Since then, a large number of Edomites stayed in this mountain range, and lived here for quite a while. But, over time, they may have decided to expand their horizons a bit.

> *...the bulk of the **Edomites lived at Mt. Seir**, southeast of Palestine. There the kingdom of Edom was established. But **the Edomites did not stay there**. The chapter shows that their leaders **ruled territory much greater** than Edom proper. Verse 37 states that the Edomites ruled land that reached **all the way to the Euphrates River**. In addition to Edom, they dwelt in what the Bible calls the land of **Temani**. This land is located near Persia and Central Asia... The Bible shows that **certain Edomites migrated northeast into Central Asia and Persia and lived among all those different people**...*
> ("East, West or Neither?", 2024, p. 2)[17]

Because of this relocation, a number of Edomites, apparently, ended up following a similar path to those Edomite Jews who ended up leaving Babylon - living in those ancient lands of Turkey.

*Our purpose here is to trace Esau's lineage through his son Eliphaz and then to his grandson **Teman**. The Bible is not specific about the hundreds of years of movement of the migrating descendants of Teman but eventually we read of a people called **Temani** in Persia and **Turkestan**. The Edomites named the Persian and Turkestan plateaus "land of Temani" (an area just to the south of Khazaria).*
("Turkey, Another Son Of Esau", 2013, p. 3)[18]

Here is the Bible verse that, seemingly, shows a relationship between those migrating Edomites and their new land: **Temani.**

*And thy mighty men, **O Teman**, shall be dismayed, to the end that every one of the **mount of Esau** may be cut off by slaughter.*
- Oba. 1:9 (KJV)

Wow. It almost sounds like a "slam dunk" here! But, if they had to leave Mt. Seir, then what may have happened here, to prompt them to have to get out of there? We actually might have a reason:

*...the Babylonians, led by Nebuchadnezzar, conquered Edom. Many of the Edomites **continued to migrate to Central Asia**, out of reach of the powerful empires emerging from Mesopotamia...*
("East, West or Neither?", 2024, p. 2)[19]

*Some historians indicate that at the fall **of Jerusalem in 586 B.C. (at the invasion of** Nebuchadnezzar) not all **Edomites** stayed in the area, many fled and migrated **northward**... The ultimate destination, or where they finally settled, is not known; it could have been in the area later called **Chazaria**...*
("The People of Mt. Seir", 2009, p. 7)[20]

The above quote seems to have said it all, and makes perfect sense here. With Nebuchadnezzar now on the march, a number of those in the path of his destruction would have, naturally, been thinking the same thing - to get out of where they were now living. A lot of physical conflicts could have been taken place in the Middle East, throughout ancient history, which prompted a number of people to take advantage of this same "escape route" that the giants, the Lost 10 Tribes, and a number of others may have ended up utilizing.

What if at least *some* of this early stock of "Turks" - who would eventually go on to end up comprising the original Khazar people - were, at least in part, those same **Edomites** who had to flee Mt. Seir? What if this new nation could have *already* had their fair share of Edomite blood and intellectual graft in their midst?

The Jewish Encyclopedia seems to have a *definitive* take on this possibility:

*The Jewish Encyclopedia states that the majority of the **stock of Khazars** came from the land of Edom. "... (Ḥasdai) Abd al-Rahman, Sultan of Cordova, in his letter to King Joseph of the Chazars (about 960 A.D.), ... speaks of the tradition according to which **the Chazars once dwelt** near the Seir Mountains." (**The Jewish Encyclopedia**, 4:3.)*
("The People of Mt. Seir", 2009, p. 7)[21]

Wow. Did that 1906, unedited text of this Jewish Encyclopedia actually say this? Apparently so. A direct quote from this work is below.

*Taking a keen interest in everything relating to the kingdom of the Chazars, (an ancient scholar and diplomat named) Hasdai begs... (the Khazarian) king to communicate to him a detailed account of the geography of his country, of its internal constitution, of the customs and occupations of its inhabitants, and especially of the history of his ancestry and of the state. In this letter Hasdai speaks of the tradition according to which the **Chazars once dwelt near the Seir (Serir) Mountains...***
("CHAZARS (The *Jewish Encyclopedia*)", 1906, p. 10)[22]

Now, nobody really seems to deny that there may, indeed, have been some *links* between those ancient Edomites and this nation of Khazaria. And, if a number of those Edomites *did* end up fleeing into this same direction (through Turkey), then <u>why</u> couldn't those same *Ashkenazi* settlers end up doing the same thing (if they so deemed it necessary)?

The Jewish Encyclopedia also seems to state how these Chazars were, not only conncected with the ancient Turks (as those early Edomites?), but was also connected with a number of ancient *Jews* themselves! According to their work, the definition of *Chazars* are:

*A People of **Turkish** origin whose life and history **are interwoven with the very beginnings of the history of the Jews** of Russia.*
("CHAZARS (The *Jewish Encyclopedia*)", 1906, p. 1)[23]

Interwoven, here! Again, straight from "out of their mouths" it seems to come.

The Yiddish Connection?

Well, what if the Khazars were, in some shape, manner or form, connected with these ancient Edomite Jews? From the Jewish Encyclopedia, once again, we have:

Jews have lived on the shores of the Black and Caspian seas since the first centuries of the common era.
("CHAZARS (The *Jewish Encyclopedia*)", 1906, p. 1)[24]

So, if this was something to be believed, and if at least *some* of these Edomite Jews were once in the area, is there more evidence to the possible migration of these individuals from Babylon, as a whole?

*Since north-east Turkey is the only place in the world where the place names of Iskenaz, Eskenaz, Ashanaz, and Ashkuz exist this strongly implies that **Yiddish** was established around the first millennium at a time when Jewish traders moved goods from Asia to **Europe**.*
("Uncovering ancient Ashkenaz - the birthplace of Yiddish speakers", 2016, p. 3)[25]

Again, as we see in the above quote, the language that of a number of people in these particular areas may have utilized - *Yiddish* - could also been used by these Kathars... and also was *connected* to these ancient migrating Edomites and Jews. According to some interpretations, we have:

> ...(the Khazars were)... a non-Semitic, Asiatic, Mongolian tribal nation who emigrated into Eastern Europe about the first century... (and they also) account for the presence in Eastern Europe of the great numbers of **Yiddish-speaking Jews** in Russia, Poland, Lithuania, Galatia, Bessarabia and Rumania.
> ("Search Willie Martin Studies", n. d., p. 1)[26]

Also:

> During the 10th, 11th 12th, and 13th centuries the rapidly expanding Russian nation gradually swallowed up the Khazarian kingdom. After the fall of the Khazarian kingdom **the people were known as "Yiddish" in Russia and Eastern Europe... The present day language of the Khazars is known as "Yiddish."**
> ("The Khazarian Empire", 2019, p. 1)[27]

So, this Yiddish language seems to have been fairly *well known* to the ancient Ashkenazi people as well. Could there have been some sort of *connection*, here?

Regardless of any type of denial, or any type of "willful ignorance" on these particular topics, we really see how there could have been another way to look at the entire ancient history of this Edomite-Jewish migration. Let's look a bit *more* into that rarely discussed history of these Khazars, and how it may have all been connected to those migrating Edomites and Jews of ancient history.

Paganism - Too Much for the King?

As we've already discovered, a number of those original Turks, who formed into this original Khazarian nation, may have already been people with **Edomite** blood, somewhere down the line. With this, it seems obvious that the morality and religious beliefs of this Khazarian people would **not** have necessarily wanted *God* as their central figure of worship, just as those ancient Edomites did not. These Edomites, and other people who ended up forming the nation, were pagans, all the way! Yet, once they began to come across these migrating Edomite Jews, a number of them may have begun to change their religious practices.

At first, those Edomites of Turkey, and others who may have first went on to comprise these Khazars, were not followers of God.

*The "Khazars"... were originally part of the Turkic speaking tribes (via those earlier migrating Edomites). They **were a pagan and sex-oriented people**...*
("The People of Mt. Seir", 2009, p. 7)[28]

Yet, history tells us that, at a certain period of time, a certain Khazarian king began to notice all of the improprieties and pagan immoralities going on around him, and wanted a few things to change.

*One of the experts on Khazars was Benjamin Freedman, a Zionist operative who walked away from Zionism in 1945 and described the Khazars as a **pagan** nation and: "The vile forms of sexual excess indulged in by the Khazars as their form of religious worship produced a degree of moral degeneracy"...*
("Khazaria Rothschild Dynasty, New World Order Ukraine and Implementation Of The Nephilim Agenda", 2022, p. 3)[29]

*This form of **worship produced to a large degree** a moral degeneracy that the Khazarian King could **no longer endure.***
("The Khazarian Empire", 2019, p. 1)[30]

Because of this king, change seemed to be in the air. What happened next - and *why* - is still under conjecture; but, according to one scholarly opinion:

*...king Bulan of Khazar apparently had a **dream**, around the year 760 A.D. He began to adopt **Talmudic** Judaism. and everybody had to be the same religion as the king. an angel came to him in a dream, exhorting him to obey the only true God promising in exchange he would bless his offspring, deliver his enemies into his hands, and make his kingdom last till the end of the world.*
("King Bulan of Khazar", n. d., p. 1)[31]

Wow. Doesn't that sound a little like that angel who visited the virgin Mary? Regardless of how much stake we might hold in this interpretation, it seemed that the king started to feel a sense of morality, and wanted to do things the right way. Whatever may have begun to pan out here, the king decided that changes was in the air. He wanted to change paganism into something that appeared to be *much more Godly*. And, at the time, there apparently were three Godly options for him to choose from: Catholicism, Islam or Judaism.

In the *American People's Encyclopedia*, we find that a choice was made:

> *In the year 740 A.D. the Khazars were officially converted to **Judaism**. A century later they were crushed by the incoming Slavic-speaking people and were scattered over central Europe where they were known as Jews.*
> ("The History of the Khazars Part One", 2020, p. 10)[32]

Could this have been, at least partly, due to a number of incoming migrants - those who may have already had the Jewish way of life and religion under their belt? It only makes sense to believe that *some* Edomite Jews may have come to the area, at least for a time… because a king wouldn't have just have easily converted his entire nation to Judaism unless there weren't already some people around, practicing the faith. Where would they have gotten the choice in the first place, if no one of the faith was even there, practicing away? Could it have been these ancient Ashkenazi who, eventually, have already migrated in, from those Turkish regions?

Either way, this edict may have easily begun to turn this entire Khazarian nation into a *new*, Edomite and Jewish powerhouse.

Welcoming in their New "Spiritual Advisors"

> *In the 7th century King Bulan…decided to abolish the practice of phallic worship…and selected the future state religion as… '**Talmudism**,' and now known and practiced as 'Judaism'.*
> ("Khazaria Rothschild Dynasty, New World Order Ukraine and Implementation Of The Nephilim Agenda", 2022, p. 3)[33]

From his decree, we see that all Khazarians were now directed into following the practice of *Talmudism*. which would eventually morph into today's conception of what **Judaism** is all about:

> ...*according to Rabbi Louis Finkelstein, in his The Pharisees: The Sociological Background of Their Faith, we do know where Judaism has come from: Pharisaism (as in **those Pharisees of Jesus' time**) became Talmudism. Talmudism became Medieval Rabbinism. Medieval Rabbinism became Modern Rabbinism and **Judaism**, but throughout these changes in name, the spirit of the ancient Pharisees survived unaltered from Palestine to Babylonia... and ultimately to the world at large...*
> ("Who's Who?", n. d., p. 1)[34]

Yes, it also seems as though these early practices of the ancient **Pharisees** still survived, just receiving a "face lift," if you will. The corruption seemed to have been ramped up, after their religious leaders migrated back to Babylon, and renamed the faith "Talmudism," after a holy book of theirs - the *Babylonian* Talmud. Go figure. Wow, it seems as though there was already a lot *more* intermingling in this particular faith - the faith that those Edomite Jews who ended up bringing with them. The Ashkenazim were, then, welcomed in by this Khazarian king.

Now, what could have happened next, as a result of all this?

Yet, Only a Moral Rationale?

> *The king then concluded that Judaism, being the foundation upon which both of the other monotheistic religions were built, would be that which he and his subjects should embrace.*
> ("The Khazar Kingdom's Conversion to Judaism", n. d., p. 2)[35]

The decision sounded noble enough of course (at least on the surface). But, as we begin to dig a little deeper, maybe there could have been a couple of *other* reasons behind his particular choice, beyond just a dream (and a bit of common sense for his people). It's quite possible that there was something even more nefarious going on here, beneath the surface. Let's see.

First, we'll take a look more into this transition to Talmudism, and what the ruling class at the time could have gotten out of this switch. It seems that the Khazarian king, at this same time, was in somewhat of a pickle. It was during the time of the Crusades, with Catholics and Muslims brutally fighting against each other all around him. And, now, the fight was slowly beginning to manifest itself into a northerly direction, towards the land of Khazaria. He must have begun to feel a little pressure - from both these advancing armies of Islam and of Roman Catholicism - to either choose a side or another. Yet, it may have just so happened that those EJCs were also migrating up from the south, looking to settle there as well (at least for a little while). How convenient for the king, and what perfect timing! Maybe, if he chose their belief as the *third* option, then one of those advancing armies would not be too upset with him (for not choosing one of them) to want to force him to become religiously *subservient*.

According to one scholar on the subject (Arthur Koestler):

> *...(Koestler's) position was that the king's conversion was essentially a **political** decision. "At the beginning of the eighth century," he writes, "the world was polarized between the two super-powers representing Christianity (i.e. Catholicism) and Islam... (and) The Khazar Empire represented a Third Force," Koestler continues, "which had proved equal to either of them, both as an adversary and an ally. But it (the Khazar Empire) could **only maintain its independence** by accepting neither Christianity nor Islam - for either choice would have **automatically subordinated it to the authority** of the Roman Emperor or the Caliph of Baghdad."*
> ("The Khazar Kingdom's Conversion to Judaism", n. d., p. 3)[36]

> *It was clear that the Khazars were determined to preserve their supremacy as a "Third Force" in the world, and undisputed leader of the countries and tribal nations... Judaism was a reputable religion with sacred books which both Christian and Mohammedan **respected**; it elevated **him above the heathen barbarians**, and **secured** him against the interference of Caliph or Emperor.*
> ("The Khazar Kingdom's Conversion to Judaism", n. d., p. 3-4)[37]

Wow. So, maybe this was (also) the result of some strategic move, based upon the circumstances of the day. Maybe it was to help the king secure his own nation, and hold onto his power - as the ruler of a nation who was, more or less, "neutral" in the whole crusade fight, all the while cleaning up the negative *pagan* elements that may have begun to plague his nation state.

*In the seventh century King Bulan, (the current king of Khazaria), decided to **end** the practice of Phallic worship and all other forms of idolatrous worship and to make one of three monotheistic religions, (which he knew very little about) the new Khazarian state religion.*
("The Khazarian Empire", 2019, p. 3)[38]

Now, those incoming EJC leaders, in actually, becoming of great importance to him, as well as his stand - helping him weasel out of that current situation he, and his country, may have been facing!

Now:

*King Bulan and his four thousand feudal nobles were promptly converted by rabbis **imported from Babylonia** for the event… The Khazarian Kings invited large numbers of Rabbis from Babylon and vicinity, to come and open synagogues and schools to instruct the population in the new state religion.*
("The Khazarian Empire", 2019, p. 3)[39]

Wow, we even see another direct link to *Babylon*, here. And, of course, these particular rabbis could have easily been amongst those who migrated into the area, from the land of Ashkenaz early on (and, ultimately, from the city of Babylon). Those corrupted EJC authorities could have easily been able to slither their way into both the political and religious structures of the Khazarian authority, to become more and more powerful. And, if there were already a number of Edomites in this land, it would have also made perfect sense for the king to go with a *brethren's* religion here, rather than choose a belief from among those feuding Catholics and Muslims:

*…if true, the Khazars would have had **a natural affinity for the Edomites and Jews** as they traveled north from Jerusalem, helping to explain why the **Khazars accepted Judaism as their national religion** rather than Mohammedism or their natural enemy Christianity.*
("The People of Mt. Seir", 2009, p. 7)[40]

Again, we see how a few more "pieces" of this historical "puzzle," and how things are all falling into place (it seems)! Could this have, indeed, been the route these ancient

Edomites and Jews have taken, to, eventually, have become known as *Eastern* European Jews, many of them who would have eventually ended up in Czarist Russia?

We recall a former quote:

> *...(the Khazars were)... a non-Semitic, Asiatic, Mongolian tribal nation who emigrated into Eastern Europe about the first century... (and they also) account for the presence in Eastern Europe of the great numbers of Yiddish-speaking Jews in* **Russia**, *Poland, Lithuania, Galatia, Bessarabia and Rumania.*
> ("Search Willie Martin Studies", n. d., p. 1)[41]

For that "Love of Money," As Well?

It also seems quite possible that there could have been even *more* reasons for Judaism as being their particular religious choice - a very *powerful* reason, mind you. Every migration into a foreign land was not always greeted with "open arms.," as how these Edomite Jews seemed to have been. And, yet, as we'll now see, there could have been something *else* that this Khazarian king felt was very advantageous about accepting this particular group of people, and their religion. It would, simply, be the ability of those particular individuals - under the religious authority behind their belief system - to be able to loan out **money** to others. It seemed that, at the time, this religion was the only belief system (out of the three) that openly allowed for the practices of ***usury*** - lending money to people with interest. Apparently, Catholicism and Islam both forbade the use of it (at least at this time). So, with their religious choice, the newly-conglomerated people of Khazaria would now be able to loan money to a number of other people, and receive a *profit* from it. Of course, if that meant a person would become more and more wealthy as a result then so be it. And, of course, this would mean that the Khazarian people, as a whole, could stand a chance to become more and more *wealthy*, over time, if they were able to loan money to more and more people around them!

What could have come out of this decision (over time), and what kind of power could it have allowed for those currently sitting in those financial "seats?"

Significances of this Color "Red"

Let's first begin by, possibly, trying to link this use of *usury* with some early *Edomites*, and also discover what the color *red - their own* color - may have to do with this entire process (if anything). Could there have been some ways of going about one's personal business, or ways of lending to people, that may, somehow, relate to that color *red*? Possibly.

Interestingly, in the Bible, we see that the word "Esau" and "Edom" both mean *red*.[42] Why? What could have been the rationale behind this fact? Well, from past volumes we could have already discovered a number of reasons *why* they were associated with this particular color: Esau, reportedly, was born with *red* hair, and a lot of it (all around his body). And, as we expand on this a bit, we also see (from the Jewish Encyclopedia) that the color *red* could stand for a few more things:

*"Edom" (lit. "red")= "**one who causes to blush**."*
("IDUMEA (The *Jewish Encyclopedia*)", 1906, p. 1)[43]

As we now see, Esau could have also gotten involved with certain practices that, quite often, make people *blush* - especially a typical person of God. They may turn bright red in their face, or *blush* (with embarrassment or shame), at what their Edomite neighbors may be doing in front of them! The Bible tells us how Esau would end up consorting with a number of pagan women, even marrying a couple of them… which ended up allowing him to choose a lifestyle worthy of sin and *shame*. Of course, his actions would also end up bringing a lot of *shame* to the rest of his family.

If we really think about it, this man was the twin brother of *Israel* himself (and the *grandson* of Abraham). With a family line such as his, one would think that he would have *known* better than to fall off of the Godly wagon… yet, he seemed to have been proud of all the nefarious acts he participated in! His descendents, as well, seemed to have followed right along with his example, following a number of pagan paths, and not really caring about the *shame* it would have brought to anyone around him.

We also recall how Esau did not really seem to have given two shakes about being the firstborn of his father Isaac, and what that all may have meant to his family. In fact, he traded this "unimportant" birthright for something easy, an easy meal - a pot of **red** beans, actually. Go figure. And, to top it all off, Esau didn't even seem to care *why* his brother was cooking those red beans in the first place! The cooking of red beans, in ancient times, may have signified that a *death* had just occurred in the family - their grandfather **Abraham** as a matter of fact! Wow. Once again, however, Esau didn't really seem to care… except only about *himself* and how he could improve his livelihood. No honor. No dignity. No concern for Godly decrees. It was all about the sacrilegious ways of living that he was now adopting - what was good for *him*, what was *in front* of him, and how *he* could benefit from any present situation, as well.

Now, we see how the color *red* may, indeed, relate to this new pathway that Esau, and his descendants, decided to go down:

Red - *Suffering, sin, worry, fear, blood*
                      ("The Scripture Speaks", 2011, p. 5)[44]

*Red in the human body is not only the color of blood but also indicative of a health problem where it means **suffering**, inflamed, anger, or a raw wound (Exodus 21:25; Isaiah 1:6, 30:27).*
　　　　　　　　　　　("Dreams, Colors, Meaning", n. d., p. 1)[45]

Because he became such an *embarrassment* to his immediate generation, and a lot of other people around him, he brought a good deal of *worry* and *suffering* to his contemporaries (especially to his own father Isaac). Could the descendants of Esau have hurt so many of his peers, in so many different ways? We know he caused a lot of bloodshed. He deceived people. He probably angered a lot of people as well, due to his mischievous acts and self-centered decisions.

From previous volumes, we've seen how the color *red* may have also been connected with Edomite *Rome*, coming out in things such as the color of their *battle* flag. How fitting! Their color, as well, was adopted by the Roman Catholic Church… utilized as *the* color of one branch of their upper religious brass (i.e. the Cardinals).

There is more: Ancient written sources also inform us that, in a spiritual sense, Esau (or Edom) could also have been related to the fallen angel **Sammael** - the angel believed to be Satan. Why? It has been stated that there were a number of angels out there - and each *nation* of people were said to have had their own corresponding angel. And *Sammael* (of course) was said to have presided over this corrupted nation of *Edom*. Wow. Go figure.

And, on this same *spiritual* level, we have:

*The ensigns of Sammael and all his princes, and all **his lords**, have the resemblance of a **red fire**…*
　　　　　　　　　　　(Eisenmenger, 1748, p. 192)[46]

Wow. We may, indeed, have another connection here, at least in the spiritual realm. As we may, once again, recall (from previous volumes), the Serpent and Sammael *both* were considered to be very emotional beings, very passionate, even "fiery" at times (much more than any other angel around them). That is why we see ancient (and modern) descriptions of this devil as an entity who is *red* in color. The color is a symbol of an individual who is extremely passionate, or emotional… *fiery* in their rhetoric! Could these attributes have been adopted by a number of Edomites, as well? Could these uses of *emotion* have been manifested in a number of the ways that the Edomites tended to engage themselves with others, or in the ways that they used to *influence* people? Could they have used passion and emotion in regards to their business practices as well? Could they have also involved themselves with certain emotions - such as animosity, underhandedness, or even extortion - to get for themselves what they've always been after? Could they use these ways to *shame* others, to embarrass them, or even to slander them (i.e. to make them ***red***), to help them get on top of any exchange, or get their *own* point across? Quite possibly, it may be all of the above.

Let's see how there might, indeed, have been some members of this Khazarian/Ashkenazi partnership who (over time) have gone on to use some of these methods in their acts of ***usury***, for example - to either get **money** for themselves, or to get whatever *they* may have wanted out of people. Let's begin by learning about, quite possibly, one of the most famous banking families out there, a family who had, over the years, become very, very wealthy.

The Beginning of Rothschild - Those "Red Shields"

Let's take a look at one (possible) example of this power of **banking** in action. Let's also discover some of those possible "signs" that could give us a little evidence of a person's *Edomite* origins (or, at least, their Edomite flare). One quick note before we continue with this expose: we may need to make it known that *every descendant* of those migrating Edomites and Jews (of course) does not have this Edomite blood, nor want to subscribe to the "Edomite" way of doing things; but, that's the beauty of this kind of deception - no one really knows "who's who," until it seeps out on occasion. What *really* matters, in this scenario, is a person's actions, or the *moral codes* they utilize – and how much of it all seems to reflect some kind of *Edomite* flavor. This is the important thing.

Now, it also makes sense to assume that: if a number of these certain (powerful and elite) individuals *truly* had a Jewish heart, and had that flare for God over the ages, then they really **wouldn't have been doing** a number of the things that they once may have did, right? It only makes sense. They would not be out to accumulate as many *material* things as they could in this world if they were truly on God's side - for *that's* not the way to God's heart. They wouldn't be out to seek after whatever's *worldly*, over their relationship with God. Yes, if they were *truly* those protégés of God they would not have acted the same ways that *Esau* could have once acted, a long time ago.

Of course, we're not saying that everyone (or even *anyone*) of the Rothschild family (or any other family) is definitely from the Edomite tribe (how would we know, after two thousand years)… but, what *does* truly matter here is their "fruits" (just as Jesus said). What is important, here, is the *graft* they may subscribe to, the way they ended up carrying themselves, or showing to others what they may *really* be made of!

With all of this in mind, let's continue, and look a little at that Rothschild banking empire, and discover at least *one* reason why they, seemingly, have ended up so fabulously wealthy.

> *Thanks in large part to the persisance of their banking empire, the Rothschild family is estimated to have a collective net worth of roughly **$400 billion**. While no individual member of the family is the richest person in the world, that collective net worth means that they live in incredible luxury, as their family* **has for generations**.
> ("The Rothschilds Have Been One of the World's Wealthiest Familes for Centuries", 2024, p. 4)[47]

With the ways that banks, sometimes, may end up working, all that glitters (assuredly) could not be gold… *every* time (especially if one family was able to amass the amount of money that these Rothschilds have). And, yes… there, apparently, **could** have been some nefarious business practices going on within the family, over their years of practicing this banking craft. One huge story involves a British Rothschild member, named *Nathan Mayer Rothschild* (around the early 19th century). As an Ashkenazi, he was also considered to be a very famous banker, as well as financier of his day. And, because of his place within England's banking system, he may have become extremely privy to a lot of timely and sensitive information.

During the time of his business practices, there was a battle going on, between the British and the French (under Napoleon Bonaparte), called the Battle of Waterloo.

Around twenty four hours before the rest of the public had real access to information about this war, Nathan, himself, came into possession of some important information: the British army had actually defeated Napoleon at the Battle of Waterloo. Yet, to prop himself up, and increase his financial holdings significantly, he told others that he understood that *Napoleon* was the one who, indeed, was victorious… which would have had a dire affect on the British stock exchange. The people reacted accordingly, and consols (i.e. government debt issues) plummeted. Their whole stock market was going down the proverbial toilet. Then, a split second before everything was too late, Nathan went and bought back a huge amount of plummeting consols and etc., for a *song*. Yes, this, of course, allowed the man, and his family, to become quite rich (or, even *more* rich), because of what he said. Again, what kind of moral code would a person have to have used, here, in order to get him so much material wealth, and so fast (via the banking route)? Does that seem like something a protégé of God would normally do?

Interestingly enough, we also see this about the Rothschilds:

> *Their name was derived from the* **'red** *shield' (*'**rotschildt**'*) that hung over the door of their shop, and had been the emblem of revolutionary Jews in Eastern Europe.*
> (Rivera, n. d., p. 24)[48]

Wow. Out of all the colors for them to choose here! Interestingly enough, we *also* recall (out of the Bible) how Isaac, Esau's father, actually **predicted** that his son, and by extension his Edomite descendants, would be able to end up amassing a *large* amount of material and worldly goods, over time and circumstances:

> *And Isaac his father answered and said unto him (Esau), Behold,* **thy** *dwelling shall be* **the fatness of the earth**, *and of the dew of heaven from above…*
> - Gen. 27:39 (KJV)

Go figure. Yes, it sure *does* sound like the way an *Edomite* might be able to make his or her way in this world, now doesn't it? Could there have been some kind of connection? Would a number of these top EJCs (*Edomites in Jewish Clothing*) be able to amass a good amount of wealth for themselves, through practices such as *usury*… by going about things according to methods that a typical *Edomite* might have used in the past (all the while claiming that *they* were those true members of this "good" family of God)? Or, do we see a number of *Edomite* "fruits" at work, here?

The (Edomite) Means to an End?

As more powerful EJCs rose within the Jewish ranks, more of them seemed to have been able to corrupt the Jewish community *as a whole*. Eventually, they believed that they would be able to fully take it over – incorporating most everyone to follow their own (Edomite) ways, and their own lifestyles. Could these banking exploits be just one example? And, wouldn't it have become harder and harder, after a while, for those *truly* in the Jewish community to do right by God, and "call them out" for their nefarious, and unbiblical actions, because the "enemies within" were just getting *too* prominent, and too powerful (overall)?

Also, with their Talmud-based (and other "mystical") interpretations of religious dogma, and their *own* religious traditions overriding a lot of what was once considered sacred and Godly, those **religious EJCs** have also been able to rise to the *top* of so much of the Jewish religious aristocracy… making everything seem as though *they* are now the true Jews, calling the shots.

Now, a number of things that seem to come out of this Edomite Jewish community do not really sound too loving, or too compassionate towards others… *especially* those considered "outside of their community," such as Christians (for example). Those "Gentiles" were often referred to by certain titles, such as the *Goyim*, *Cuthean* and even (sad to say) the *cattle*.

Here are a few sample quotes from a number of respected, or even "holy works," in the past (often viewed as the interpretations or traditions of high-ranking officials, certain religious elites, etc.), in regards to the uses of *money*:

*...it is permitted to lend to gentiles **and apostates** with **usury**... nowadays it is permitted.*
- Shulchan Arukh Yoreh De'ah 159:1[49]

*It is forbidden to steal even if it is a small amount... Anyone who steals... is obligated to pay... Note: a gentile's mistake, for example to mistake in counting or repaying his loans, **is permitted**, and provided that he doesn't know... And there are those who say it is forbidden to mislead him except if he makes the mistake on his own, and then **it's allowed**.*
- Schulchan Aruch Choszen Hamiszpat 348[50]

*...(and, in regards to the withholding of wages of a hired laborer) for a gentile to do so to another gentile and for a gentile to do so to a Jew is prohibited, but for a Jew to do so to **a gentile is permitted.***
- The Babylonian Talmud Sanhedrin 57a[51]

With regard to robbery... it is permitted for a Jew to rob a gentile.
- The Babylonian Talmud Sanhedrin 57a[52]

*...He (God) arose and **permitted**... their (i.e. a Gentile's) **money to the Jewish people**, so that in certain cases Jews are not liable for damage caused to gentiles.*
- Baba Kamma 38a[53]

What kind of attitudes are these? They really do not sound like something coming from those holding onto the Godly birthright! They really don't sound like how a person should be talking, and acting, as those special protégés of God, right? At least that's not the ways Jesus would have wanted people to act. It doesn't sound like what would have come out of the Bible, as well. It's more like a number of those Edomite "fruits" coming to the human surface, once again, and emanating out of certain individuals.

Expelled From a Number of Countries... Why?

Interestingly, we also see that:

Between the years 250 CE and 1948 CE *- a period of 1,700 years - Jews have experienced more than **eighty expulsions** from various countries in Europe..."*
("Why Do People Hate The Jews?", n. d., p. 1)[54]

Wow. That does not sound too good. Now, why would so many people have done this to those Edomite Jews over the years? And, yes, if we really think about this: a degree of *sympathy* may even need to have been drawn, in this case. It all sounds so horrible to do to a particular group. Now, why would so many people throw out an entire nation of migrants who just may have wanted to live nearby, and (presumably) live *innocently* amongst them? Diversity could be a good thing at times, for sure. Why be so antagonistic towards one particular group of people… something that would have ended up with *eighty* expulsions from so many different countries? That's quite a number. Is it all because of one party, or is it only from the other… or, could it be a *combination* of the two?

Again, the logical question here is: what may, in fact, have been *the deeper, probable story* behind all of these expulsions (if there really was just one)? Was it purely out of racism, unjustified hate or anti-Semitism? Was it "just because" a number of mean people decided they had nothing better to do? Was it because a number of people, in eighty countries, were acting as Christian or Roman Catholic *bigots* - harboring an ingrained hatred towards anyone with Jewish (or Edomite) blood? Was it because those Edomite Jews were descendants of the crowd who set out to crucify Jesus? Or, possibly, was it something that resulted from the overall *attitudes* of these Edomite Jews towards other people around them - *especially* coming from those elites and powerful EJCs? The answer, in actuality, may have been *all* of the above. **All** of these scenarios might have had some relevancy in all of what happened in these cases, each to a varied degree.

Searching for that definitive answer, indeed, becomes the "elephant in the room." Yet, with all of the background information we now have available to us (in regards to this Edomite infiltration) then maybe there **could have been** a lot more Edomite *flavor* injecting itself into a number of these living situations… affecting things a lot more than we may have ever assumed before!

We see here that the Bible - in the *Torah* no less - does not speak very highly about anyone profiting from usury, and utilizing certain banking practices (such as how those Rothschilds may have acted over the years):

*He shall lend to thee, and thou **shant not** lend to him…*
- Deut. 28:44 (KJV)

This does not seem to be a very effective way to relate with other people around one. Once again, a big problem with those political and religious elements of this Edomite and Jewish combination may lie with the number of *traditions* and *reinterpretations* (of Scripture) that may have gone on, throughout the years. The problem lies when those of a particular Edomite *flavor* began to insert their own value system into the picture, *trumping* the very Bible that was once considered so sacred!

After a while, a number of those Edomite elements, coming to the surfaces of everyday life, could easily begin to bring out dissention, and mistrust in a number of people… doubting the inner heart and soul of a person proclaiming such things. In other words, if people put out the image of Godliness, and do something else, then problems may arise. Eventually, a lot of people may become affected by these little deviations… a lot are affected by the actions of a few.

Maybe, animosity begins to swell on *both* sides. Maybe the loaning of money, intertwined with certain other styles of banking, could have "set" a few people off, creating anger and mistrust. Maybe, neighboring people just decided, in their own minds, to let their *prejudices* get the better of them… even though they were, in no way, directly affected by those Edomite "fruits." Neither would help out the *cohesion* needed between two different peoples, in order for them all to get along.

Of course, it's also true that Catholicism and a good number of Protestant faiths have convinced people to despise these Edomite Jews, for whatever religious reasons. They ended up detesting anyone who didn't necessarily like Jesus, and that's wrong too.

It's truly sad when two groups of people get into these kinds of situations, and cannot get along. It's also sad how a small percentage of those at the top - those top echelons of this Edomite Jewish conglomeration - turned into "bad apples" over the years, hurting the reputations of the *entire* group. It's also sad how a vast majority of that particular group might be just trying to do what *they* were always told was right, or Godly… not understanding how those *Kenites*, those *pagans* as well as those *Edomites* have all crept in, and corrupted so much of what lies in front of them.

God hates the counterfeits. He did not like Esau, and what *he* had brought to the world's stage. God also seems to dislike those who take it upon themselves to propagate this up-and-coming *White Horse* system - which involves one acting as though they are righteous, or holy, but, deep down inside, they are not really feeling it! Once again, it all involves taking advantage of the masses - those who are just trying to find their way to God, and putting them on another, different track. Once again, it's so sad, but (so often) true: a number of "bad apples" have really hurt this Jewish community.

There are reasons why there were over eighty expulsions of these people in the past… and, sometimes, it's not as "cut and dry" as one might think.

Chapter 12

Ushering in those (Catholic) "Dark Ages"

Now that we've discovered some more elements that may appear to "glitter" in this whole Edomite takeover of the ancient Jewish nation (and not exactly be "gold"), we'll need to return, once again, to that *other* powerhouse of Edomite origin - Edomite *Rome* (under *Zepho's* doing). Next, we'll need to return to our chronological timeline, and head back to that Edomite-led empire - since their transformation into the fledgling Roman Catholic Church (of the 4th century). It's equally important to understand the *Roman* side of this Edomite infiltration as well, to be able to see how the unholy (masking as holy) **White Horse** would be able to take off, even further (and what *systems* it would be able to **manifest itself** as, over the years).

With all of this said and done, let's return to the time just after the establishment of the Roman Catholic Church. The religious "overlords," of course, hoped that their newly-formed church would be able to (at least) hold a candle to their former Roman glory (as a political and militaristic empire). But, at first, things did not seem to go too easily for them. There were just so many variables in the picture now - disgruntled populations, internal corruptions, invasions from "savages" or "barbaric peoples" on the outside, etc. And, yes, there were *still* a good number of *true* Christians out there (as well), who didn't exactly want to adhere to this new (Christian and pagan) conglomerate. Even beyond all of this, there would soon be an up-and-coming (and, indeed, *monumental*) force of ***Islam*** coming into the picture, with people conquering lands and winning souls over (all for the sake of a new religion). Yes, it would become a very "rocky" start for this new version of the Roman Empire (now turned Catholic) to get on board. They just couldn't seem to quickly elevate this *religious* empire to the same heights as what gave them their former glory... at least not *yet*.

To add insult to injury, the "Christianized" Roman Empire would even be forced to "splinter off," due to some disagreements within the original church. Now, the empire of Catholicism was forced to split into *two*, never to really unite as it had been before. One half remained this "universal," Roman Catholic Church... a church which inhabited the (former) western lands that were once part of the original Roman Empire. The other church began to inhabit the Eastern side of the old empire, calling itself the *Eastern Orthodox Church*.

> *...Eastern Orthodox Christian (Catholic) Constantinople in the East was the most advanced and civilized world for almost 1,000 years after it was founded by the Emperor Constantine in the early 4th century until its collapse in 1453 by Islamic Jihad.*
> ("Buck Sexton Traces Parallels Between Fall of the Roman Empire, Rise of the Ottoman Empire and What's Happening Today", 2013, p. 1)[1]

After their split, the Eastern Orthodox side would end up taking a horrible beating, (after being continually *beat down* by Muslim forces over the ages). Eventually, they would be gone, overthrown, leaving only this *western* element to stand strong. This western side of the former Roman Empire would, also, end up being associated with something else, a particular way of living: "**Western civilization**."

Even though it had now splintered, and one half was cut off, the Roman Catholic, or Western side of the faith, still wanted to "soak up" all of the Christian "air" in the room, assimilating everything and everyone formerly considered "Christian" into its own clutches! And, because of this, the Western Roman church would, ultimately, end up attempting to squash anyone (and anything) *close* to their own faith... that may have objected to them, or not been on their same wavelength (and this included anything and everyone in the **Jewish world** as well).

Over the years, a *dark* shadow had come over most everyone and everything even in the *vicinity* of this church, because of its new stance. It simply wanted to rule, and stay strong... and, did not want to lose any more of their former empire. The church began to clamp down on any and all of those naysayers out there - *especially* the true Christians who were continually objecting to their conglomerated Christian view. Even things such as the *Bible* was becoming a threat to them (and their authority), because of the information inside... which may have started to appear a bit *contradictory* to what this conglomerated church was trying to accomplish:

> *Enter into the world of saints and martyrs wrestling against the powers and principalities of the **Dark Age**, when the Bible was outlawed by the Roman Church and those who dared to handle it faced imprisonment, torture and death.* ("The Untold History of the Bible", n. d., p. 1)[2]

Again, Rome wasn't relying on just political pressure here, or some kind of militaristic push (at least not as much)… they were trying to gather their successes by using priests and popes, and a new religious order. They were using fears and intimidations. They wanted to push their own ways onto the people… as the *only* ways that anyone should be hearing about.

This meant that any "barbarians" or "savages" - as well as any true Christians (still holding onto the Bible, and the pure elements of the faith they once had - need to have been dealt with. Persecutions began. The church, also, eventually began to *strongly* discourage the use of the Bible (by any "commoners"), with the rationale that: "the public probably won't understand it anyhow, so why not leave it up to the (elite) experts out there." With these new way of Christendom (i.e. *forcing* people to come to only *them*), things seemed a lot more like the iron-fisted ways of the old Roman Empire. The so-called "Dark Ages" were beginning to come upon so many people in these areas:

> *These "Dark Ages" would commonly be considered an early part of the period known as the Middle Ages, starting as a time of turmoil and instability. "During this time **Rome and other cities deteriorated because of the invasions of barbarians from northern and central Europe**."*
> ("What were the Dark Ages?", 2022, p. 1)[3]

This time (for Rome) it wasn't as easy as just marching into a town, and physically taking it over - there was a lot of psychology (and religious fears) going on. They needed to intimidate, and do their tortures in small doses. Minds were being twisted. People were confused. That's why this time period was famously known as the "Dark Ages":

> *Often the term Dark Ages refers to the initial five hundred years following the fall of Rome in **476**. It is thought of as beginning ar**ound A.D. 450 and continuing till A.D. 1000**.*
> ("What were the Dark Ages?", 2022, p. 1)[4]

And, around the year 800 A,D. - in order to help them "speed up" their process of keeping everyone under their thumb - the "Holy Roman Empire" was established. Wow, what a name! Talk about evolving from one stronghold into another!

And, as we've also mentioned a bit earlier (of which will talk more about in the future), there were Muslim caliphates, becoming a "thorn in the side" of this Roman force. Both factions (the Catholics and the Muslims) were trying to conquer their own immediate world, and expand upon it. The Muslim belief was a bit different than Judaism, Christianity and Catholicism however, yet *still* they believed they deserved to have a number of sites around the Middle East that they considered hold, and wouldn't mind *fighting* to keep the control of such areas.

True Christians, however, *still* seemed to have been able to continue as a "thorn in their side," as well. And, on top of this, it's also interesting to see how there were a vast number of *other* people in the area - considered to be "barbarians" or "savages" - who, in actuality, were probably those *Scythians* (or *Cimmerians*) of ancient times… migrating through those former Roman lands. And, yes, as we might remember (from previous volumes) **they** were the people who were already linked with those migrating **Lost 10 Tribes** (of Israel)! Yes, go figure. There's actually so much for us to ponder here, with all of this new information: if those "barbarians" of that late Roman age were, in actuality, the Lost 10 Tribes of Israel - attacking and trying to dismantle this old Edomite stronghold - then, once again, it shows us more of the "back and forth" that could have actually occurred between those two (Edomite and Israeli) factions! How fascinating, if one thinks really about it. God *does* truly work in some mysterious ways (unbeknownst to most of us, so often).

Feudalism

Even though this new Roman conglomerate was continually being attacked on the outside, they did begin to make some progress, in regards to being able to control a number of their constituents, on the *inside*. A technique that this Catholic regime was able to capitalize on - throughout these early years of going "back and forth" - was their ability to apply a sense of *feudalism* to those underneath them.

> ***Feudalism*** *was a combination of legal, economic and military customs that flourished in medieval Europe between the 9th and 15th centuries.*
> ("Feudalism", n. d., p. 1)[5]

To allow for a way to have people monitor *themselves*, through a person's own fear of religious reprisals, the Catholic Church, at first, began to micromanage their constituents, and do it on a *local* level (at least for a while). This whole "big brother" approach may, eventually, get people so accustomed to having somebody else who's "looking over their shoulder" that they, over time, their fears may become automatic, and *self-regulated*. If the church could accomplish this, their choice - to migrate into a *religious-based* governing authority - may have, indeed, been worthwhile.

To begin their experiment, they would need to "parse out" their lands into small sections. They would, then, assign a few religious authorities to govern each area, as well as a few secular leaders over the same plots of land - called them "feudal lords." Of course, this could have also been where we get the term *landlord* today! The top elites of the Catholic Church (in Rome) would, however, be far away from a lot of this all; but, they *still* would be able to hold great sway over their regional leaders in the field. It was, truly, a "top-down" approach. And, of course, those on "the bottom" of this food chain would become known as those European *serfs*, or *peasants*. It, eventually, did turn out to be a very way to manage a good number of people... with only a *small* number of those at the top. It also helped to keep their multitudes *docile*, needy and uneducated, because they did not have a very good chance at any upward mobility... all they had was a heavy hand over them, as well as those newly adopted fears of religious reprisals (if they dared step out of this new and debilitating *system*).

Eventually, the people would end up so *broken* that they were practically zombies. The church's plan was working. It would now be all about self-moderation and submissiveness, rather than about force. If so a majority of these people were too uneducated to read anything (like the Bible), then how were they able to know anything better for them, in the future? What a racket.

Of course, it was a lot more than just about the church promoting religion, or "spiritual traditions," here... it was a way of dominion and control. And, again (as we've mentioned about that assimilation of Edom into early Judaism and the Jewish people), it's not the Catholic *serfs* and *peasants* who were the problem with this whole set up, but, the small amount of those at the top - directing everything. It's so much about *power* here; it always has been (with so much of humanity). Just look at a number of those medieval churches, and how grandiosely they were constructed. It took so much time, dedication and money to put a number of these religious structures together, and to adorn them in the magnificent ways that they appeared. The reasons for this were obvious: to lead people in such *awe* that they couldn't help but think this church was the way to go, and you better not try to deviate from their authority!

Somebody was profiting from this kind of set up (and a number of them *still* do). It's sad that, quite probably, about 97% of the people to these Christian systems of influence -

especially the Catholic church - are well-wishing, spiritual individuals. They just seem to be caught up in a White Horse *system* (of manipulated Christianity). And, once again, our issue and concern does not lie with these people "on the bottom," it's really about those few at the *top* - those belonging to the long line of this "Ebonite-infused" leadership.

The whole dynamic of the old Roman Empire had changed, with these new "ways of working":

> *Since there was no longer an imperial authority with the power to protect the citizens of the cities, the urban population declined sharply during this period of history. Another consequence of the lack of a* **strong central power** *was the development of the feudal system especially from A.D. 900-1150. During this feudal age, most* **(Catholic) parishes had rural populations, and towns tended to be smaller and less numerous. Castles and walled towns were guarded by the feudal lord's armies and provided security and safety to the peasants and townspeople from the invading barbarians**.
> ("What were the Dark Ages?", 2022, p. 1)[6]

Through this Catholic blueprint, a lot of it seemed to have been working… maybe a little too well. Other elements, however, were not working as well, however - people were starting to become so poor and sedentary that they really didn't have much chance to keep funding the Catholic regime. One's own drive to achieve was stifled, and a lot of people ended up looking *to the church* for their assistance out of it all (which they couldn't really provide). It was like things were grinding to a halt; and the church did not want to feel like everyone around them were nothing but a charity case.

These conditions seemed ripe for outside invasions. Outside "barbarians" and "savages" were taking notice of these fragmenting policies, and how weak so many seemed to have been. Of course, a church was not going to be able to protect them… because their world was, now, all about religion, rather than wars. And, because of this all, the church may have ended up needing to adopt some kind of *fighting* force to help them. It wasn't going to continue on with just feudalism alone.

That "First (Roman) Reich"

*The First Reich was the **Holy Roman Empire**... 800 - 1806. Charlemagne (Charles the Great) was crowned emperor by Pope Leo III in Rome on Christmas Day 800, this is normally seen as the founding of the Empire...*
("The First and Second Reich", n. d., p. 1)[7]

Most of us have heard of the "Third Reich" - a title that reflects something out of 20th century Nazi Germany. And, Nazi Germany, as most of us know, was considered a military "machine." Yet, as we begin to discover the possible origins of these particular words, let's see how there could have, indeed, been a "First Reich" here, and what it all may have meant.

As we've already just understood, the western end of this divided (and religious) regime would be now known as that "**Holy** Roman Empire." It was not *exactly* assuming the same military direction as their earlier incarnation (as a brute, military force of the Roman Empire); but there may have been some desire to "scale up" their military prowess somewhat, in order to keep this feudal conglomerate intact, and safely functioning.

We've also mentioned that up-and-coming *Islamic* force, riding the heels of this Roman religious machine - a large, militant group of individuals (from areas such as ancient Arabia) doing their own version of land-acquisition and missionary work. When in front of Rome's religious machine, these people would not just "roll over" (unlike those feudal peasants). They played for keeps. It seemed as though when they wanted something (such as land) they were more than willing to fight for it, and get it. Something needed to be done in the Catholic world. No more passive fears being distributed… solely.

Soon, the *Crusader* movement was about to be born - volunteer militants under this whole Catholic *umbrella* - vowing to take on a military stance for their church, and for their loving pope. The Catholics powers that be, at this time, began to recruit a vast number of subjects to assist them at slowing down these invading Muslims, or even taking them out. And, around 1096 A.D., a bunch of crusading knights were sent to areas in the Middle East, to reclaim a number of "holy sites" from the Muslims. By 1100, they were gathering some victories, opening up areas for Catholicism to reign, once again. Yet, things didn't go particularly too well, over time. There was some "back and forth," in regards to who was in charge of what. And, although those Crusaders assured the church *some* levels of victory, for certain periods of time, the movement as a whole was not very strong. The church *still* felt the need for some kind of **permanent**, militaristic force, in order for them to help the church do their "dirty work." They needed a force that would be able to help them to, not only stop this Muslim expansion, but also solidify that fragile hold that they still may have had over their subjugated populations.

Enter the *Knights Templar*.

Need For a "Knights Templar"

To make a long story short, we now need to introduce another important (and very *powerful*) player in this whole "Edom-verses-Israel conflict": the *Templars*, the Knights of the Temple of Christ (i.e. the *Knights Templar*), or even those *Poor Knights of Christ*.[8] Via the blessings of that current leader of the Catholic Church - the pope - a group of militaristic individuals would soon come together. These individuals were purposely chosen to have more of a *military* edge to them. The Templars were assigned to, not only work on that prevailing Muslim threat, but also to *temper* any rebellions actions from other human "threats" out there, such as those nearby "barbarians," any Edomite Jews in the vicinity, as well as any of those pesky, *real* thinking Christians. They, in only a short time, would start to become *the* powerhouse of the early Middle Ages - acting as the Catholic Church's own "military machine."

It started off as nine knights from France.[9] These monks all decided that *they* were, indeed, the ones that should take up this cause. With vows of poverty, chastity and obedience, they obeyed the pope, and became only answerable to *him*. Interestingly enough, these monks seemed to have a dual identity - they were also allowed to *kill*![10] It's almost as though the pope gave them the "green light" to go out and "kill for Christ," whenever necessary, to do whatever they needed to accomplish their goals.[11]

After those earlier Crusaders were somewhat successful in conquering parts of the Holy Land (in the time of approximately 1100 A.D.), a number of crusading knights began to reclaim (or hold onto) a number of Christian "holy sites."[12] It was also around this time that the Catholic Church came up with another *brainchild*: not only were their pewsters to believe that their church was in possession of a number of Christian "holy sites," as well as authentic Christian relics, they were also encouraged to *go see* these things, and marvel after them (any of them who had a bit of money, that is). The church began to hold onto areas such as where Jesus was said to have been crucified (for example). A number of *pilgrimages* was now about to begin!

Another move that, seemingly, would be good for the church, they now were able to convince a number of parishioners to turn themselves into pilgrims, and go all the way to a number of these holy sites (some of them being a great distance away), just to see and experience them. The primary arrival point was, supposedly, the Church of the Holy Sepulchre (built on the site where Jesus was, supposedly, said to have been nailed to the cross).[13] Eventually, the church would even offer *indulgences* to their pewsters: a promise to intercede with God for the remission of their individual sins… if they only ended up taking the journey. So, as a result, a number of people *did* end up making long, arduous journey into these particular areas, trying their best to be "good Catholics."

Yet, some problems did end up arising because of this all. There were robbers and thieves discovering an opportunity here - to take money from these pilgrims along the way, or even do worse! It was not a safe journey. The crusaders of the time would not really be able to do a lot to protect them, not *totally*… because they had enough on their hands already (i.e. fighting the Muslims). Of course, this would end up to be a perfect chore for those up-and-coming *Knights Templars*.

The Knights Templars would end up taking on this role, and, as a result, would actually become extremely good at it. They would go on to allow pilgrims safe passage, along the majority of their travels - through some very interesting ways to protect them. Of course, for all of this protection, there was a *price* to be had; and *this* price would end up catapulting those Knights Templars into something big… *really* big.

(Another) Early Form of Banking?

What these pilgrims had ahead of them was nothing short of extremely difficult: it, quite often, manifested as a very *long* trek, through difficult terrain and hot climates (never mind the bad people they may have come across). That was the least of their worries… at least at *first*. But, as the trek became more of a *standard*, the people that the pilgrims ended up facing would become one of their *biggest* concerns. Now, a "wonderful" idea was conjured up, in order to help out these travelers: the Knights Templars would take all of the money from these pilgrims, at the beginning of their trek; and, at various points of their trek, they would give them *a certain* form of money to be able to use… something that meant something to these pilgrims, as well as to the Templars, but **not** to the would-be robbers.

The templar representative would give each individual pilgrim a "payment note," or "check" if you will, so that they wouldn't get their money taken away… it was a medieval version of a *travelers check* And, yes, this would continue on (throughout the length of their journey). When the pilgrims ended up reaching their destination, the Templars were there, and would give them the cash that was due them at the time (minus their *fee*, of course). It served to protect a vast number of people (and benefited these Templars in the process).

And, since a pilgrim had already put up their home and property as collateral (to be able to participate in this "travelers check" program), something would happen, if the pilgrim ended up *dying*, or was killed, on his or her journey: all proceeds would end up going to these Templars! Wow. Imagine the potential for these Templars to benefit from all of these people, travelling abroad! Yes, as a result of this early way of banking, as well as their ability to seize properties (from any pilgrim who may have died), the Templars were soon able to become very wealthy, in a very small amount of time. Just like those EJCs (in Khazaria), the Knights Templar were also able to accumulate wealth and power through financial exchanges.

Over time, the Templars became so powerful that they even would begin to bankroll princes and kings, as well.[14] Over time, the Templars became so powerful that the church even became a little worried; and, as a result, the strict discipline that the Templars once had to the church was now beginning to **erode**. After a while, the pope and the upper political "crust" began to feel as though they created a monster - a monster which needed a little bit of adjustment, in order to stop it all from "getting out of hand."

Eventually, the pope was rarely able to tell these Templars what to do; the kings of the area, assuredly, could just *forget* about trying to lord over them as well.

> *...they may have owned up to 15000 properties, and paid no taxes, since they were a religious order… (and) they became the most prominent **bankers** of their age.*
> - In Search of History (A&E Networks, 2000)[15]

Over (and Under) the Temple Mount

Along with the power that they began to maintain in areas such as Europe, they were enjoying a bit of authority in the Holy Land as well. Because of all this unbridled power, the Templers may have started to go "a little rogue," in a sense. They began to "do their own thing," even thought they were supposedly accountable to Rome, and to the pope. For a while, they began to search out more power - this time, it was power in the esoteric or spiritual world. They had begun to want to learn some things that the Catholic Church wasn't exactly teaching, such as necromancy, divination and other occult arts… all for the sake of advancing themselves *even further*. While in the Holy Land, they began to consort with a few "questionable" figures - some of those who gathered their power through various *pagan* outlets, or sources from the "Other Side."

That wasn't good, especially for an order that, supposedly, came from a "Christian" foundation. Yes, even though these Templars were supposed to be serving Catholic constituents, as the "long arm" of Christian law, they were beginning to fall to those seductive pagan elements out there - via a few corrupted religious elites (such as corrupted EJCs, corrupted Pharisee or Sadducee types, corrupted Muslim religious leaders, etc. As we recall, Judaism was continually under attack by pagans and Kenites since the Old Testament, and were also being twisted around by those Edomites of Jesus' time, so there was already a lot of (mystical or occult) corruption in the faith. Islam seemed to have had their share of corrupted elites too, at the time, because *paganism* was already prevalent in a number of Muslim lands… before it even became a religion (and, of course, old religions "die hard"!)

A number of these ancient faiths seemed to have had *some* pagan infiltrations already, and their leaders may have had *some* secrets to share with these Templars, if the price was right! Word is, the Templars were able to barter a number hidden, supernatural secrets, and gain even *more* power - all against the what the Catholic Church may have originally wanted out of them.

> *…were they "a shadowy sect with a clandestine quest," or were they simply "pious soldiers of Christ?"*
> - In Search of History (A&E Networks, 2000)[16]

What made things even more volatile, these Templars, eventually, were able to discover a way to look *underneath* that famous Temple Mount (in Jerusalem). Apparently, there were tunnels under the place where that famous Temple of Solomon was built. Word seemed to have gotten out that there could have been some riches hidden underneath it all - very valuable and significant relics (such as the Ark of the Covenant, the Holy Grail, etc.)… and, now, it may have been within the Templar's reach.

They had to start digging. Imagine the potential for more power here… if they had the Ark of the Covenant or the Holy Grail? They were not going to let this opportunity pass them up, if they could help it. And, tradition states, they may have actually *found* some things in these tunnels (just what they found, or how they may have found, is not really known to almost everyone)!

When word got out about what the Templars were doing in the Holy Land, the church was being pushed beyond their "breaking point." And, on top of all this, the king of France may have also found himself *very* indebted to these Templars, which was an embarrassment to him, and to his nation (it seemed).[17] But, what if some change was in the air?

More Power, Less Feudalism… Bad for Church Leaders

Around 1126 A.D., things started to change, and few of the top Templars had to returned to France, because the Templars were beginning to lose control of the Holy Land. It would soon begin to fall back under Muslim control. And, because of this defeat, a good number of Templars would have to retreat, back into Europe… all the while bringing their riches and everything else they had along with them. They were watched nervously by European kings. And, as humans often do, they became haughty, arrogant and self-centered, and didn't really have a lot to do (since their expulsion). Since they were now back in France, the opportunity had arisen for them to seize a lot of land in the country… practically enough to form *their own nation* (if they so desired). They had already amassed so much land there, and had the king in their "back pocket" (because he ended up owing *them* money), that they were practically taking over the area.

With all of this potential in their hands, it's perfectly understandable to see how the king of France, and the pope, decided to take action.[18] No more of their feudal authority (if this was going to happen)… nothing but *losses* for the church. The current king of France, *Philip IV* - cold and calculating as he was - decided to "pull the rug out" from underneath the unchecked power of these Templars.

The Big Betrayal of 1307

The pope and the church's top leaders, with the assistance of the French and the French King, began to work together. They began to accuse a few of those top Templars of *heresy* - of communing with evil people, learning a number of black, satanic arts, and being willing participants in a number of sexual deviations. They were also accused of worshiping a false, demonic idol (during the time that they were communing with those corrupted religious leaders inside the Holy Land). Where all of this was true or not, it did not really matter. They still were considered *heretics* - even though they may have, indeed, started to go down some very dark pathways (for the sake of power).

So, the time had now come for the "great takeover" of the Knights Templar, to "rein everything in." And, on **Friday the 13th**, 1307, the king of France, with the blessing of Pope Clement V, arrested those major Templar leaders, *all around* the Holy Roman Empire! It was an ambush. This would be the day that the Templars found their lands being taken away, their money stolen from them, and the entire order being dissolved into nothingness.[19] The church charged these Templar authorities with no less that 127 blasphemous crimes, and escorted a number of them to the torture chambers… in the same manner as what would happen to people in the up-and-coming Inquisition. The future of the Templars was not be good, at least for now.

But, this would not be the end of the Templars, however. The word *already* seemed to have been out, that the church and the king were after them, so it was not possible for *all* of those Templars to be caught off guard. And, a number of them, most probably, ended up being about to *do something* about what was in front of them - and get out of the area with an enormous cache of treasure! Some valuables may have went aboard a few ships, and sailed up to the Britain, Scotland, Portugal, or even to northeastern parts of America (near Nova Scotia). Yes, some got away.

But, still, two hundred Templar leaders, by this time, had been rounded up, and were burned at the stake. And, yes, this was why *Friday the 13th* was thought to be such an "unlucky" day, over time. It sure wasn't good for those Templars!

Yes, the whole power structure of Medieval Europe was now changing. No longer were the Knights Templar able to operate as before. They were, essentially, cut off at the heels, with the proverbial "rug" being pulled out from underneath them. The King of France and the pope were back on top, not having to owe anyone anything! The Templars lost so much of that land that they had accumulated over the years. But, were the Templars gone forever? That would be the question.

To the Templars of the time, it was a horrible double-cross. Yet, all in all, it may not have been over for those Knights Templars, at least not for ever. The remaining knights had to go into hiding… for now. But, *they* were truly out for revenge here, and wanted to regain a lot of their former glory. And, the rest of the story is not far away. We will begin to look at what may have happened *next* for the Templars very soon.

But, for now, we need to see how that - at least for a few *hundred years* - the Catholic brass felt pretty confident that they had dispersed, or killed, enough Templars to *not* have to worry about them anymore. But, if we think about it: both sides may have learned something about this experience. On the Templar side, they may have realized that: if they ever had the chance to regroup again, it would be best to not be in the *same* guise. And on the church's side, they may have realized that: if they ever wanted to form a group like the Templars again, they had to watch them, and make sure that they never got out of control (as they once did). They needed to be able to watch out for any new threats to the church, and target them early.

Now, around the 12th Century, plans were already in the works to put an end to any number of those possible threats to the church *early on* - to be able to "clamp down" on any of those "savages," those uncivilized "barbarians," and those pesky (yet *true*) Christians who always seemed to have been out there, **protesting** this conglomerated, Christian faith known as Catholicism.

Enter the *Inquisition*.

An Inquisition of True Christians

Now, to continue solidifying their hold over the people, as well as to, possibly, shut down any future insurrections (such as what the Knights Templers had already done), the church was now beginning to engage themselves with acts to torture or intimidation, in order to keep their people in line. They also began to execute a number of those so-called "heretics," or "non-believers" - *anyone* outside of, or acting contrary to, that Catholic belief system. It seems that there was one group, however, which continued to be a thorn in their side. They continued to rise to the top of their "hit list," as a shot of cream would continue to rise in a glass of milk:

> *...while most modern believers are unaware of it, the Great Inquisition began - not over Muslims, Jews or witches - but rather,* **because of Bible believing Christians...** *the Inquisition was launched* **to stamp out** *the preaching of the* **true Gospel** *and the knowledge of the* **Word of God**.
> ("The Untold History of the Bible", n. d., p. 1)[20]

The church did not like to be exposed, nor would it want to get that close to being usurped again (at least that's what may have been the driving force for a lot of their actions, here). Yes, it seems as though their Edomite (and pagan) sides were beginning to leak out of them, quite a bit. A lot of future aggressions were in the air... practices that didn't seem too "church like," to say the least.

Over the years, as one may begin to figure, that "holy" empire of Rome extended into most of Europe. As a lot of the known world was becoming more "civilized" under the Roman Catholic thumb, the church couldn't *directly* get their mitts on every area of the former empire, such as the British Isles. In these nation/states, there existed a strong British (and Christian) Church, and they did not exactly suckle off the Roman teat. These people, of course, would have been a target of Catholic disapproval.

There were also other people, within the European continent itself, who would also fall into a similar "targeted" category: the (Christian) Waldenses, the Albigenses and the Anabaptists for example. These groups seemed to have represented Christianity in more of a *pure* form, without all of the intrusive paganism allowed.

If we really think about it, we have theorized, in volumes, that the Lost 10 Tribes could have went into Europe, helping to form into certain countries. There were a number of true Christians in these lands. And, even though a vast number of people in these same lands wanted the same kind of conversion into Christian ideals, the Catholic authority had hold over a great deal. If we think about it, this could *actually* reflect the beginning of those Lost 10 Tribes wanting to return to the "Godly fold" (through whatever version of

Christianity that they were currently involved in)? Could Jesus' conversation, about asking his people to go out, and start to bring back the "lost sheep," be coming to pass here, in one way or another?

> *"(Jesus speaking)…but go rather to the lost sheep of the **house of Israel**. And as ye go, preach, saying, The kingdom of heaven is at hand."*
> *- Mat.* 10:6 (KJV)

It now makes perfect sense, once we understand that those Lost 10 Tribes actually went to these areas, and were also beginning to convert to some kind of Judeo-**Christian** ethic - the fulfillment of this particular prophecy, plain and simple! What an exciting time it was - the uniting of the lost tribes of Israel, through Jesus' calling! Even a number of those in the last two tribes were being converted, and being known as "Messianic Jews." Yet, even though this may have been going on, there always seemed to be pagan and Edomite factions in their midst, working to corrupt (or, at least, slow down) this process.

Now, we are beginning to see a number of attempts by this *White Horse* to come to fruition, and work on this unification process. The Catholic Church already had a number of pagan elements within. And, if anything, this unification gives us new insight on the reasons for the early **Inquisition**, assuredly.

Most of us may have already know of the Inquisition (especially the Spanish Inquisition), or, have at least heard of it. Of course, many historians *today* would want us to believe that the Inquisition involved "only a few thousand" deaths, rather than the millions of probable deaths that it entailed. Regardless of these attempts to downplay the numbers (even to a few thousand), that's still a massive amount of people to be tortured and killed… all because they did not want to convert to any type of *Christian* faith (or conglomerated religion). Again, these seem to be Edomite "fruits" for sure, because no *true* leader of a Christian faith should subject someone else to torture of any kind, just because they do not choose to be Christian, or be of a Christian faith. The argument of even a few thousand is ludicrous. The choice should be between them and God… using Jesus' sacrifice as the pathway to their atonement. Simple.

These Bible-reading, ideologically-pure (or, "true") Jews and Christians did not want to follow along with any of this Edomite corruption, or may have already sensed a number of *pagan* elements intertwined in what Catholicism was pushing. Many individuals knew that it wasn't all quite *pure*, and were not about to convert to such a conglomerate. So, because of this, the church decided that they had no other use for these "heretics" now, and wanted them either "reeducated," or removed. Even before the ultimate betrayal of these Knights Templar, steps seemed to have already been dreamed up, to do such a thing - eradicate anyone **protesting** their "universal" conglomerate of Christianity. And, roughly, from the late 12th century, all the way up to the early **19th century**, Inquisition mandates were issued, and carried out, throughout a lot of Catholic-controlled Europe.

During this time, a number of different tactics of "persuasion" were being enacted, such as the placing of people onto torture racks, pulling sackcloth from out of their throats, putting them in iron maidens , etc… all to "make" people accept the religious ways that they were promoting. So, now, anyone from Waldenses to witches would have been elevated to their "hit list." Now, what kind of soul-winning was that? Who goes out and has to *force* people to convert to your faith, or die? If we really think about it, any religious leader *truly* of God - truly Jewish or truly Christian - would not want to even contemplate the torturing of anyone else, just to *make* them follow what you may believe it. As we recall, "Ye shall know them **by their fruits**!"

The Unofficial Birth of "Protestantism"

Because of all this going on, a number of people protested what the Catholic Church was been doing. The only thing that a number of persecuted people could really do here, given these new parameters, was to **speak out**, against the Catholic Church - hence, we have the beginnings of the **Protestant** Movement. A number of these individuals did not want to follow the dogmas of this conglomerate as pillars to their salvation. They had a feeling, deep down in their hearts, that this conglomeration wasn't the way to go. They also may have wanted to read the Bible on their own, and see what it *really* may have had to say (and not just *blindly* following the feelings of a number of church aristocrats at the time). They truly felt that God was calling them elsewhere.

Maybe, a number of people out there also strived to be able to read the Bible, and teach it to a number of others. Maybe, a number of them really began to like what the Bible had to say about things, rather than their Magisterium or church tradition… such as not being saved by *works*. Maybe they began to think their salvation came through their faith in God, and through Jesus' sacrifice (and this *only*)… and not through the petitions of a Catholic priest. Maybe they didn't need all of those extras thrown at them. Maybe they didn't need to have to bow down to those "Christianized" icons (such as the pagans would). Maybe they didn't need to pray to "little deities" (such as the saints), but only need to pray to God Himself. Maybe they didn't think that three needed to be a female "co-savior" or "co-redeemer" (such as the pagans had) - something that wasn't Biblical to begin with. Maybe they didn't want to participate in Catholic-inspired holidays, as well… most of which, once again, had pagan origins and other pagan elements to them, nor did they want to go to a number of churches built over early *pagan* sites. Maybe these individuals were after the fundamental teachings of the Bible, and what those early propagators of the faith have said - the ones under the direction of Jesus himself, rather than the interpretations and traditions of certain religious elites.

The only thing for them to do next was to turn their backs on these corrupted elements, or even expose them… no longer would they want to drink the "intoxicating beverage" that the Roman church was pouring out to the populous. Enter this longstanding feud between the "holy mother" and a number of Protestant churches being formed, and established. More on these dissentions in just a bit. But, for now, we'll need to discover how there would be a number of these protesting "fronts" emerging… against this Roman stronghold. One would be the battle between the Catholic Church and anything Islamic. There, also, would be (as we might recall) that longstanding battle of wits between those two Edomite brethren - the Edomite Romans and the Edomite-infiltrated Jews (or EJCs). **Now**, there would be yet *another* battle - a battle between these Edomite factions within the Christian faith and *true* thinking Jews as well as Christians. From this point on, a mishmash of "back-and-forth" confrontations would brew, and continue brewing, amongst a number of entities… some that weren't even too easily defined.

The "Catholic-Run" Middle Ages

Moving on, a little forward in time, and we run into the *Middle Ages*. Most of us have probably already heard, at least somewhat, about the *Middle Ages* (or the *Medieval Period*). It was said to have lasted from the 5th to the 15th century A.D. - a time when human achievements were starting to amplify *around* this Roman machine (at least in some respects). People were beginning to come out of the Dark Ages. Interestingly enough, it was also around this same time that a good number of the people *objecting* to the Catholic Church were beginning to take up steam as well.[21]

Still, the Inquisition allowed the Catholic Church hold onto most of its power (at least, for a while). Yet, some changes would be just over the horizon, changes that would be thought of as a "game changer," in regards to this whole "back and forth" between the Catholic Church and a number of those dissenting groups. This time, however, things would begin to swing in favor of those dissenting groups out there. Times, indeed, were changing (as we soon shall see).

So, let's continue on, and discover a little bit more about what may have been going on at this time. We'll also begin to discover just *who* may have decided to unite, *once again*, to take on the church. Yes, the Roman Edomites of Zepho would soon have to confront another **powerful** group of individuals - remnants of a group that they may have already encountered a few hundred years earlier. It seemed to have been a group dead set on taking *back* a lot of what they may have originally considered as *theirs*! Yes, that new group could have originally come from under that same Catholic *umbrella*… only *renamed*.

Their "Change of Image"

A couple of hundred years have passed, since that infamous *Friday the 13th* betrayal of the Knights Templars (in 1307 A.D.). Around the beginning of the 15th century, those tides of change seemed to have been in the air. People were beginning to think a bit differently about their present *spiritual* situations, and why the church had maintained such an influence over them… and they didn't like a lot of it. And, as we already may know, a number of protesting individuals would not be very interested in staying in their situations. What could have been the major elements behind a couple of big changes, in regards to this Roman Catholic Church?

Interestingly enough, it would be around this same time that certain remnants of a particular group that the Roman Catholic once knew - their old nemesis the *Knights Templar* - may have actually been poised to make return, in a very *subtle* way. The Catholics of old, as one might recall, didn't exactly finish the job of wiping out these early Templars. A number of them may have had fled, and ended up relocating out of Catholic-controlled Europe. And, of course, it's easy to assume that: any people coming into their fold since this time would have felt a desire for some kind of revenge. And, for a good number of years, they may have had to live in silence. But, no longer. **Now** seemed to have been a good time for all of this hidden Templar momentum to come back, and take up steam once again.

Now, remnants of this order may have been ready to make their move, to get back "on top" (as much as they once were). And, on top of this all, we'll soon see that they may have even begun to align themselves with *another* very powerful group of the day… a group that may also have felt dispossessed by this Roman Catholic regime (and one that we've already discussed). Who might these individuals be, on top of this all?

Their Return… As "Freemasons"?

It's interesting to see that, around this same time, a group of powerful and influential people would begin to rise up, and make their names known. This group, collectively, were known as the *Freemasons* (or, simply the *Masons*). They, quite rapidly, began to establish themselves as the "new force" on the block, as far as power and prestige. In actuality, a number of these Freemasons began to rise up - almost *unanimously* (and from a whole number of different areas). But, how could this have happened back then? There was no internet, and no phones back then, no real way to broadcast one's own intentions to a wide range of people (at least not that easily)… unless there may have been a little something going on "behind the scenes." Could there have been an *underground network* of former Templars already out there, entrenched within a number of different areas, all waiting for the signal to come back to the "surface," and call themselves the *Freemasons*?

It seems highly likely that these Templars remnants would not have wanted to take any betrayal lying down. Maybe the ones who escaped their early tyranny would have, over the years, wanted to rebuild themselves, and their entire order, into something better, initiating new members along the way. Maybe they needed to remain a "secret society" until it was time for them to rise up, once again, and (publically) be able to challenge this Catholic Church (once again). A few interesting things about these **Freemasons** are: they surely do have a number of *Templar* references and symbolism about them, and seem proud of it.

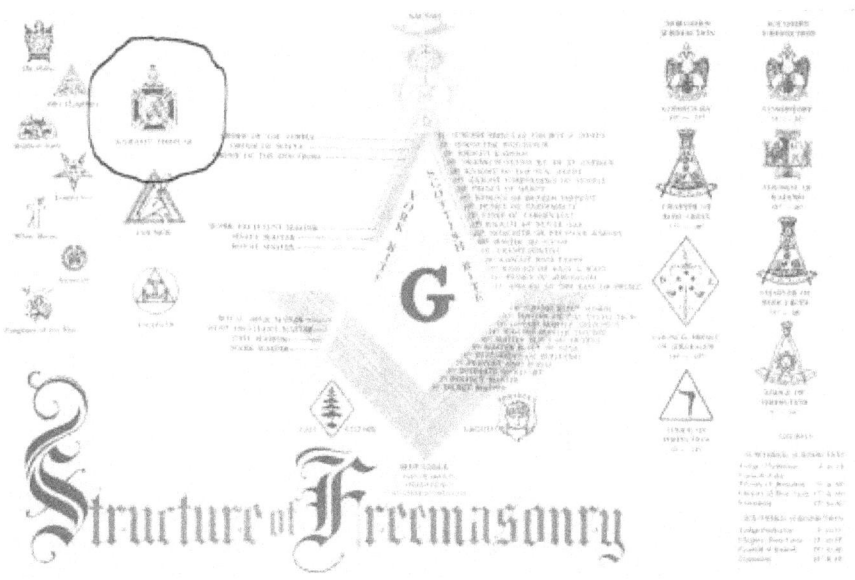

KNIGHTS TEMPLAR

Could they have once been of this early group?

Since this early time, we may notice how that Freemason footprint is in a number of different towns and cities, all across the United States (as well as certain parts of Europe). The Freemasons, at least for a while, seemed everywhere, in a whole number of communities, in a whole number of towns. Today, when someone first drives into an individual town or community, they may often see the familiar plaque of the Masonic order, right next to the other signs or emblems that represent the establishments within a local community:

And, what does this symbol represent, exactly? It, of course, tells us that there is a local chapter of the Masonic order in town. Interestingly enough, these individual chapters do seem to come complete with their own *temples*. Wow. It almost seems as to be a *religion* of sorts, now doesn't it? Either way, all of these many chapters originated from somewhere, and from something. Maybe there was some kind of connection here, with elements of our past.

Either way, just who were (and still *are*) these Freemasons, and how would this particular secretive society become so prolific, powerful and prominent - even with that Catholic Church potentially on their heels? How could it have become so powerful, and so influential over the ages, to be able to find itself in so many different locals?

Apparently, certain historians of this Masonic craft seem to openly admit that their society could have, indeed, risen out of the ashes of those Knights Templar. Still others are not sure where it all came from. Yet, even though their early history might be a bit murky, there's still a number of interesting elements of this society that could tell us a little about what they *really* may have been all about (early on), or what they could have been based upon.

One of the most prominent speakers of Masonic lore, way back in the 1800's, had this to say about their most famous emblem:

Albert Pike *had reconfirmed this fact by quoting Levi in his book, Liturgy of the Ancient and Accepted Scottish Rite of Freemasonry, IV to XIV: 'In the centre of this Blazing Star Freemasons place the letter* **G**. *It signifies* **Gnosis** *and* **Generation**, *the two sacred words of the* **ancient Kabala**'...
("The Letter "G" in Freemasonry Signifies Gnosis", 2015, p. 5)[22]

Wow. Now we see a few elements of this ancient craft, and how it could have been associated with a number of *mystic* elements of ancient Judaism (via the Jewish *Kabbalah*). Interesting, to say the least. But, where and how would these Masons have come up with this information, and *why*? We already recall how those Knights Templars may have also received a lot of *mystical* information from their stay in the Holy Land, a long time before this. Could there have been a connection?

On top of these elements, we also have parts of the Masonic order seemingly dedicated to some mystical elements of *Islam* as well. In one level of the Masonic hierarchy, we have the "Shriners" (i.e. the men who wear those funny little hats):

Once again, with the Shriners (a.k.a. the "Nobles of the Mystic Shrine"), we may want to ask ourselves: why would Freemasonry contain mystical elements (or symbols) of ancient *Islam* here, as well? Could it be have been because those former Templars, in times past, gathered a lot of mystical or esoteric elements from both of *these* faiths, while in the Holy Land? Once again, could there have been a connection? What if a few *pagan* elements have found their way into this secret society, just as some parts of ancient Judaism and Islam have?

Also, if we really think about this: Freemasonry prides itself as being a *secret* society. Now, why would a society such as this *have* to be secretive? They project an image of being something truly good - a society available for *all* the different faiths. But, why would any good society need to *hide* anything, anything at all… if it was nothing but pure and innocent? Makes no sense… unless there *are* a number of things inside of it that aren't exactly *Kosher* - things that the order may not exactly want to be connected with. If something is really good and open, then it really *should be* good and open, for all to see.

In Masonry, we can see one example (of probably a number) of things that might just seem a little *beyond* what a typical Christian may think is Godly: take the sacred name of their god, for example (according to "Royal Arch Masonry"). The name of the Masonic "god," as a confection of three syllables, seems to stand for three different deities, and is read as *Jahbulon*. This term, apparently, has been in use all the way up to the 1980s. And now, we see (according to a number of them) what the title supposedly stands for:

JAH (as ***Jah***) — - This name of God is found in the 68th Psalm, v. 4, the God of the Hebrews

BAAL OR BEL (as ***Bul***) — - This word signifies a lord, master, or possessor, and hence it was applied by many of the nations of the East to denote the Lord of all things, and the Master of the world.

ON (as ***On***) - — - This was the name by which JEHOVAH was worshipped among the Egyptians.[23]

Interesting, and innocent on the surface. But, as we recall, from past experiences, we already know who a couple of those deities are… and they're not really Godly (or Christian). First, most of us know that *Jah* (or *Yah*) is the shortened version of the God of the Bible - Yahweh (or Jehovah). So, that's spot on. Good.

The other two, however, are a lot different, and have some potential issues. What we *really* may have here, in regards to the three, are:

JAH = ***Jahweh*** (or *Jehovah*), the God of the Hebrews
BUL = ***Baal***, the ancient Canaanite fertility god associated with 'licentious rites of imitative magic'
ON = ***Osiris***, the ancient (and "paganized") Egyptian "father" god, the god of death and the underworld[24]

Bal or *Baal* is, in actuality, the *Serpent* (as we may recall). Osiris, that famous Egyptian god, was the *pagan* deification of that famous "father" god of Egypt, Mizraim (as we may also recall) - and *not* Jehovah. Doesn't all of this sound a little familiar - just as how the Catholic Church decided to mix all that is Godly (and the Bible) with a few things that are pagan?

A number of top Masonic leaders may make references to King Solomon (in the Bible), as well as one of his laborers (i.e. Harim Abif), as a couple of people that their craft was modeled after; but, they also make mention of their influences from (pagan) Egypt, as well as from pagan *Nimrod* (i.e. the leader of Babylon)… even honoring him as another early "founder" of the craft!

*The Legend of the Craft in the Old Constitutions refers to **Nimrod** as one of the founders Of Freemasonry. Thus in the York Manuscript. No. 1, we read: 'At ye makeing of ye Toure of Babell there was Masonrie first much esteemed of, and the King of Babilon yt was called **Nimrod was A Mason himself** and **loved well Masons**.' And the Cooke Manuscript thus repeats the story: 'And this same **Nembroth** (or **Nimrod**) began the towre of babilon and he taught to his werkemen the craft of **Masonrie**, and he had with him many **Masons** more than forty thousand. And **he loved and cherished them well**' (see line 343).*
("Nimrod", n. d., p. 1)[25]

Now, what is this craft all about? Is it Godly or some kind of *pagan* conglomerate (once again)? There is, in actually, so much *more* to this Masonic society and its possible pagan affiliations, but, it reality, the rest of it could be classified as being outside the scope of this volume. What we need to understand about it (for the present volume) is: it could have, quite possibly, been the reunification of those former Knights Templars, operating as a "revived" (and secretive) organization. And, we also need to understand that they, as well, could have had some pagan elements to them, just like the Catholic Church. And, thirdly, we need to know that there may have indeed been some *obvious* reasons why this order, *from the start*, already seemed to have had some ingrained prejudice against the church… as a whole.

And, to top it all off, it makes perfect sense for these former Templars to begin to seek out anyone who may *also* have had a beef with this Catholic Church, once upon a time… to help them with their quest for revenge. Over the years, there was another enemy of this Catholic Church out there - one who, assuredly, wouldn't mind saying, "the enemy of my enemy is *my* friend." What about the those powerful **EJCs**, or Edomite Jews, out there, in the same boat as these former Templars? What a coming together of "like minds" (and "like funds") that would have been! As we recall, they *both* had begun to be very *savvy* with early forms of banking.

Yes, the two would have found it of *greatly* advantageous to begin working together, if they so could. They had a common enemy, and they both could have reaped some rewards for the usurping of this Roman Catholic Church… so why not?

Actually, there *did* appear to have been some kind of "coming together of the minds" here; and the two indeed may have decided that "two heads were definitely better than one" (and definitely more advantageous). So, now, let's begin by taking a look into how this new conglomeration would start to go down, and how their end goal of taking out the Catholic Church would start to be accomplished.

Chapter 13

Sciences, Explorations, and Reformations

Certain decisions had to have been made, regarding how to take down this religious powerhouse, and they needed to do it subtly and effectively. A new partnership, apparently, was established, with the two anti-Catholic forces looking for a number of ways to act as *one*. The battle lines were (subtly) beginning to be defined... at least *subtly* to the public at large! Probably, the majority of the populous, at the time, did not have a real clue to the monumental struggle that was about to begin... for control and dominance "at the top." For the rest of the world, it was just seemed as though a number of random events were in the air, changes that may have just began to "sprout up," organically. Yet, now, we'll begin to see how there could have *indeed* been a lot more to a number of those "organic" changes of the time (brought about, and fomented, through this new struggle out there).

A number of upheavals against the Roman Catholic Church were now set to begin, via a number of different facets. The former Templars (as the Masons), along with their new EJC allies on board, were destined to become a great force. The financial means of these two groups, over time, would have allowed for this rebellion to get off of the ground. Hopefully (for them), their new union (and the funds that they were able to accumulate) would be able to make a few "cracks" in this huge, Roman "apple cart."

The timeframe of this upheaval, and how it was about to function, was to begin around the early 16th century. Interestingly enough, history tells us that there *was* a number of changes around this time, and a widespread sense of *anarchy* against the Roman Catholic church. Go figure. What perfect timing for all of this, right?

There, now, seemed to have been a number of "dissentions," popping up all over Europe. And, even though a number of "revolutions" may have been already underway, most of them, in one way or another, seem to have been united - *against* the powers of the church (as we soon shall see).

The beginnings of this new era - known as the ***Renaissance*** - was thought to have been ignited by a particular Catholic dissenter, named Martin Luther (in 1517). Once a devout monk, Luther began to be very distraught with what the Roman Catholic Church was teaching their people, and publically posted his grievances on a door, for all to see. Other dissenters, such as John Calvin, would join in on the fight. But, as we've already understood, there may have been a few *other* forces out there, gently "greasing the skids" for more of this to keep taking place... truly working "behind the scenes."

Let's look at a few of those avenues that the former Templers and EJCs could have ended up taking, here. And, while doing so, we'll begin to see that a number of their attempts - to usurp all things Catholic - would end up being very effective (over a period of time).

Yet, on another (entirely different) extreme, we'll also begin to see how a number of common people in the area would end up getting a lot closer to the Bible, and the right ways to God, because they were able to "break free" from this Catholic hold. They began to go down a number of different Protestant pathways, back into the direction of God and the Bible. Either way, the Reformation seemed to have been funneling a vast number of people *away* from this Catholic juggernaut, and towards something else.

For such a long time, Zepho's Rome seemed almost impenetrable, all the while squashing a number of those who dared to stand up, and oppose them. But now, something different was in the air. There were so many dissentions springing up. It would have almost seemed a little overwhelming to the church as a whole. Even the inquisition would begin to lose its hold.

Let's see more of how it was all beginning to pan out.

> *One of the first **assaults** on the Roman Catholic hold on the majority of Europe began with two movements - the time period of the **Renaissance**, and the Age of **Discovery** (or **Exploration**).*
> ("Middle Ages", n. d., p. 1)[1]

The above movements could have easily been the brainchild of those two enemies of the Catholic Church. This Renaissance (or *Reformation*) was often characterized as a number of advancements in science, the arts, education, etc. It seemed to have sparked a "new age" of enlightenment or understanding. Those taking a *Protestant* stance, especially, were starting to feel a lot more emboldened. More and more people were beginning to read the Bible. Former peasants were now being more and more educated about their world at hand... and began the slow crawl out of their former *feudalistic* past.

This movement, as well, helped to open up a couple of new "ages," one being the Age of Discovery (or Exploration), as mentioned above. Now, it wasn't only about people wanting to get more and more information about their world, it was also a number of them desiring to venture out, away from their "comfort zones," to do something special in this world. A number of people began to travel abroad, investigating, exploring and discovering new things:

> *The Age of Discovery, or the Age of Exploration (approximately from the beginning of the 15th century until the middle of the 17th century), is an informal and loosely defined term for the period in European history in which extensive overseas exploration emerged as a powerful factor in European culture...*
> ("Age of Discovery", n. d., p. 1)[2]

Talk about breaking free of Catholic feudalism!

Yes, it was also around this same time (interestingly enough) that a couple of *other* things were beginning to sprout up. These times also represented:

> *...**the beginning of globalization**. It also marks the rise of the widespread adoption of **colonialism** and **mercantilism** as national policies in Europe.*
> ("Age of Discovery", n. d., p. 1)[3]

Globalism? What a familiar topic we so often hear about (in today's world). It, now, seems to have become a part of a number of different conversations we find ourselves in. Yet, *why* would globalism have been instigated so far back, in this early time? Let's begin to dig a bit further, to find out some of the reasons.

We, first, understand how colonialism and mercantilism may have been the result of a number of people desiring to go out, and discover new places. But, what about those feelings of globalism, or globalization? Could the origins of this movement have something to do with a number of these attempts - by former Templars and EJCs - to take out their biggest rival (all the while, working to eventually unite almost everyone under their *own*, controlling thumb)? We'll eventually be able to start seeing a few links, here.

That Famous "Reformation" (With a Pinch of Paganism)

First, let's look a little more into what the general populations (of this time) would have wanted to do with a lot of their "newfound" knowledge. As we begin to look more into this Reformation, we may begin to wonder just where those EJCs and former Templars could have received a lot of this new information… the information now being injected into a number of societies. Of course, as we might already recall: those EJC religious elites may have had some help from a number of *pagan* Kenites, as well as whatever they picked up in *pagan* Babylon; and those Knights Templar may have received a good deal of *their* esoteric knowledge from some top religious elites (such as such as those EJCs and Islamic religious elites), back in the Holy Land (a number of years ago). But, of course, this "new" information was probably nothing of the kind, but really based upon this mystical, *occult* information of old.

We will hear of advancements in astronomy. But, we also can think of this particular study as having a base in pagan *astrology*. We will hear of advancements in *chemistry*. But, we also can think of this study as having a base in ancient pagan *alchemy*, as well. A lot of it seemed to have had *pagan* elements, or pagan sources, somewhere down the line. Could this "new" renaissance age be just a regurgitation of older (and, often *pagan*) knowledge and information that was, once, reserved only to the elites of a number of ancient religions? Was a lot of this "new age" only a "rebooting" of a vast number of nefarious spiritual (and pagan) elements of our past - dominated by those of the "Other Side" (such as fallen angelic entities, demonic spirits, etc.).

Again, the surge of knowledge inside of this early Renaissance period may have made a lot of sense - once we begin to *link* their "new" information with a lot of that same "old" information already in the hands of those former Templars and EJCs. As the Bible says, "there is nothing new under the sun" (*Eccl.* 1:9). Things just seem to get regurgitated over the years... but, for the most part, it usually something of these same old *pagan* origins.

"Propping Up" the Protestants

Also, if one wants to cause *division* within this Roman Catholic Church, they might begin by attempting usurp the *foundations* of this particular faith, or even expose some of the nefarious elements within it. And, yes, those *Protestants* out there - the ones now protesting the Catholic faith's dogma and theology - were now considered very good candidates to be "propped up," and thrown into the religious *forefront* of this religious fight (by former Templars and EJCs).

These former Templars and EJCs couldn't just unleash these mystical or pagan elements to the people alone. There needed to have been *some* Christian involvement in the works... pointing accusatory fingers at the faith, as well. This way, there could be attacks from *two* fronts, working to wear down the faith faster. Yes, there may have been good reason why this reformation was also called the "**Protestant** Reformation!"

As we could piece together, Martin Luther, and other such as John Calvin, were a few early pioneers in this religious resistance, and were even those who had protestant *branches* named after them (such as the *Lutherans*, the *Calvinists*, etc.)!

The entire Catholic Church was, most probably, a little taken back by the veracity of the resistance out there, at the time, and probably needed to soften a few of their policies a bit, such as the Inquisition. Their hold was slowly loosening.

To the number of Protestant people out there (especially), *this* seemed to have been their chance... to be able to fight back. They've been oppressed for so many years, and now the "faucets" of discontent were turned on, going full blast. Again, the funny part about this all was: so many of these protesting individuals, most probably, did not have any idea that they, essentially, were being "set up," or **utilized**, as religious "fodder" by one unified Edomite group against another... and, in a number of respects, these people are *still* being utilized in this same way (as we'll eventually see)!

Bibles Back into Their Hands

The momentum seemed to be heading "off of the charts." Now, with knowledge and learning on an massive upswing, this seemed to have been *another* powerful modem to take on those traditions and the Magisterium of the Catholic Church. One thing began to stand out, as *the* book for people to now be able to read: yes, it was the **Bible** itself! Yes, *now* was the perfect time for people to begin to learn - for themselves - how to elevate their own lives, and live according to God's direction. Now was the time for people to be able to read things *on their own*, as well as, quite probably, to discover a number of *pagan* elements within this Roman Catholic belief system.

Initially, as one might expect, there was already a good deal of push back, by those Roman Catholic authorities:

> *Throughout the Middle Ages, the Papal Inquisition forbade* **biblical translation**, *threatening imprisonment and death to those who disobeyed.*
> ("A Lamp in the Dark: The Untold History of the Bible", n. d., p. 1)[4]

And, of course, all of this may seem a little odd to so many of us today - discovering a number of church officials out there, trying to stop their own parishioners from reading their *own* holy book. Yes, today, it doesn't really seem to make a lot of sense. But, of course, it may have made perfect sense back then: it was their attempts to try and keep their people under their control, uneducated - not really having a chance to learn much for themselves (at least religiously). Yes, this Holy Mother needed to be needed!

At the time of the Reformation, however, the church was still trying to pull this off - not only attempting to keep their parishioners from learning very much, but also trying to slow the migration of their populations *away* from their (former) feudal existences! And, of course, what better way for them to stifle any advancements in education (as well as in migration) than to sabotage any early printings of the Holy Bible.

And, of course, it would have been in the best interests of any *enemy* of that Roman Catholic authority to do just the opposite: to get a vast number of Bibles out there, into the hands of lay people. Now, with the eager help of a good number of early Protestant pioneers (such as John Wycliffe, William Tyndale and others), this task was slowly becoming a reality. A number of these individuals, indeed, worked feverishly, and even (sometimes) under the threat of their own imprisonment (or death)... all to translate a book known as the Bible (into the various languages around ancient Europe). We can't help but think about an earlier section, of which we may have already learned that: sometimes, people try to do things for their own benefit, or do it for something *nefarious* or even evil; but, in the end, it all ends up working for good, or the good of God's people. This seems to have been *another* classic case.

> *Once the common people were able to read the Bible, the* **world was turned upside down** *through the Protestant Reformation. The Reformers subdued whole kingdoms by preaching the grace of God, and* **exposing** *the unbiblical doctrines of Rome.*
> ("A Lamp in the Dark: The Untold History of the Bible", n. d., p. 1)[5]

What a thorn brewing in the side of this Catholic Church! It was as if the proverbial rug was slowly being pulled out from underneath them! Those EJCs and former Templars probably knew that this would began to spread the Protestant resistance like wildfire, and gave people some good ammunition to go on. They probably understood the passions of these people who, for so very long, felt the sting of so much oppression from their common enemy (ever since the beginning). They probably also understood that these people wouldn't particularly mind making a few sacrifices for this new cause... even up to their deaths.

One of the earliest Bibles produced was called the *Wycliffe Bible*, by John Wycliffe. Things were starting to take off. There was a translation of William Tyndale out there, as well (in 1536). With Tyndale, however, he was burnt at the stake (for merely attempting to do something positive). What a reason for him to die like that. Regardless, the work that he was doing, as well as others, helped to bring a vast amount of people out of the proverbial gutter, and onto better things. Next would be the formation of the King James Version (in 1611), which would have ended up becoming very, very popular, over the centuries. The distribution of Bibles was pushing through, regardless of any initial rebuttals that the Catholic Church could put out there.

New times - and new ways of thinking - were definitely coming about, and *not* just from this Protestant movement! We've already mentioned how there would be *other* disciplines or ways of thinking being inserted into this whole "anarchy" mix, as well - all to usurp this Catholic Church. The former Templars and EJCs probably figured that: their whole anti-Catholic movement would, most probably, flow a lot *better*… if even *more* elements were being added into the overall mix (beyond a bit more paganism and Christianity). Enter the Godless disciplines of *science* and *secular humanism*.

Science and Secularism - Two Decimating Factors

Now, we'll begin to see how a few more additions to their ideological *arsenal* would, in so many ways, help them with their causes (even more). Welcome the disciplines of science, as well as secularism - man's *reason* or *rationalizations* as being the "measure of all things" (as compared to the God of the Bible). Yes, unleashing *these* upon Western civilization world, assuredly, be able to start taking the place of a number of views held by the Roman Catholic Church at the time (as we shall soon see)! Yes, it would soon become *man's* views, as well as his scientific assumptions, trumping most any (and all) *Catholic* views, or views of God.

Interestingly enough, after the beginning of the Protestant Reformation we do see a very dramatic rise in how science and technology was unleashed upon the world. And what timing that was! Add in the Protestant movement and we have a number of different "fronts" here, opposing the Catholic Church - so many opposing fronts that the Catholic Church might not have had a clue which one to begin fighting first!

As a new, atheistic "faith," science would begin to do a number on almost anything actually promoting Christian ideals, such as Catholicism. The belief in *man*, as well - as the measure of all things - would soon begin to fill the void that God once had in people's hearts, as well as minds… thanks to all of the doubt in things such as the spiritual world (that science was now providing). See how it all works?

Inserting something Godless and man-centered would, assuredly, help to take their fight to a "next level," a level beyond what almost any protestant out there could actually accomplish, that's for sure! Now, a person doesn't even have to be religious to take a side! Imagine how many *more* people these former Templars and EJCs could get into the fight this way! The Catholic Church would, in good time, begin to have enough people out there - thinking things *contrary* to their teachings - to start giving them a good fight!

Of course, expanding upon these ways of thinking (and learning) could have also helped a number of people to get out of their former statuses of serfdom, or feudalism. From free-thinking and science comes innovation and technology; and from these things, there, naturally, comes a rise in capitalism and free markets. As people begin to profit from their knowledge, it, naturally, expands to others… giving a whole number of individuals a way out of their former, impoverished states. But, of course, this was all well planned. The unleashing of all this knowledge and potential - at just the right time - would have consequences for those currently holding the reins of power.

Sadly, though, a rise of science and technology would, naturally, begin to wear down one's ability to believe in the real Creator of the universe, and accept *His* role in one's everyday life. By one beginning to learn (and understand) basic scientific principles, as well as preparing great works of art, the feats of *man* were beginning to **condition** a person into thinking more about everything in the world around them (everything *other* than the God of the Bible). Enter the world where *mankind* - on a grand scale - was beginning to serve (or worship) the *creature* (or, elements of *creation*), rather than the Creator (Rom. 1:25)! People, eventually, would begin to believe in *man* as the way to salvation, and the way to solve all of their problems - rather than though Jesus' sacrifice (taking away the sins of the world). Again, it would soon be all about what the *creation* has to offer one… nothing really about the Creator.

Man (& His Rationales) Vs. God

*Humanism is a democratic and ethical life stance, which affirms that human beings have the **right** and responsibility to give meaning and shape to their own lives. It stands for the building of a more humane society through an ethic based on **human** and other natural values in the spirit of **reason** and free inquiry **through human capabilities**. It is not theistic, and it **does not accept supernatural views** of reality.*

("Humanism", n. d., p. 2)[6]

Wow. These ways sure seem to be out to *replace* God, and His authority over all the world. Soon, there really would be **no need** to concentrate on anything like God, the spiritual or religion... and this *includes* the Catholic Church! Science, now, cannot really prove that all of what the church talks about, so why put any stock in any of it? Wow. If we think about it: once again, if the forces of the "Other Side" could get rid of the belief in the supernatural, or spiritual, world, then they could be able to "call the shots"... with impunity! How interesting, but it really *does* make sense (for some) to be able to blot a lot of this out. With a number of these new parameters, it's almost like an individual trying to convince other people that the devil exists. But, now, because science cannot *prove* it... the evil gets a pass.

As we see, so much of this has deeper rationales, and a deeper agenda behind it all. There are so many levels! Human reason, subjective rationalizations, as well as adherence to a number of scientific "laws of this universe" would eventually go on to *erase*, and even replace, the laws of religion, the Bible, and of God. Science would become the new "authority" (or "god") out there, with the interpretations **of** *man* as having the "final say"... just what the former Templar / EJC "doctors" may have "ordered."

Science - The New "God"

Yet, a number of those sciences out there, being what they are, *might* actually have some subtle connections with the spiritual world itself (believe it or not). For example, we need to ask ourselves: just *where* did so many ancient civilizations receive their advancements in geometry, mathematics, astronomy, chemistry and the like? How were they able to build so many ancient, and monumental, structures with their (supposed) primitive knowledge and limited means of production? Why was there such a quick rise in the arts, the sciences as well as a number of technological advancements in certain areas of history, *as well as* the Renaissance? How about in the last 70 or 80 years - with computers, transistors, satellites, robots, the internet, etc.? Where did that all come from... so quickly? A little over a century ago, most people were traveling with a horse and buggy, and didn't have electricity. But, look at us now! Why such a massive jump, once again, in our modern day? Why all of the "ups and downs?"

All of this seems to go completely *contrary* to what a typical evolutionist might want to map out for our human existence (if we think about it). Advances should be slow, extremely slow... but sure. Was there something more to all of this? Well, we do know that a number of corrupted religious dignitaries may have done some seeking of their own... and not from the Godly side of the universe. A number of power-hungry intellectuals, in the past, have (most probably) consorted with entities of the "Other Side" in their search for knowledge and power. We know a lot of this happened. Enoch and other ancient texts plainly say how people committed fornication for a lot of this "forbidden knowledge" - the forbidden **arts** and **sciences** of fallen, terrestrial angels, demons, powers and principalities - all forces of this "Other Side."

> *For we wrestle not against flesh and blood, but against principalities, against powers, against the **rulers of the darkness** of this world, against **spiritual** wickedness in high places.*
> - *Eph.* 6:12 (KJV)

They are out there.

But, how about this "burst of knowledge" during the Renaissance? Where did these people get such a rapid influx of understanding... unless a lot of it was just brought, from the shadows, onto the public scene (by those elite EJCs and former Templars, of course)? We, now, have an answer (something that actually makes a lot of sense): a lot of this may have actually come from these particular parties (and the people before from) who ended up communicating with nefarious beings and spiritual sources (even ancient giants).

Even in the Middle Ages we hear of a number of people dabbling in astrology, occult alchemy, and the like. They were getting into some really *dark* things at this time, for the sake of knowledge. Where did this all come from?

People just don't wake up one day and "discover" geometry, physics, and astrology. They don't just scratch their heads and come up with these advanced sciences. An apple doesn't just fall on one's head and allows them to think of everything! It only makes sense to believe that these contrary institutions were behind so much of the "independent" thinking at the time (and we know the reasons *why* it was all introduced).

The Real Instigators?

We're not saying that a number of people don't have "epiphanies" on their own. but, most probably, the lion's share of so many of these advancements in the Middle Ages may have, in actuality, had some "coaching" from some kind of former Templar (or Masonic) leak, or from an EJC "higher up." Take Isaac Newton (for example). We recall that the man was accredited for the discovery of gravity, all the while sitting under a tree. When the apple fell on his head, he (supposedly) had an epiphany. Wow. Could a falling apple have been the *only* factor behind this great discovery; or, could it, partially, be the fact that he, and a number of other "early thinkers" of the time, were actually *Masons* (i.e. the former Knights Templar)? Could a number of people, with a number of their great "discoveries" (of this age), have had a little "help" along the way, or behind the scenes? Could something a little higher than them be the ones calling a number of those shots, here? We already know the reasons *why* they would want to.

Once, there were a number of religions laws in the Bible, such as the books of Leviticus and Deuteronomy (in the Old Testament), and these were considered the laws that God wanted the ancient Jews to follow, and respect. Later, as we introduce Jesus onto the scene, as the son of God, and discover *his* new ways of working and relating to one another, those could be the new laws of the Christian belief. But *now*, with the agnostic laws of **science** coming onto the scene, and those elements of man's reasoning on an upswing, *they* were now to become the new *laws* - poised to replace those former laws of the religious, or supernatural world. And, where would God be in this whole new scientifically-run world? Of course, **nowhere**.

Eventually, the laws of *science* would begin to have the final say, in regards to how people should think or what they should believe in; and, a number of these people should really have to get the "approval" of the scientific community, as well as the approval of this new "god" of humanism, of political correctness (i.e. collective *human* interpretations about one's world), in order to continue believing in something, accepting it, or support it.

After this begins to take precedence, almost everything else in our world, from that point on, begins to *narrow* (such as what might comprise the supernatural, or spiritual, world). Everyone ends up "bowing" to these parameters, or else they will be laughed at, scorned, or even ridiculed. What a devious plan they came up with, to not only take out Roman Catholicism, but also all *true* Judeo-Christian values. It started working back then, in this early time… and *still* works today!

Yet, these EJCs and former Templars assuredly knew that this supernatural world existed. They knew about angelic beings, or divine elements of our current existence… for their top predators (most probably) received a lot of their information from this particular realm (in the first place)! Claiming it "doesn't exist" (in the end) really helps them out. It allows them to work their "magic" over the populous, and over anyone who might be church-bound - all under the cover of *dark* forces in, around, or underneath this present fallen world of ours.

A Flat (or "Geocentric") Earth?

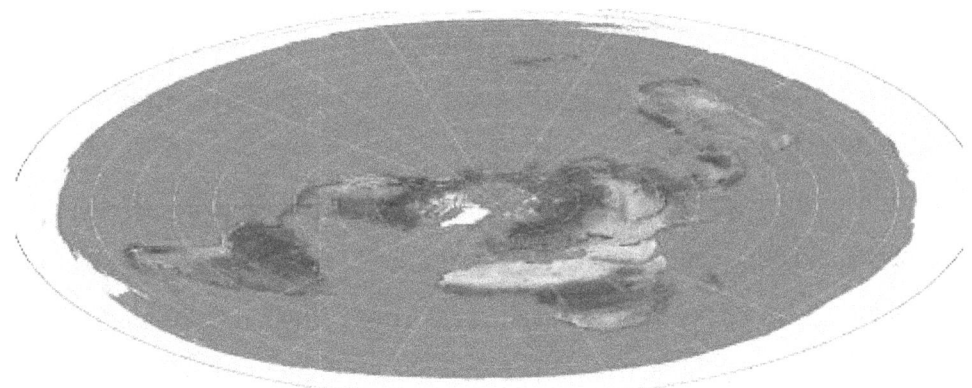

There are a number of examples of these new laws of *science*, and how they would have slowly begun to "take over" conversations, as well as belief systems - a number of them originating right around this same time as the Renaissance period (go figure)! One example of this has to do with the entire *earth* itself, and where everything (including the universe) may have come from!

It was around this same time that: no longer would the narrative about our earth (and our universe) be thought of as: "in the beginning, **God** created the heaven and the earth." No. According to the new scientific "god," a spiritual being could not have created something like this! No. The God of the Bible, most probably, doesn't even really exist, so how could He be responsible for anything? And, since God could not be proven, then that leads the creation of our world "wide open" to other interpretations. And, with *science* now beginning to set the stage for a number of new interpretations out there, then there must have been some kind of **self**-directed motive behind the formation of our earth, and the universe itself. In other words, everything must have all come together - somehow - *by itself*. Makes it for something to really believe in now, doesn't it?

Yes, with this new "god" in tow, the "old," traditional ways of the Bible, and of the Christian or Catholic church, may need to get tossed aside… in favor of everything just deciding to create itself. Wow. Even the *authority* over creation, and the story behind the origins of everything (including us) is now "up for ideological grabs."

How did we really come into existence? How did it turn out the way they did… if it wasn't for some kind of divine intervention? Did life originate from a number of *chemicals* that, somehow, decided to mix together? And, what would have caused all of this to happen in the first place? If we stand "outside of the box," and just try to look at what (the ancient and) modern scientists are really trying to say here, most of us will see how far-fetched it all sounds.

But regardless, there now seemed to have been some stiff competition, in regards to what the church had once said. Another battle was on! Using *the Bible* as religious justification, however, we do seem to have a number of Christian theologians (including those inside the Roman Catholic Church) claiming something very different: that our earth was *not* really considered one planet (out of a number of them), all circling around some kind of *self-made* sun, all within some kind of self-formulated solar system. No, our earth was shaped - more or less - like a *dome*… a kind of vaulted *terrarium*, if you will.

It had an upper sky, a middle portion (of land and soil), and a lower level portion of subterranean existence, lying underneath the surface of this earth. This, of course, would have been considered the *Darkness*, or the underworld.

The whole thing would have looked something like this (if we view it from the "outside looking in"):

Yes, if this was indeed the concept that the Bible was alluding to, then our whole biosphere would appear to be a dome of sorts, with an atmosphere over top of the land - a biosphere that almost was, intentionally, *put there*, or set into place, by some kind of intelligent design. No, it wasn't round. It was not a sphere, a sphere which, somehow, was directed to come together by itself and rotate (at over one thousand miles an hour) around a sun that decided to create itself. It was (and, supposedly, is) a stationary and *flat* plane.

Of course, this all may sound a bit hard to fathom... *especially* because, for the last three or four hundred years of education, we've been taught us there is really **no other way** to perceive this particular scenario (as anything different). Today, it seems almost *laughable*, or even sacrilegious (to society at large), to contemplate anything *other* than their being nine (or so) planets revolving around the sun - that's how *deep* it all has become ingrained within our minds. And, of course, with science as the new "god" here, the "correct" interpretation lies within the thoughts of a number of learned individuals, not the Bible. Now, it *has* to be something like what they say or it's no good. Any other type of theory - other than our universe, somehow, deciding to create *itself*, over a long period of time - is not viable.

Was the world flat, with a heaven above and a underworld (i.e. hell) below (as the Bible seems to allude to), or was everything the result of a *fluke*, if you will, by which a "big bang" decided to dictate that everything was going to start creating itself, creating life on its own, eventually turning our earth in a life-supporting sphere? Yes, things like a universe decided to create itself get harder and harder to swallow... especially after we begin to look at it "outside of the box." Did it all just happen, without any type of divine intervention?

Just think about it: the way our earth all seems to come together is very fascinating. There are so many systems out there that just seem to "coexist." Flora and fauna just seem to work. Oxygen and carbon dioxide seems to also work together (in their own ways). And, let's not forget about the weather - it works throughout the world as if it's almost *alive*. Yes, it's just so incredible to think that all of these systems could have actually resulted from some kind of *explosion*, an explosion from *nothing*, which caused everything (and everyone) to, eventually, come into being, and turn the world into what it is today (and, all on its *own*). Really now?

Of course, where might a number of these scientific teachings have their roots in, or be associated with? As we already could already assume, it sure wouldn't have been the Bible. The Bible, on the opposite extreme, tends to lean us towards believing that the earth was a prize of God's creation. It was indeed something special, reserved for a particular life form destined to live in, and rule over, this "vaulted terrarium" - *man*. Yes, it was to be a specially-designed place for God to put the zenith of His creation. But, of course, if we think about it: these aristocratic elites - if they were working under something that was not necessarily Godly - would, naturally, want us to believe *the opposite*. As we recall, it's either one way or the other. If it is something of the "Other Side" then, naturally, it would begin to point one towards all the opposite that is God, and, once again, we seem to see that here.

Now, science (and those intellectuals fronting it) are trying to say that our earth, and even our entire human race, is *not* something "prized." In fact, it is more like the *opposite*. Both are nothing but some kind of insignificant specs, in a whole universe of possibilities! Most of us have heard something up this same line: Our earth is nothing but one of many, many possible worlds in the universe. It's no big deal. According to the "flat earth" theory (as it would have eventually become known as), our earth was *specially* formed, and formulated for living beings, such as mankind, to thrive in. Unlike those who interpret science, our world was considered the **center** of God's handiwork (and not the sun). The earth, also, was *not* just some small, insignificant planet (amongst the millions upon millions of them out there); and, it didn't just become the home of the human race because, somehow, everything just "lucky" turned out in the favor of life.

And, on top of this all, mankind was supposed to be God's *prize* creation, and this whole living cosmos being set into place for one important reason: to revolve *around* the human existence, giving us a place to live in and enjoy. At least before the Fall, the world was supposed to be a place for mankind to reside in, to care for, as well as be responsible for. Yes, *humankind* was to be "on top" of the entire game here, above the plants, above all of the animals. This, again, is almost the **opposite** of what we're being taught today (by the scientific elite).

Today, we're being assured that man came about as some fluke of evolution, or through some incredible stroke of "luck," and that we're just some insignificant speck in the whole scheme of things. We just became "lucky" (and undeserving) enough to rise up, above other animal species. Forget about man having a soul (at least, according to them)… our mind is not really anything special as well (just above an intelligent ape, for the most part). Again, it's almost two *opposing* views here: a divine God extorts His prize creation in a world fashioned especially for His prized human race, *or* the world we see about us came about, by incredible chance (or even by "dumb luck"), to be able to form life, and thrive… *on its own*.

As we now see, once again, there seems to have been a famous person behind a lot of this shift (towards science) - *Nicolaus Capernicus*. Capernicus was one of the most prominent promoters of this new "planet" theory: the earth, as a spinning globe, continually revolved around the sun - the opposite of what a believer in the "flat earth" theory might think. And, interestingly enough, this may was also believed to have been a sun-worshiper during his life, an occultist, as well as a **Freemason**![7] Wow, fancy that! Where could Capernicus have received a lot of this background information for these "new ways" of looking at the universe around him? Was it all organic?

If man, and his home base of *earth*, are both **insignificant** specks in the whole scene of things, then, that also can make **God** (and the number of people and churches who may also believe in him) as insignificant *specs*, as well. These people, obviously, must be living in the "Dark Ages" (or the Middle Ages) and need some kind of "refresher course" on reality. Of course, this stand diminishes the authority of any church calling itself Christian, as well as the Roman Catholic Church. Ah, yes, the former Templars and EJCs, again, were getting what they wanted.

The Stars, the Planets… and Galileo

In today's world, as stated, most of us seem to have been force-fed, and subsequently bound to the unshakable "truth" that the earth is nothing but a huge, spinning ball, spinning at ten thousand miles an hour, and flying about the sun at some in some ridiculous speed. And, of course, a "big bang" of atoms decided to explode. Now, from what we know about a typical explosion (in our world), an explosion does not bring everything together, nor does it help to bring about life, after the detonation occurs - it, in fact, does just the *opposite*. Go figure.

Yet, if we begin to step back, and look at all of what they're trying to "spoon-feed" us, the whole theory might sound a little ridiculous - especially contrasting it with the possibility of a supernatural deity out there, using intelligent design to lay everything out. But, of course, new people would come onto the scene, theorizing that a number of flaming chucks of rock would eventually turn into planets, and begin their revolutions around another flaming object (i.e. the sun).

It's interesting that: once **again**, we have a few famous people of the era, like *Johannes Kepler* (one of the founders of modern astronomy), as well as *Galileo Galilei* (the famous Italian astronomer who made a number of discoveries with his own telescope). Both of them began to study the stars, and come up with *other* theories about our world, and our universe. And, of **course**, both of them were known to be Freemasons! Smell something a little *suspicious* here?

Of course, there were (and are) so many geniuses out there, many who are also sticking to these *scientific interpretation*s like there's no other way. But, as one could say: intelligence doesn't necessarily mean that a person has got it right:

> *"You can have a lot knowledge, but if you don't have wisdom to **apply** that knowledge, what good is that?"*
> - Steve Quayle

Learned minds may have been taught a number of things, and how things *should be*, or should have originated. They may be extremely knowledgeable in what they've been instructed, but... who teaches *them*? We must remember: a vast number of these educated peoples are taught by those who get *paid* for thinking, or saying, things in a certain light. A lot of them get paid by certain "higher ups" (such as in the government); and, these governing officials pay people to think and say what *they want* them to say! It's as simple as that.

Do we sense something, quite possibly, a little more *political*, and even a little more *nefarious*, that what we might see on the surface? There's politics in everything, even *behind* the sciences. And, so much of it began in the Renaissance - to, most probably, help a couple of opposing forces gain victories over the Catholic Church, or any other Christian church. Don't be fooled.

The "De-Evolution" of Mankind

These deceptions go beyond just the creation of the universe. What about man? How did *he* and *she* come about? Again, was there some kind of intelligent design here, in the forming of human beings (with a soul), or, was it the result of a few *neophytes* who, somehow, found a way to escape from their former ape family? The theory of **evolution** was another concept that, eventually, became popular. Of course, it would also become a tool to help usurp the Christian and Catholic churches as well (if used properly). Once again, this belief (according to a number of people who are out there who may be propagating it) seems to revolve around the concept of how "little" or "insignificant" we, as a human race, truly are. To them, in the whole scheme of the universe, we are only considered insignificant specks, who, somehow, just made it to the big time.

One way or another, it seems that we are continually being pulled *away* from anything that may point towards God as the Creator, and His prized creation. Again, evolution seems to represent the *opposite* of all that. In actually, it, more often, parallels a *pagan* viewpoint on the world, if we really think about it! It really seems to follow right along with this whole pattern of reincarnation - man continually improving himself, or evolving into something better all by himself. Wow, what a concept! It makes perfect sense though, if the mindset of a number of these scientific elites are contrary to God, and the Bible, then what seems to be right there, accepting their rationales with open arms? Of course, paganism.

In no way were Adam and Eve placed in some garden, where everything seemed wonderful and right. And, because of man's sin, there began to be ushered into our world a steady stream of *degeneration*, as a result. No, according to these learned individuals, everything seemed to have worked in the **opposite** way: mankind *began* as something less than human - a degenerate; and (through some quirk of fate) would start his journey "towards the stars." As time when on, he (and his entire world) would eventually become *better* and *better*, and not *more* and *more* polluted (as a result of sin). Man was truly evolving into something *higher*! In the physical world, he was evolving into a higher being, with better intellect. In the spiritual, man was also, eventually, evolving - into a "god." And, of course, all of this was happening *on its own*.

The funny thing about all of this: we can see, all around us, that things are a little different than what they may be saying, overall. Is everything - our environment, our entire human existence, etc. - *truly* getting better, or becoming "higher" (i.e. a better place to live in), or are there a vast number of things out there that seem to be getting *worse* for us? Again, it seems as though it's not pointing towards something like they're saying.

Any environmentalist will tell us that our earth is, indeed, *not* getting much better; in fact, it seems to be getting worse, overall - pollution is increasing, air, water and material sources are being contaminated. With all of these things going on, the earth seems to suffer overall, people and societies seem to be more and more unstable as well. Should we call that evolution, or quite the opposite? We really need to see our world for what it currently is today, and where we're currently heading. It seems a lot more like, in times past, we had a world that was a lot more pure, and a lot less tainted…. and, that would seem to fit, right along with or Adam and Eve story (and how things began to fall apart after the Fall)!

These people seem to spout one thing, but the environment around us tells us another! You really can't hide a lot of what we *really* see. It seems our trajectory is not spiraling (or evolving) upward, but, rather, our world is suffering death pangs. It's really falling apart; and we're not heading towards perfection, or self actualization… but darkness, blackness and a vast number of imperfections.

"Evolving Connections"

But, of course, they press harder. Eventually, we'll have the English biologist Charles Darwin (back in the 1800s) attempting to claim that mankind has been, and still *is*, on the upswing. Our human race, along with members of the animal kingdom, is evolving into something better. Yet, as we look deeper into things here, history seems to tell us that Darwin's cause was, at least in part, financed by one of those famous (EJC?) banking gurus - the **Rothschilds**. Once again, we have the infamous "Red Shields" becoming involved. Wow. Once again - go figure! Why would bankers really need to care about financing this theory of evolution anyway? What interest was it for them? Are we starting to sense a few *nefarious* things going on, behind the scenes (throughout those Middle Ages and beyond)? Why would these people need to insert *themselves* into an ideological movement such as this, unless there may have been some reason for them to benefit from it? There's nothing, really, in this extremity of the world that would be of much interest to bankers.... unless it had something to do with a movement that may have been near and dear to their own (Edomite?) hearts.

Now, once again, if this was true, we see members of the former Templars, as well as members of the EJCs, working together - using their influence to *take down* all that was Catholic, as well as Christian (and prop something else up)! Of course, there's reasons for everything... and, it's not just all about philanthropy! Also, we could keep remembering what Jesus said here, in these situation: ye shall know them *by their fruits*!

If we really think about it, what kind of Godly person - whether they be a true Christian, Israeli or Jew - would *actively* want to deny God in the first place, let alone sponsor anyone who actively seeks to promote theories that's seem to directly contradict the God of the Bible? Darwin surely didn't believe that God "created the heavens and the earth!" Again, it seems as though a few Edomite "colors" may have been showing, here!

Again, it seems as though these insertions were, eventually, set out there to replace a person's fear of God, as well as the worship of Him, and change it into something of *man's interpretation* (or, even man-centered). And science, once again, becomes the "last word," assisting in this interpretation. These ways, eventually, become the "only way" to look at our own world, as well as interpret it. Mankind, now, takes it upon himself to become the *only* controller of his own destiny, as well as the only decider of what is right or wrong. Now, it's all about replacing the "old" religion (of Christianity or Catholicism) with a "new," secular religion - the reverence (or worship) of *one's own self*.

And, as we recall: the ultimate reason behind the insertion of so many *alternative* viewpoints about our world - for so long - seems to stem from a darker origin:

> *But they are trying to spread this lie that conservatives, of course, are Cro-Magnon or Neanderthal and that **we're anti-science and backwards and so** forth, and by the way, that, if you don't know, **is rooted in their bias and bigotry against Christianity**. They happened to believe that Christians don't believe in science because science conflicts with the Bible and God, and they **don't think** the two can go together.   - The Rush Limbaugh Radio Program (9/03/15)*[8]

Science could - very easily - work with Judeo-Christian ideals... if a number of their people would actually want to be *open* to what the Bible has to say, that is. But, as most of us know, *politics* often seem to be involved in so many different elements of our world. And, of course, anything that might be a little *different* than whatever these Former Templars and EJCs may have wanted to spout out over the years - *especially* anything of a **Christian** or Catholic tone - now needs to be immediately disregarded, or even scrubbed (all for the sake of "scientific continuity").

It seems that there's so many smart people out there, who are not open to anything other than what they've been taught. It's almost as if they had blinders on. They want to only look in one direction - in a direction that won't upset any (funding) "apple cart." It's sad; but these people, like all people, have to pay their bills, and probably have children to raise.

Yet, what does that do for us, as a human race in general? Are we truly "evolving," as they say we should be, or is everything "de-evolving," as a result of the Fall? Are things truly getting worse for our world, and for our societies at large? If man's rationality and reason were the keys to overcoming almost every problem out there, then why haven't we been on an incline, with a steady "ascension" towards a divine state of living and being? The answer is obvious - because the things they are shoveling, such as paganism and humanism, are, indeed, not able to make one perfect; but, in reality, they are taking us in the *opposite* direction. The "proof" is all around us.

With natural selection, can animals eventually change what they are, or do they still breed the same type of individual, in the end? Does a giraffe - with a long neck - still sire another giraffe (with a slightly longer neck the next time), or do the offspring begin to turn into something else? It really doesn't become a new creature, even over time, because the DNA that's passed along is coded for the *same* animal. That is what the Bible calls "kind after kind."

Also, how could one feel like they are a "higher" creature by experiencing some kind of mutation within themselves? How does that work? Mutations usually don't turn someone into something better (even over time). As we see today, it always seems to turn out as something *worse*. What happens when we think of something that has been "mutated" today (due to excessive radiation, too much EMF exposure, etc.)? Again, evolutionists try to tell that the *opposite* is true: as we *mutate* we could, somehow, end up as something better, and God's "kind after kind" plan for life on earth really doesn't exist (except that, it really does). Again… it's either one way or another.

The Humanism & Paganism (of Cain)… Interwoven In it All

Speaking of their quest to take down *all* of what is Catholic or Christian (with a number of these alternative theories), we may also be able to assume that: *something* would need to "fill in the gaps" here, whenever someone takes God out of the picture, or out of our heart. When the object of one's moral intention, as well as veneration, are not in the direction of the God of heaven, then something (or *someone*) has to fill in the void, here on earth. Why not make it *mankind* himself (and *his* interpretations of the world)? Why not allow *man* to become the final arbitrator of what's right and wrong, what's good or evil? Of course… we may be able to turn it into man-centered "religion" of sorts - a secular belief of *self-worship* (that, for the most part, originated with Cain and his early world views)! Go figure.

To explain all of this a little bit more, we may need to recall how this originated with, or was made extremely popular by, **Cain**, as well as his father the **Serpent**. Consider the two, and the pagan belief system they helped to generate, as the *antithesis* of all that would have been Godly. The back-and-forth between these two sides, of course, was nothing new. We've seen incidents of these self-serving rationales all the way back in the Old Testament:

In those days there was no king in Israel: every man did that which was right in his own eyes.
– Judg. 21:25 (KJV)

Woe unto them that are wise in their own eyes, and pudent in their own sight!
– Isa. 5:21 (KJV)

Be not wise in thine own eyes: fear the LORD, and depart from evil.
– Prov. 3:7 (KJV)

All of this sounds pretty straightforward, and also contrary to the ways of God. And, of course, we must not also forget what the Serpent said to Eve, all the way back in the Garden of Eden:

*"...your eyes shall be opened, and ye shall be as gods, **knowing good and evil**."*
- Gen. 3:5 (KJV)

Again, why *not* take God's place, here (as a "god"), and understand the ways of the world ourselves? If we take God out of most everything then we really don't have another viable entity to make up all the rules… or *do* we? Of course, man would become the "judges" over people, except over their own upper echelons, those making up all of these rules! Yes, now we see the real reason why there was so much time, effort and financial expenditures utilized for this particular battle (between those former Templars, the EJCs, and the Roman Catholic Church). Big stakes here… especially when you want to be "god." Hey, the popes were already given that honor, in a way, why not some other people? The rest of these top Edomites began to want their own "cut," in this whole "deity" thing!

And, of course, it only makes sense to emphasize with **Cain** and the Serpent, were the first to push this kind of thinking - with the Serpent beginning it all back in the Garden, and Cain allowing a lot of his own self-centered thoughts to challenge God (after he had just killed Abel)… which was, thereafter, immortalized by a number of his followers. The pagan religion was on!

And, yes, with the help of those fallen Nephilim and their giant mixed offspring - spreading this movement in almost every direction - it "boomed" ever since! As we may also recall, it had gotten so bad, so quickly, that, in the antediluvian world, God had to practically wipe out almost everything, and everybody (through the Flood of Noah).

And, by the time the Renaissance began to roll around, we already have a number of people in high positions of power, dictating their edits over a large portion of populated areas… spewing these *same* things. At first (of course), the goals of one side was to usurp the Catholic Church (as we already know). But, later on, these techniques began to work so well that these powers that be decided to keep it all going. It's almost like a genie being let out of a bottle… you can't easily put it back.

But, why try to contain these new movements anyway? They were slowly attempting to put an end to anything and everything Judeo-Christian, and that would eventually be on the agenda of all those who dislike God, and do not want to follow what He says.

Well, is *all* human thought (and interpretation) bad? What about logic and reason? What's wrong with using the left side of our brain here? Weren't these supposed to be more akin to *God* anyhow (in a whole number of ways)? Well, using reason, rationality and logic could be good… but, *not* all the time, or when it begins to deny the sovereignty and existence of God Himself.

Let's look at those **Freemasons**, for example (as the revived Knights Templar). They often seem to teach their people that the uses of human *reason* and *intellect* are good, *very* good. But, as we'll soon begin to see, Masonry also seems to take *God* out of the overall picture (once again), and replaces it with man.

> *Philosophy for a Freemason is an activity of human intelligence inspired by free thought and guided by the humility **of the intellect**; It is the art of thinking that is inspired by the exercizes of **reason** taken to the limit of its critical possibilities, free from any dogma that conditions reason…*
> ("Philosophy in the Life of a Freemason", 2024, p. 3)[9]

> *Human nature **is also worshiped** by some as "Deity," as are **Knowledge and Reason**.*
> ("The Bible - Word of God Verses Errors of 'Freemasonry'", 2024, p. 3)[10]

As we see, it almost exclusively seems to be about *man* here, and the limits of his *own* intellect - not much room for God.

> *In sum, a Mason understands that an intuitive idea can be developed by reason and logic into the search for more **light**.*
> ("Reason, Intuition, and Freemasonry", n. d., p. 3)[11]

Well, what is this *light*, or *illumination* one may need to seek now, if God's really isn't in the picture? Just where might one go to get the ideas for their own (intellectual) advancement? What about any "lights" out there, in the world around us, to utilize? What *wisdom* could some of these intellectuals be referring to,, here - could some of it be the *wisdom* of the Serpent? They sure do like to bring ancient (pagan) Egypt up a lot, as a society that they, in many ways, model themselves after. Could there be a connection?

We also know that Lucifer - that ancient god of this world - could also be able to manifest himself into an "angel of **light**." We already recall where the Knights Templar may have obtained a lot of their esoteric or advanced knowledge from (in the past) - the wisdom of those fallen Nephilim, their giant offspring, and a number of those elements emanating from the "Other Side." So, if a lot of this could have been so, why not start assembling a lot of these missing pieces together?

Paganism (Once Again) on the Rise

Beyond the worship of *self*, we've seem to have a subtle revival of that ancient *pagan* religion of Cain and the Serpent, as well. As we may already recall, a number of those "novel" scientific theories that came into existence - such as astronomy, chemistry, evolution, etc. - seem to have had some kind of *pagan* associations, or parallels a lot of what *paganism* might actually say! Beginning with the Renaissance, a number of people would begin to focus more on their *created* world around may have to give them rather than what the Creator of it all might really have to say.

Yes, this leads us back to that one verse in the Bible (as we recall):

Who… worshipped and served the creature more than the Creator…
  - *Rom.* 1:25 (KJV)

It seems like the people out there, propagating science, may need to tell others (as well as themselves) how they should focus on whatever's of this *lower* world, or use whatever's of their world around them, to solve a lot of their problems. Interestingly enough, *paganism* would use spirits (or elementals) of this lower world as well, to help them find ways to achieve their innermost wants and desires. It's all this lower world, and not God.

This seems to sprout some other interesting takes on science, as well as this lower world. Today, for example, we hear a lot about people referring to the concept of *climate change*, and how important it should be to the populous at large. Yet, if we really think about it, a number of people seem to have become obsessed more *with the earth* itself, and how to "revere" it, rather than even the *people* of our earth, and the well-being of the human populous. Once again, it seems upside down - people seem to care more about the world we live in (and even the animals), rather than caring about the welfare of God's crowning glory. Mankind, now, seems destined to the bottom of their "compassion" barrel. But, why… why would the earth require so much of our attention?

Surely, the earth *does* seem to be suffering, with so many people inhabiting it, sucking up so many of the resources, and spreading so much pollution around. And, to some individuals, caring for "Mother Earth" (or, the environment) needs to be first and foremost! To some people, It's almost as if the concern for "Mother Earth" parallels how one would engage in a *religion* - a reverence for *mother nature*, or *Mother Gaia*. And, once again, if we really begin to look deeper into a few things, we'll see that this sort of reverence is nothing really *new*. It's actually a lot older, and a lot more *pagan*.

The pagans of old definitely involved themselves in the worship of our natural world (or nature), and this had been going on for many, many years. Only, their ancient "mother of nature" (or "mother nature") was none other than that great "mother" of the ancient pagan world - ***Eve*** herself! Yes, as we recall (from previous volumes), *Eve* (in pagan theology) was elevated to that great "mother" goddess of all the earth, as well as the Serpent being elevated to that great "father" god over all the sky (and beyond). Since Eve was the "mother" of all nature, we see the origins of "mother nature."

Again, it's all based on pagan *ancestor worship*, regurgitated and now repackaged as some kind of *new*, political stance, when (of course) it's just something of those same old occult origins. Once again, human reverence has been shifted, directed at something or someone else… anything other than God!

Yes, they say that "politics makes strange bedfellows." And, in the case of these former Templars and EJCs, it's perfectly natural for them to allow pagan elements to just "pop up" in a whole number of (ancient and modern) places, now… working to assist their attempts to diffuse (and eventually *eliminate*) everything that may have been, at one time, *truly* of God, and of the Bible.

Chapter 14

Beginnings of "Western Civilization"

Next, we may have heard a lot about the term "Western civilization" in our world of today, and how it's being used to describe the statuses of certain modern societies. But, where might have this term have come from, and what could it have to do with our conversation at large?

Interestingly enough, a good first question, regarding this term, might be: why was it considered to be "*Western* civilization" in the first place? What's the "*west*" all about? Well, if we follow along these same battle lines (i.e. between the former Templars, the EJCs, and the Roman Catholic Church) we might begin to see how the Catholic Church, once, would have viewed an "advanced" society, or a "civilized" way of life (according to them). Yes, to them, this kind of "Western civilization" was practiced by the people of their lands - the *Western* half of this early Holy Roman Empire exactly, and the term stuck, ever since.

In actuality, it seemed that the Roman Catholic Church began to have a number of internal difficulties after a while, and was forced to split into two. For a while, we had the "Eastern" and "Western" sides of the Roman empire. And, a while later, the Eastern half of this empire would eventually be taken over by the Muslims. The Western half, and their ways of "civilization," would end up being the only ones left. So, for the most part, what we now consider "Western civilization" was, most probably, once a reflection of the times, and particular ways of life, of this side of Catholic Europe.

Of course, those early Catholics would have considered both sides of their original religious empire as being "civilized," or "first-world," with the people outlying it all as, more or less, the "barbarians," or even "savages." To them, *their* civilization was the one and only, the only civilized ways. Never mind if they might have contain pagan elements - the same as their "uncivilized" human fringes. They just "did it better."

Of course, this makes sense, however. There are not a lot of civilizations out there (past or present) who do not really think of *their* ways of life as inferior. They, for the most part, believe that their ways are the best (at least, the best *for them*). The Romans were no exception. Regardless of their view of the outside world, and who were the real "barbarians" here, the people inside of this empire (as well as the church) did some pretty horrific things to other people, throughout the ages: they crucified people; they threw Christians to the lions (while spectators watched and cheered); they also tortured (and killed) a huge number of so-called "heretics" (through events such as the Inquisition).

Of course, "civilization" is often dependants on one's own point of view. Enjoying the spectacle of people being ripped apart by hungry lions is not much better than the ancient Aztec pagans tearing the hearts out of sacrificial victims, just as it's not much better than the scalping of people, or cannibalism.

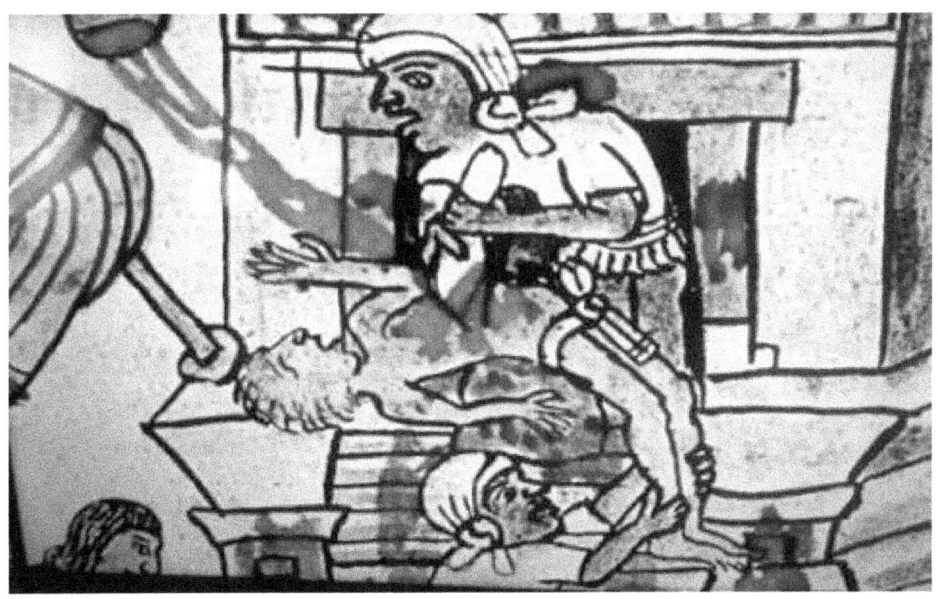

All of these practices, in actuality, seem to reflect a number of (earlier) *pagan* views of "civilization," as we now notice.

And, we also know how the Roman Catholic Church sprung up from the dissolution of a former *pagan* empire, with a number of their former pagan ways of civilization not totally disappearing… just being "Christianized." And, regardless of their Christian face (or flavor), they still believed that they were the civilized ones out there, with their religious conglomeration in tow. With this, they began to set up *their* canon law as the "law of the lands." And, in actuality, a number of European countries *still* utilize these same canon laws of times past, as part of their present governing authority!

Regardless of that, with the Renaissance, people were entering a *new* era of thinking and living - a new manner of *civilization* if you will. People were trying really hard to rise above their feudal overloads, and come out of the oppressive Middle Ages. As we may already recall, a vast number of people were becoming more educated, more cultured, and more and more independent. Still, these new ways of living and looking at one's world would become overshadowed, at least in a number of areas, by those *older* ways of how Catholics viewed "Western civilization." Yet, the church was still following after them, trying to keep the people under their *old* version of what they believed the "straight and narrow" should really be.

Let's take a look at a few of those societal elements of "Western civilization," and what it was all about historically:

> *Western civilization traces its roots back to Europe and the Mediterranean. It is* **linked to ancient Greece, the Roman Empire** *and with Medieval Western Christendom (i.e.* **Roman Catholicism***) which emerged from the Middle Ages to experience such transformative episodes as the Renaissance, the (Protestant) Reformation, the Enlightenment, the Industrial Revolution, scientific revolution, and the development of* **liberal democracy***.*
> ("History of Western civilization", n. d., p. 1)[1]

Wow... a whole number of things to digest, here. First, we see how these "new" ways of (Catholic-influenced) working and living may have, in actuality, had a number of links to those *old* **pagan** empires of ancient Greece and Rome. Ok, we have paganism here, once again, as an underbelly of this whole thing!

Apparently, this was nothing new - conquering empires often absorbed the overall essence (as well as the religious beliefs) of the empire that they previously conquered. Yet, as we see at the end of the above quote, there was something *new*, here, it seems. Among all of those other "classical" elements that may have made comprised Rome's view of civilization, we now discover a couple of *new* elements to it all - at least new to those people of the Renaissance. Those former Templars and the EJCs, most probably, felt the need to insert these at the time. Once again, we notice the *final* elements of Western civilization:

> ...*the development of* **liberal democracy**.
> ("History of Western civilization", n. d., p. 1)²

Those terms surely might seem a bit familiar to many of us today… especially in the world we live in? Well, what about *liberalism* and *democracy*? Aren't they supposed to be good and noble things? There's nothing nefarious about a person subscribing to these viewpoints, right? Yes, it sure seems to be that way, at least according to what we've been fed (over the many years)!

But, could there have been a little *more* to these concepts? Could these noble subjects have, possibly, been "hijacked" for some other end-result, maybe to be utilized in that never-ending battle between those two warring (Edomite) factions? There definitely may have been a deeper agenda to this sudden rise in the ways people viewed liberalism and democracy… much more than we may have ever thought, or believed. It's quite possible that liberalism and democracy were ejected out there, into the mainstream populous, to further *oust* the church's role as the decider of men's lives, and of their futures (as we soon shall see). Could there have been some kind of "deeper layer" to this all… something that might sound like some kind of "White Horse" tactic?

The United States, for example, used to pride itself as a nation with a Judeo-Christian foundation; but, as we notice, it also has buildings mirroring (or, even paying *homage to*) ancient **pagan** Greek and Roman architecture - especially with their government buildings! Now, why would that be? Why profess that you are Christian but seem to show great reverence to ancient pagan societies? Interestingly enough, we notice that how number of US officials are out there, bragging about how much of a *democracy* the nation also is. Could there be some kind of White Horse "shell" going on - proclaiming your Judeo-Christian values on the outside, while emanating pagan elements from the inside? Is this, again, some of the deeper *"fruits"* of certain governments bleeding through?

If we think about it, we'll soon be able to see a lot of elements of this "new age" of enlightenment and renaissance, within Western civilization, are nothing but those regurgitated pagan and occult practices of old, just "repackaged," with a better looking (and Judeo-Christian) cover. Again, it often seems to look wholesome, or even "Christ-like," but so much of it has a pagan core. And, once again, it's may have been used to be able to thwart Roman Catholicism, or any other kind of Protestant belief out there. It worked for Judaism, with the influx of those Kenite and Edomite elites into their midst; and now, they figured they could do the same with anything holding Christian values. We can bet that *this*, most probably, was a major reason behind so much of the fervor about liberalism and democracy during this Renaissance period, and beyond.

There are reasons for everything. Don't be fooled.

Liberalism and Democracy... Humanism in Disguise?

Interestingly enough, we may recall that:

> *Humanism is a **democratic** and ethical life stance, which affirms that human beings have the right and responsibility to give meaning and shape to their own lives.*
>
> ("Humanism", n. d., p. 2)[3]

Wow. What role would one's church - or any church, mind you - have in this process? That would be none. And, as we recall from previous volumes, we might re that (Cain's) humanism would have, indeed, been another "spoke" of this complicated wheel of *Mystery Babylon*! Again, it seems that we now we see the *White Horse* at work, and expanding.

But, wait a minute... aren't these words supposed to spark something "warm and fuzzy," inside our heads? To be liberal is to be free, right? And, who would want to be subjected to someone else, or be oppressed? Democracy, also, is supposedly a great way to govern populations, right? It's good that everyone has a say, and can vote on something. To have *democracy* in government is a great way to govern, right? With people coming together, and deciding their *own* futures, no authoritarian (or authoritarian church) could overshadow them, and dictate their free wills… right? What's really could be so *wrong* about these approaches, if we think about it?

Again, they are not wrong… on the surface. But, as we dig a little deeper into it all, we may, first, need to recall just *where* these ideals could have originated, and *why* they could have been injected back onto the scene… at that particular time. First, we notice that both of these styles of thinking seem to rely more on the opinions of *humankind*, rather than of anything objective, such as the Bible, or God. Because of this, people may begin to feel more of a need to rely on the *state*, or on those governing over them, for their help in daily life (of course, once again, it's not God). Again, as nice as it all might sound on the surface, there may be some kind of *deeper* motivation to these ways of thinking, as we are now seeing. Do we follow man (and his ways), or do we follow God?

Of course, it's nice for people to be able to make their own decisions, and have their own opinions, but… about *everything*? Isn't there a higher standard out there, or a higher authority over mankind… or *should* there be? In regards to a humanistic view of thinking, however, it seems that the opposite is often true: that whatever ends up to be the "best-sounding" ideologies of the time, or the most *popular* ones, may often begin to win out over the minds of the people. In essence, with (Cain's) humanism, there really is no *absolute* right and wrong, no objective laws to become the standard of mankind;. it's all about relativity, it's all about being subjective. It's about one's own opinion, as well as what might be popular at the time. It, ultimately, seems to be about which purveyor of (collective) thought would "win out" over any other. And, of course, what if those former Templars and EJCs were "at the top" of the ideological heap, here… pushing a lot of the most popular agendas? And what if their agendas might entail getting rid of the power of the Catholic Church, as well as Christianity in general? Humanism becomes another weapon in their arsenal because of this, assuredly.

Again, in some respects, these concepts sounds good and worthy. But, if there's nothing objective, and nothing absolute over us all (such as a heavenly God), then people could easily begin to think that almost *anything* was game, as far as morality. Besides, who's to tell them something differently? We recall Cain (from previous volumes), and some of the thoughts *he* had after the murder of Abel. He began to have things so twisted around in his head, after a bit of thinking, that it almost seemed as though Abel's murder was *his own* fault, or even God's fault for not accepting Cain's sacrifice! Yes, things can get quite twisted in the human mind, if allowed to go unabated. Imagine if we had a *questionable* group of human thinkers at the top, dictating what the new "right" and "wrong" parameters may now be?

Again, as we've seen the rapid rise of a number of new Renaissance factions, we need to include the rise of *liberalism* and *democracy*, as well. Yet, as we're now beginning to see, these could also have a dark underbelly (if utilized improperly). It also makes us to wonder: maybe this fronting of *liberalism* and *democracy* was, indeed, another couple of arrows in the "quiver" of war… aimed directly at the Roman Catholic Church, and all of Christendom. There were inserted, largely, for *nefarious* reasons.

And, with all of these additions in tow, this whole movement - the new, and *altered*, vision of what Western civilization was now to be viewed as - seemed to have been "taking off," if you will (during the time of the Renaissance). The entire conglomerate was now "on fire":

> *Since the oldest known records of civilization, advanced societies have risen and have fallen, but none have advanced* ***so rapidly*** *as western civilization. For thousands of years humankind existed in mostly agrarian societies… Empires would rise and fall making great achievements in architecture and culture, yet* ***none so profound nor as rapid as what western civilization has achieved in such a short period of time****…*
> ("Forbidden History of the Aryan Race Unabridged", n. d., p. 1)[4]

The (Unsuccessful) Counter-Offensive

After the addition of all these additional elements into the collective consciousness, the "universal" church of Rome was not very happy (obviously), and was not about to take it all lying down (at least, that was their plan). They, then, vowed to make at least some kind of a comeback. Yet, with the momentum already so pushing straight at them, and very hard, it was already proving to be very difficult to get anything off the ground. The "cats" were truly out of the bag here… and the peasants were beginning to enjoy a better (and, quite often, *ungodly*) life! People were no longer in the mood for feudalism, nor were they in the mood to be dictated. It was near impossible to put this genie back in the bottle.

Yet, the church still had to try. And now, to begin their retaliatory "roll out," they began to recruit a number of high ranking priests to help them out, very savvy priests.

Enter the *Jesuits*:

> *...in 1540 the Society of Jesus was founded by Ignatius Loyola for the purpose of **overthrowing the Protestant Reformation**, and to ultimately **subvert the Bibles** produced by the Reformation...*
> ("The Untold History of the Bible", n. d., p. 1)[5]

> *...(as the Bible version)... known as the bestselling book of all time, the King James translation is seen as the crowning achievement of the Reformation, and a uniting text for English Protestantism. Because of its symbolism, Rome and the Jesuit Order have always hated this Bible... In response, the **Vatican would launch a Counter Reformation to destroy the work of the Reformers...*** ("The Untold History of the Bible", n. d., p. 1)[6]

We recall that, throughout its long history, the Roman Catholic Church, already, did not have a lot of use for those pesky (and *true* believing) Protestant sects out there, as well as any of those true thinking Jews out there, proclaiming the Torah and even the Messiah (without all of those additional (rabbinic) interpretations or *mystical* (or occult) additions). For a while, they really enjoyed stopping anyone from interpreting the Bible in any other way... except *their* way. But now, since the Bible was getting out there, and people were discovering a few things out for themselves, the church was no longer able to tell people to just sit down, and be quiet. These Jesuits had to work on a new level.

It was now time for the Jesuits to enact their own attempts at *subtle* warfare, in a coinciding period known as the "Counter-Reformation." The battle royal had now begun, on a number of *subtle* levels (even though the common people may have not had a clue to what kind of battle was actually raging on around them, behind the scenes).

*This final victory over the Lord's Protestant Reformation, will be the climax of the Jesuits' quest to submit **all nations** to the Temporal Power of the Pope in a worldwide fascist, military police state, maintained by the Jesuits' International Intelligence Community - the Holy Office of the Inquisition - grinding the "**liberals**" and "**heretics**" of all nations to dust.*
(Phelps, 2007, p. 74)[7]

Notice the final line here. We see that: beyond their attempts at subverting a number of "heretics" out there (as was done in the past), they, now, had begun to set their sights on any and all of those "liberals" out there as well! Go figure. Of course, this was because they wanted to slow down any advancements of those humanistic *ways of Cain*.

The Maximization of "Discovery" and "Exploration"

As we know, a subtle was raging, between those different Edomite front groups. And, by the time these Jesuits came onto the scene, the damage to the Catholic Church was already starting to show. It was already looking as though there wasn't a lot for them to do to stop this momentum… not anymore. It's was almost as though these movements were beginning had taken on a life their own, and were too big (and popular) to tame down.

One thing that seemed to have been making things a bit worse here (for those Jesuits) were the number of people who sought after *true* Christian ethics and morality. It seemed as though: once people began to follow what the Bible truly had to say (and not just the interpretations of the church), the people began to prosper. There was something *huge* in the air here - and it would commonly became known as the "Protestant work ethic." Yes, since protestant ideologies were beginning to take hold over the people, they were beginning to be "won over" to the concept of inscribing Biblical values into their everyday working lives. Of course, if we see a majority of people wanting to follow Judeo-Christian values, such as hard work, honestly, and being kind to one another, a group of people couldn't help but end up prosperous! Yes, they say that "a rising tide raises all ships," and there were a lot of "ships" around, beginning to "rise" all over the place.

Over time, things were beginning to get a lot better for those living in these new eras, with so many emerging out of their old feudal ways. And, yes, it wasn't just the Protestants who were benefiting from all of these changes. Still, if we really think about it, these "Protestant" ways of thinking, living and working - especially those coming directly out of the Bible - could have easily gave a number of people the "green light" to do a vast number of great things.

With all of this, let's begin to expand a bit *more* on a couple of those new "ages" coming into Western civilization. Enter in the ages of *Discovery* and *Exploration*. If we add in a number of people, with a good amount of will and bravery, we, then, get a population beginning to ponder what it may be like to just get out there, and explore a vast number of new things. Enter a good number of people who felt the desire to travel abroad, and travel to the furthermost reaches of the earth. Enter those who wanted to expand the flags of their own nations as well. The Catholic regime already had control over most of the European continent, but not the rest of the world. So, around this time, a good number of individuals - many not directly related to this Catholic regime - began to venture out of their comfort zone, and seek out new land, new riches and resources. And, of course, they, often, were doing this to enrich their *own* selves as well.

There was *colonialism and mercantilism* going on. Trade and commerce began to flourish; and the world just seemed to "come alive." Of course, all of this would help the former Templars and EJCs to put another "nail in the coffin" in the church's ability to *overshadow* people, and ultimately control what they were doing. So many were going in so many different directions now! New horizons were being established; and there were new goals in mind. So many things were going on, other than people just sitting there, being subjected to the overwhelming desires of their former Catholic feudal lords.

The "Work Ethic" That Worked... A Little Too Well?

Those ages of Discovery and Exploration surely would have allowed for the expansion of so many, as well as the expansion of other things, such as the sciences, the arts, and even a number of **Protestant** ideals. And now, this brings us to another interesting question (in regards to the Protestant Reformation and the Renaissance): was

God behind a lot of this societal prosperity, because so many people were beginning to come back to the Bible, and to **Him**, once again?

A number of people, at this time, *were* beginning to read the Bible, and follow that so-called "Protestant work ethic." They began to desire to make the most out of their lives, and expand their horizons. Could these people have become "blessed" - in an *esoteric* way - by their choices to, once again, go after the Bible? Could they have become "rewarded" for their efforts? Were the "dots" being connected here - people being rewarded by trusting, and being obedient to, that one and only God? This seems to be the big question we are facing now.

Of course, a number of these kind of thoughts, today, might not sit very well with a number of people out there today (especially those who, of course, seem to have a desire to lean away from God, and apart from the Holy Scriptures). And, yes, it might seem perfectly understandable that so many of us (today) wouldn't exactly feel good about being subjugated, or exploited, by any other nation. No one wants to be on the receiving end of those individuals who want to go out, and expand their empire. Makes total sense, if we really think about it.

It also makes sense that: those humanistic concepts of "liberalism" and "democracy" seem to come up, again and again, all over our modern world. Today, people want to be *free* to live out their own lives, and be able to vote in whatever way they might want. Understandable. But, as we should also understand, these thoughts may not have always been the prevailing thoughts (in a lot of people). In fact, it was probably something a bit different… that is, until the former Templars and EJCs decided it was time for a change. Up to the Renaissance (and somewhat beyond), it may have been acceptable for one nation to travel aboard, and, not only engage themselves in trade with other people in other areas, but, also, to attempt to conquer them, or colonize them.

Today, one might shudder at the thought of such things. The concept of conquering another nation, or any type of "imperialism" or "colonization" (as they're called) are, so often, considered to be *wrong* at their very core! Yet, once again, we may need to understand that today's ways of thinking are actually a reflection of today's standards and values (and not the standards of way back when). And, just because most of us may not think in this way (today) doesn't mean that practices such as these were not socially acceptable, or as something justified. That is the real thing for us to realize here: there were a number of people out there, during these times, that may have done whatever they did - not because they were "intentionally" striving to be evil, or wanting to do something wrong - but because they were doing what was considered the trend to do.

Ultimately, can *we always* judge the deeds of those in the past according upon a number of social parameters we have in right front of us? If a number of people smoked cigarettes in the 20th century, is it fair for us to point fingers at them, saying they were wrong, based upon what we might know? It doesn't sound fair. Doctors, about 80 years ago, even publically went on record recommending certain cigarettes, saying how glamorous it was for them to be able to smoke them!

In the last century or so, we've also seen a number of people openly pushing radioactive things, or other deadly things, to the public at large, as if they were something desirable, or what they were pushing had something good about them:

Of course, neither of these options would fly in today's world; but, once again that's because we're looking at it by today's standards.

These concepts seem to be very applicable here, in regards to our current discussion, because a majority of people, back then, *did* seem to condone the migration of their own people into other lands, exploring them, and even conquering them. As well, the people who successfully participated in these conquests, when they returned home, were often heralded for their efforts, even celebrated as "heroes." That's just the way it was.

One more thing: if we dig a little deeper into this whole thing here: most nations, today, didn't just obtain their own land by migrating somewhere, and simply *asking* the indigenous people ahead of them (if there were any) to "be nice," and let them in. They didn't just hope the people already there would "move over," and allow them to intermingle, or even take over. No, it usually didn't happen that way (for the most part)! So many nations (in our distant past) did have to *fight*, in order to obtain whatever land and resources that they now have. And, again, if that's the way it was (with so many nations), how much could we condemn a number of individuals for the ways they had once lived?

If we might also recall, just after the time of Noah's flood, Noah was the one who dictated where a vast number of people should end up moving to, in individual groups; yet (as we may also recall), not all people ended up going to the places they were supposed to go, nor did a number of them want to *stay* in the areas that they were told to. Could this have been the beginning of all of this conflict, between ancient nations?

In the Bible, we also discover how **Israel** had to engage a number of their neighbors, quite often, for them to obtain the land that they, eventually, were able to settle in. They needed to battle a number of hostile (as well as *pagan*) nations, to be able to move into the land promised to them (by Noah, as well as God). These lands, of course, were already taken over by pagans and giants alike. Maybe, as far as these Israelites were concerned, God might not have been particularly happy with a number of those pagans, giants and Canaanites who invaded the land, and decided to take over - the land that Noah dictated to those sons of Shem instead (i.e. Israel). Maybe, because of their defiance, God did not really care about turning His back on them… just as *they* had turned their backs on Him, by becoming pagan, and doing evil. Yes, there's, often, more to stories of the Bible than we're given.

It's also obvious that: there were a number of **pagan** nations out there, as well, in the most ancient of days, openly looking for ways to conquer other lands around them, turning their captors into slaves! We mustn't forget about those ancient histories of Greece, Rome, and even the Aztecs (for example). These pagan empires (among many) would become particularly wealthy by pillaging and plundering neighboring nations, so it wasn't just those ancient Israelites out there, becoming violent and aggressive towards their neighbors (not by a long shot). It's just plain to see: it really doesn't matter *who* was out there, conquering whomever - and it really didn't even matter what *faith* they may have professed at the time - most nations (or empires) involved themselves in some kind of aggression, for one reason or another. It was, so often, a fact of life, and of *faith*.

So, with all of this, we are, now, able to see that there's a bit *more* to our world than just a number of quick assumptions on what's right or wrong (in today's world). And, we also see that there's really not much room for *anyone* to claim total innocence here, in regards to those thoughts of colonialism, imperialism, or what have you. No one can really go off and claim that: "*our* group never did anything *like that*."

And, on top of it all, we may now be led to that age-old question: should we condemn Israel (or any other nation that may have been "holding the flag" for the Bible, or any Godly ways) as "horrible" individuals, because they needed to resort to violence for some reason, or desired to be victorious over other nations? What about those at the time of the Renaissance? What if some of these conquerors were Christian? Was it *still* "right" for any nation to be able to travel out, into the world, and conquer other lands, or set up shop? **Or**, was it all evil (according to today's standards)? Once again, the answer is: it all depends on how one looks at a particular situation, or what *their* interests might have been about a topic.

The "Right to Conquer"?

Either way we might think about these practices, we now begin to discover that, soon after the Renaissance became more and more popular, a number of nations (such as France, Spain and Portugal, to name a few), began to take it upon themselves to venture out, and conquer new lands… and venture out they did! Yes, a number of those Catholic nations eventually decided it was time for them to take action, and go out into their world. But, there was also a *Protestant* nation out there, that ended up becoming extremely noteworthy for their ventures abroad, and this would be the nation of *Great Britain*.

Yes, in an era that did not go into a tizzy about any kind of exploration, conquest or colonization, the Protestant nation of *Great Britain* seemed to have stood out, in a major way! They actually became so powerful (as an empire) that a saying was developed about them, over time: "**the sun never set on the British empire**!" Wow. If we really think about this, the saying could have assuredly become a matter of pride and accomplishment for those British people themselves. They would establish colonies throughout the world, from America to Asia… and become extremely wealthy and powerful because of it! And, of course, even though this kind of talk might sound a bit "exploitive," or even unsavory (nowadays), we know that it was once considered to be *advantageous* for the British people to be in this situation.

Now, as we begin to think about this further, could the people of Britain - utilizing that Protestant work ethic - have begun to be feel a bit "**blessed**" by God, because of how far they were able to expand themselves out (as an empire), and reap the benefits from it? But, on the other hand, what a nation for those former Templars and EJCs to indirectly "prop up" here, with the new ways of Renaissance, to take on the Catholic machine! Yes, these former Templars and EJCs may have, indeed, helped to start the "engine" of Catholic division and separation (through countries such as Great Britain), which would, then, allow for that "Protestant work ethic" to be ignited, and become the "fuel" for their overwhelming successes abroad! Naturally, those early Brits must have felt pretty *good* about what they were able to accomplish, and where their new empire was going (with this new "formula" in tow). They must have felt as though their allegiance to God was beginning to pay off (with so much additional land and resources allotted to them). Yet, on the other extreme, they may not have understood how they were actually being *used*, as well, for the new, anti-Catholic movement that was already being laid out.

But, in all of this, one could figure out that: those Masons and EJCs were only able to set up this nation for success… something *else* had to take it from there! The people couldn't just have accomplish so much, as an empire, by doing nothing. Could their successes have been due to, in part, their Protestantism, or their Godly work ethic?

There may be even *more* to this all: from previous volumes, we might recall that the nation of Great Britain (as well as a number of other European nations) could have, actually, been remnants of those Lost 10 Tribes of Israel… beginning to come *back* into God's fold (through their utilization of Christian beliefs and Godly values). What if these people of promise were actually becoming successful in their attempts... because they were coming back in favor with God?

Yes, by adding *these* obscured elements into the whole "confrontation" scenario (between Esau and his brother Israel) the plot may *really* thicken... even more! If Britain, indeed, was considered the land where the descendants of ***Ephraim*** ended up in, then how would it look to see this particular empire being able to expand as much as it did? Was it considered *blessed* by God, maybe? Their successes may have, indeed, looked good to a number of Protestants in those days, assuredly... even if they did not fully understand, or even know about, their **Israeli** connections.

To help support this claim, we, already, may have understood (from previous volumes) that the word *Britain* could have stemmed from words meaning: the "men of the covenant." And, we also know that Ephraim was considered the descendant of Jacob who carried on Israel's birthright. Wow. If we put a lot of this together - things start to make sense.

If the people of Britain could have been thought of as "coming back to God" (through their adoption of Christian values around this time), then seeing them actually being able to form a huge empire might start to make sense. What if their birthright, or "covenant," with God seems to have been a reflection of what was promised to this particular descendant of Jacob (a long time ago)?

The Bible has this prediction about Ephraim (as well as his brother Manasseh):

*...he (Manasseh) also shall become a people, and he also shall be **great**: but truly his younger brother (Ephraim) **shall be greater than he**, and his seed shall become **a multitude of nations**.*   - Gen. 48:19 (KJV)

Are we talking about Britain, and the British Empire, here - as the "multitude of nations?"

Who knows? *Something* allowed them to become very successful during the time of the Reformation (and beyond). Could their adherence to the Bible, as well as the "Protestant work ethic," have been a part of it all? Is there some kind of "unsung rule" of

God's universe here: that, if someone works hard and does the right things in life, God will want to *reward* him or her (in one way or another)?

Doing Better Than (Most) Anyone Expected

Well, we've heard about Great Britain (or *Ephraim*). What about that brother of Ephraim - *Manasseh*? The above prediction (in the Bible) stated that his descendants would become *great* as well! Could there have been something to the fact that a number of people, upset with the corruption that was also following England (at this time), would want to "come out from her," and settle in one of her many colonies? One major group of people, of course, would end up becoming known as the *Puritans*, and their destination would have been the shores of (what would have eventually been) the United States. But, once again, why would a number of Puritans feel so strongly about leaving Britain, and relocating all the way across an ocean? Maybe, in an esoteric way, this could have been the manifestation of *Manasseh* coming out of his brother Ephraim, deciding to go onto another path, and forming into another nation.

Interestingly enough, we now see that there may have indeed been a few problems in Protestant England (along with all of the good), most probably because there were Masonic elements already in the country, and in the government (due to those Knights Templar escaping to the British Isles, way back in the early 1400's).

The Bible seems to lead us to believe that the brothers - Ephraim and Manasseh - would become *close* in a number of ways, even though they may have be separated themselves into two people! Could England be Ephraim and those American colonies (soon to be the United States) be Manasseh (in blood and graft)? And, if these were both plausible possibilities, would their adherence to that "Protestant work ethic" be an esoteric part of their present (and future) successes?

Since these two (future) nations would end up prospering (due to the ramifications of this Renaissance), and were also considered to be Protestant areas (during these early times), could they have also been "set into place" by a number of Masonic individuals who ended up permeating the governments of these two lands, as well? And, if so, were those former Templars and EJCs working to take advantage of their own successes, over time, to take down the Roman Catholic Church? It's entirely possible.

And, if this was so, then what would happen to this whole charade if the two (Christian) lands began to be a little too *powerful* (over time)? What if the work ethic of these two lands allowed their people to, practically, "take on a life of their own" (and not continue to be used as pawns as easily)? It would become as a lion who escaped his cage, and did not want to be confined to any cage anymore. What to do now?

Well, the first thing that those former Templar/EJC elites would need to do would be to *slow down* the progress of these Protestant people a bit, to "curve" the ways of God… so they don't become as successful, in the end. And, in order to accomplish their objectives, the Edomite powers that be needed to distort, confound, as well as dilute, the *spiritual* momentum of this Protestant reformation, a little at a time. They couldn't do it too much, or too quickly, because people may be able to spot a rat. They needed to keep their people continually able to do damage to Rome, all the while reducing the potential for an increase in the Protestant momentum. How would the pull this off?

Back and Forth… With the Illuminati

Now, in order to accomplish their anti-Catholic goal, as well as take true Christianity *down* a few pegs, those ruling elites needed to start steering the people of those Protestant lands into some *other* direction… leading by deception.

> *The world is governed by **far different** personages from **what is imagined by those who are not behind the scenes**.*
> - Benjamin Disraeli (nineteenth century British prime minister, in a speech to Parliament)[8]

The above quote really says it all, in regards to what had been going on (behind the scenes), as well as what's going on today! Most of us have heard of a "shadow government." The time had come, it seemed, for a number of *ultra-elites* (of those former Templars and EJCs) to start *consolidating* their power, and initiate a "top down" approach to rule, and manipulation. They hoped that this would allow them to accomplish their new tasks at hand. And, a lot of this began to foment (seriously) around the year 1776 A.D. Now, doesn't *that* year sound a bit familiar?

Yes, many of us may have heard of that secretive organization known as the *Illuminati*. As we'll now see, the Illuminati could have been considered a small group of intellectuals, with a vast amount of power and resource behind them, beginning to use their weight to make changes in the world around them. These people were considered (or, more likely, they considered *themselves*) the "crème of the crop," as far as what their place would have been in society… and called themselves the "Illuminati" because of their supposed ability to be *illimuintated*, or receive *illumination* from many high-level, esoteric sources. These were indeed the top thinkers of the time… originating (for the most part) from the former Templars and the EJC.

Because of their origins, this new secret society could have been thought of as a "secret society *within* a secret society." And, being accredited as the founder of this high-level organization, we have it originatating with one man:

> ***Freemasonry*** *originated… as part of the* **ancient Egyptian occultism**. *Building on that, in 1776, law professor* **Adam Weishaupt** *founded the Illuminati.*
> (Gouws, n. d., p. 1)[9]

There are those out there who say that the Rothschilds (once again) had become a part of this whole establishment, assembling it together. Go figure! And, looking for a person to spearhead this new leadership project, they reportedly backed the recruiting of a man named Adam Weishaupt, son of a Jewis rabbi.

> *Judaism and even Jewishness itself was infiltrated and overtaken a long time ago by a… man called Sabbatai Zevi… who was proclaimed messiah around (approximately) the year 1666… Sabbatai was succeeded by another 'messiah' called* **Jacob Frank who apparently instructed Adam Weishaupt** *to found the original Bavarian Illuminati in 1776.*
> ("#3664: The Satanic Jewish Messiah of 1666 - Audio DVD", n. d., p. 1)[10]

Interestingly enough, Weishaupt was also believed to have, at one time, been a *Jesuit* priest as well (at least for a time). Wow, what a combination here! Could this man have, possibly, become disparaged by the Catholic Church, and decided to switch sides? Either way, it seems that, with his unique past, as well as with all of his powerful connections, Weishaupt seemed to have been the perfect person for the job.

And, interestingly enough, Weishaupt's goals of his new Illuminati was to accomplish a number of things such as the following:

> *Its aim was to **replace Christianity** by a **religion of reason**, to **destroy the sovereignty of nations** and thus to **control** the world.*
> (Gouws, n. d., p. 1)[11]

Wow. What an end goal here! Of course, we also see their goal of "replacing Christianity." Makes total sense here, for the particular time. Could this have been because the Protestant work ethic was working well, maybe a little bit *too* well?

This, also, sounds like a number of people striving to establish some kind of "universal" government, uniting a lot of people from a lot of different factions. This time, however, it wouldn't have been the "universal" Catholic Church, attempting to unite people of all faiths… it would be those *former Templars* and *EJCs* being at the "top" of that proverbial hill, uniting people in other ways!

Now, according to their new goals, their wish would be to replace *any* religious faith, which would, then, turn belief systems of the world into something more of a *man*-based faith, or belief in his intellect. In other words, the new belief system would be modeled after the **humanism** of Cain - replacing Christianity, and God in general, with a religion of human *reason* and interpretation. Of course, this sounds totally typical, knowing what we already know… with those particular elitists, now, substituting themselves as the new "gods" of this world, the ones being given credit for:

> *…receiving illumination, being **enlightened** by mystical reason… (and adopting the teachings of) radical French philosophers… and other **anti-Christian** doctrines.*
> (Gouws, n. d., p. 1)[12]

Again, things usually head us towards one direction or another - towards something of the Christ or something of the antichrist! Take out anything religious, and the new ways of human enlightenment and salvation seem to lie upon *their own* elitist rationalizations, perceptions and interpretations. Of course, as long as *they* are the ones "on top" (in situations such as this), then that works for them. Also, it seems that: as long as what they promote is something that's *anti-Christian*, that's all that really matters to them too (at least as far as their new agenda is concerned)!

They may have, for a time, been using Protestantism to help them take down the Catholic faith, but their new approach, as these new ways of looking at things, may need to be spliced in - to slowly begin to take down those Protestant ways of doing things. They, ultimately, couldn't have had the Protestant work ethic continuing on, the way it had been, and working so well. According to the new rules, no Protestant, nor person of God, should be allowed to stand on their feet for *too* long, only to serve their interests and agenda (i.e. continually taking down the Roman Catholic Church). These people, for the most part, were only considered "tools," in a much bigger fight.

Of course, establishing this Illuminati made perfect sense to them, and understanding why *they* would want to establish a "one-world government" makes perfect sense as well… as long as it's all under *them*. There would no longer be any more judges in the picture, no more gods… but them (and what *they* worshipped). Of course, once they're able to succeed in taking out their formidable enemy (the Catholic Church), and, eventually slowing down the Protestant movement into practically nothing, then **nothing** would really be left to challenge them, and their authority over the world. So, why not begin to push *humanism* on all of the populous, as the new (and stellar) method of achieving something higher?

One famous (and modern) writer, as well as TV personality, gave his interpretation about what a number of people behind the Illuminati may have actually wanted to accomplish, way back then (and all the way up to **today**). He said that this particular group of individuals:

*"...felt they could create a **better world**. They wanted to abolish all monarchies, **religion**, private property and nation states and replace them with a utopian society… infiltrating the houses of power…"*
   - *Brian Meltzer's Decoded* (A&E Networks, 2010)[13]

Again, to a number of people out there (especially today), these goals may actually sound noble, and good! An "utopian society," of course, sounds good, as well… especially *for the people at the* top (running it all). It also seems to sound like a number of these individuals were (and are) just out to make the world "a better place." How flowery. But, of course, the question beckons: why would the people in charge have to come from a *secretive* society - only to accomplish social work? It makes no sense. Of course, there's always seems to be something deeper to a lot of the "philanthropy" we see around us. A lot of times, there's something advantageous for those who are promoting certain things. Also, if movements such as the Illuminati were only out for philanthropy, then why would anyone have to have anything *secretive* about them, or emerge out of secretive institutions?

Mother Teresa, if we think about it, did not really seem to have anything to hide. She actually was out there, living "in the trenches," and helping people out… not looking down upon it all, viewing things from some mansion on a hill. No grandstanding here. No secret initiations. No nothing… except a person who was "practicing what they preached."

1776 - Significant For a Couple of Reasons

There seemed to have been some more interesting things going on, around the same time that this Illuminati was established. In 1776, there seemed to have been *another* major power player here, emerging onto the world's scene… and it was also Protestant, just like Great Britain (at least for a while). And, eventually, the governing party of *this* new nation would push for it to become mighty - even mightier than what came out of that old British Empire. Yes, it seems as though these former Templars and EJCs have finally hit the jackpot - developing a major bulwark here (in regards to their ability to challenge Catholic Rome).

One of the most interesting elements of this particular nation lies in the *year* it was established… the same year as the beginning of the Illuminati. What a coincidence! And, yes, anyone with a knowledge of the history would be able to recognize this date… as the year when the United States was founded - those colonies who, initially, broke apart from Masonic Britain (just as how the descendants of *Manasseh* could have broken apart from Ephraim, and established their own nation). Do we sense a "hidden hand" at work here, manipulating a number of things into place?

Yes, could the establishment of this particular country have, indeed, been a part of some bigger agenda… of anti-Catholic domination? As we begin to dig deeper, it does seem as though these Former Templars and EJCs were making another bold move… to enable another large force of individuals (in the land of Manasseh?) to come together, and, slowly, become strong enough to aid Britain in taking on this Catholic foe in Europe? Was this *another* great, Protestant "machine" in the making?

And, if we really think about it, a lot of these changes could have actually been a fulfillment of some Bible prophecy here, in regard to those missing tribes of Israel:

*And I will make of thee a **great** nation, and I will belss thee, and make thy name great; and thou salt be a blessing…*
- Gen. 12:2 (KJV)

We already have Britain becoming known as *Great* Britain, and the United States, of course, seemed to be destined for greatness, as well. And, on top of this, a similar thing would end up happening with the government of this new nation as what may have already happened to the government of Great Britain… and that would be Freemasons in positions of power. But, *this* time, the government of the United States would be organized a lot *differently* - actually, unlike anything the world had ever seen before. Yes, it would be set up differently, but still, deep down inside, it would contain those same old *Masonic* elements within it, working, once again, behind the scenes.

Yes, the new "constitutional republic" would be thought of, in a number of interesting ways, was a "great experiment." And, since enacted, a lot of it seemed to work for a good number of people (at least at first). No more kings to rule over them! No more harsh authoritarians. And, best of all (at least for those in charge), *no* more Catholic Church in charge.

The concepts of *individual liberties* and *freedoms* would soon began to ring, throughout this new nation, and it all sure sounded good to a lot of people living there, including those descendants of the pilgrims. Yet, as great as so much of this early U.S. was beginning to churn out, could there have been a lot *the same* going on, as far as the ruling party under the surface?

> *"The history of our (American) revolution will be one continued **lie** from one end to the other."*   - *John Adams* (former president of the U.S.)[14]

Yet, America would end up being a "shining beacon on a hill," for a good long time, a place where a lot of people would eventually want to move to. Just look at all of people *still* wanting to migrate to this land, and live here, today! Yes, *something* must have been exceptional about this place, making it great.

Living in this country allowed the populous to establish their own parcels of lands, and stay on their own property. This gave a number of them the leverage to borrow money (against their home), and allowed them to be able to use this money to invest in their own business, or in something that would help them become more *independently* wealthy (and not slaves to the government). The middle class, as a result, would begin to expand, and even end up thriving. No more reliance on the government, nor on religion. No more feudalism in this land… this "experiment" seemed destined for success.

As well, the strength of a number of people in this country would be in their Protestant faith, and their Protestant work ethic. Once again (as Jesus said), we would know a person by their fruits… and the United States was becoming quite fruitful! Neighbors would be out there, helping neighbors; families would be helping families; people would go to church on Sunday, and "loving thy neighbor" in the process. It seems that those descendants of Manasseh (in blood and graft) were beginning to realize their full potential, and becoming the best that they could be. In a nutshell, their Judeo-Christian moral code could have, indeed, been a huge part of what would allow America to become so different, and so exceptional.

> *...this (United States) is a country that was founded and expanded and grew, (as from the) foundations of Western civilization... (and the) **Judeo-Christian** ethic...*   - *The Rush Limbaugh Radio Program* (4/4/18)¹⁵

Again, with the Protestant work ethic blooming, and the people beginning to prosper, what about the people behind the governing body (especially those working in the shadows)? What would they need to do now, and what changes would they need to put into place soon, when they began to feel the need to capitalize on whatever *they* believed they should, naturally, get out of this country, *as well as* from the people?

Corruptions Within "The Great Experiment"

It's also interesting to see that, today, we could picture the United States and Great Britain as, for the most part, two Protestant nations (at their core); and, they are considered to very close to one other (in a whole number of ways)... just as two brethren (i.e. Ephraim and Manasseh) would have been!

And, we'll also soon see how the Masonic-backed governments of *both* would, eventually, come to the decision that: it was time to "rein in" some these successes a bit, and "take their cut." As we've already discussed, they couldn't just let these nations get *too* successful, and get too out of hand. So, as a result, subtle manipulations (and takedowns), over the years, may have now been in order!

The powers that be figured that: if they could keep these two countries on a "short leash," if you will - by allowing them to grow (at least to a degree), and become more powerful - then, all they would need to do, over the years, would be to slowly feed the nation a little bit of moral "arsenic" (or poison), so that it would weaken the nation, just enough, to keep in under their thumbs!

Of course, we're not saying that a majority of those American founders (including Washington, Jefferson, Franklin, as well as a number of those signers of the Declaration of Independence) were horrible people, or had only *evil* inside of their hearts; but (of course), it needs to be known that every one of these individuals were Freemasons, or former Templars! Go figure. And, of course, there may have been the presence of a number of *Illuminati* involving themselves in the American experiment as well.

Well, what would be a few ways they could "put the reins" on a country, such as the United States. They, obviously, couldn't just let the people be too happy, and have *too much* freedom overall… at least, **not under** the Protestant work ethic!

So, one way they would begin to work on the people would be to insert a couple of additional elements of Western civilization that we've already talked about - those concepts of *liberalism* and *democracy*. Now (and for a long time in the future), the two concepts would began to be brought *back* into the forefront of conversations and public discord. We already know that the country was, at least partially, founded on Judeo-Christian principles, principles which inserted *God* into almost everything. Now, the concepts of *liberalism* and *democracy* would also see the light of day, intermingling with all of this Godly talk (even thought they seem to be of a *secular* or *humanistic* origin). In other words, when these parallel topics were brought up, and focused on, the thought of *God* was, usually, not there. Yes, it's almost like substituting the freedom that one finds with following God with another style of freedom - the freedoms that one might feel through the adoption of some kind of *secular* or *liberal* value system (i.e. with humanism, or some kind of *human-based* interpretation).

These other concepts were, slowly, being inserted into the populous - as tares would be inserted next to the pure wheat - to corrupt it, as well as slowly replacing it! This is nothing new. Eventually, anything that may also have a connotation with God, or the Bible, has to be (slowly) be stripped of all the "Godly" elements, or diluted to a point where it doesn't matter, and usually replaced with a number of secular, or humanistic, elements. That's how it works. Even pagan elements would slowly begin to seep in, and "fill" the missing "gaps." And, interestingly enough, we'll now begin to see how a number of these *other* elements have been set up, all along the passage of time (even since the founding of the nation), to allow these elites the ability to subtly *replace* anything Godly, or of the Bible, when the time came to pass.

Today, we hear element of secular humanism, liberalism and democracy mentioned as often as we hear "pass me the butter"… and this is not by accident. And, as we also may notice - God seems to have been taken out of most everything, just to be "politically correct." This, as well, was not done by accident.

There are pagan elements around us, as well, ready to "fill in the gaps" whenever Godly elements are taken out of the American experience... and, yes, this was also not done by accident. As we look at some examples of pagan elements already inserted into the country (since its founding), let's begin by looking at a very famous symbol of the United States.

It's not too hard to figure out that, at one time, a good number of English and American people - being the Protestants that they were - valued **liberty** and freedom... with these values being *under God*, that is. But, as we now are beginning to see, their new game would be: change the perception of one's own liberty and freedom, from something that was from *God* into something that was from *something else*. And, of course, with God now out of the picture, there would be a number of **pagan** elements, already set in place (and all around the country), ready and willing to "fill in" any of the missing gaps of Godliness, here.

Some of those pagan *changelings* may have already been, strategically, set into place, around important areas of the United States ("hidden in plain sight," as well):

Of course, we have the Statue of *Liberty* - which, in actuality, served as a representation of that ancient **pagan** goddess *Libertas* (complete with the sun rays upon her head). Fancy that! No God in this landmark, that's for sure (even though it was supposedly set up as an major emblem of *freedom*... valued so much by the United States). And, of course, this statue was designed by a famous Frenchman, and *Mason* (named Frederic Auguste Bartholdi).

Libertas, as we might also recall (from previous volumes), was nothing but an ancient representation of that "paganized" goddess *Eve* (from the Bible). She was, ultimately, the goddess who did stand for a number of "freedoms" out there... but, these were the freedoms associated with mankind leaving the ways of God, and following the *new* ways of the Serpent (in the Garden of Eden). Yes, this actually represented a "celebration" - of how the Serpent supposedly "freed" Eve (and all of mankind) from their spiritual "bondage," away from an oppressive God. Yes, these icons of *Libertas* are nothing but a twisted, immortalized view of the Fall of man... from a **pagan** perspective.

Also, smack dab in the middle of some land, quite near the U.S. *Capital* building, we have another **pagan** symbol:

Again, the phallic symbol symbolizes the sexual instrument that was used (by the Serpent) to help him convince Eve to follow his ways. In other words, he *wholly* seduced Eve (even sexually), convincing her to turn away from God. Yes, it's all pagan here, and it's all contrary to God… all hidden in plain sight.

Yes, what a thing to celebrate here: *sex*, the loss of human purity, and the adoption of those fallen ways of this world… all within a Christian country no less? Do we sense some "baiting and switching" going on here?

And (of course), the human *by-product* of the sexual interchange (between Eve and the Serpent) would turn out to be none other than one of the founders of this entire pagan movement (as well as of humanism): **Cain**, of course. Yes, the whole story of *paganism* seems to be subtly there even, in the United States and other Protestant nations… just waiting to be absorbed into all things once Godly.

Also, no wonder why so many pagans, from the 4th century onward, tried to downplay or silence any talk about fallen angels being able to produce children with mortal women… the powers that be wouldn't have been able to insert these strategic symbols as easily as they now were able to… if people had understood the truth. This knowledge would, indeed, begin to blow their cover!

Interestingly enough, there seems to be even more "proofs" to these pagan infestations (inside a Christian country). As we look at the capital city of the United States (i.e. Washington D.C.) we'll begin to discover that there could have even been a *pentagram* laid out amongst the number of major building in the city (via certain streets), if one "connects the dots" (and, of course, the layout of these streets was designed by a Mason)!

How's that for a governing body, riding the coattails of Christian values - a major sign of the evil one, quite possibly, on their capital streets? How lovely.

As we also may recall, the major governmental buildings of the U.S. are, so often, modeled after those of ancient (and *pagan*) Greece and Rome:

Once again, *why* pay homage to these particular ancient empires? Were a number of these things set into place by random choice; or, were they (quite possibly) brought about to honor those *real* forces behind those deeper, governing parties? Could *these* be what a number of individuals - in the shadows of Christian governments (such as the United States) - are actually be holding a lot *more* dear, deep down inside (other than their devotion to submit to a heavenly God)?

A number of Masonic historians have openly claimed that the foundations of their secret craft were, in part, based upon the Bible, as well as on the Solomon's Temple (in Jerusalem). Yet, other Masonic historians have given credit to *Nimrod* as one of their early founders. Now, why *Nimrod*... a front man of ancient *Babylon*? A number of other scholars have claimed that their craft has roots in the ancient (and pagan) empire of **Egypt**. Well, just what is it, here... a Christian secret society or a pagan secret society?

When we look at the back of our basic monetary unit - where governments and empires alike (throughout the ages) have placed their heroes, gods, or whatever *they* consider honorable or noteworthy - we see it adorned with an important *Masonic* symbol:

Fancy that. Yes, once again, we see the reverse side of that great seal of the United States - an unfinished *pyramid* (of ancient and *pagan* Egypt)! Go figure. And, of course, surrounding this great seal are the Latin words: Novus ordo seclorum, which, actually, may give us the *real* end-goals of those who put it there. The words, translated into English, could mean "a new order for the ages." But, the words could also be interpreted as to mean something else: a "new order for the world" or "**new world order**!" Yes, a number of things do seem to be interrelated here, and interconnected.

It, now, seems as though we are beginning to see why those ruling parties (working in the shadows) seem to prefer pagan elements and symbols to be set up, all around them, tactically placed all over their new, "Christian" nations. It's not only about allowing for *something* to fill in those religious "gaps" (once they start to kick God and the Bible out of everyday life), but also to allow them to petition the deities behind paganism (i.e. those forces of the "Other Side"), to give them some kind of "divine favor." Of course, this is all for a reason: to help them get their "job done." Yes, there, so often, is a method to so much of this "madness." And, nothing is ever really done by chance… nothing.

The moral foundations of England and the United States may have allowed the countries to start out as Godly nations, with Judeo-Christian principles; but, it was just a cover (for what was really waiting in the shadows). Eventually, things in these countries would become more and more about man's reason, more about *mankind* becoming the measure of all things (through Cain's *humanism*), and, especially, more about the pagan religion (i.e. the religion of Cain and the Serpent)… seeming more about most *anything*, but that one **God** above.

Chapter 15

Bringing Down the Protestants

*Have not I commanded thee? Be **strong** and of a **good courage**; be not afraid, neither be thou dismayed: for the LORD thy God is with thee whithersoever thou goest.*   - Josh. 1:19 (KJV)

With all of the pressure that was about to be applied - to Catholics and Protestants alike (to, ultimately, take them both down) - God still desires for us to remain strong, dignified and courageous. He does not us to be weakened in any way; and, if we do feel end up feeling weak (temporarily), He does not want us to remain there. Yes, it all makes sense, if one really thinks about it… or *does* it?

Interestingly enough, when we look around us today, when was the last time that we've heard people sing "Onward Christian Soldiers," or hear a sermon about how *strong* a good warrior for Christ should be, or how much we should *fight* the enemy? No. So often, it's about a whole number of *softer*, politically correct things, such as *love*, *worship*, *overcoming hardships*, *dealing with one's personal demons*, etc. Well, why do things seem to be so different today? Was it all by design, a while ago?

Those former Templars and EJC leaders - with their two powerful nations (the United States and Great Britain) in tow - would considered their plight to be on an upswing, in regards to how much power and influence they were now able to throw around. They, indeed, were gathering a good deal of material resources, as well as human strength, from these nations, all the while (subtly) working on their ability to use them to eventually take on the Catholic Church… and maybe even *win*.

Yet, the process of utilizing the strengths of other people - those holding onto that Protestant work ethic - would actually become a little dangerous. It was almost like holding onto a lit firecracker, and not throwing it, because of the chance that these Protestants would, indeed, become stronger and stronger, and a little out of *their* control. Although they were, initially, setting up these Protestants to prosper (as a tool against their enemy Rome), they couldn't allow them to become *too* strong, or too Godly… at least not beyond what these elites could handle. So, now, steps had to have been taken, in order to keep the grinding wheel of prosperity to a manageable state.

To assure that these Protestants were used for *only* what those elites intended them to be used for, a few things had to be "adjusted," in regards to their Christian foundation:

> *The doctrines of Calvin and Luther, which formed and forged the **pilgrim** and **puritan doctrines**, and those men who came over here as covenanters, built up a great land they called the Kingdom. But this "Kingdom" was now beginning to **fade**. It was now beginning to be replaced by a "New Gospel" **not** taught by the Messiah, and the political and social life began **to change** right along with it.*
> ("The Jewish-Created Scofield 'Bible'", n. d., p. 1)[1]

Now, a few "anti-Christian" changes were becoming established, in order to meet the challenge. But, just *how* would these opposing parties (to God) accomplish their directive? How do you stop this Protestant "train," once it leaves the station and begins to gather more and more momentum? It's hard to slow down people, once they begin to believe in something (and begin to like what they're seeing). It's hard to slow down a group of individuals, once they begin to see the ramifications of what they've believed in, all along. The (slow and eventual) takedown of these people would, indeed, have to be accomplished through the manipulation of one's *faith*, and it would have to be done over time... diluting substance and confusing religious dogma. It would involve the *weakening* one's moral foundation, causing one's resolve to become unreliable over time, and, eventually, wither to pieces. So, in order to make all of this work, and on a vast scale, change would naturally have to begin at the *top* (of the Protestant religious hierarchy). Again, all of this would take a bit of time; but, if handled correctly, it would begin to work on a whole number of people - turning devout warriors of God into spineless jellyfish; turning convicted scholars into conflicted malcontents; etc. And, this (eventually) would also begin to serve as their *new* formula: continually bringing new Christians from faith into fear; from strength into weakness; and from vitality into impotence. That's why we see such different themes in our religious churches and institutions today/

Again, these manipulations would have to begin with those at the top, and their ability to preach dogma to others. But, how would these former Templars and ECJs be able to work over a such vast number of prosperous people in the first place? How could so many even fall for these manipulations? Along with time, it took a bit of brainwashing. These elites understood the power of the human mind. They also understood: if they could influence those *shepherds*, first and foremost, to walk down a different pathway, then their sheep would, most often, follow right along… even over a cliff if necessary! So, yes, *these* would be the individuals that had to have been concentrated on. And, after the corruption of these religious dignitaries was set in place, an *alternate* system of thought and practices would, eventually, begin to arise.

So, let's begin to see how all of these changes would have went down, by looking at a few of ways that those Protestant "shepherds" - as well as their Protestant "sheep" - would have been targeted..

Untermeyer, Schofield… And Influential EJCs

The time had truly come for those former Templars and EJC elitists to start twisting things around a bit - to dilute, diminish, and ultimately corrupt those true theologies of God, as well as the Bible. They would be able to accomplish this, in part, by subtle word changes (in the Bible), or with additional information added onto the Bible. And why not? These elitists, most probably, did not think too much about what the Bible may have had to say anyhow.

Still, any attempts to change these Christian foundations, early on, would not have been very welcome. A good number of people, naturally, would want to go on the defensive. Those that read the Bible, at least during these earlier times, seemed extremely passionate about keeping everything pure and consistent. They now had the Word of God, and were not about to lose it.

Regardless, even though a number of them really treasured what they now had, the former Templars and EJCs were still be able to (slowly) dilute a few things, here and there, after a bit. Some different theological "ink" was, assuredly, being added to that pure glass of Christian "water" - namely the "ink" of man's reason and rationality, and a little bit of paganism as well.

Eventually, these additions would begin to tear at the very fabric of what made the people of these Protestant lands so prosperous, powerful and individually successful:

> *The French author, Alexis de Tocqueville, wrote* **Democracy in America** *when he traveled here in the first third of the 19th Century. In ringing tones he sang the praises of America's invulnerable strength and spirit. He attributed its greatness to its citizens' sense of* **morality**... *(and) is credited with this familiar quote: AMERICA IS GREAT BECAUSE SHE IS GOOD, AND IF AMERICA EVER CEASES TO BE* **GOOD**, *SHE WILL* **CEASE TO BE GREAT**... *De Tocqueville could see the power of America, but he could not have known in 1830 that she was soon to* **be under an attack aimed at** *its churches and the* **very sense of morality** *that he extolled.*
> ("The Jewish-Created Scofield 'Bible'", n. d., p. 1)[2]

These attacks would make sense for the time, totally, and we know *why* they were done. And, yes, it all did begin to work, slowly starting to dismantle America's "greatness," a little at a time. And this process would need to continue in this way, bit by bit, and piece by piece. So, now, let's begin to see an example of how those powers that be were able to turn the "waters" of Biblical understanding and acceptance into something a little bit "muddier."

A lot of this initial corruption began after the time of a particular king of England, named *King James*. The king was listening to his subjects, and decided to take their quests for a protestant Bible up a notch. He began to declare that **all** of his subjects should be able to have access to a Bible if so desired. And then, he began to commission a number of learned individuals to work on what would have soon been known as the *King James Bible* - a very famous Bible indeed!

Yes, this was his attempt to have the original tongues of the Bible translated into English, as accurately and as succinctly as (flawed) human beings were able to do. This original version, for a few hundred years, seemed to have become the "go to" version for a vast number of Protestants - a Biblical "staple" if you will. And, throughout the years, the faith of many people remained fairly solid, because they, not only had a Bible in their own hands, but also in their own language… and they all would have had **one** with the *same* words to read together! No room for confusion here.

Yet, as we already know, the time had come for those former Templar and EJC elites to do some damage, and start their infiltration process. Next, we'll see an example of how one educated Protestant leader was recruited by a few of these elites, and used to help them bring about a couple of changes in the Bible (*slowly* but surely).

Now, to explain the story in a nutshell, we are introduced to a very powerful man named *Samuel Untermeyer*. He was thought to be a Jewish man; but, of course, how he ended up carrying himself (and his value system) in regards to this particular situation did not seem to end up being very Godly! As we'll soon see, we may even need to question whether he, in actuality, could have been one of an ***Edomite*** flavor, or Edomite graft. True Jews would, most probably, not want to be pushing things that Untermeyer was (for the most part). But, whatever was behind his motivation, Untermeyer would eventually meet up with an American preacher, one with "questionable" moral attributes in his own right, named *Cyrus Scofield*. After their meeting, the two eventually ended up striking up a good working relationship. Scofield, a struggling preacher, seemed to have hit religious "gold" with his new confidant, and liked some of the things that he was being offered.

Untermeyer was also thought to be a "Zionist" (loosely defined as a person who sports a strong belief in a homeland for the Jewish people). This, of course, all sounds good on the surface. It sounds like a noble cause. But, once again, after we begin to peel off a few layers of what's going on, and see the direction by which he begins to take pastor Scofield, we may begin to question his ulterior motives, as well as his sincerity as a true Jewish person, who's under God (as we soon shall see).

To help Scofield achieve the "big-time" as a pastor, Untermeyer pulled a few strings, which ended up allowing the man to become a major Protestant influencer, over time. But, *why*? What was Untermeyer's motives for Scofield, here?

> *Untermeyer did more than introduce Scofield to his wealthy and influential Zionist circle in New York. Soon the Kansas con man was off on a lavish tour of Europe, including an important visit to Oxford University where plans were made for the publication of his **new reference Bible**.*
> ("The Jewish-Created Scofield 'Bible'", n. d., p. 1)[3]

Yes, plans were in the works to manipulate the "old" King James Bible (at least a little bit), and start the process of "dumbing down" the populous.

After their initial meeting in New York, Scofield found himself heading off to England, around the early part of the 1900s. The areas of which he ended up travelling to (especially around the British city of *London*) were already considered hotbeds of Freemasonry, **banking**, and *Rothschild* influence. Fancy that! Scofield's new friends ended up bringing him to Oxford University (which, supposedly, was another Rothschild-supported institution), in order to begin work on a "slightly-modified" version of the KJV Bible, complete with specific linear *notes* alongside the words, as well as some *different* interpretations of the material at hand... and Scofield was to be the one to bring it to America.

Of course, this was all supposedly done to "assist" the reader in understanding a number of passages in the Bible a little better (at least, according to *these people*). Yes, the "new and improved" King James Bible was now underway - with attempts by the former Templars and EJCs to *modify* the current Bible into something that reads slightly different than people may have been used to before.

Cyrus Scofield, a forger, felon and trained lawyer, had been hired by the Rothschilds to write this dispensational **reinterpretation** *of biblical events and Christian doctrine.*
  ("Christian Zionism: Cyrus Scofield Was Rothschild Puppet", 2020, p. 1)[4]

Yes, this Bible would end up being a transformation of that immensely-popular King James Bible into the *Schofield Reference Version* (of the King James Bible)! And, yes, this was only the beginning. Of course, today, we often have a number of educated people out there, claiming that a "new look" of the King James was actually needed... to help "clear up" a number of confusing passages in the book, or make the Bible "easier to read." But, was this whole process a little *tilted*, in fact... in the direction of those former Templars and EJCs? Could a number of those "extra" elements have been, subtly, inserted, in order to *sway* the reader into some other theological direction, or even in the direction of something ungodly (or, at least, something different than what they may have always been used to)?

If a number of EJC elites were, indeed, influencing Untermeyer into convincing Scofield to join a different cause, then could this new Bible actually end up helping out those individuals who may have desired the insertion of a number of Zionist-friendly notes into the Biblical margins?[5] It sure seems so.

> *...Scofield produced a revolutionary book that radically changed the context of the King James Version. It was designed to **create a subculture around a new worship icon, the modern State of Israel... (representing)** the highly political movement... openly called "Christian Zionism."*
> ("Zionists Behind The Scofield 'Bible' - It's Powerful Effect On Modern Christianity", 2015, p. 2)[6]

> *The purpose of Samuel Untermeyer, and the... (EJCs?) associated with him, was to find a way to get fundamental Christians **to have an interest in, and support for, the international Zionist cause**. This was an idea they had to keep the lower and middle-class Christians **in line**.*
> ("The Jewish-Created Scofield 'Bible'", n. d., p. 5)[7]

As we've mentioned earlier, a number of people (at least early on) were not very keen on any Biblical additions and changes. They were quite worried about any manipulations of Bible wording, or any type of interpretation (at least for a time). In fact, not many would allow the actual words of the Bible to be changed (at least not yet). In fact, there was even a curse in the Bible (in the Book of Revelation) about those who may think about changing around the words of the Good Book:

> *...if any man shall add unto these things, God shall add unto him the plagues that are written in this book: and if any man shall take away from the words of the book of this prophecy, God shall take away his part out of the book of life...*
> - *Rev.* 22:18-19 (KJV)

Wow. It seems as though the writer of Revelation already knew that this may indeed happen in the future. And, yes, with a good number of people out there, and understanding the full meaning of this verse, it would not have been exceptionally easy for any authority figures to just waltz in, and start changing around the *actual* words of the Bible... without a fight. So, as a response to this, the powers that be may have strived to do the next best thing: the manipulation of a few *meanings* inside the Bible (by adding a number of "explanatory" margins)!

> *Scofield... wisely chose not to change the text of the King James Edition. Instead, he added hundreds of easy-to-read footnotes at the bottom of about half of the pages and, as the Old English grammar of the King James Edition becomes increasingly difficult for progressive generations of readers, students* **become increasingly dependent** *on the modern language footnotes.*
> ("The Jewish-Created Scofield 'Bible'", n. d., p. 7)[8]

Of course, a lot of this manipulation, in order to be successful, would take a bit of time, as well as a bit of "smooth talking." People really needed to be very subtle (as a Serpent) to manipulate this English Bible (at least early on). Still, as how a serpent would be able to sneak up on its prey, there was an ace up in the sleeves of these anti-Bible elites. It takes a little common sense to understand that: languages can change over time; and, because they may, a number of nefarious individuals might be able capitalize on this process. They may be able to use this as an opportunity to find ways to *change around* the words of the Bible! Yes, this was another way "in."

By the early 20th Century, a number of people would begin claiming that the King James Bible, itself, was now a little "passé," or "old fashioned" (because of its 17th Century wording). Now (according to some), it was time for updating, or even some "reinterpretation" because of this! Go figure. And, yes, this (of course) would open the floodgates of new versions to be out there, challenging the rock-solid verbiage of that old King James.

Now, more changes to the English Bible were on their way, with a good number of "new versions" being injected into the mainstream... all for the sake of "readability," or some kind of "political correctness." But, of course, there's consequences to almost every action... and the consequences for adding and taking out words here, in regards to what that English King James translation said, may have indeed damaged the cohesiveness of what the populous was able to enjoy in times past (as we'll soon see)!

Outside of Their Bible - "Dangerous"?

Things were, indeed, beginning to change, as a result of a number of upcoming manipulations. The floodgates of mistrust and misinterpretation were also beginning to seep into the minds of Protestant Christians. Along with a number of *new* interpretations being inserted into the margins of versions such as that Scofield version, and a number of *different* English versions being uploaded onto the public at large (such as the NIV, the NASV, etc.), the "apple cart" of Protestant understanding was truly becoming upset.

It's obvious to see what the powers that be were doing - adding a lot of new information (via reinterpretations), as well as changing the English wording (via a number of new translations). All of this, of course, was not only done to make things "easier to read" (or provide people a "new and improved" version), but to confuse things a bit, or sow the seeds of theological doubt. People no longer couldn't be as confident than they may have been before… and that, of course, was all by design: to "corral" the powers of God and His Word a bit; to slow up Christian expansion. And, the worst part about a lot of this corruption is: it usually begins at the *top*, and works its way down - with the "Shepherds" charged with helping out all of the seekers below.

Interestingly enough, we may already be seeing how a number of those efforts (to twist or dilute the power of Christianity) could have been prophesied by the Bible… as coming from those at the top:

> *For the time will come when they will not endure sound doctrine; but after their* ***own*** *lusts shall they* ***heap to themselves teachers****, having itching ears...*
> *- 2 Tim.* 4:3 (KJV)

> *For false Christs and false prophets shall rise, and shall shew signs and wonders, to seduce, if it were possible,* ***even the elect****.*
> *- Mark* 13:22 (KJV)

Eventually, the "end game" of what a number of those corrupted elites have wanted is clear: to have people believe the Bible *as they see it*, or according to how *they* may want to present it. So, now, if people begin to accept *their* version of the Bible (as the only reference to look to), then there would no longer be much room for anything else out there to study! *Their* Bible, along with *their* own interpretations of this Bible, would be the only true "keys to the kingdom." And, yes, a lot like the Catholic Church (of old) used to do, the religious elites of the time were beginning to the same. It's, now, all about them, and their interpretations.

Yet, what about the numerous ancient texts out there, texts that may not have necessarily been on the same level as the Bible (such as the Book of Enoch, for example)? Are these no longer considered viable, or even worth a reading? Are they worthless… if they're not currently something that the establishment may support! See where this all may be going?

Soon, we have people being taught that there is only *one* way - the present, *established* way that was set up around them! Of course, this, then, would become the *only* means for a person to study, and to learn (which would, as well, keep them *needing* to rely on their "Shepherds"). What a racket. And, because of this structure change, we have a number of people eventually having thoughts such as the following:

> *"**I was always told** that anything outside of the Bible was considered **mysticism** and is **dangerous** to study as it **would cause confusion**."*
> - "Amy" (via an incoming email to the author's website, dated 10/21/16)

Dangerous? To who… *them*? Yes, this particular word - *dangerous* - seems to be quite telling. Now, why would people be continually be taught that they need to foment this perception? Of course, it's because those elect want to be the "one and only source." And, with their role as the "one and only" authoritative figure over Scripture, *any* other text are considered "off limits," or considered *untrustworthy* (for whatever reason). Of course, simply reading these alternate texts is not necessarily a sin, nor does it represent a person's attempt to elevate the texts to the same level as the books of the Bible. Yet, this perception still persists. What's dangerous, really, are those who only want us to go to *them*, and not be able to use that spirit of discernment… that God gives to a whole number of us.

Isn't this what we are put on this earth for, anyway… to make advancements in our own understanding? How could we do this - if there are so many restraints placed upon us, continually being initiated by people trying to be "helpful," or trying to save us from ourselves? Isn't our journey through life to "seek" and "find" (Mat. 7:7)? Of course, their narrative would be that it's all about helping the seeker to go through life without a lot of "pollution;" but, God gave us some mental *tools*, in order to help us out along the way. He gave us a mind capable of critical thinking, and independent thought. Could the deepest part of their actions, here, *really* be about trying to *control* some kind of narrative? Of course, to those who want to regulate (or even *diminish*) true Christianity and Judeo-Christian values, all of this makes sense. They want us to come to *them* (for spiritual fulfillment), and then let "let sleeping dogs lie" about the rest of it (not questioning anything that may require some independent research or study).

But, as long as God gives us a conscious mind, and the spirit of curiosity or *discernment*, we should be able to seek out truths… not bound by those who, ultimately, may want to subtly stifle it.

Interestingly enough, there *are* a number of ancient complementary texts out there, which relate to the Bible, as well as a number of Bible mysteries. It's fascinating to take a look at a number of these tidbits of information, to give us help with Biblical interpretation. Of course, we are not elevating these texts as canon, none of them, but there really should be nothing wrong with being able to look at these pieces of information, and gather insight from them. We can decide (with God's help) what might make sense.

What about that *Book of Enoch*, for example, once found right alongside a number of Bible books (in the Dead Sea Scrolls)? Could the book give us some information on the books of Scripture, possibly helping us figure out a few mysteries that may have continued on, without this information? In one example (of many), we'll take a look at a story in Genesis (in Gen. 4:23). It was the Biblical account of *Lamech* (a descendant of Cain), and how he felt a sense of lamentation for what he just did. We see here, in the Bible, that he reached a point of crying out, to anyone around him, exclaiming how much he was in anguish. Yet, the Bible does **not** give us any more information about this story… nothing to help us identify what he may have actually did, nor why he was lamenting! Nothing. Now what? Why would this story even be in the Bible, if there was no clue about where one could go next, to figure out what the end of the story (and even the moral of the story) may have been? In the divinely inspired Word of God, you think it would have been in there... for us to learn something, or get something out of it. Of course, if we look at a few alternative sources out there, the answers are provided for us to ponder.

Again, just looking at these sources isn't betraying anybody (except, maybe, those who are dead set on controlling the narrative). We are not elevating these text on the same level as Scripture, so why not?

It even says, in the Bible itself:

*It is the glory of God to **conceal** a thing: but the honour of kings is **to search out** a matter.*   - Prov. 25:2 (KJV)

But, of course, the elites would like us to believe that we should only be looking to something *they* recommend, or approve. With their policy, of course, if we have a question (such as what Lamech did and why was he lamenting) - and there's not a clear answer in the Bible - then should we just chalk it up as one of those "mysteries" of the Bible (that we're not supposed to know), and call it a day? To people who enjoy thinking like sheep, and being led everywhere, this might work. But, for the rest of us, it almost seems nonsensical for God to put a story in there, and **not** provide us any way to seek out the answers surrounding it. We are strong. We could figure out a number of things. We can decide on what information is good and what information doesn't sound too savory.

Do we sense an *agenda* going on here, quite possibly?

Somewhere - Between "Fear" and "Faith"

Now, with their ability to cement a number of Bible interpretations as *their* own, the weakening of the people at large continues. Now, just like the Catholic Church had done early on, the "peasants" of this time were discouraged from participating in any real kind of critical or independent thought, and encouraged to go to their religious elites for help in their spiritual fulfillment.

Their next step, after pulling the informational "rug" out from underneath the populous, would be to start *weakening* one's own *drive* or *spirit*! First to confuse, then to weaken.

With this next barrage coming onto the scene, the challenged Christian would soon find themselves sinking in a "quicksand" of unanswered questions, a rise in self-doubt, and a skepticism of their own faith. Soon, their "helmet of salvation" (in Eph. 6:17) would begin to slip off; and their "sword of the spirit" would become a little dull. No more would "Onward Christian Soldiers" be their battle cry! Almost anything promoting strength, self-reliance and freedom were beginning to fall by the wayside… in exchange for *other* topics of conversation. Of course, it was all done for a good reason - a part of their ultimate plan (of stagnation, and eventual Christian dissolution).

Now, instead of showing Christian people how *powerful* they could become, once they apply the use of the Bible and the Protestant work ethic, a lot of it becomes downplayed. Instead of showing to people the confidence they could feel as a child of God, they are led towards a faith that's about as strong as a house of cards.

Christian countries, such as Britain and the United States, were once prime examples of how **strong** (and prosperous) a nation *could have been* (under the umbrella of Godly worship); but, now, due to these shifts, the opposite would be more of the norm.

Of course, if we really think about it, those Israelites of the past - way back in Biblical times - were fighters, *real* fighters. They had enemies to take out, and they did what they had to do. They responded to the number of assaults on their lives and livelihood as God directed! They would not crumble, or run into a dusty corner. Yes, they had God on their side, and they knew it. And, adorned with this fortitude, they would win a number of battles, and meet their goals. Today, however, we don't have to fight a lot of these same physical battles (of course), but we may need to fight a good number of *theological* ones. That's where the fight has transposed to.

And now, with *today's* way of going about things, it seems almost stylish to concentrate on almost anything **bu**t being a strong warrior for God. Weakness is good. Weakness is acceptable. Assurance in who you are, in what you are, and in what you stand for (as a soldier of God) has slowly been transformed into something else - a "four-letter word" known as ***hope***!

Stuck Inside that "Four Letter Word"

Today, how often do we hear about this word? In Christian circles, it appears to be quite a bit. But, why do we seem to concentrate on *hope* so much, rather than concentrate on what we could actually do with our *own* strengths or abilities? Of course, we need to be relying on God, regarding either situation. But, why does *hope* seem to come up, so much nowadays? What else could *we* do, besides just think about that? There's surely more to our lives than just hope, a lot more... hopefully.

It's fascinating, once we think about it: how many things around us seem to be almost *reversed*, or even turned upside down! To be valiant is often considered toxic, or even narcissistic; to take action in our own lives seems as though it could be excessive, or even violent; to fight back is not really considered to be of immense value anymore. Lamenting on our own situations, as well as focusing our thoughts on how far we may have fallen, seem to be taking up a lot of our time. Again, why have things changed in this way? Victimization becomes, more or less, a big topic of conversation. It's almost as if we're stuck.... in between thoughts of fear and faith. And, of course, for those who might, eventually, want us to get "out of their way," **this** would have been the perfect mindset for us to direct a number of our thoughts.

Today, we are beginning to see people actuality believing that it might be *good* to feel broken, or sad inside. Existing in this lowly state (somehow) shows a *closeness* to God, or proves to others that we are His child. It also helps us to see the wonders of this God, and His work over the human race (once our hopes are fulfilled). Yes, all of this does has some merit, but, what about the rest of it? What about our actions? Does God want us to go to those states of mind, and just wait for a miracle?

Of course, everyone has trials and tribulations in life; but Christianity does not, necessarily, have to be associated with *only* passiveness, weakness and stagnation. Idleness is not really a virtue. "Treading water" - through the result of inaction - does not really help out anybody... except those who want us to remain there!

One also does not need to be *broken* to "find religion," or achieve some kind of dignity in their personal life. Why is "down," now, turned into something that is considered "up?" Nowadays, things are eventually becoming so lopsided (in these *other* directions) that a number of us might even be convinced that, somehow, being a Christian (of old) is a little unsavory! It's old-fashioned, or even *bigoted*! Who knows what kind of hurtful or racist thoughts might coming into our heads, if we stayed with the Christianity of our forefathers?

Essentially, to take us down even further, we are also being told to, nowadays, to just shut up, and take our well-deserved medicine (for, once, being a part of that *bigoted*, or biased, faith of old). We are now instructed to *respect* all other religions out there (so many of them pagan), and not be "too preachy" with our own. Yet, as we also see: those same parameters, so often, do not seem to be mutually pushed upon other people, of other religions. So much of what we hear is about some kind of Christian-based bullying, or hate. Again, why is that? How come other (often *pagan*) religions no not have to follow the exact same protocols as modern Christianity does, it seems. Could there be something *deeper* going on, possibly?

On top of this all, we also see that a number of people, all around us, are out there, claiming that Judeo-Christian values are nothing really special at all, nothing any better than a number of other religious theologies out there (of course, a number of them with **pagan** elements).

Again, looking at all of this from "outside the box," it really does seem to be about taking the Christian person, and their faith, *down* a number of notches. Today, there is not too much that these people seem to be deserving of, except, of course, that four letter word - ***hope***!

"Turning the Other Cheek"... For Whom Exactly?

> *But I tell you, **do not resist** an evil person. If anyone slaps you on the right cheek, turn to them the other **cheek** also.*   - Mat. 5:39 (NIV)

As those twists of Christian morality seem to be getting a bit worse (over time), so do the chances for a Christian to remaining strong, and confident in what they believe in. The more restraints and convoluted interpretations get thrown into the whole theological mix here, the harder it is for a typical Christian to remain steadfast, and stand on solid ground. A typical Christian may end up feeling as though they need to, somehow, feel meek, or even defenseless, in order to "fit in" with the desires of the rest of the world around them! Feeling blessed by God, and **enjoying it**, now seems to be something that was ill-gotten, or even not deserved. Self-confidence or assurance becomes redefined as narcissistic, arrogant and, utterly, immoral. And, as a result of all this, the typical Christian rarely ends up feeling a desire to stand up for themselves, or for what they believe in. The pressures of political correctness seem to push a vast number of people in the direction of a number of things *against* the God of the Bible. And, because of this all, the typical Christian begins to lose a lot of his or her own drive, or ability to "fight back."

In one major example of how subtle "reprogramming" could begin to affect a typical Christian, and their resolve, we may recall a very popular phrase uttered by a good number of Christians today: **"turn the other cheek."** Yes, Jesus said this (in Mat. 5:39), so it must have been something of importance. And, yes, many of us have already interpreted this saying as: when a person harasses you (or "slaps" you on one side of your face) you should react in a very humble way, turning the other cheek, to let them "slap" you on the other side, too! Sounds noble, and totally Christian nowadays (it seems). Through our modern interpretation, many people believe that: for the sake of Jesus' testimony, we, essentially, should allow others harass us, if they so want to, and just "take it" (by turning the other cheek). This shows them that we abide by a new "Christian" principle… in the example of Jesus. But, is that really right?

Does this modern interpretation mean that we should be *so* humble, as to not resist most any desire to confront an attacker, or fight back? Should we just allow other people to "slap" us around, without a reply? Should we just look the other way, and "take it?" It sure seems to be that way. Or, was there something a bit *more* to what Jesus said, here… more than just having to "take it" all? It, actually, sounds a lot like the example of an army cadet, uttering a quote to his drill master (after being slapped): "Thank you for the strike Sir. May I have another?" Quite possibly, this was **not** how the verse was originally intended to be followed. Let's see if there could, indeed, be *another* way to it all.

Even though the process of reinterpreting this verse might, on the onset, seem to be a little complex, it's a really good way for us to see how those "powers that be" were able to "pull the wool" over a typical Christian's eyes (once again), and see how their *new* interpretations would continue to weaken the populous. The real meaning of this phrase should become fairly clear, once we take into account the number of *others* meanings of the Greek here, as well as the context by which the verse was a part of. Let's take a look at it all.

Jesus, in his Sermon on the Mount, was going through a number of hypothetical situations, giving scenarios as well as solutions. A number of Jesus' examples, it seemed, could, actually, be segregated into a whole "block" of verses, with each block corresponding to one particular moral lesson. In regards to this "turn the other cheek" scenario, Jesus seems to have been trying and help a number of people establish a *gauge*, by which they would be able to respond to certain situations a little bit differently. He begins by recalling a typical human response to a behavior that may have been fairly well-known (in the past), and then suggests a new way of handling the situation. And, as we proceed, it should all make sense (soon enough).

We'll begin by looking at how the context of this particular block was laid out (adding in a bit of commentary on each). First, we see that Jesus' opening statement may have been referring to a very familiar practices of the time:

"You have heard that it was said, 'Eye for eye, and tooth for tooth'...
- Mat. 5:38 (NIV)

In the next verse, we run into that "turn the other cheek" scenario:

*"But I tell you, do not **resist** an evil person. If anyone slaps you on the right **cheek**, turn to them the other **cheek** also."*
- Mat. 5:39 (NIV)

Via another version:

*"But I say unto you, That ye resist not evil: but whosoever shall smite thee on thy right **cheek**, turn to him the other also."*
- Mat. 5:39 (KJV)

Next, we need to understand that the English word for "check," here, was only in the original Greek verbiage *one* time (in this verse)... not twice! Now, that's very strange, here. Why would a number of English versions (such as the above) insert the second "cheek" in the verse... if it wasn't originally in the original Greek?

It seems fairly obvious that this second "cheek" was added (at the end of the verse) to make the verse "easier" to read, or to understand... at least to make it read more like what *they* might want it to read.

Second, another key element, in regards to the understanding of this verse, revolves around the English word *resist* (located at the first half of the verse):

*"But I tell you, do not **resist** an evil person..."*
- Mat. 5:39 (NIV)

Now, if we really think about it, it wouldn't really make any sense for Jesus to say something contrary to the rest of Scripture, now would it? Would he really want us to *not* resist evil, or *not* resist an evil person? At least that's what the translation seems to be saying, here (in the above). Would Jesus really want us to just sit back, and let evil "do their thing?" The Bible continually tells us the opposite: to resist evil, and all of its forms. We are not even look in the direction of it (if possible)! So, there seems to be some a little bit of a conflict here... until we realize just *who* may actually be doing some of that "interpreting" for us, and *why* they would.

Could the verses be telling us *not* to resist evil, or could they be telling us to *change the **manner of how** we resist the evil*? Yes, as we soon shall see, there may indeed be something more to this all. And, yes, we'll also realize that these verses may actually relate to a person's *intent* - their intent to retaliate (at whomever might have been initiating a provocation). So, to understand it all fully, let's explain things a little bit more,.

As we move on, we now may be able to understand that:

He (Jesus) is speaking to believers who will experience persecution and hate from the world (Matthew 5:11–12).

("Matthew 5:39", 2024, p. 3)[9]

And, because of this, the original Greek word for the (translated English word) *resist*, here, could actually have related to *how* one decides to fight back. A person would usually want to respond to another person in kind, once jested or treated unfairly. And, as we'll now see, there are a few *other* word that could have been inserted, instead of this English word *resist* (in the original Greek). The word could also mean: to "take a complete stand against;" to "forcefully declare one's person conviction;" or (in a military sense) "to strongly resist an opponent."[10] These three meanings, indeed, seem to say it all: the phrase doesn't necessarily mean to "not resist" someone (or, not to do anything). Yes, with a number of these *other* meanings, inserted back into the English translation, we could now see that the first half of this verse could actually be interpreted in another way: Jesus was not saying something like: "do not resist an evil person;" but, rather, he was saying to "not respond to an evil person in such as forceful, or militaristic, way!"

But I tell you, do not **react so strongly (or forcefully) to** *an evil person (as you may have done before)…*

- *Mat.* 5:39 (in retranslation)

Again, this also seems to make total sense (if we really think about it). And, if we begin to retranslate this verse a little bit differently, we now have Jesus commenting on that whole "eye for an eye" scenario: "You may have heard about that saying, 'an eye for an eye.' But I tell you, do not **react so strongly (or forcefully) to** an evil person. Do not try to take one's eye out, the same way that he may have tried to take out yours."

Now, with this possibility in tow, we'll need to move on, and take a look at the middle of the verse (around the "whosoever shall smite thee on thy **right cheek**" mark), to see what this may *actually* mean. Now, we'll look at what one of our modern translations might have presented for this particular part:

Mat. 5:
38 *"You have heard that it was said, 'Eye for eye, and tooth for tooth'*
39 *But I tell you, do not resist an evil person.* **If anyone slaps you on the right cheek**…"[11]

Next, as we'll now discover, the second part of the verse may not even be talking about a person slapping another person. Let's see.

But, wait a minute here. Wasn't the entire verse about a person being able to slap us, and our being able to react in a humble way, allowing them to slap us, once again, on the other cheek? Not necessarily. Now, as we take a look at the interlinear breakdown of this entire section, we'll see that the original Greek may, in actuality, point towards a person *striking back* at someone else:

◀ **Matthew 5:39** ▶

436 [e]	3588 [e]	4190 [e]	235 [e]	3748 [e]	4771 [e]	4474 [e]
antistēnai	tō	ponērō	all'	hostis	se	rhapizei
ἀντιστῆναι	τῷ	πονηρῷ .	ἀλλ' ,	ὅστις	σε	ῥαπίζει
to resist	the	evil [person]	Instead	whoever	you	shall strike
V-ANA	Art-DNS	Adj-DNS	Conj	RelPro-NMS	PPro-A2S	V-PIA-3S

Yes, it actually says: "whomever **you** shall strike (back)…" It's not talking about being slapped one time, and then inviting another!

Now, as we continue on with this verse, we'll begin to see what that whole "right cheek" element of the phrase might be about. We'll begin to discover that the "striking" or "slapping" of a person, on their right cheek. was, most probably, a *figure of speech* - a symbol of one's aggressiveness towards another human being:

*In the ancient world, the **right** hand was always assumed to be dominant. Jesus specifically refers to the "**right cheek**," here. That implies a backhanded movement: to slap someone on the right cheek, with the right hand, is more **intimidation and abuse** than mayhem.*
                                             ("Matthew 5:39", 2024, p. 3)[12]

Next, it is our *reaction* to whatever kind of hypothetical "slap" we get that becomes important, here. What Jesus was probably referring to, here, relates to the *way* a person wants to retaliate to whatever evil, intimidation, or abuse that might come their way. And now, in the retranslation of the verses (following along these same lines), we now have:

<u>Mat. 5</u>:
38 *"You have heard that it was said, 'Eye for eye, and tooth for tooth'*
39 *But I tell you, do not **react so strongly (or forcefully)** to an evil person (as you may have done before); instead, whenever you decide to strike back (to insult them, or humiliate them, back)…"*
                                             (in retranslation)

Now we're getting pretty close to the end of this whole block, and what the overall meaning of the verses may be. As we get into this last phrase, we recall what was projected to be *their* meaning of the entire verse black (according to one modern English translation):

*"But I tell you, do not resist an evil person. If anyone slaps you on the right cheek, **turn to them the other cheek also**."*
                                             - *Mat.* 5:39 (NIV)

Yet, as we get to the gist of our retranslation here, we'll need to recall how there was actually **no** second "cheek" in the original Greek language… it was added, after the fact. And, of course, the reason that there was not really a second "cheek" in this verse was, most probably, because the verse was not referring to a person being "slapped" here, and then "turning the other cheek."

So now, to finish our reinterpretation, we'll discover how Jesus may have actually been suggesting that: "instead of trying to 'slap' someone back (as a reply to some evil action), do not do it in the same way you have done before (as in "an eye for an eye"). **Try some other way - *convert* or *change*** the perceived manner of your reply." In other words, do not "return fire with fire" as aggressively (or even harder) as you would have before. Turn the tables a bit, if possible. Try to handle the situation in another way.

And, yes, although this reinterpretation might seem to be a little bit complex (at least on the surface), it is important for us to get a grasp on it all, to help us understand what they may actually be trying to do to us, and our power. Now, looking at the verse - with our *new* retranslation in tow - and we have:

<u>Mat. 5</u>:
38 *"You have heard that it was said, 'Eye for eye, and tooth for tooth'*
39 **But I tell you, do not <u>react so strongly</u> (or forcefully) to an evil person; instead, whenever you decide to strike back, you turn it around upon him, or even try to do something a little bit differently.*"*
(in retranslation)

In other words, Jesus, most probably, was asking us to (do our best to) **not** stoop to their level, if at all possible. Sometimes, it's unavoidable; and we have to respond appropriately; yet, quite often, "an eye for an eye" isn't always the best choice. You may need to do what you have to do, of course, in certain circumstances, but try to provide a reaction in the *right* spirit of the situation!

This seems to have been a much *better* interpretation of this block, and it also doesn't seem to sound contradictory to the Bible in any way. It also allows you to show your dignity as a person, by *trying* to respond a little bit differently, and even better. On top of it, it doesn't mean that you have to have your hands at your sides, and turn your other "cheek"… to get slapped once again!

Yes, this alternate interpretation *does* seem to be quite different than what a number of modern versions may have it as, and a lot different than was (continually) pushed upon so many of us! Yes, we are not passive jellyfish; we are not to just sit there, waiting for our next blow to come. We also discover that: we might need to be confrontational at times, or even need to fight back - to hold onto our dignity. Yes, even though we may need to do what we have to do (at times), we should also do it in a dignified manner.

> *In short, **Christ's command here does not mean "you must do nothing while someone beats you into a bloody pulp"**... The proper Christian response to discrimination, mocking, or insults is to simply let it go... **turn abuse upside down**...*
>
> ("Matthew 5:39", 2024, p. 3)[13]

Yes. Turning your usual response "upside down" here, or trying to do things a little bit differently, makes total sense.

But, if this meaning was really the case (in regards to these particular verses), then the next question that still may be looming out there is: *why* haven't we heard of things being interpreted in this way before? Why were we basically being told to just sit there, and take things from other people… without really being able to display any kind of spine or backbone? Of course, it's not too hard to figure out the answer to this question, once we realize just *who*, we may really be up against, and *what* they want out of the entire situation.

Yes, there's nothing really wrong with showing the world that you are a *humble* Christian, and don't really want any confrontation. But, once again, that doesn't mean that others should be able to do whatever they want with you, and walk all over you… shaming you into oblivion. Ultimately, as we now see: it's not about a *lack* of resistance (whenever evil decides to confront you), it's about a **dignified** resistance. We could still do whatever may we need to do, in order to protect and preserve ourselves (as well as stand up for our faith). We can still be a mighty soldier for God, if need be… we just shouldn't be ignorant about our responses to anything evil, coming our way.

"Sell-Outs" of this Modern Age

Another question that might, naturally, arise (because of this all): why would top level Christians be pushing things (like the above) onto their pewsters? It may sound nice and flowery (on the surface), but it doesn't really help out the entire Christian condition overall. Why would we see so many Christian dignitaries out there, trying to push a number of these *other* meanings into Bible verses (such as the above)? Well, if there are a number of those out there who may **not** necessarily favor the faith of Christianity, we would really expect nothing less from them.

One who is more concerned with *bringing* down the people of the faith would continually be searching for different ways to *weaken* its people. It only makes sense, right? And, what better way to continue weakening a population than to try and convince the individual that they *should* just allow themselves to get "slapped" - not once, but again and again, and not even do anything about it!

No. The Bible doesn't want situations to end up like this. The Bible doesn't want us to become poor, nor be put down... all the while believing that it's some kind of "Biblically-condoned" action. The Bible doesn't really support things like flagellation (which involves the repeated whipping of one's self, in order to achieve some kind of "divine" favor). None of that. The Bible does not want us to be *content* with being weakened, with feeling down, or feeling afraid either. We shouldn't feel content with being in those states of mind. They do nothing to help us achieve God's purposes for our own lives, nor do they assist us with our abilities to *succeed* (in this fallen, evil world).

God really wants the *opposite* for us, and our lives: He wants us to be happy. He wants us to be successful, and feel blessed by our works (without a lot of the *shame*). But, of course, with the winds of change being what they are (today), we should understand why there were (and are) so many attempts to push people in these opposite directions. Yes, it seems obvious that the former Templars and EJCs have really "done a number" on so many of those Christian believers out there, as well as the entire Christian experience... all without a lot of them even knowing it. And, on top of this all, these same were being used to help these elites *take down* the Roman Catholic Church, in whatever ways possible. What a racket.

Yes, there are a great number of corrupted elements within Protestantism now, just as there had been in the early Roman Catholic Church. It's almost everywhere, in today's day and age (and, so much of it right under our noses). So, as we now begin to spot a lot of those corrupted "fruits" out there, rotting away the pureness of the whole Christian faith, we might also begin to discover how the Bible could have predicted a lot of this! Yes.

As we look at a few verses, we may be able to decipher a bit more about "who" may be responsible for "what," in regards a lot of this Judeo-Christian corruption. It may also help us to see how much of a dark underbelly these two faiths are now acquiring.

> *But there were false prophets also among the people, even as **there shall be false teachers** among you, who privily **shall bring in** damnable heresies, even denying the Lord that bought them…*   - 2 Pet. 2:1 (KJV)

> *Then the LORD said unto me, The prophets prophesy lies in my name: **I sent them not**, neither have I commanded them, neither spake unto them: they prophesy unto you a false vision and divination, and a thing of nought, and the **deceit of their heart**.*   - Jer. 14:14 (KJV)

There were false prophets in the past… and this trend would continue onto today. But, wait: could all of this *really* be going on (unbeknownst to so many)? Could a number of our Christian elect - the preachers, pastors, priests and rabbis and even teachers of the faiths - *really* have been subjugated to a lot of corruption (from those people over and *above* them)? So many seem very nice. They sound compassionate, helpful and are out there to help us, right? Maybe some are. Yet, we've still seen how the Bible had a number of things to say about a number of these individuals.

Again, we are not out to condemn the thoughts and agendas of **each and every** preacher out there, for there are assuredly a number of them who are out to follow God's will, or want to follow after His heart. But, that doesn't mean that there weren't many more who have made up their minds to follow these corrupted Edomite front groups, and whatever they wanted them to preach.

<u>Jer. 23</u>:
16 *Thus saith the LORD of hosts, Hearken not unto the words of the prophets that prophesy unto you: they make you **vain**: they speak a vision of their own heart, and **not** out of the mouth of the LORD.*
17 *They say still unto them that **despise** me, The LORD hath said, Ye shall have peace; and they say unto every one that walketh after the imagination of his own heart, **No evil shall come upon you**.*

A number of them will begin to give you *their own* interpretations of God's Word, and tell you that there's nothing really wrong (or evil) about what they are doing now, or saying to you. They will make you *vain*, or try to have you to concentrate more on *yourself* (rather than Him). Sound familiar?

Pastors or preachers may, now, begin to add *science* into most every concept they come across… even beginning to question the existence of the Garden of Eden, the Flood of Noah's etc., referring to them as "legends" or "cautionary tales." They may attempt to mesh Scripture with secular humanism, or even begin to add a few elements of paganism into the mix… all to sound a bit more "compassionate," "inclusive" or up "with the times." And, of course, we already *know* who was (and still is) behind a number of those additional elements.

The "workers of change" (on the side of those former Templars and EJCs) are truly helping to bring the *White Horse* to its current form - training others to preach things the way that they want. And (as previously mentioned in this volume), we may recall the two "atrocities" of this White Horse: **hunger** and **famine**. It seems clearer and clearer now - those particular elites want to keep as many Christian people as they could stuck in "spiritual poverty," or be subjected to some manner of intellectual "starvation."

Eventually, the preachers and pastors underneath them would have to help them pass on this same mindset (in one way or another), until most everyone becomes more and more accepting of those new ways of this "upper crust":

*The prophets prophesy falsely, and the priests bear rule by **their** means; and my people **love to have it so**…*   - Jer. 5:31 (KJV)

How sad. People would even end up *looking forward* to what these new ways might have to offer them! Yes, the White Horse has been under development for a very, very long time, and, now, it's beginning to work, quite well.

Yet, once again, the Bible seemed to have known that this would happen… it says that there would be a great deal of corruption in the faith, in our latter days. And, there would also be a good number of "wolves" out there, dressed up in sheep's clothing:

*My people hath been lost sheep: **their shepherds have caused them to go astray**, they have turned them away on the mountains: they have gone from mountain to hill, they **have forgotten their restingplace**.*   - *Jer.* 50:6 (KJV)

*Beware of false prophets, which come to you in sheep's clothing, but inwardly they **are ravening wolves**.*   - *Mat.* 7:15 (KJV)

Sad to say, but, we already know the reason so many of them do this: because they are after *their* share of the wealth… dripping from that corrupted "cup" of the ancient **Whore of Babylon**, still alive in a number of (religious and political) systems we now have, all around us, today. That famous verse in Revelation seems to make a lot more sense now, knowing what we know:

*And upon her forehead was a name written, **MYSTERY, BABYLON** THE GREAT, THE MOTHER OF HARLOTS AND ABOMINATIONS OF THE EARTH. And I saw the woman **drunken** with the **blood** of the saints, and with the blood of the martyers of Jesus…*   - *Rev.* 17:5-6 (KJV)

Yes, that whore of Babylon has been utilized by a whole number of corrupted individuals… many who have "sold" their souls for the vast number of material riches our corruption the world might have to offer. So many have become "drunk" off of their attempts to achieve, in actuality, the ultimate end-goal of their own enemies (i.e. Christian destruction)! Go figure.

Materialism - The Age-Old Aspiration (of Cain)

*…prophesy against the shepherds of Israel, prophesy, and say unto them, Thus saith the Lord GOD unto the shepherds; Woe be to the shepherds of Israel that do feed themselves! should not the shepherds feed the flocks? **Ye eat the fat**, and ye clothe you with the wool… but ye **feed not** the flock…*   - *Ezek.* 34:2-3 (KJV)

It doesn't really take a rocket scientist to see that there is a lot going wrong, here. We have so many Protestant elites *looking* as though they were (and are) pursuing Godly goals, but showing their "fruits" of something a little bit different. A number of preachers and pastors have, indeed, fallen into this trap (subtly)… seeking out **material** things, and asking their constituents to keep giving them more and more money in the process.

Interestingly enough, as we continue to look into the Bible, we'll discover this verse:

Every man according as he purposeth in his heart, so let him give…
- 2 Cor. 9:7 (KJV)

It all sounds pretty straightforward. But, *still*, we come across a number of religious authorities throwing around that old "ten percent" requirement (in the Old Testament). Of course, to a number of individuals out there, this requirement may sound a little bit better… if they're able to ask us for a specific amount, or percentage (rather than just having us donate "the best that we could"). However, if we believe that the New Testament is the "new" way to go (rather that strictly following those old laws of that Old Testament), then the former verse should, hypothetically, be able to *trump* this Old Testament requirement.

The modern religious elite may even attempt to shame an individual (subtly), by reciting verses such as the following:

Thou shalt not muzzle the ox when he treadeth out the corn.
- Deut. 25:4 (KJV)

In other words, some of them may (politely) claim that: if you don't give them a good amount of money, then **you** might actually be slowing down "Godly progress" (i.e. the muzzling of the ox), or (somehow) you may be preventing "God's will" from coming true. *Really* now?

Of course, while we access each particular situation, we might need to take into account the total amount of money that certain elites get to "skim off the top" (of each donation), as well as how much money they may have already accumulated over time. Do preachers really need to become fabulously wealthy as a result of their positions? Should preachers or pastors have huge homes, large parcels of land, and even private jets? Of course, there's nothing wrong with being successful (and not being ashamed about it), but, a man of the cloth may need to understand that their particular choice of employment shouldn't involve how much money you could accumulate overall. A shepherd, in many ways, needs to be *closer* to his sheep, to seem like someone to look up to (at least, in this field of work). That's just the way it is.

. Of course, all of these material possessions do not really seem to fit the mantra of a *humble* servant of God. People are really watching.

*For they that are such serve not our Lord Jesus Christ, but **their own belly**; and by **good words and fair speeches** deceive the hearts of the **simple**.*
- Rom. 16:18 (KJV)

<u>2 Pet. 2:</u>
2 *And **many** shall follow their pernicious ways; by reason of whom the way of truth shall be evil spoken of.*
3 *And through **covetousness** shall they with feigned (i.e. artificial, contrived) words make **merchandise of you**…*

The Bible also seems to make it clear that: a number of preachers (in the future) will be able to accumulate a *lot* of material things (such as money)… making "merchandise" of you the whole time! Indeed, there is a point where one's "fruits" may begin to sound a little contradictory to what they say they are, or may preach to others. Yes, people are watching.

When a number of religious elites end up taking these stands, and begin to fall into a world of corruption, a number of them (most probably) do not realize (nor care) what their actions may be doing to their congregations at large. They're only human, and, of course, they are subjected to human desires and needs just like the rest of us. But, what good is a corrupted shepherd to the number of sheep who follow him?

*And they were scattered, because there is there is **no shepherd**… My sheep wandered through all the mountains, and upon every high hill: yea, my flock was scattered upon all the face of the earth, and none did search or seek after them.*
- Ezek. 34:5-6 (KJV)

Yes, it's getting bad for the "sheep" out there, and these systems of the **White Horse** are truly coming to fruition... acting like Christ, but *not quite*. And Jesus, of course, being the *true* figure to rightfully to sit upon a "White Horse" (at the moment of his return), seems to have had the best rebuttal, in regards to a number of those corrupted religious elites out there - corrupting their populations at large (via one way or another):

*Woe to you, scribes and Pharisees, you hypocrites! You traverse land and sea to win a single convert, and when he becomes one, you make him **twice as much a son of hell** as you are!* - *Mat.* 23:15 (KJV)

Yes, these deceptions, no matter their reason, have truly hurt (and will continue to hurt) everyone in the Judeo-Christian ethos, and entire Christian populations are, indeed, being brought *down*! No one - no one other than *Jesus* Christ himself - could really have pointed it all out in a better way (than the above).

Chapter 16

Making their Moves… Whilst Covering Their Backsides

But, what if there, *still*, were a good number of individuals out there who, over time, were able to stick with the Bible, and continued to read it, as well as understand it (regardless of a number of those societal pressures around them)? These individuals were not about to accept this corruption, nor were they to fall to the material temptations of this fallen world. Yes, there still seemed to have been a number of "thorns" out there, sticking into the sides of those elite who, ultimately, were not (and are not) on the side of God.

In this part, we've learned a lot about those former Templars (now believed to have become the Freemason order), and what they may have wanted to accomplish in this world (since being betrayed by the Roman Catholic authority). We've also discovered how those Edomites corrupted the pure Jewish people, with a number of Edomites transforming themselves into the "EJCs." We discover how a number of pagan (and occult) elements have been inserted into the faiths of Judaism and Christianity as well, along with elements of Cain's humanism. And, any *true* warrior of the faith should understand that there was (and still is) a good deal of "smoke and mirrors" out there, in our world, infecting the true faith. And, in **no way** would God have wanted any of these additional elements to be blended into the Judeo-Christian theological mix.

Yes, there are "mystical" elements in modern Judaism (for example), which really do not seem to be from God. There's mystical elements in what the former Templars have adopted, over the years. Kenite scribes have, over the years, been able to corrupt the Israeli priesthood, as well. A number of pagan elements have found their ways into the two faiths (coming from ancient Rome, Babylon and a number of other surrounding places). And, of course, a lot of this information ultimately originated with that "forbidden" knowledge, brought to the world by those fallen, terrestrial angels of old, as well as their giant offspring. Yes, these individuals were, most probably, the *real* sources of so much of that "**mystical**" information that has crept up, and began to be blended into the pure faiths.

Whereof what's past is prologue…
 - Willaim Shakespeare

How true this is! A lot of this "new" is nothing but a reflection of that same "*old*" thing… sometimes, the same, *very* old thing. Yes, the battle lines for our conflict have, apparently, been laid out, a few millennia ago (coming from to the time of Shem, from Noah, even from Adam and Eve)! Yes, once again, we are seeing the past mirroring the present.

And, as we may also recall (from previous discussions), father Shem may have said something to pregnant Rebecca (Isaac's wife), way back in the earliest of time, while two children were inside her womb (i.e. Jacob/Israel and Esau/Edom):

"My daughter, I confide a secret to thee. See to it that none finds it out. Two nations are in thy womb, and how should thy body contain them, seeing that **the whole world** *will not be large enough for them to exist in it together peaceably?"*
(S. Baring-Gould, 1881, p. 217)[1]

How true that prediction seems to be **now**, in our day and age! Yes, the struggle between these Israelites (and Jews) and their Edomite brethren was anything but new, and nothing less than a massive, worldwide conflict. It, indeed, has been going on for a long, long time… and, yes, it did seem (and *does* seem) to encompass the whole of our Western World, the Middle East, and so much more!

And, as we may also begin to understand (in regards to this whole Jewish-Edomite conflict): this whole discussion is not about baseless claims of a "Jewish conspiracy," with attempts to take over the world; but there *is* a conspiracy **someone** out there, trying to do lot of that. And, we also know that: a number of individuals situated at the top of this same conspiratorial "heap" were (and are) **not even really Jewish**, but, in some way, are from an *Edomite* flavor (i.e. either through blood or through graft)! It's all about infiltration.

Also, it's not necessarily about a number of baseless claims about "secret societies" out there, such as the Knights Templar, the Freemasons or the Illuminati, with their attempts at world-domination, or the destruction of the Roman Catholic Church. So much of this, in fact, would actually be going on "behind the scenes." Why, of course, would a number of those "secret societies" need to be, and need to remain, so secretive… if there was nothing like these things on their agenda? What is there to hide anyway, if they're only out to help people become better citizens, or provide some kind of philanthropic relief? Again, one doesn't have to *hide* good deeds. Only those who work in the dark, or are up to nefarious things, would rather be allowed to go back *into* the dark, and stay within it, whenever necessary.

And, as well, we've already mentioned that it's not *every* person, within a number of these above groups, that are on the warpath against all things Godly, or of the Bible. In fact, it's just, perhaps, an extremely **small** minority - maybe even around 3-5% of the total people involved (the *top* 3-5% in most cases). It's so sad because the corrupt few at *the top* often set the standards - and the reputations - for those considered "beneath them."

We, as well, need to remember that this volume is actually an *expose'* - on the infiltrations and corruptions of the entire Judeo-Christian ethos, or ways of God. There truly is a battle going on, between the two (Edomite and Israeli) brethren. And, those **Edomites** (in either blood or graft), as well as their fellow pagans, were (and are) the ones who are, most probably, behind the vast majority of world's problems. Once again, we also need to remember: it's not the *majority* of people out there, trying to live out their lives according to what they believe in, or were taught… it is (for the most part) *the leadership*.

Still, we do seem to have a way to identify a lot of what's going on, inside a person's heart, no matter where they may come from, and that's by their "**fruits**." Yes, whatever eventually comes out of them gives us the evidence of what side they might *really* be on, regardless of any outer "shell."

Making Sure Their Enemy Stays Weak…

And, yes, there still seems to be a number of *real* Israelis out there, or real Christians, who are not going to fold (to the pressures of the "Other Side") very easily. That's why things had to have been done… so stealthily, and over a long period of time. They could not allow these people to figure out what they *really* may have been up against, all of these years. And, just as what probably happened to those migrating Lost 10 Tribes of Israel, the desires of these ungodly front men would seem to continue, in this same way, against their enemies… slowly, but surely, *removing* any evidence that could have been advantageous to their enemies (no matter what it might have been).

…While "Propping Up" Everybody Else!

And, one good way, for them, to keep up with their "anti-God" processes, over the years, would be to (simply) **crowd** their enemies out of existence, just as those Edomites had begun to do to those two tribes of Judah and Benjamin (ever since the beginnings of their assimilation process)! This time, in the *Christian* era, their efforts would have needed to be expanded on (quite a bit), to crowd out practically *anyone* holding onto that Judeo-Christian ethic. A number of other elements of the human experience (such as humanism and paganism) would, now, have to come into the picture - to help them out with their *saturation* process. Essentially, it would involve that old "squeeze play" - getting rid of true Jews and Christians by the assimilation of so many *other* thoughts and ideologies onto the world's stage!

Yes, we do seem to observe this going on today, on a massive scale! And, yes, there does seem to be a deeper reason to why there's so much talk about "multiculturalism" or "unity" in today's conversation. Of course, it all *does* sound good, in a whole number of respects… allowing every person a chance to have a shot at representation and relevant dialogue. Inclusion and equity, indeed, are hot topics in today's world. And, as a result of all these additions, a number of individuals who are **not** necessarily true Jews or true Christians should also be heard from, respected, and taken into account (as people)… with their own, individual beliefs to be respected and taken into account, as well!

Again, a lot of this might sound very good on the surface. But, once again, we may need to keep an eye out for just *how much* true Jewish and Christian values are being "crowded out" in this entire process… to the point of where anything of God seems to have lost any real sense of value, or exceptionalism. Yes, in all of this "inclusion," there may actually be some *deeper* purposes to movements such as this… at least to those anti-God elites out there.

Make no mistake: the elites of this White Horse would rather have practically *anyone* on top of the governing (or informational) heap here, in our modern world, than anyone who may be of God, or one holding onto some kind of Judeo-Christian *flavor*. It's all because these other individuals wouldn't be considered as much of a *threat*… to them, of course. Sad but true.

Conglomerating it into What <u>They</u> Want

Next, to work on the finalization of any "White Horse" goals, those powers that be (who are against God) would need to have other people look at them as if *they* were (and are) the people who are "doing the right thing," or are only out for "good." Cain's *humanism* would, of course, become more prevalent around this time.

Yes, in order for all of their goals to come true, it's almost as if these elites are creating an antichrist "cake" (if you will). First, on top of any Judeo-Christian foundation, they will need to add a number of pagan elements. As well, they'll toss in a number of *human* interpretations (coming from secular humanism, or some manner of politically correct thought). Toss in a dash of science, and stir everything up. Add a layer of Biblical "reinterpretation" (such as with those linear notes of the Scofield Reference Bible), as well as a layer of *multiple Bible versions*, and we have a cake ready to go… complete with the "sweet frosting" of censorship on top (i.e. the crowding out of anything contrary to their agenda)!

As well, in the wake of the Renaissance, we are about to witness their attempts at *globalization* - the beginnings of a world takeover (with *their* interests leading the way). As we may recall (from a previous chapter), we have:

*The Age of Discovery, or the Age of Exploration (approximately from the beginning of the 15th century until the middle of the 17th century), is an informal and loosely defined term for the period in European history in which extensive overseas exploration emerged as a powerful factor in European culture and which was the **beginning of globalization**. It also marks the rise of the widespread adoption of colonialism and mercantilism as national policies in Europe.*
("Age of Discovery", n. d., p. 1)[2]

And, to top it all off, there seemed to have been *another* ideology out there, to be inserted into this whole "baking" process. It would be a plan to help those powers that be solidify their own desires to take out most anything considered purely Jewish, or purely Christian. In fact, their new plan could even be referred to an "**evil plan**," if you will (as we'll soon see).

*...they **plan** evil against you... they devise mischief...*
- *Psa.* 21:11 (ESV)

Hopefully (for these people), it would allow them a chance to *speed up* the process of diverting the entire world's population in the *opposite* direction of all things Godly, all the while helping them reach their goal… of world domination.

We recall the goals of the Illuminati, for example:

"*...to abolish **all** monarchies, religion, **private property** and **nation states** and replace them with a utopian society… infiltrating the houses of power…*"
- *Brian Meltzer's Decoded* (A&E Networks, 2010)[3]

*…to **replace Christianity** by a **religion** of reason, to destroy the sovereignty of nations and thus to **control the world**.*
(Gouws, n. d., p. 1)[4]

We, interestingly enough, may now be able to incorporate *these* goals with that "*evil* plan" of the Bible, and begin to discover how this would have eventually been brought to the people of the world:

> *Woe to them that **devise iniquity**, and **work** evil upon their beds! when the morning is light, they practise it, because it is in the **power of their hand**. And they covet fields, and take them by violence; and **houses, and take them away**: so they **oppress** a man and his **house**, even a man **and his heritage**... **this time is evil**.* - *Micah* 2:1-3 (KJV)

Does this echo a lot of what we are seeing around us, today? We already are seeing examples of people wanting to take away a man's *house* (for the sake of "environmentalis"), or even attempting to take away a man's **heritage** (by "unifying" the peoples of the world). The Illuminati, as we've just seen (in the above), also brought up the desire to abolish private property rights, as well as to take away the sovereignty of one's former nation (to bring everyone into their "utopia"). And, of course, if they are able to successfully take away one's own property rights, as well as their national sovereignty, surely they'll be able to take away one's adherence to those Judeo-Christian values! And then, of course, if the God of the Bible was taken out of almost everything, then they - as members of the *state* - would naturally have to be thought of as the new "gods" of this world (backed by those occult forces of the "Other Side," of course)! What a racket!

In the next part, we'll begin to look a bit more into what this "evil plan" could have eventually manifested itself into, and how it will play out over time. And, once we begin to understand how everything would begin to work, and how it would all work so *cohesively* (against all things Godly), we'll soon be able to put "two and two" together, and discover how it all, collectively, would be considered the *rise of Mystery Babylon*.

More to come on all of this, in *Part 2*.

- End of Part 1-

Endnotes

Chapter 1

1. *Rev.* 6:2-8 (KJV).
2. Blue Letter Bible, *chloros*, 1, blueletterbible.org/lang/lexicon/lexicon.cfm?Strongs=G5515&t=KJV (accessed Jan. 16, 2020), *Rev.* 6:1-8.
3. Christianity.com, *What are the Four Horsemen in the Apocalypse During the End Times?*, 1, https://www.christianity.com/wiki/end-times/who-are-the-four-horsemen-in-revelation-their-meaning-and-significance.html (accessed Jan. 16, 2020).
4. Blue Letter Bible, *deber*, 1, https://www.blueletterbible.org/lexicon/h1698/kjv/wlc/0-1/ (accessed Jan. 16, 2020).
5. World Population Review, *World Population by Country*, 1, worldpopulationreview.com (accessed Mar. 12, 2019).
6. Merriam Webster Dictionary, *paganism*, 1, https://www.merriam-webster.com/dictionary/paganism (accessed Mar. 12, 2019).
7. World Atlas, *The 10 Largest Religions in the World*, 22, www.worldatlas.com/articles/largest-religions-in-the-world.html (accessed Dec. 15, 2022).
8. Reddit, *What percentage of the world is Pagan?*, 1, reddit.com/r/Wicca/comments/ryjrk/what_percentage_of_the_world_is_pagan/ (accessed Mar. 12, 2019).
9. Blue Letter Bible, *dabar*, 1, https://www.blueletterbible.org/lexicon/h1696/kjv/wlc/0-1/ (accessed Jan. 16, 2020).

Chapter 2

1. The Sheila Zilinsky Show, *Steve Quayle - Little Creatures: The Gates of Hell are Opening* sheilazilinsky.podomatic.com/entry/2015-02-24T16_40_16-08_00 (accessed Mar. 12, 2019).
2. Brad Steiger and Sherry Steiger, *Conspiracies and Secret Societies* (Canton, Michigan: Visible Ink Press, 2006), 308.
3. Elizabeth Clare Prophet, *Fallen Angels and the Origins of Evil* (Gardiner, Montana: Summit University Press, 2000), 38.

Chapter 3

1. Sage Journals, *Global Catholicism: Diverse, Troubled, Holding Steady*, 4, https://journals.sagepub.com/doi/full/10.1177/23969393211051444 (accessed Mar. 12, 2019).
2. Wikipedia, the free encyclopedia, *Protestantism*, 1, en.wikipedia.org/wiki/Protestantism (accessed Mar. 12, 2019).
3. Merriam Webster Dictionary, *anti*, 1, https://www.merriam-webster.com/dictionary/anti (accessed Mar. 12, 2019).
4. The Free Dictionary, *anti*, 1, http://www.thefreedictionary.com/anti (accessed Mar. 12, 2019).
5. Ralph Edward Woodrow, *Babylon Mystery Religion* (Riverside, California: Ralph Woodrow Evangelistic Association, 1993), 127.
6. Psychology Today, *Your Lizard Brain: The limbic system and brain functioning*, 1, (psychologytoday.com/blog/where-addiction-meets-your-brain/201404/your-lizard-brain (accessed Jan. 16, 2020).
7. PsychCentral, *The Lizard Brain and the Resistance*, 1, blogs.psychcentral.com/creative-mind/2011/04/the-lizard-brain-and-the-resistance/ (accessed Jan. 16, 2020).
8. Mazzastick, *The Reptilian Brain in Humans*, 11, mazzastick.com/are-you-behaving-like-a-reptile/ (accessed Jan. 16, 2020).
9. Mazzastick, *The Reptilian Brain in Humans*, 3, mazzastick.com/are-you-behaving-like-a-reptile/ (accessed Jan. 16, 2020).mazzastick.com/are-you-behaving-like-a-reptile/ (accessed Jan. 16, 2020).
10. Dr. Taylor Marshall, *Lizard Brain: Seth Godin's Christian Theology*, 1, taylormarshall.com/2013/07/lizard-brain-seth-godins-christian-theology.html (accessed Jan. 16, 2020).
11. Mazzastick, *The Reptilian Brain in Humans*, 8, mazzastick.com/are-you-behaving-like-a-reptile/ (accessed Jan. 16, 2020).mazzastick.com/are-you-behaving-like-a-reptile/ (accessed Jan. 16, 2020).
12. PsychCentral, *The Lizard Brain and the Resistance*, 1, blogs.psychcentral.com/creative-mind/2011/04/the-lizard-brain-and-the-resistance/ (accessed Jan. 16, 2020).
13. Mazzastick, *The Reptilian Brain in Humans*, 1, mazzastick.com/are-you-behaving-like-a-reptile/ (accessed Jan. 16, 2020).https://www.mazzastick.com/are-you-behaving-like-a-reptile/ (accessed Jan. 16, 2020).
14. Mazzastick, *The Reptilian Brain in Humans*, 9, mazzastick.com/are-you-behaving-like-a-reptile/ (accessed Jan. 16, 2020).mazzastick.com/are-you-behaving-like-a-reptile/ (accessed Jan. 16, 2020).
15. Mazzastick, *The Reptilian Brain in Humans*, 8, mazzastick.com/are-you-behaving-like-a-reptile/ (accessed Jan. 16, 2020).mazzastick.com/are-you-behaving-like-a-reptile/ (accessed Jan. 16, 2020).
16. Dr. Taylor Marshall, *Lizard Brain: Seth Godin's Christian Theology*, 1-2, taylormarshall.com/2013/07/lizard-brain-seth-godins-christian-theology.html (accessed Jan. 16, 2020).
17. Mazzastick, *The Reptilian Brain in Humans*, 9, mazzastick.com/are-you-behaving-like-a-reptile/ (accessed Jan. 16, 2020).mazzastick.com/are-you-behaving-like-a-reptile/ (accessed Jan. 16, 2020).

¹⁸ Mazzastick, *The Reptilian Brain in Humans*, 1, mazzastick.com/are-you-behaving-like-a-reptile/ (accessed Jan. 16, 2020).https://www.mazzastick.com/are-you-behaving-like-a-reptile/ (accessed Jan. 16, 2020).
¹⁹ Mazzastick, *The Reptilian Brain in Humans*, 1, mazzastick.com/are-you-behaving-like-a-reptile/ (accessed Jan. 16, 2020).https://www.mazzastick.com/are-you-behaving-like-a-reptile/ (accessed Jan. 16, 2020).
²⁰ Mazzastick, *The Reptilian Brain in Humans*, 1, mazzastick.com/are-you-behaving-like-a-reptile/ (accessed Jan. 16, 2020).https://www.mazzastick.com/are-you-behaving-like-a-reptile/ (accessed Jan. 16, 2020).
²¹ Mazzastick, *The Reptilian Brain in Humans*, 7, mazzastick.com/are-you-behaving-like-a-reptile/ (accessed Jan. 16, 2020).mazzastick.com/are-you-behaving-like-a-reptile/ (accessed Jan. 16, 2020).
²² Mazzastick, *The Reptilian Brain in Humans*, 6, mazzastick.com/are-you-behaving-like-a-reptile/ (accessed Jan. 16, 2020).mazzastick.com/are-you-behaving-like-a-reptile/ (accessed Jan. 16, 2020).
²³ Mazzastick, *The Reptilian Brain in Humans*, 5, mazzastick.com/are-you-behaving-like-a-reptile/ (accessed Jan. 16, 2020).mazzastick.com/are-you-behaving-like-a-reptile/ (accessed Jan. 16, 2020).
²⁴ Mazzastick, *The Reptilian Brain in Humans*, 8, mazzastick.com/are-you-behaving-like-a-reptile/ (accessed Jan. 16, 2020).mazzastick.com/are-you-behaving-like-a-reptile/ (accessed Jan. 16, 2020).
²⁵ Mazzastick, *The Reptilian Brain in Humans*, 1, mazzastick.com/are-you-behaving-like-a-reptile/ (accessed Jan. 16, 2020).mazzastick.com/are-you-behaving-like-a-reptile/ (accessed Jan. 16, 2020).
²⁶ Mazzastick, *The Reptilian Brain in Humans*, 3, mazzastick.com/are-you-behaving-like-a-reptile/ (accessed Jan. 16, 2020).mazzastick.com/are-you-behaving-like-a-reptile/ (accessed Jan. 16, 2020).
²⁷ Mazzastick, *The Reptilian Brain in Humans*, 9, mazzastick.com/are-you-behaving-like-a-reptile/ (accessed Jan. 16, 2020).mazzastick.com/are-you-behaving-like-a-reptile/ (accessed Jan. 16, 2020).
²⁸ Mazzastick, *The Reptilian Brain in Humans*, 1, mazzastick.com/are-you-behaving-like-a-reptile/ (accessed Jan. 16, 2020).https://www.mazzastick.com/are-you-behaving-like-a-reptile/ (accessed Jan. 16, 2020).
²⁹ Dr. Taylor Marshall, *Lizard Brain: Seth Godin's Christian Theology*, 2, taylormarshall.com/2013/07/lizard-brain-seth-godins-christian-theology.html (accessed Jan. 16, 2020).
³⁰ St. Ephrem the Syrian, *Selected Prose Works*, Section 2, 22(2), trans. Edward G. Mathews, Jr. and Joseph P. Amar (Washington, D. C.: The Catholic University of America Press, 1994), 125.
³¹ St. Ephrem the Syrian, *Selected Prose Works*, Section 2, 22(2), trans. Edward G. Mathews, Jr. and Joseph P. Amar (Washington, D. C.: The Catholic University of America Press, 1994), 129.
³² Merriam Webster Dictionary, *psychopath*, 1, https://www.merriam-webster.com/dictionary/psychopath (accessed Oct. 17, 2018).
³³ Tools For Freedom Store, *#3058: How to Defend Yourself Against Psychopaths*, n. d., 1, toolsforfreedom.com/How-to-Defend-Yourself-Against-Psychopaths-DVD-p/3058.htm (accessed Oct. 17, 2018).
³⁴ Quora, *Do wolves ever kill more than they can eat at one time?*, 1, https://www.quora.com/Why-do-wolves-kill-maul-multiple-sheep-but-not-eat-them (accessed Apr. 04, 2022).
³⁵ Drug Abuse in Scripture, *The Biblical Tare of Saint Matthew's Gospel*, 2, http://www.drugabuseinscripture.co.uk/html/the_tare.html#.VmZvhtpzM2x (accessed March 24, 2011).

Chapter 4

¹ Merriam Webster Dictionary, *titan*, 1, https://www.merriam-webster.com/dictionary/anti (accessed Mar. 12, 2019).
² *The Dennis Prager Radio Program*, AM 560 The Answer (Chicago, IL: WIND, January 2, 2024).
³ Dr. Justin Prock, *Who's Who?*, 1, https://www.justinprock.com/2021/10/09/i-know-the-blasphemy-of-them-which-say-they-are-jews-judahites-and-are-not-but-are-the-synagogue-of-satan-part-1-introductions/ (accessed Oct. 17, 2018).
⁴ Anno Mundi Books, *The Travels of Noah into Europe*, 1, annomundi.com/history/travels_of_noah.htm (accessed Apr. 04, 2022).
⁵ McClintock and Strong Biblical Cyclopedia, *Shepherd Kings*, 1, https://www.biblicalcyclopedia.com/S/shepherd-kings.html#:~:text=Shepherd%20kings%2C%20a%20series%20of%20foreign%20rulers%20in,requires%20a%20somewhat%20fuller%20consideration%20of%20this%20topic (accessed Dec. 15, 2022).
⁶ McClintock and Strong Biblical Cyclopedia, *Shepherd Kings*, 1, https://www.biblicalcyclopedia.com/S/shepherd-kings.html#:~:text=Shepherd%20kings%2C%20a%20series%20of%20foreign%20rulers%20in,requires%20a%20somewhat%20fuller%20consideration%20of%20this%20topic (accessed Dec. 15, 2022).
⁷ Stumbough, Virginia. "Fairies Were Real." *Fate*, Nov. 1957.
⁸ Mysterious World, *The Kurgans*, 9, mysteriousworld.com/Journal/2003/Summer/Giants/#TheKurgans (accessed Apr. 04, 2022).
⁹ Mysterious World, *The Kurgans*, 9, mysteriousworld.com/Journal/2003/Summer/Giants/#TheKurgans (accessed Apr. 04, 2022).
¹⁰ Cradle of Civilization, *On the origin of the Aryans*, 5, https://aratta.wordpress.com/2015/10/14/on-the-origin-of-the-aryans/ (accessed Mar. 12, 2019).
¹¹ iThought, *"Aryan Invasion Theory" - The Greatest flaw in our Indian History?*, 3, https://rajkhandelwal.wordpress.com/2012/06/24/aryan-invasion-theory-the-greatest-flaw-in-our-indian-history (accessed Mar. 12, 2019).

[12] Good Reads, *Michael Tsarion Quotes*, 8, https://www.goodreads.com/author/quotes/850488.Michael_Tsarion?page=3 (accessed Mar. 12, 2019).
[13] Wikipedia, the free encyclopedia, *Behistun Inscription*, 1, en.wikipedia.org/wiki/Full_translation_of_the_Behistun_Inscription (accessed Mar. 21, 2019).
[14] Archaeology Wordsmith, *The Kurgans*, 1, archaeologywordsmith.com/search.php?q=barrow (accessed Jan. 16, 2020).
[15] "The Reptilians", *Ancient Aliens*, The History Channel, Season 8, Episode 5, 2014.
[16] Mysterious World, *The Kurgans*, 9, mysteriousworld.com/Journal/2003/Summer/Giants/#TheKurgans (accessed Apr. 04, 2022).
[17] Mysterious World, *The Kurgans*, 9, mysteriousworld.com/Journal/2003/Summer/Giants/#TheKurgans (accessed Apr. 04, 2022).
[18] Mysterious World, *The Kurgans*, 9, mysteriousworld.com/Journal/2003/Summer/Giants/#TheKurgans (accessed Apr. 04, 2022).
[19] Mysterious World, *The Kurgans*, 9, mysteriousworld.com/Journal/2003/Summer/Giants/#TheKurgans (accessed Apr. 04, 2022).
[20] Dr. Michael S Heiser, The Myth of Double Row Teeth and Elongated-Skull Nephilim, drmsh.com/the-myth-of-double-row-teeth-and-elongated-skull-nephilim/
[21] Marzulli, L.A.. (n. d.). *On the Trail of the Nephilim: The Mysterious Moundbuilders*.
[22] Marzulli, L.A.. (n. d.). *On the Trail of the Nephilim: The Mysterious Moundbuilders*.
[23] BibleVerseStudy.com, *Haran - Where & Who?*, 1, https://www.bibleversestudy.com/acts/acts7-haran.htm (accessed Mar. 12, 2019).
[24] Timeless Myth, *Creation of Gods and Mankind*, 35-36, https://www.timelessmyths.com/classical/creation.html (accessed Mar. 21, 2017).
[25] R. E. Asher, *National Myths in Renaissance France* (Edinburgh: Edinburgh University Press Ltd., 1993), 203.
[26] Timeless Myth, *Creation of Gods and Mankind*, 36, https://www.timelessmyths.com/classical/creation.html (accessed Mar. 21, 2017).

Chapter 5

[1] Wiktionary, *atlas*, 1, https://en.wiktionary.org/wiki/atlas (accessed Jan. 16, 2020).
[2] Wikipedia, the free encyclopedia, *Ad*, 2, https://en.wikipedia.org/wiki/%E2%80%98Ad (accessed Mar. 21, 2017).
[3] Mom.com, *Hena*, 1, https://www.babynamewizard.com/baby-name/girl/hena (accessed Mar. 21, 2017).
[4] Wiktionary, *las*, 1, https://en.wiktionary.org/wiki/las (accessed Mar. 21, 2017).
[5] Wikipedia, the free encyclopedia, *Pillars of Hercules*, 1, https://en.wikipedia.org/wiki/Pillars_of_Hercules (accessed Mar. 12, 2019).
[6] Brad Steiger and Sherry Steiger, *Conspiracies and Secret Societies* (Canton, Michigan: Visible Ink Press, 2006), 40.
[7] Wikipedia, the free encyclopedia, *Athens*, 3, https://en.wikipedia.org/wiki/Athens (accessed Jan. 16, 2020).
[8] Space Intelligence, *Plato's Story of Atlantis*, 4, https://spaceandai.com/project/platos-story-of-atlantis/ (accessed Jan. 16, 2020).
[9] Space Intelligence, *Plato's Story of Atlantis*, 5, https://spaceandai.com/project/platos-story-of-atlantis/ (accessed Jan. 16, 2020).

Chapter 6

[1] Space Intelligence, *Plato's Story of Atlantis*, 5, https://spaceandai.com/project/platos-story-of-atlantis/ (accessed Jan. 16, 2020).
[2] Ignatius Donnelly, *Atlantis: The Antediluvian World* (New York: Harper & Brothers, 1882), 78
[3] Mysterious World, *The Kurgans*, 9, mysteriousworld.com/Journal/2003/Summer/Giants/#TheKurgans (accessed Apr. 04, 2022).
[4] Humans are Free, *America May Derive From Peruvian Name*, 1, humansarefree.com/2012/03/america-may-derive-from-peruvian-name.html (accessed Mar. 21, 2017).
[5] The Night is Coming, *America/Amaruca - Land of the Plumed Serpent 2013*, 1-2, https://endoftheage.blogspot.com/2013/10/americaamaruca-land-of-plumed-serpent.html (accessed Mar. 12, 2019).
[6] Wikipedia, the free encyclopedia, *Toltec*, 1, https://en.wikipedia.org/wiki/Toltec (accessed Mar. 12, 2019).
[7] Ignatius Donnelly, *Atlantis: The Antediluvian World* (New York: Harper & Brothers, 1882), 105.
[8] Ignatius Donnelly, *Atlantis: The Antediluvian World* (New York: Harper & Brothers, 1882), 332.
[9] Ignatius Donnelly, *Atlantis: The Antediluvian World* (New York: Harper & Brothers, 1882), 168.
[10] Ignatius Donnelly, *Atlantis: The Antediluvian World* (New York: Harper & Brothers, 1882), 175-176.
[11] Sydney Bristowe, *Sargon the Magnificent* (London: The Covenant Publishing Co., 1927), 163.
[12] Marzulli, L.A.. (n. d.). *On the Trail of the Nephilim: The Mysterious Moundbuilders*.
[13] Marzulli, L.A.. (n. d.). *On the Trail of the Nephilim: The Mysterious Moundbuilders*.
[14] Ignatius Donnelly, *Atlantis: The Antediluvian World* (New York: Harper & Brothers, 1882), 106.
[15] Mysterious World, *The Kurgans*, 9, mysteriousworld.com/Journal/2003/Summer/Giants/#TheKurgans (accessed

Apr. 04, 2022).
16 Ignatius Donnelly, *Atlantis: The Antediluvian World* (New York: Harper & Brothers, 1882), 172.
17 Dr. Michael S Heiser, *The Myth of Double Row Teeth and Elongated-Skull Nephilim*, 2, drmsh.com/the-myth-of-double-row-teeth-and-elongated-skull-nephilim/ (accessed Sept. 19, 2017).
18 Dr. Michael S Heiser, *The Myth of Double Row Teeth and Elongated-Skull Nephilim*, 2, drmsh.com/the-myth-of-double-row-teeth-and-elongated-skull-nephilim/ (accessed Sept. 19, 2017).
19 ATS: above top secret, *The Smithsonian cover-ups*, 1, http://www.abovetopsecret.com/forum/thread741628/pg1 (accessed Apr. 04, 2022).
20 ATS: above top secret, *The Smithsonian cover-ups*, 1, http://www.abovetopsecret.com/forum/thread741628/pg1 (accessed Apr. 04, 2022).
21 ATS: above top secret, *The Smithsonian cover-ups*, 1, http://www.abovetopsecret.com/forum/thread741628/pg1 (accessed Apr. 04, 2022).
22 Star Myths of the World, *The Smithsonian Cover Up*, 7, starmythworld.com/mathisencorollary/2014/04/the-smithsonian-cover-up.html (accessed Sept. 19, 2017).
23 ATS: above top secret, *The Smithsonian cover-ups*, 1, http://www.abovetopsecret.com/forum/thread741628/pg1 (accessed Apr. 04, 2022).
24 ATS: above top secret, *The Smithsonian cover-ups*, 1, http://www.abovetopsecret.com/forum/thread741628/pg1 (accessed Apr. 04, 2022).
25 Marzulli, L.A.. (n. d.). *On the Trail of the Nephilim: The Mysterious Moundbuilders*.
26 Marzulli, L.A.. (n. d.). *On the Trail of the Nephilim: The Mysterious Moundbuilders*.
27 ATS: above top secret, *The Smithsonian cover-ups*, 2, http://www.abovetopsecret.com/forum/thread741628/pg1 (accessed Apr. 04, 2022).
28 ATS: above top secret, *The Smithsonian cover-ups*, 2, http://www.abovetopsecret.com/forum/thread741628/pg1 (accessed Apr. 04, 2022).
29 ATS: above top secret, *The Smithsonian cover-ups*, 2, http://www.abovetopsecret.com/forum/thread741628/pg1 (accessed Apr. 04, 2022).

Chapter 7

1 R. E. Asher, *National Myths in Renaissance France* (Edinburgh: Edinburgh University Press Ltd., 1993), 199.
2 Wayne Simpson, *Noah: Founder of Civilizations* (Springdale, Arkansas: Lightcatcher Books, 2009), 6.
3 Wayne Simpson, *Noah: Founder of Civilizations* (Springdale, Arkansas: Lightcatcher Books, 2009), 7.
4 *An Historical Treatise of the Travels of Noah Into Europe: Containing the First Inhabitation and Peopling Thereof*, trans. Richard Lynche (1601), 11.
5 *An Historical Treatise of the Travels of Noah Into Europe: Containing the First Inhabitation and Peopling Thereof*, trans. Richard Lynche (1601), 15.
6 *An Historical Treatise of the Travels of Noah Into Europe: Containing the First Inhabitation and Peopling Thereof*, trans. Richard Lynche (1601), 11.
7 name doctor, *Sabatius*, 1, http://www.name-doctor.com/name-sabatius-meaning-of-sabatius-55978.html (accessed Sept. 19, 2017).
8 Wikipedia, the free encyclopedia, *Sabazios*, 1, en.wikipedia.org/wiki/Sabazios (accessed Sept. 19, 2017).
9 name doctor, *Sabatius*, 1, http://www.name-doctor.com/name-sabatius-meaning-of-sabatius-55978.html (accessed Sept. 19, 2017).
10 Name Meaning, *Saba*, 1, https://www.thenamemeaning.com/saba/ (accessed Apr. 29, 2023).
11 Anno Mundi Books, *The Travels of Noah into Europe*, 2, annomundi.com/history/travels_of_noah.htm (accessed Apr. 04, 2022).
12 R. E. Asher, *National Myths in Renaissance France* (Edinburgh: Edinburgh University Press Ltd., 1993), 199, 205.
13 *An Historical Treatise of the Travels of Noah Into Europe: Containing the First Inhabitation and Peopling Thereof*, trans. Richard Lynche (1601), http://www.annomundi.com/history/travels_of_noah.htm (accessed Dec. 7, 2007), 15.
14 R. E. Asher, *National Myths in Renaissance France* (Edinburgh: Edinburgh University Press Ltd., 1993), 199, 201; Wayne Simpson, *Noah: Founder of Civilizations* (Springdale, Arkansas: Lightcatcher Books, 2009), 19.
15 Wayne Simpson, *Noah: Founder of Civilizations* (Springdale, Arkansas: Lightcatcher Books, 2009), 14.
16 R. E. Asher, *National Myths in Renaissance France* (Edinburgh: Edinburgh University Press Ltd., 1993), 203.
17 *An Historical Treatise of the Travels of Noah Into Europe: Containing the First Inhabitation and Peopling Thereof*, trans. Richard Lynche (1601), 15.
18 R. E. Asher, *National Myths in Renaissance France* (Edinburgh: Edinburgh University Press Ltd., 1993), 203.
19 R. E. Asher, *National Myths in Renaissance France* (Edinburgh: Edinburgh University Press Ltd., 1993), 203.
20 Annius of Viterbo, *Berosus, The fourth book of Berosus, the Babylonian, on ancient times*] R. E. Asher, *National Myths in Renaissance France* (Edinburgh: Edinburgh University Press Ltd., 1993), 203.
21 Annius of Viterbo, *Berosus, The fourth book of Berosus, the Babylonian, on ancient times*] R. E. Asher, *National Myths in Renaissance France* (Edinburgh: Edinburgh University Press Ltd., 1993), 207.
22 Annius of Viterbo, *Berosus, The fourth book of Berosus, the Babylonian, on ancient times*] R. E. Asher, *National*

Myths in Renaissance France (Edinburgh: Edinburgh University Press Ltd., 1993), 205.

[23] *An Historical Treatise of the Travels of Noah Into Europe: Containing the First Inhabitation and Peopling Thereof*, trans. Richard Lynche (1601), 15.

[24] R. E. Asher, *National Myths in Renaissance France* (Edinburgh: Edinburgh University Press Ltd., 1993), 207.

[25] R. E. Asher, *National Myths in Renaissance France* (Edinburgh: Edinburgh University Press Ltd., 1993), 207.

[26] *An Historical Treatise of the Travels of Noah Into Europe: Containing the First Inhabitation and Peopling Thereof*, trans. Richard Lynche (1601), http://www.annomundi.com/history/travels_of_noah.htm (accessed Dec. 7, 2007), 11.

[27] R. E. Asher, *National Myths in Renaissance France* (Edinburgh: Edinburgh University Press Ltd., 1993), 201.

[28] R. E. Asher, *National Myths in Renaissance France* (Edinburgh: Edinburgh University Press Ltd., 1993), 201.

[29] R. E. Asher, *National Myths in Renaissance France* (Edinburgh: Edinburgh University Press Ltd., 1993), 201.

[30] *An Historical Treatise of the Travels of Noah Into Europe: Containing the First Inhabitation and Peopling Thereof*, trans. Richard Lynche (1601), 24.

[31] Ignatius Donnelly, *Atlantis: The Antediluvian World* (New York: Harper & Brothers, 1882), 174.

[32] Wayne Simpson, *Noah: Founder of Civilizations* (Springdale, Arkansas: Lightcatcher Books, 2009), 9, 19.

[33] Anno Mundi Books, *The Travels of Noah into Europe*, 3, annomundi.com/history/travels_of_noah.htm (accessed Apr. 04, 2022).

[34] R. E. Asher, *National Myths in Renaissance France* (Edinburgh: Edinburgh University Press Ltd., 1993), 203.

[35] R. E. Asher, *National Myths in Renaissance France* (Edinburgh: Edinburgh University Press Ltd., 1993), 201.

[36] Wayne Simpson, *Noah: Founder of Civilizations* (Springdale, Arkansas: Lightcatcher Books, 2009), 20.

[37] R. E. Asher, *National Myths in Renaissance France* (Edinburgh: Edinburgh University Press Ltd., 1993), 201.

[38] Wayne Simpson, *Noah: Founder of Civilizations* (Springdale, Arkansas: Lightcatcher Books, 2009), 20.

[39] Gen. 46:31-34.

[40] Wikipedia, the free encyclopedia, *Hyksos*, 15, https://en.wikipedia.org/wiki/Hyksos (accessed Jan. 16, 2020).

[41] Wayne Simpson, *Noah: Founder of Civilizations* (Springdale, Arkansas: Lightcatcher Books, 2009), 20.

[42] Anno Mundi Books, *From Noah to Dardanus (according to Annius)*, 3, annomundi.com/history/travels_of_noah.htm (accessed Apr. 04, 2022).

[43] R. E. Asher, *National Myths in Renaissance France* (Edinburgh: Edinburgh University Press Ltd., 1993), 207.

[44] *An Historical Treatise of the Travels of Noah Into Europe: Containing the First Inhabitation and Peopling Thereof*, trans. Richard Lynche (1601), 11.

[45] R. E. Asher, *National Myths in Renaissance France* (Edinburgh: Edinburgh University Press Ltd., 1993), 205.

[46] R. E. Asher, *National Myths in Renaissance France* (Edinburgh: Edinburgh University Press Ltd., 1993), 209.

[47] R. E. Asher, *National Myths in Renaissance France* (Edinburgh: Edinburgh University Press Ltd., 1993), 209.

[48] Anno Mundi Books, *From Noah to Dardanus (according to Annius)*, 3, annomundi.com/history/travels_of_noah.htm (accessed Apr. 04, 2022).

[49] Anno Mundi Books, *From Noah to Dardanus (according to Annius)*, 5, annomundi.com/history/travels_of_noah.htm (accessed Apr. 04, 2022).

[50] Wayne Simpson, *Noah: Founder of Civilizations* (Springdale, Arkansas: Lightcatcher Books, 2009), 12.

[51] Wayne Simpson, *Noah: Founder of Civilizations* (Springdale, Arkansas: Lightcatcher Books, 2009), 12.

[52] R. E. Asher, *National Myths in Renaissance France* (Edinburgh: Edinburgh University Press Ltd., 1993), 209.

[53] R. E. Asher, *National Myths in Renaissance France* (Edinburgh: Edinburgh University Press Ltd., 1993), 211.

[54] *An Historical Treatise of the Travels of Noah Into Europe: Containing the First Inhabitation and Peopling Thereof*, trans. Richard Lynche (1601), 15.

[55] R. E. Asher, *National Myths in Renaissance France* (Edinburgh: Edinburgh University Press Ltd., 1993), 201.

[56] Anno Mundi Books, *From Noah to Dardanus (according to Annius)*, 3, annomundi.com/history/travels_of_noah.htm (accessed Apr. 04, 2022).

[57] R. E. Asher, *National Myths in Renaissance France* (Edinburgh: Edinburgh University Press Ltd., 1993), 213.

[58] *An Historical Treatise of the Travels of Noah Into Europe: Containing the First Inhabitation and Peopling Thereof*, trans. Richard Lynche (1601), 15.

[59] R. E. Asher, *National Myths in Renaissance France* (Edinburgh: Edinburgh University Press Ltd., 1993), 213.

[60] *An Historical Treatise of the Travels of Noah Into Europe: Containing the First Inhabitation and Peopling Thereof*, trans. Richard Lynche (1601), 15.

[61] *An Historical Treatise of the Travels of Noah Into Europe: Containing the First Inhabitation and Peopling Thereof*, trans. Richard Lynche (1601), 15; Wayne Simpson, *Noah: Founder of Civilizations* (Springdale, Arkansas: Lightcatcher Books, 2009), 13; *An Historical Treatise of the Travels of Noah Into Europe: Containing the First Inhabitation and Peopling Thereof*, trans. Richard Lynche (1601), 11; Alexander Hislop, *The Two Babylons or the Papal Worship: Proved to be the Worship of Nimrod and His Wife* (Neptune, New Jersey: Loizeaux Brothers, 1916), 243.

[62] *An Historical Treatise of the Travels of Noah Into Europe: Containing the First Inhabitation and Peopling Thereof*, trans. Richard Lynche (1601), 15.

[63] *An Historical Treatise of the Travels of Noah Into Europe: Containing the First Inhabitation and Peopling Thereof*, trans. Richard Lynche (1601), 15.

⁶⁴ Anno Mundi Books, *From Noah to Dardanus (according to Annius)*, 3, annomundi.com/history/travels_of_noah.htm (accessed Apr. 04, 2022).
⁶⁵ R. E. Asher, *National Myths in Renaissance France* (Edinburgh: Edinburgh University Press Ltd., 1993), 209.
⁶⁶ Anno Mundi Books, *The Travels of Noah into Europe*, 4, annomundi.com/history/travels_of_noah.htm (accessed Apr. 04, 2022).
⁶⁷ Anno Mundi Books, *The Travels of Noah into Europe*, 3, annomundi.com/history/travels_of_noah.htm (accessed Apr. 04, 2022).
⁶⁸ R. E. Asher, *National Myths in Renaissance France* (Edinburgh: Edinburgh University Press Ltd., 1993), 209.
⁶⁹ R. E. Asher, *National Myths in Renaissance France* (Edinburgh: Edinburgh University Press Ltd., 1993), 211.
⁷⁰ Anno Mundi Books, *From Noah to Dardanus (according to Annius)*, 2, annomundi.com/history/travels_of_noah.htm (accessed Apr. 04, 2022); R. E. Asher, *National Myths in Renaissance France* (Edinburgh: Edinburgh University Press Ltd., 1993), 211.
⁷¹ Anno Mundi Books, *The Travels of Noah into Europe*, 4, annomundi.com/history/travels_of_noah.htm (accessed Apr. 04, 2022).
⁷² R. E. Asher, *National Myths in Renaissance France* (Edinburgh: Edinburgh University Press Ltd., 1993), 211.
⁷³ *An Historical Treatise of the Travels of Noah Into Europe: Containing the First Inhabitation and Peopling Thereof*, trans. Richard Lynche (1601), 23.
⁷⁴ R. E. Asher, *National Myths in Renaissance France* (Edinburgh: Edinburgh University Press Ltd., 1993), 201.
⁷⁵ *An Historical Treatise of the Travels of Noah Into Europe: Containing the First Inhabitation and Peopling Thereof*, trans. Richard Lynche (1601), 22.
⁷⁶ Anno Mundi Books, *The Travels of Noah into Europe*, 4, annomundi.com/history/travels_of_noah.htm (accessed Apr. 04, 2022).
⁷⁷ Anno Mundi Books, *The Travels of Noah into Europe*, 5, annomundi.com/history/travels_of_noah.htm (accessed Apr. 04, 2022).
⁷⁸ *An Historical Treatise of the Travels of Noah Into Europe: Containing the First Inhabitation and Peopling Thereof*, trans. Richard Lynche (1601), 24.
⁷⁹ *An Historical Treatise of the Travels of Noah Into Europe: Containing the First Inhabitation and Peopling Thereof*, trans. Richard Lynche (1601), 24.
⁸⁰ *An Historical Treatise of the Travels of Noah Into Europe: Containing the First Inhabitation and Peopling Thereof*, trans. Richard Lynche (1601), 25.
⁸¹ Wikipedia, the free encyclopedia, *Osiris*, 1, https://en.wikipedia.org/wiki/Osiris (accessed Apr. 04, 2022).
⁸² *An Historical Treatise of the Travels of Noah Into Europe: Containing the First Inhabitation and Peopling Thereof*, trans. Richard Lynche (1601), 21.
⁸³ *An Historical Treatise of the Travels of Noah Into Europe: Containing the First Inhabitation and Peopling Thereof*, trans. Richard Lynche (1601), 24.
⁸⁴ R. E. Asher, *National Myths in Renaissance France* (Edinburgh: Edinburgh University Press Ltd., 1993), 221.
⁸⁵ *An Historical Treatise of the Travels of Noah Into Europe: Containing the First Inhabitation and Peopling Thereof*, trans. Richard Lynche (1601), 58.
⁸⁶ Anno Mundi Books, *The Travels of Noah into Europe*, 5, annomundi.com/history/travels_of_noah.htm (accessed Apr. 04, 2022).
⁸⁷ Anno Mundi Books, *From Noah to Dardanus (according to Annius)*, 2, annomundi.com/history/travels_of_noah.htm (accessed Apr. 04, 2022).
⁸⁸ Anno Mundi Books, *The Travels of Noah into Europe*, 5, annomundi.com/history/travels_of_noah.htm (accessed Apr. 04, 2022).
⁸⁹ *An Historical Treatise of the Travels of Noah Into Europe: Containing the First Inhabitation and Peopling Thereof*, trans. Richard Lynche (1601), 58.
⁹⁰ Anno Mundi Books, *From Noah to Dardanus (according to Annius)*, 2, annomundi.com/history/travels_of_noah.htm (accessed Apr. 04, 2022).
⁹¹ The Conte de Gabalis (1913): *Hercules*, 1, sacred-texts.com/eso/cdg/cdg57.htm (accessed Apr. 29, 2023).
⁹² *An Historical Treatise of the Travels of Noah Into Europe: Containing the First Inhabitation and Peopling Thereof*, trans. Richard Lynche (1601), 58.
⁹³ Anno Mundi Books, *From Noah to Dardanus (according to Annius)*, 5, annomundi.com/history/travels_of_noah.htm (accessed Apr. 04, 2022).
⁹⁴ *An Historical Treatise of the Travels of Noah Into Europe: Containing the First Inhabitation and Peopling Thereof*, trans. Richard Lynche (1601), 60.
⁹⁵ R. E. Asher, *National Myths in Renaissance France* (Edinburgh: Edinburgh University Press Ltd., 1993), 221.
⁹⁶ Anno Mundi Books, *From Noah to Dardanus (according to Annius)*, 5, annomundi.com/history/travels_of_noah.htm (accessed Apr. 04, 2022).
⁹⁷ *An Historical Treatise of the Travels of Noah Into Europe: Containing the First Inhabitation and Peopling Thereof*, trans. Richard Lynche (1601), 36.
⁹⁸ Anno Mundi Books, *From Noah to Dardanus (according to Annius)*, 2, 5,

annomundi.com/history/travels_of_noah.htm (accessed Apr. 04, 2022).
[99] R. E. Asher, *National Myths in Renaissance France* (Edinburgh: Edinburgh University Press Ltd., 1993), 215.
[100] *An Historical Treatise of the Travels of Noah Into Europe: Containing the First Inhabitation and Peopling Thereof*, trans. Richard Lynche (1601), 23.
[101] Wayne Simpson, *Noah: Founder of Civilizations* (Springdale, Arkansas: Lightcatcher Books, 2009), 19.
[102] Moses Khorenats'i, *History of the Armenians (Translated by Robert W. Thomson)* (London, England: Harvard University Press, 1978), 101-102; R. E. Asher, *National Myths in Renaissance France* (Edinburgh: Edinburgh University Press Ltd., 1993), 201.
[103] *An Historical Treatise of the Travels of Noah Into Europe: Containing the First Inhabitation and Peopling Thereof*, trans. Richard Lynche (1601), 23.
[104] R. E. Asher, *National Myths in Renaissance France* (Edinburgh: Edinburgh University Press Ltd., 1993), 215.
[105] *An Historical Treatise of the Travels of Noah Into Europe: Containing the First Inhabitation and Peopling Thereof*, trans. Richard Lynche (1601), 23.
[106] R. E. Asher, *National Myths in Renaissance France* (Edinburgh: Edinburgh University Press Ltd., 1993), 215.
[107] Alexander Hislop, *The Two Babylons or the Papal Worship: Proved to be the Worship of Nimrod and His Wife* (Neptune, New Jersey: Loizeaux Brothers, 1916), 236; Moses Khorenats'i, *History of the Armenians (Translated by Robert W. Thomson)* (London, England: Harvard University Press, 1978), 102.
[108] *An Historical Treatise of the Travels of Noah Into Europe: Containing the First Inhabitation and Peopling Thereof*, trans. Richard Lynche (1601), 24.

Chapter 8

[1] S. Baring-Gould, *Legends of the Patriarchs and Prophets and Other Old Testament Characters* (New York: American Book Exchange, 1881), 217.
[2] Church News, *Scirbes were masters of Hebrew law, writings through diligent study*, 1, https://www.thechurchnews.com/1994/11/12/23256241/scribes-were-masters-of-hebrew-law-writings-through-diligent-study/ (accessed Apr. 29, 2023).
[3] S. Baring-Gould, *Legends of the Patriarchs and Prophets and Other Old Testament Characters* (New York: American Book Exchange, 1881), 217.
[4] *The Alex Jones Radio Program*, infowars.com (Texas: December 7, 2016).
[5] aish, *Nimrod*, 4, https://aish.com/nimrod/ (accessed Apr. 29, 2023).
[6] *The Book of Jasher*, 36:23, trans. Albinus Alcuin (Pomeroy, Washington: Health Research, 1966).
[7] *The Book of Jasher*, 57:2, trans. Albinus Alcuin (Pomeroy, Washington: Health Research, 1966).
[8] Daat Emet, *Esau, Edom, Rome, and the Christians*, 2, http://daatemet.org.il/en/question/esau-edom-rome-and-the-christians/ (accessed Mar. 21, 2017).
[9] House of Cards, *Zepho, Balaam, Jannes & Jambres pt 1*, 3, https://houseofcardsbook.wordpress.com/2015/12/20/zepho-balaam-jannes-jambres-pt-1/ (accessed Jan. 16, 2020).
[10] House of Cards, *Zepho, Balaam, Jannes & Jambres pt 1*, 1-3, https://houseofcardsbook.wordpress.com/2015/12/20/zepho-balaam-jannes-jambres-pt-1/ (accessed Jan. 16, 2020).
[11] *The Book of Jasher*, 58:14, trans. Albinus Alcuin (Pomeroy, Washington: Health Research, 1966).
[12] Daat Emet,, *Esau, Edom, Rome, and the Christians*, 2, http://daatemet.org.il/en/question/esau-edom-rome-and-the-christians/ (accessed Mar. 21, 2017).
[13] House of Cards, *Zepho, Balaam, Jannes & Jambres pt 1*, 2, https://houseofcardsbook.wordpress.com/2015/12/20/zepho-balaam-jannes-jambres-pt-1/ (accessed Jan. 16, 2020).
[14] *The Book of Jasher*, 60:4-6, trans. Albinus Alcuin (Pomeroy, Washington: Health Research, 1966).
[15] House of Cards, *Zepho, Balaam, Jannes & Jambres pt 1*, 4, https://houseofcardsbook.wordpress.com/2015/12/20/zepho-balaam-jannes-jambres-pt-1/ (accessed Jan. 16, 2020).
[16] simplybible.com, *The Error of Balaam*, 1, https://www.simplybible.com/f416-2pet-the-error-of-balaam.htm (accessed Mar. 12, 2019).
[17] Bible Study Tools, *Important Reminders From the Story of Balaam and His Talking Donkey*, 1, https://www.biblestudytools.com/bible-study/topical-studies/important-reminders-from-the-story-of-balaam-and-his-talking-donkey.html (accessed Mar. 12, 2019).
[18] Got Questions, *Who was Balaam in the Bible*, 4, https://www.gotquestions.org/Balaam-in-the-Bible.html (accessed Mar. 12, 2019).
[19] Got Questions, *Who was Balaam in the Bible*, 1, https://www.gotquestions.org/Balaam-in-the-Bible.html (accessed Mar. 12, 2019).
[20] Jewish Encyclopedia, *BALAAM*, 11, https://www.jewishencyclopedia.com/articles/2395-balaam (accessed Mar. 21, 2017).
[21] House of Cards, *Zepho, Balaam, Jannes & Jambres pt 1*, 3, https://houseofcardsbook.wordpress.com/2015/12/20/zepho-balaam-jannes-jambres-pt-1/ (accessed Jan. 16, 2020).
[22] Daat Emet, *Esau, Edom, Rome, and the Christians*, 2, http://daatemet.org.il/en/question/esau-edom-rome-and-the-christians/ (accessed Mar. 21, 2017).

²³ *The Book of Jasher*, 64:5-6, trans. Albinus Alcuin (Pomeroy, Washington: Health Research, 1966).
²⁴ *The Book of Jasher*, 64:1-2, trans. Albinus Alcuin (Pomeroy, Washington: Health Research, 1966).
²⁵ Ken Johnson, *Ancient Post-Flood History* (Ken Johnson, 2010), 81.
²⁶ Daat Emet, *Esau, Edom, Rome, and the Christians*, 2, http://daatemet.org.il/en/question/esau-edom-rome-and-the-christians/ (accessed Mar. 21, 2017).
²⁷ Wikipedia, the free encyclopedia, *History of Rome*, 2, 32, en.wikipedia.org/wiki/History_of_Rome (accessed Mar. 21, 2017).
²⁸ Daat Emet, *Esau, Edom, Rome, and the Christians*, 2, http://daatemet.org.il/en/question/esau-edom-rome-and-the-christians/ (accessed Mar. 21, 2017).

Chapter 9

¹ Daat Emet, *Esau, Edom, Rome, and the Christians*, 2, http://daatemet.org.il/en/question/esau-edom-rome-and-the-christians/ (accessed Mar. 21, 2017).
² The People of Mt. Seir, *The People of Mt. Seir*, 5, peopleofmtseir.blogspot.com (accessed Sept. 19, 2017).
³ Louis Ginzberg, *The Legends of the Jews Volume I: From the Creation to Jacob*, trans. Henrietta Szold (Baltimore, Maryland: The Johns Hopkins University Press, 1909), 314.
⁴ Jewish Encyclopedia, *HYRCANUS, JOHN (JOHANAN)*, 1, http://www.jewishencyclopedia.com/articles/7972-hyrcanus-john-johanan-i (accessed Mar. 21, 2017).
⁵ The People of Mt. Seir, *The People of Mt. Seir*, 5, peopleofmtseir.blogspot.com (accessed Sept. 19, 2017).
⁶ Laura Sanger, *The Roots of the Federal Reserve* (Dallas, Texas: Relentlessly Creative Books, 2020), 191.
⁷ The People of Mt. Seir, *The People of Mt. Seir*, 6, peopleofmtseir.blogspot.com (accessed Sept. 19, 2017).
⁸ Jewish Encyclopedia, *EDOX, IDUMEA*, 8, jewishencyclopedia.com/articles/5434-edox-idumea (accessed Mar. 21, 2017).
⁹ Encyclopaedia Judaica Vol. 6, *EDOM* (Jerusalem, Israel: Encyclopaedia Judaica Company, 1971), 378.
¹⁰ Flavius Josephus, *Jewish Antiquities Book 13.9.1*.
¹¹ Josephus, *Jewish Antiquities Vol. 7* (London, England: William Heinemann Ltd, 1957), 256-60.
¹² Laura Sanger, *The Roots of the Federal Reserve* (Dallas, Texas: Relentlessly Creative Books, 2020), 258.
¹³ *Psa.* 137:7-8 (NIV)
¹⁴ Josephus, *Jewish Antiquities Vol. 7* (London, England: William Heinemann Ltd, 1957), 256-260.
¹⁵ Jewish Encyclopedia, *EDOX, IDUMEA*, 8, jewishencyclopedia.com/articles/5434-edox-idumea (accessed Mar. 21, 2017).
¹⁶ Jewish Encyclopedia, *EDOX, IDUMEA*, 8, jewishencyclopedia.com/articles/5434-edox-idumea (accessed Mar. 21, 2017).
¹⁷ Wikipedia, the free encyclopedia, *Judea (Roman province)*, 1, https://en.wikipedia.org/wiki/Judea_(Roman_province) (accessed Sept. 19, 2017).
¹⁸ The Standard Jewish Encyclopedia (Garden City, New York: Doubleday & Company Inc., 1966), 593.
¹⁹ Laura Sanger, *The Roots of the Federal Reserve* (Dallas, Texas: Relentlessly Creative Books, 2020), 192.
²⁰ Reasons for Hope: Jesus, *What Do We Know about Judas? This Might Surprise You*, 2, https://reasonsforhopejesus.com/what-do-we-know-about-judas/ (accessed Feb. 5, 2019).
²¹ Bible Gateway, *Encyclopedia of the Bible - Kerioth*, 1, https://www.biblegateway.com/resources/encyclopedia-of-the-bible/Kerioth (accessed Feb. 5, 2019).
²² Reasons for Hope: Jesus, *What Do We Know about Judas? This Might Surprise You*, 3, https://reasonsforhopejesus.com/what-do-we-know-about-judas/ (accessed Feb. 5, 2019).
²³ Dr. Justin Prock, *Who's Who?*, 1, https://www.justinprock.com/2021/10/09/i-know-the-blasphemy-of-them-which-say-they-are-jews-judahites-and-are-not-but-are-the-synagogue-of-satan-part-1-introductions/ (accessed Mar. 12, 2019).
²⁴ Reasons for Hope: Jesus, *What Do We Know about Judas? This Might Surprise You*, 3, https://reasonsforhopejesus.com/what-do-we-know-about-judas/ (accessed Feb. 5, 2019).
²⁵ Biblical Hermeneutics, *Have the prophecies about Edom been fulfilled?*, 3-4, https://hermeneutics.stackexchange.com/questions/78772/have-the-prophecies-about-edom-been-fulfilled (accessed Dec. 15, 2022).
²⁶ Jewish Encyclopedia, *EDOX, IDUMEA*, 8, jewishencyclopedia.com/articles/5434-edox-idumea (accessed Mar. 21, 2017).
²⁷ The People of Mt. Seir, *The People of Mt. Seir*, 6, peopleofmtseir.blogspot.com (accessed Sept. 19, 2017).
²⁸ S. Baring-Gould, *Legends of the Patriarchs and Prophets and Other Old Testament Characters* (New York: American Book Exchange, 1881), 217.
²⁹ Jewish Virtual library, *Origins of the Name 'Palestine' and Palestinian Nationalism*, 2, https://www.jewishvirtuallibrary.org/origin-of-quot-palestine-quot (accessed Dec. 15, 2022).
³⁰ Jewish Virtual library, *Origins of the Name 'Palestine' and Palestinian Nationalism*, 2, https://www.jewishvirtuallibrary.org/origin-of-quot-palestine-quot (accessed Dec. 15, 2022); Christianity.com, *Palestina and Palestine (Smith's Bible Dictionary)*, 1, https://www.christianity.com/bible/dictionary/smiths-bible-

dictionary/palestina+and+palestine.html (accessed Dec. 17, 2023); Washington Report On Middle East Affairs, Zionisms Original Sin: Ignoring the Fact That Palestine Was Fully Populated, 4, https://www.wrmea.org/israel-palestine/zionisms-original-sin-ignoring-the-fact-that-palestine-was-fully-populated.html (accessed Apr. 29, 2023).

[31] Think-Israel, *The History and Meaning of 'Palestine' and "Palestinians"*, http://www.think-israel.org/katz.palestine.html (accessed October 15, 2021).

Chapter 10

[1] The Fall of Rome and the End of Civilisation (Ward-Perkins, 2005), 220; UKEssays.com, *The Fall of Rome and the End of Civilisation*, 1, https://www.ukessays.com/essays/history/barbarians-roman-civilisation-8420.php (accessed Apr. 7, 2018).

[2] Wikipedia, the free encyclopedia, *Sola scriptura*, 1, https://en.wikipedia.org/wiki/Sola_scriptura (accessed Feb. 5, 2019).

[3] Got Questions, *Does the Bible promote or prohibit praying to angels?*, 1, https://www.gotquestions.org/praying-to-angels.html (accessed Feb. 5, 2019).

[4] Stack Exchange, Why is the Book of Enoch not regarded as canonical?, 9, https://christianity.stackexchange.com/questions/8576/why-is-the-book-of-enoch-not-regarded-as-canonical (accessed October 15, 2021).

[5] Koinonia House, *Michevious Angels or Sethites?*, 2, https://www.khouse.org/personal_update/articles/1997/mischievous-angels-or-sethites ex khouse.org/articles/1997/110/ (accessed Sept. 19, 2017).

[6] DouglasHamp.com, *Part Six: The Sons of God According to Ancient Sources*, 7, douglashamp.com/part-six-the-sons-of-god-according-to-ancient-sources/ (accessed Mar. 21, 2017).

[7] Elizabeth Clare Prophet, *Fallen Angels and the Origins of Evil* (Gardiner, Montana: Summit University Press, 2000), 16.

[8] Daat Emet, *Esau, Edom, Rome, and the Christians*, 2, http://daatemet.org.il/en/question/esau-edom-rome-and-the-christians/ (accessed Sept. 19, 2017).

[9] Daat Emet, *Esau, Edom, Rome, and the Christians*, 2, http://daatemet.org.il/en/question/esau-edom-rome-and-the-christians/ (accessed Sept. 19, 2017).

Chapter 11

[1] JewishHistory.org, *The Origins of Sephardim and Ashkenazim*, 1-2, https://www.jewishhistory.org/sephardim-and-ashkenazim/ (accessed Feb. 5, 2019).

[2] The People of Mt. Seir, *The People of Mt. Seir*, 6, peopleofmtseir.blogspot.com (accessed Sept. 19, 2017).

[3] Foundation for the Advancement of Sephardic Studies and Culture, *What does Sephardi Mean? Who are the Sephardim?*, 1, http://www.sephardicstudies.org/intro.html (accessed Sept. 19, 2017).

[4] JewishHistory.org, *The Origins of Sephardim and Ashkenazim*, 2, https://www.jewishhistory.org/sephardim-and-ashkenazim/ (accessed May. 1, 2018).

[5] Merriam-Webster, *Ashkenazi*, 1, https://www.merriam-webster.com/dictionary/Ashkenazi (accessed Mar. 12, 2019).

[6] Wikipedia, the free encyclopedia, *Ashkenazi Jews*, 1, https://en.wikipedia.org/wiki/Ashkenazi_Jews (accessed Mar. 12, 2019).

[7] The Conversation, *Uncovering ancient Ashkenaz - the birthplace of Yiddish speakers*, 2, https://theconversation.com/uncovering-ancient-ashkenaz-the-birthplace-of-yiddish-speakers-58355 (accessed Feb. 5, 2019).

[8] Aeon, *How DNA traced the Ashkenazic Jews to northeastern Turkey*, 1-2, https://aeon.co/ideas/how-dna-traced-the-ashkenazic-jews-to-northeastern-turkey (accessed Apr. 7, 2018).

[9] Middle East Eye, *Ashkenazi Jews descended from ancient Turkey: New research*, 2, https://www.middleeasteye.net/news/ashkenazi-jews-descended-ancient-turkey-new-research (accessed Feb. 5, 2019).

[10] Aeon, *How DNA traced the Ashkenazic Jews to northeastern Turkey*, 1-2, https://aeon.co/ideas/how-dna-traced-the-ashkenazic-jews-to-northeastern-turkey (accessed Apr. 7, 2018).

[11] Orange Street Congregational Church, London, *The Khazars*, 1, orange-street-church.org/text/khazar.htm (accessed Sept. 19, 2017).

[12] Israelite Knight, *Khazars*, 1, https://israeliteknight.com/khazars.htm (accessed Aug. 26, 2018).

[13] Gaf.news, *The Khazarian Empire*, 1, https://gaf.news/2019/11/24/the-khazarian-empire/ (accessed Aug. 26, 2018).

[14] Radio Christianity, *The History of the Khazars Part One*, 3, http://radiochristianity.com/the-history-of-the-khazars-part-one/ (accessed Aug. 26, 2018).

[15] Era of Light, *Khazaria Rothschild Dynasty, New World Order Ukraine and Implementation Of The Nephilim Agenda*, 1, https://eraoflight.com/2022/04/11/khazaria-rothschild-dynasty-new-world-order-ukraine-and-implementation-of-the-nephilim-agenda/ (accessed Apr. 29, 2023).

[16] The People of Mt. Seir, *The People of Mt. Seir*, 7, peopleofmtseir.blogspot.com (accessed Sept. 19, 2017).

[17] the Trumpet, *East, West or Neither?*, 2, https://www.thetrumpet.com/8717-east-west-or-neither (accessed Aug. 26, 2018).

18 Studies in the Word of God, *Turkey, Another Son of Esau*, 3, http://www.studiesintheword.org/Turkey.htm (accessed Feb. 5, 2019).
19 the Trumpet, *East, West or Neither?*, 2, https://www.thetrumpet.com/8717-east-west-or-neither (accessed Aug. 26, 2018).
20 The People of Mt. Seir, *The People of Mt. Seir*, 7, peopleofmtseir.blogspot.com (accessed Sept. 19, 2017).
21 The People of Mt. Seir, *The People of Mt. Seir*, 7, peopleofmtseir.blogspot.com (accessed Sept. 19, 2017).
22 Jewish Encyclopedia, *CHAZARS*, 10, http://jewishencyclopedia.com/articles/4279-chazars (accessed Sept. 19, 2017).
23 Jewish Encyclopedia, *CHAZARS*, 1, http://jewishencyclopedia.com/articles/4279-chazars (accessed Sept. 19, 2017).
24 Jewish Encyclopedia, *CHAZARS*, 1, http://jewishencyclopedia.com/articles/4279-chazars (accessed Sept. 19, 2017).
25 The Conversation, *Uncovering ancient Ashkenaz - the birthplace of Yiddish speakers*, 3, https://theconversation.com/uncovering-ancient-ashkenaz-the-birthplace-of-yiddish-speakers-58355 (accessed Mar. 12, 2019).
26 Israelect.com, *Search Willie Martin Studies*, 1, https://israelect.com/reference/WillieMartin/Jews_Are_Not_Israelites.htm (accessed Apr. 29, 2023).
27 Gaf.news, *The Khazarian Empire*, 1, https://gaf.news/2019/11/24/the-khazarian-empire/ (accessed Aug. 26, 2018).
28 The People of Mt. Seir, *The People of Mt. Seir*, 5, peopleofmtseir.blogspot.com (accessed Sept. 19, 2017).
29 Era of Light, *Khazaria Rothschild Dynasty, New World Order Ukraine and Implementation Of The Nephilim Agenda*, 3, https://eraoflight.com/2022/04/11/khazaria-rothschild-dynasty-new-world-order-ukraine-and-implementation-of-the-nephilim-agenda/ (accessed Apr. 29, 2023).
30 Gaf.news, *The Khazarian Empire*, 1, https://gaf.news/2019/11/24/the-khazarian-empire/ (accessed Aug. 26, 2018).
31 Killhell.com, *King Bulan of Khazar*, 1, https://killhell.com/?p=3016 (accessed Mar. 21, 2017).
32 Radio Christianity, *The History of the Khazars Part One*, 10, http://radiochristianity.com/the-history-of-the-khazars-part-one/ (accessed Aug. 26, 2018).
33 Era of Light, *Khazaria Rothschild Dynasty, New World Order Ukraine and Implementation Of The Nephilim Agenda*, 3, https://eraoflight.com/2022/04/11/khazaria-rothschild-dynasty-new-world-order-ukraine-and-implementation-of-the-nephilim-agenda/ (accessed Apr. 29, 2023).
34 Dr. Justin Prock, *Who's Who?*, 1, https://www.justinprock.com/2021/10/09/i-know-the-blasphemy-of-them-which-say-they-are-jews-judahites-and-are-not-but-are-the-synagogue-of-satan-part-1-introductions/ (accessed Mar. 12, 2019).
35 Hope of Israel Ministries, *The Khazar Kingdom's Conversion to Judaism*, 2, https://www.hope-of-israel.org/KhazarConversion.html (accessed Feb. 5, 2019).
36 Hope of Israel Ministries, *The Khazar Kingdom's Conversion to Judaism*, 3, https://www.hope-of-israel.org/KhazarConversion.html (accessed Feb. 5, 2019).
37 Hope of Israel Ministries, *The Khazar Kingdom's Conversion to Judaism*, 3-4, https://www.hope-of-israel.org/KhazarConversion.html (accessed Feb. 5, 2019).
38 Gaf.news, *The Khazarian Empire*, 3, https://gaf.news/2019/11/24/the-khazarian-empire/ (accessed Aug. 26, 2018).
39 Gaf.news, *The Khazarian Empire*, 3, https://gaf.news/2019/11/24/the-khazarian-empire/ (accessed Aug. 26, 2018).
40 The People of Mt. Seir, *The People of Mt. Seir*, 7, peopleofmtseir.blogspot.com (accessed Sept. 19, 2017).
41 Israelect.com, *Search Willie Martin Studies*, 1, https://israelect.com/reference/WillieMartin/Jews_Are_Not_Israelites.htm (accessed Apr. 29, 2023).
42 Jewish Encyclopedia, *IDUMEA*, 1, jewishencyclopedia.com/articles/8060-idumea (accessed Sept. 19, 2017).
43 Jewish Encyclopedia, *IDUMEA*, 1, jewishencyclopedia.com/articles/8060-idumea (accessed Sept. 19, 2017).
44 Colors in Scripture, *The Scripture Speaks*, 5, http://www.biblenews1.com/colors/colorsa.html (accessed Sept. 19, 2017).
45 Spiritcommunity.com, *Dreams, Colors, Meaning*, 1, spiritcommunity.com/dreams/colors/meaning.php (accessed May. 1, 2018).
46 Johann Andreas Eisenmenger, *The Traditions of the Jews, Contained in the Talmud and Other Mystical Writings* (London: J. Robinson, 1748), 192.
47 Msn.com, *The Rothschilds Have Been One of the World's Wealthiest Familes for Centuries*, 4, https://www.msn.com/en-us/money/personalfinance/the-rothschilds-have-been-one-of-the-world-s-wealthiest-families-for-centuries/ar-BB1iUXUO (accessed May. 1, 2024).
48 David Allen Rivera, *Final Warning: A History of the New World Order* (INGSOC), 24.
49 Sefaria, *Shulchan Arukh, Yoreh De'ah 159:1*, https://www.sefaria.org/Shulchan_Arukh%2C_Yoreh_De'ah.159.1?lang=bi&with=all&lang2=en (accessed Feb. 5, 2019).
50 Sefaria, *Schulchan Aruch, Choszen Hamiszpat 348*, https://www.sefaria.org/Shulchan_Arukh%2C_Choshen_Mishpat.348.2?lang=bi (accessed Feb. 5, 2019).
51 Chabad.org, *Sanhedrin 57a (The Babylonian Talmud)*, https://www.chabad.org/torah-texts/5458278/The-Talmud/Sanhedrin/Chapter-7/57a (accessed Feb. 5, 2019).
52 Sefaria, *Sanhedrin 57a (The Babylonian Talmud)*,

https://www.sefaria.org/Sanhedrin.57a.17?lang=bi&with=all&lang2=en (accessed Feb. 5, 2019).
53 Sefaria, *Baba Kamma* 38a, https://www.sefaria.org/Bava_Kamma.38a.4?lang=bi (accessed Feb. 5, 2019).
54 Simpletoremember.com, *Why Do People Hate The Jews?*, 1, simpletoremember.com/vitals/Why_Do_People_Hate_The_Jews.htm (accessed Mar. 12, 2019).

Chapter 12

1 Blaze media, *Buck Sexton Traces Parallels Between Fall of the Roman Empire, Rise of the Ottoman Empire and What's Happening Today*, 1, https://www.theblaze.com/news/2013/08/21/buck-sexton-traces-parallels-between-fall-of-the-roman-empire-rise-of-the-ottoman-empire-and-whats-happening-today (accessed Feb. 5, 2019).
2 Sky Watch TV Store, *The Untold History of the Bible*, 1, https://www.skywatchtvstore.com/products/the-untold-history-of-the-bible?_pos=1&_sid=a3bab8859&_ss=r (accessed Mar. 12, 2019).
3 Got Questions, *What were the Dark Ages?*, 1, https://www.gotquestions.org/dark-ages.html (accessed Mar. 12, 2019).
4 Got Questions, *What were the Dark Ages?*, 1, https://www.gotquestions.org/dark-ages.html (accessed Mar. 12, 2019).
5 Wikipedia, the free encyclopedia, *Feudalism*, 1, https://en.wikipedia.org/wiki/Feudalism (accessed Mar. 12, 2019).
6 Got Questions, *What were the Dark Ages?*, 1, https://www.gotquestions.org/dark-ages.html (accessed Mar. 12, 2019).
7 Axis History, *The First and Second Reich*, 1, https://www.axishistory.com/about-ahf/125-germany-unsorted/germany-unsorted/4865-the-first-a-second-reich (accessed Mar. 12, 2019).
8 "The Knights Templar", *In Search of History*, The History Channel, Season 8, Episode 6, 2000. *In Search of History* (A&E Networks, 2000).
9 "The Knights Templar", *In Search of History*, The History Channel, Season 8, Episode 6, 2000.
10 "The Knights Templar", *In Search of History*, The History Channel, Season 8, Episode 6, 2000.
11 "The Knights Templar", *In Search of History*, The History Channel, Season 8, Episode 6, 2000.
12 "The Knights Templar", *In Search of History*, The History Channel, Season 8, Episode 6, 2000.
13 "The Knights Templar", *In Search of History*, The History Channel, Season 8, Episode 6, 2000. *In Search of History* (A&E Networks, 2000).
14 "The Knights Templar", *In Search of History*, The History Channel, Season 8, Episode 6, 2000. *In Search of History* (A&E Networks, 2000).
15 "The Knights Templar", *In Search of History*, The History Channel, Season 8, Episode 6, 2000. *In Search of History* (A&E Networks, 2000).
16 "The Knights Templar", *In Search of History*, The History Channel, Season 8, Episode 6, A&E Networks, 2000.
17 "The Knights Templar", *In Search of History*, The History Channel, Season 8, Episode 6, A&E Networks, 2000.
18 "The Knights Templar", *In Search of History*, The History Channel, Season 8, Episode 6, 2000. *In Search of History* (A&E Networks, 2000).
19 "The Knights Templar", *In Search of History*, The History Channel, Season 8, Episode 6, 2000. *In Search of History* (A&E Networks, 2000).
20 Sky Watch TV Store, *The Untold History of the Bible*, 1, https://www.skywatchtvstore.com/products/the-untold-history-of-the-bible?_pos=1&_sid=a3bab8859&_ss=r (accessed Mar. 12, 2019).
21 Wikipedia, the free encyclopedia, *Middle Ages*, 18, https://en.wikipedia.org/wiki/Middle_Ages (accessed Mar. 12, 2019).
22 Gnostic Warrior, *The Letter "G" in Freemasonry Signifies Gnosis*, 5, https://www.gnosticwarrior.com/g-2.html (accessed Apr. 29, 2023).
23 Everything Explained Today, *Jahbulon Explained*, 1, http://everything.explained.today/Jahbulon/ (accessed Apr. 29, 2023).
24 Wikipedia, the free encyclopedia, Jahbulon, 2, https://en.wikipedia.org/wiki/Jahbulon (accessed Apr. 29, 2023)
25 Masonic Encyclopedia, *Nimrod*, 1, https://masonicshop.com/encyclopedia/topics/entry/?i=2619 (accessed Apr. 29, 2023).

Chapter 13

1 Wikipedia, the free encyclopedia, *Middle Ages*, 1, https://en.wikipedia.org/wiki/Middle_Ages (accessed Dec. 15, 2022).
2 Wikipedia, the free encyclopedia, *Age of Discovery*, 1, https://en.wikipedia.org/wiki/Age_of_Discovery (accessed Dec. 15, 2022).
3 Wikipedia, the free encyclopedia, *Age of Discovery*, 1, https://en.wikipedia.org/wiki/Age_of_Discovery (accessed Dec. 15, 2022).
4 Sky Watch TV Store, *A Lamp in the Dark: The Untold History of the Bible*, 1,

skywatchtvstore.com/collections/audio-dvd-media/products/a-lamp-in-the-dark-the-untold-history-of-the-bible (accessed Mar. 12, 2019).
[5] Sky Watch TV Store, *A Lamp in the Dark: The Untold History of the Bible*, 1, skywatchtvstore.com/collections/audio-dvd-media/products/a-lamp-in-the-dark-the-untold-history-of-the-bible (accessed Mar. 12, 2019).
[6] Wikipedia, the free encyclopedia, *Humanism*, 2, en.wikipedia.org/wiki/Humanism (accessed Mar. 12, 2019).
[7] Bit Chute, *Freemason and Jesuit Copernicus - The Heliocentric Deception*, https://www.bitchute.com/video/CEK5EWhtiSJE/ (accessed Mar. 19, 2024).
[8] The Rush Limbaugh Show, *Mars Attacks: How Lies and Distortions About This Show Get into the Low-Information Bloodstream*, 5, http://www.rushlimbaugh.com/daily/2015/09/30/mars_attacks_how_lies_and_distortions_about_this_show_get_into_the_low_information_bloodstream (accessed Sept. 30, 2015).
[9] The Square Magazine, Philosophy in the Life of a Freemason, 3, https://www.thesquaremagazine.com/mag/article/202109philosophy-in-the-life-of-the-freemason/ (accessed Dec. 15, 2022).
[10] Menorah Ministries, *The Bible - Word of God - Verses - Errors of "Freemasonry"*, 3, https://www.menorah.org/errorsoffreemasonry (accessed May. 1, 2018).
[11] Reason, Intuition, and Freemasonry, *Reason, Intuition, and Freemasonry*, 3, https://static1.squarespace.com/static/5fb291eddf5bb83bda005e70/t/5fe9fc0d64b17f175179b33e/1609169935313/reason,+intuition,+and+freemasonry.pdf (accessed May. 1, 2018).

Chapter 14

[1] Wikipedia, the free encyclopedia, *History of Western civilization*, 1, en.wikipedia.org/.../History_of_Western_civilization (accessed Apr. 04, 2022).
[2] Wikipedia, the free encyclopedia, *History of Western civilization*, 1, en.wikipedia.org/.../History_of_Western_civilization (accessed Apr. 04, 2022).
[3] Wikipedia, the free encyclopedia, *Humanism*, 2, en.wikipedia.org/wiki/Humanism (accessed Mar. 12, 2019).
[4] Archive.org, *Forbidden History of the Aryan Race Unabridged*, 9, https://ia800401.us.archive.org/8/items/aryanity-forbidden-history-of-the-aryan-race_202305/2728.pdf (accessed Apr. 29, 2023).
[5] Sky Watch TV Store, *The Untold History of the Bible*, 1, https://www.skywatchtvstore.com/products/the-untold-history-of-the-bible?_pos=1&_sid=a3bab8859&_ss=r (accessed Mar. 12, 2019).
[6] Sky Watch TV Store, *The Untold History of the Bible*, 1, https://www.skywatchtvstore.com/products/the-untold-history-of-the-bible?_pos=1&_sid=a3bab8859&_ss=r (accessed Mar. 12, 2019).
[7] Eric Jon Phelps, *Vatican Assassoms* (Newmanstown, Pennysylvania: Lowvehm Publishing, 2007), 74.
[8] rense.com, *The Enlightened Ones: The Illuminati and the New World Order*, 1, https://rense.com/general94/enlightened.htm (accessed Dec. 15, 2022).
[9] Scribd.com, *Cecil John Rhodes and the Agenda of the New World Order Concerning Africa*, 1, https://www.scribd.com/document/77529916/Cecil-John-Rhodes (accessed Mar. 19, 2024).
[10] Tools For Freedom Store, #3664: The Satanic Jewish Messiah of 1666 - Audio DVD", n. d., p. 1, https://www.toolsforfreedom.com/The-Satanic-Jewish-Messiah-of-1666-Audio-DVD-p/3664.htm (accessed May. 1, 2018).
[11] Scribd.com, *Cecil John Rhodes and the Agenda of the New World Order Concerning Africa*, 1, https://www.scribd.com/document/77529916/Cecil-John-Rhodes (accessed Mar. 19, 2024).
[12] Scribd.com, *Cecil John Rhodes and the Agenda of the New World Order Concerning Africa*, 1, https://www.scribd.com/document/77529916/Cecil-John-Rhodes (accessed Mar. 19, 2024).
[13] "Statue of Liberty", *Brian Meltzer's Decoded*, The History Channel, Season 1, Episode 3, 2000.
[14] The New Yorker, *The Divider*, 1, https://www.newyorker.com/magazine/2008/03/17/the-divider (accessed Dec. 15, 2022).
[15] The Rush Limbaugh Show, I Still Can't Believe How Ignorant Journalists Are About Easter, 2, https://www.rushlimbaugh.com/daily/2018/04/04/still-cant-believe-ignorant-journalists-easter/ (accessed Apr. 6, 2018.

Chapter 15

[1] Hope of Israel Ministries, *The Jewish-Created Scofield "Bible"*, 1, https://www.hope-of-israel.org/createdbible.html (accessed Feb. 5, 2019).
[2] Hope of Israel Ministries, *The Jewish-Created Scofield "Bible"*, 1, https://www.hope-of-israel.org/createdbible.html (accessed Feb. 5, 2019).
[3] Hope of Israel Ministries, *The Jewish-Created Scofield "Bible"*, 1, https://www.hope-of-israel.org/createdbible.html (accessed Feb. 5, 2019).
[4] Veterans Today, *Christian Zionism: Cyrus Scofield Was Rothschild Puppet*, 1,

https://www.sefaria.org/Sanhedrin.57a.17?lang=bi&with=all&lang2=en (accessed Feb. 5, 2019).
[53] Sefaria, *Baba Kamma* 38a, https://www.sefaria.org/Bava_Kamma.38a.4?lang=bi (accessed Feb. 5, 2019).
[54] Simpletoremember.com, *Why Do People Hate The Jews?*, 1, simpletoremember.com/vitals/Why_Do_People_Hate_The_Jews.htm (accessed Mar. 12, 2019).

Chapter 12

[1] Blaze media, *Buck Sexton Traces Parallels Between Fall of the Roman Empire, Rise of the Ottoman Empire and What's Happening Today*, 1, https://www.theblaze.com/news/2013/08/21/buck-sexton-traces-parallels-between-fall-of-the-roman-empire-rise-of-the-ottoman-empire-and-whats-happening-today (accessed Feb. 5, 2019).
[2] Sky Watch TV Store, *The Untold History of the Bible*, 1, https://www.skywatchtvstore.com/products/the-untold-history-of-the-bible?_pos=1&_sid=a3bab8859&_ss=r (accessed Mar. 12, 2019).
[3] Got Questions, *What were the Dark Ages?*, 1, https://www.gotquestions.org/dark-ages.html (accessed Mar. 12, 2019).
[4] Got Questions, *What were the Dark Ages?*, 1, https://www.gotquestions.org/dark-ages.html (accessed Mar. 12, 2019).
[5] Wikipedia, the free encyclopedia, *Feudalism*, 1, https://en.wikipedia.org/wiki/Feudalism (accessed Mar. 12, 2019).
[6] Got Questions, *What were the Dark Ages?*, 1, https://www.gotquestions.org/dark-ages.html (accessed Mar. 12, 2019).
[7] Axis History, *The First and Second Reich*, 1, https://www.axishistory.com/about-ahf/125-germany-unsorted/germany-unsorted/4865-the-first-a-second-reich (accessed Mar. 12, 2019).
[8] "The Knights Templar", *In Search of History*, The History Channel, Season 8, Episode 6, 2000. *In Search of History* (A&E Networks, 2000).
[9] "The Knights Templar", *In Search of History*, The History Channel, Season 8, Episode 6, 2000.
[10] "The Knights Templar", *In Search of History*, The History Channel, Season 8, Episode 6, 2000.
[11] "The Knights Templar", *In Search of History*, The History Channel, Season 8, Episode 6, 2000.
[12] "The Knights Templar", *In Search of History*, The History Channel, Season 8, Episode 6, 2000.
[13] "The Knights Templar", *In Search of History*, The History Channel, Season 8, Episode 6, 2000. *In Search of History* (A&E Networks, 2000).
[14] "The Knights Templar", *In Search of History*, The History Channel, Season 8, Episode 6, 2000. *In Search of History* (A&E Networks, 2000).
[15] "The Knights Templar", *In Search of History*, The History Channel, Season 8, Episode 6, 2000. *In Search of History* (A&E Networks, 2000).
[16] "The Knights Templar", *In Search of History*, The History Channel, Season 8, Episode 6, A&E Networks, 2000.
[17] "The Knights Templar", *In Search of History*, The History Channel, Season 8, Episode 6, A&E Networks, 2000.
[18] "The Knights Templar", *In Search of History*, The History Channel, Season 8, Episode 6, 2000. *In Search of History* (A&E Networks, 2000).
[19] "The Knights Templar", *In Search of History*, The History Channel, Season 8, Episode 6, 2000. *In Search of History* (A&E Networks, 2000).
[20] Sky Watch TV Store, *The Untold History of the Bible*, 1, https://www.skywatchtvstore.com/products/the-untold-history-of-the-bible?_pos=1&_sid=a3bab8859&_ss=r (accessed Mar. 12, 2019).
[21] Wikipedia, the free encyclopedia, *Middle Ages*, 18, https://en.wikipedia.org/wiki/Middle_Ages (accessed Mar. 12, 2019).
[22] Gnostic Warrior, *The Letter "G" in Freemasonry Signifies Gnosis*, 5, https://www.gnosticwarrior.com/g-2.html (accessed Apr. 29, 2023).
[23] Everything Explained Today, *Jahbulon Explained*, 1, http://everything.explained.today/Jahbulon/ (accessed Apr. 29, 2023).
[24] Wikipedia, the free encyclopedia, Jahbulon, 2, https://en.wikipedia.org/wiki/Jahbulon (accessed Apr. 29, 2023)
[25] Masonic Encylopedia, *Nimrod*, 1, https://masonicshop.com/encyclopedia/topics/entry/?i=2619 (accessed Apr. 29, 2023).

Chapter 13

[1] Wikipedia, the free encyclopedia, *Middle Ages*, 1, https://en.wikipedia.org/wiki/Middle_Ages (accessed Dec. 15, 2022).
[2] Wikipedia, the free encyclopedia, *Age of Discovery*, 1, https://en.wikipedia.org/wiki/Age_of_Discovery (accessed Dec. 15, 2022).
[3] Wikipedia, the free encyclopedia, *Age of Discovery*, 1, https://en.wikipedia.org/wiki/Age_of_Discovery (accessed Dec. 15, 2022).
[4] Sky Watch TV Store, *A Lamp in the Dark: The Untold History of the Bible*, 1,

skywatchtvstore.com/collections/audio-dvd-media/products/a-lamp-in-the-dark-the-untold-history-of-the-bible (accessed Mar. 12, 2019).
5 Sky Watch TV Store, *A Lamp in the Dark: The Untold History of the Bible*, 1, skywatchtvstore.com/collections/audio-dvd-media/products/a-lamp-in-the-dark-the-untold-history-of-the-bible (accessed Mar. 12, 2019).
6 Wikipedia, the free encyclopedia, *Humanism*, 2, en.wikipedia.org/wiki/Humanism (accessed Mar. 12, 2019).
7 Bit Chute, *Freemason and Jesuit Copernicus - The Heliocentric Deception*, https://www.bitchute.com/video/CEK5EWhtiSJE/ (accessed Mar. 19, 2024).
8 The Rush Limbaugh Show, *Mars Attacks: How Lies and Distortions About This Show Get into the Low-Information Bloodstream*, 5, http://www.rushlimbaugh.com/daily/2015/09/30/mars_attacks_how_lies_and_distortions_about_this_show_get_into_the_low_information_bloodstream (accessed Sept. 30, 2015).
9 The Square Magazine, Philosophy in the Life of a Freemason, 3, https://www.thesquaremagazine.com/mag/article/202109philosophy-in-the-life-of-the-freemason/ (accessed Dec. 15, 2022).
10 Menorah Ministries, *The Bible - Word of God - Verses - Errors of "Freemasonry"*, 3, https://www.menorah.org/errorsoffreemasonry (accessed May. 1, 2018).
11 Reason, Intuition, and Freemasonry, *Reason, Intuition, and Freemasonry*, 3, https://static1.squarespace.com/static/5fb291eddf5bb83bda005e70/t/5fe9fc0d64b17f175179b33e/1609169935313/reason,+intuition,+and+freemasonry.pdf (accessed May. 1, 2018).

Chapter 14

1 Wikipedia, the free encyclopedia, *History of Western civilization*, 1, en.wikipedia.org/.../History_of_Western_civilization (accessed Apr. 04, 2022).
2 Wikipedia, the free encyclopedia, *History of Western civilization*, 1, en.wikipedia.org/.../History_of_Western_civilization (accessed Apr. 04, 2022).
3 Wikipedia, the free encyclopedia, *Humanism*, 2, en.wikipedia.org/wiki/Humanism (accessed Mar. 12, 2019).
4 Archive.org, *Forbidden History of the Aryan Race Unabridged*, 9, https://ia800401.us.archive.org/8/items/aryanity-forbidden-history-of-the-aryan-race_202305/2728.pdf (accessed Apr. 29, 2023).
5 Sky Watch TV Store, *The Untold History of the Bible*, 1, https://www.skywatchtvstore.com/products/the-untold-history-of-the-bible?_pos=1&_sid=a3bab8859&_ss=r (accessed Mar. 12, 2019).
6 Sky Watch TV Store, *The Untold History of the Bible*, 1, https://www.skywatchtvstore.com/products/the-untold-history-of-the-bible?_pos=1&_sid=a3bab8859&_ss=r (accessed Mar. 12, 2019).
7 Eric Jon Phelps, *Vatican Assassoms* (Newmanstown, Pennysylvania: Lowvehm Publishing, 2007), 74.
8 rense.com, *The Enlightened Ones: The Illuminati and the New World Order*, 1, https://rense.com/general94/enlightened.htm (accessed Dec. 15, 2022).
9 Scribd.com, *Cecil John Rhodes and the Agenda of the New World Order Concerning Africa*, 1, https://www.scribd.com/document/77529916/Cecil-John-Rhodes (accessed Mar. 19, 2024).
10 Tools For Freedom Store, #3664: The Satanic Jewish Messiah of 1666 - Audio DVD", n. d., p. 1, https://www.toolsforfreedom.com/The-Satanic-Jewish-Messiah-of-1666-Audio-DVD-p/3664.htm (accessed May. 1, 2018).
11 Scribd.com, *Cecil John Rhodes and the Agenda of the New World Order Concerning Africa*, 1, https://www.scribd.com/document/77529916/Cecil-John-Rhodes (accessed Mar. 19, 2024).
12 Scribd.com, *Cecil John Rhodes and the Agenda of the New World Order Concerning Africa*, 1, https://www.scribd.com/document/77529916/Cecil-John-Rhodes (accessed Mar. 19, 2024).
13 "Statue of Liberty", *Brian Meltzer's Decoded*, The History Channel, Season 1, Episode 3, 2000.
14 The New Yorker, *The Divider*, 1, https://www.newyorker.com/magazine/2008/03/17/the-divider (accessed Dec. 15, 2022).
15 The Rush Limbaugh Show, I Still Can't Believe How Ignorant Journalists Are About Easter, 2, https://www.rushlimbaugh.com/daily/2018/04/04/still-cant-believe-ignorant-journalists-easter/ (accessed Apr. 6, 2018).

Chapter 15

1 Hope of Israel Ministries, *The Jewish-Created Scofield "Bible"*, 1, https://www.hope-of-israel.org/createdbible.html (accessed Feb. 5, 2019).
2 Hope of Israel Ministries, *The Jewish-Created Scofield "Bible"*, 1, https://www.hope-of-israel.org/createdbible.html (accessed Feb. 5, 2019).
3 Hope of Israel Ministries, *The Jewish-Created Scofield "Bible"*, 1, https://www.hope-of-israel.org/createdbible.html (accessed Feb. 5, 2019).
4 Veterans Today, *Christian Zionism: Cyrus Scofield Was Rothschild Puppet*, 1,

https://www.veteranstoday.com/2020/10/17/christian-zionism-cyrus-scofield-was-a-rothschild-puppet/ (accessed Feb. 5, 2019).
[5] Christian Observer, *Zionists Behind The Scofield 'Bible' - It's Powerful Effect On Modern Christianity*, 2, https://christianobserver.net/the-scofield-bible-its-powerful-effect-on-modern-christianity/ (accessed Dec. 15, 2022); Veterans Today, *Christian Zionism: Cyrus Scofield Was Rothschild Puppet*, 2, https://www.veteranstoday.com/2020/10/17/christian-zionism-cyrus-scofield-was-a-rothschild-puppet/ (accessed Feb. 5, 2019).
[6] Christian Observer, *Zionists Behind The Scofield 'Bible' - It's Powerful Effect On Modern Christianity*, 2, https://christianobserver.net/the-scofield-bible-its-powerful-effect-on-modern-christianity/ (accessed Dec. 15, 2022).
[7] Hope of Israel Ministries, *The Jewish-Created Scofield "Bible"*, 5, https://www.hope-of-israel.org/createdbible.html (accessed Feb. 5, 2019).
[8] Hope of Israel Ministries, *The Jewish-Created Scofield "Bible"*, 7, https://www.hope-of-israel.org/createdbible.html (accessed Feb. 5, 2019).
[9] Bible Ref, *Matthew 5:39*, 3, https://www.bibleref.com/Matthew/5/Matthew-5-39.html (accessed Dec. 15, 2022).
[10] Bible Hub, *436. anthistemi*, 2, https://biblehub.com/greek/436.htm (accessed June, 20, 2017).
[11] *Mat.* 5:38-39 (NIV).
[12] Bible Ref, *Matthew 5:39*, 3, https://www.bibleref.com/Matthew/5/Matthew-5-39.html (accessed Dec. 15, 2022).
[13] Bible Ref, *Matthew 5:39*, 3, https://www.bibleref.com/Matthew/5/Matthew-5-39.html (accessed Dec. 15, 2022).

Chapter 16

[1] S. Baring-Gould, *Legends of the Patriarchs and Prophets and Other Old Testament Characters* (New York: American Book Exchange, 1881), 217.
[2] Wikipedia, the free encyclopedia, *Age of Discovery*, 1, https://en.wikipedia.org/wiki/Age_of_Discovery (accessed Dec. 15, 2022).
[3] "Statue of Liberty", *Brian Meltzer's Decoded*, The History Channel, Season 1, Episode 3, 2000.
[4] Scribd.com, *Cecil John Rhodes and the Agenda of the New World Order Concerning Africa*, 1, https://www.scribd.com/document/77529916/Cecil-John-Rhodes (accessed Mar. 19, 2024).

www.ingramcontent.com/pod-product-compliance
Lightning Source LLC
Chambersburg PA
CBHW081124170426
43197CB00017B/2738